MICROPROCESSORS AND MICROCOMPUTERS

FOR ELECTRONICS TECHNICIANS

EDWARD J. PASAHOW

W9-DIU-134

MICROPROCESSORS AND MICROCOMPUTERS
FOR ELECTRONICS TECHNICIANS

EDWARD J. PASAHOW

San Diego Community College
San Diego, California

Gregg Division, McGraw-Hill Book Company

New York   Atlanta   Dallas   St. Louis   San Francisco   Auckland   Bogotá   Guatemala
Hamburg   Johannesburg   Lisbon   London   Madrid   Mexico   Montreal   New Delhi
Panama   Paris   San Juan   São Paulo   Singapore   Sydney   Tokyo   Toronto

For Rosemarie, with Love and Admiration

Sponsoring Editor: Mark Haas
Editing Supervisor: Karen Sekiguchi
Design Supervisor: Caryl Spinka
Production Supervisor: Kathleen Morrissey
Art Supervisor: Howard Brotman

Cover Designer: David Thurston

Library of Congress Cataloging in Publication Data

Pasahow, Edward.
  Microprocessors and microcomputers for electronics technicians.

  Includes index.
  1. Microcomputers. 2. Microprocessors. I. Title.
TK7888.3.P33   621.3819′58   80-14761
ISBN 0-07-048713-8

CONTENTS

PREFACE

This book is intended for students in a two-year electronics technology degree program who wish to gain in-depth, practical knowledge of microprocessors and microcomputers. Engineers, technicians, and computer specialists will also find this material directly applicable in working with microcomputers. Coverage emphasizes the hardware aspects of these small systems, but enough discussion on software topics is supplied to demonstrate the interactions between the two.

In selecting the microcomputer on which to base such a book as this, the author has essentially three choices: use a generic microprocessor, range through a large number of different processors trying to communicate the "flavor" of each, or analyze a particular processor in detail. Regardless of the way taken, shortcomings become all too readily apparent. The generic processor does not support lab experiments nor does it prepare students for real-world situations. Skipping from one processor to another is guaranteed to hopelessly confuse the reader and also makes experimentation difficult. In picking a single processor, the risk is that it may not be the one confronting the student on the job.

Given this type of choice, one can only take a deep breath and plunge ahead. The single processor approach was the one used in this book. The reasons for this choice are based on my belief that it results in the most favorable outcome. First, if a widely used processor is adopted, many will find the book useful. Second, symbology and terminology that are commonly accepted by industry can be employed. Third, of course, the experiments can be run using a processor likely to be found at most colleges. And, finally, the student acquires knowledge that can be readily utilized.

Having committed the first sin of making such a choice, the next one becomes even more grievous. Which microprocessor should it be? This decision was not made blindly. Hundreds of instructors and heads of electronics departments throughout the country were surveyed. Over 70 percent recommended the 8080A. Another significant fraction proposed the quite similar 8085 or Z80. Thus the reason for all that is to follow.

Signal flow diagrams are shown in the context of tying together what the processor is currently doing with the signals present on the system buses. The integration of experiments with the text provides a unique opportunity for hands-on experience with the concepts presented. State-of-the-art devices are used as examples throughout together with such important software techniques as top-down design, reentrant code, and recursive subroutines.

Mathematics is limited to basic algebra, and an understanding of integrated circuits, in general, is assumed. Beginning chapters provide an overview of microprocessors followed by a study of number system concepts. Many students will have had earlier courses on this subject, so the chapter can serve as a review. (On the other hand, it is a complete development to serve the student who has never been introduced to number systems other than decimal.)

An outline of programming sets the stage for the assembler and machine code listings used in the experiments and examples. The 8080A supplies the basis for an architectural description which leads into detailed consideration of the instruction repertoire, explanations of how the instructions are used, means of input and output, and interfacing to external devices. With this preparation, the student should be comfortable analyzing microcomputer components and circuitry as well as writing diagnostic software routines.

The ideas and suggestions of many co-workers have assisted a great deal in writing this book. The same can be said for manufacturers of the devices, whose technical publications formed the foundation for this effort. Finally the assistance of Myrna Davis in typing portions of the manuscript is gratefully acknowledged.

Edward J. Pasahow

1

AN INTRODUCTION TO MICROPROCESSORS AND MICROCOMPUTERS

A remarkable change has occurred in the electronics industry during the last decade. Previously the number of computers in the world had been counted in the thousands, but with the invention of the microcomputer that quantity has reached the millions, and the number continues to grow. Technicians who design, build, or maintain electronics equipment will be seeing microprocessors in their work with increasing frequency. An understanding of microcomputer components, circuitry, and signal flow will become as fundamental to a technician's job as is a knowledge of Ohm's law and resistor theory. An understanding of microcomputers requires some familiarity with programming features, as well as the hardware, to aid you in assessing problems and localizing faults.

CHAPTER OBJECTIVES

Upon completion of this chapter, you should be able to:

1. Define the terms "microcomputer" and "microprocessor."
2. List the components of a typical microprocessor.
3. Name the data and instruction registers usually found within a microprocessor.
4. Explain the operations performed in the arithmetic and logic section.
5. Distinquish between the various flags used in the status register.
6. Describe how a microprogram controls the sequence of events to be executed.
7. Describe the timing and the sequencing of instruction execution.
8. Draw a block diagram of a microprocessor.
9. Describe memory usage in a microcomputer.
10. Discuss bit-sliced microprocessor architecture.
11. Distinguish between programmed input/output, interrupt servicing, and direct memory access.
12. Describe the most commonly used microprocessor products now available from manufacturers.

MICROPROCESSORS AND MICROCOMPUTERS

A *digital computer* is an electronic device which can receive, store, manipulate, and send binary data. The data is manipulated as specified by a series of instructions, called a *program,* which is also stored in the computer. A digital computer consists of control, arithmetic and logic, memory, input, and output elements.

There is a special class of digital computers called *microcomputers,* which are based on *microprocessor* integrated circuits (IC). To perform its functions, the microcomputer requires input/output logic, read-only memory, power supplies, an oscillator, and possibly random-access memory, in addition to the microprocessor. Figure 1-1 shows an example of a microcomputer based on the 8080A microprocessor.

The microprocessor unit (MPU), is made up of one or more programmable integrated circuits containing control, arithmetic, and logic sections as well as a portion of the input/output logic and sometimes memory. Providing some or all of the arithmetic and control sections of a computer, microprocessors come in a variety of *word sizes* ranging from 4 to 16 bits.

In this chapter we will use a typical 8-bit microprocessor to study the capability and operation of these devices and then take a look at some examples of microprocessors. The concepts in this chapter provide an overview of the remainder of the book, so many of the examples are of a general nature. Details in later chapters will explain how or why the operations are actually carried out.

MICROCOMPUTER CHARACTERISTICS

The most common microcomputers work with binary numbers 8 bits long. This grouping of data into 8-bit units is an example of the *word size* of the computer. The 8-bit data unit is also often called a *byte,* so referring to a 1-byte computer is the same as saying that the computer has an 8-bit word size. Because the microprocessor and the memory in the microcomputer must work with the same data, they usually have the same word size.

Microprocessors are usually manufactured as dual in-line packages (DIPs). Typically, a microprocessor is a 40-pin DIP. One or more pins are dedicated to power supply inputs. (For instance, the 8080A uses 3 pins for the power supply voltages.) One pin is used for ground and another two for the clock input. Frequently, 16 pins are needed for the memory address output. Data input/output (I/O) uses an-

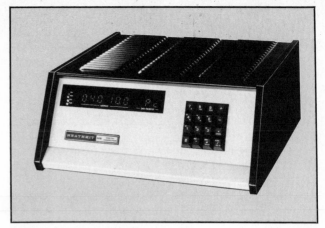

Figure 1-1. The Heathkit H8 Microcomputer *(Courtesy of the Heath Company).*

other 8 pins. One or more pins are needed to determine whether the memory reference is to be reading or writing. The remaining pins are associated with other control signals used for input, output, and timing.

The interconnection of various components of a microcomputer is shown in Fig. 1-2. The MPU acts as the controller for the system. Either *read-only memory* (ROM) or *random-access memory* (RAM) or both may be used as storage. General types of input/output transfers can be implemented. The simplest is an I/O interface to the peripheral device. (Some peripheral equipment that you may be familiar with includes magnetic tape cassettes, printers, cathode-ray-tube (CRT) terminals, and floppy disks.) When faster data transfer is necessary, interrupt logic or direct memory access may be used.

The key to a flexible microcomputer architecture is the use of *bidirectional buses* between the microprocessor and the other components. Most of the buses are *three-state* buses; that is, a device can set its output signals to high, low, or high-impedance states. In the latter case the device is essentially disconnected from the bus. Three different microcomputer buses are required, although some designs may *multiplex* two types of information over a single set of bus lines.

The *data bus* is an 8-bit bidirectional three-state bus. All data moving between the microprocessor and the other components travels along this path. Examples of data bus usage include reading data from memory to the microprocessor, storing results calculated by the microprocessor back into memory, fetching instructions from memory for the microprocessor to execute, and transferring data from the MPU to or from peripheral devices.

The number of parallel bits in the *address bus* depends on the maximum memory capacity that a microprocessor can use. Frequently the address bus

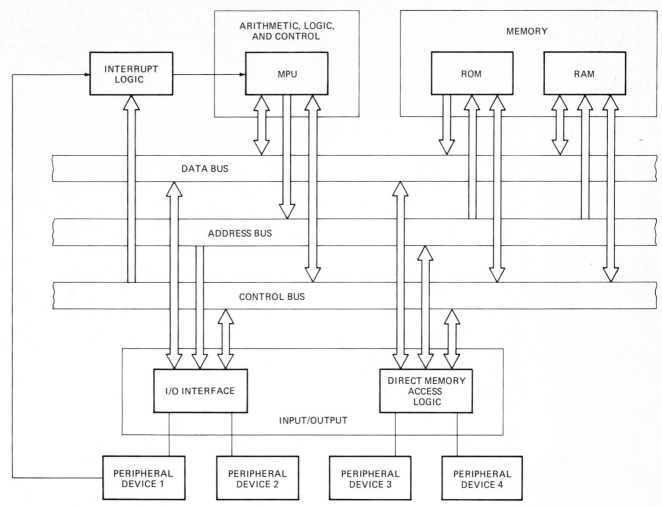

Figure 1-2. Architecture of a Typical Microcomputer.

is 16 bits wide. This bus is three-state. The address bus specifies the source or destination address for data. With 16 bits, there are 65,536 possible addresses (2^{16} = 65,536). The address can indicate either memory or an I/O device.

Each operation to be performed is under the direction of the *control bus.* The number of control lines varies a great deal from microprocessor to microprocessor, but generally there are 10 to 12 lines. These lines carry discrete signals, so they are usually not three-state. The sequence and nature of the operation are specified by setting the correct control line; for example, ''read data from RAM to the microprocessor'' may be one control line, and ''send

data to the peripheral device from the MPU'' could be another. Table 1-1 lists the data and address bus widths for some of the microprocessors that we will discuss later in this chapter.

Microcomputer Characteristics Review

1. Define the characteristics of a digital computer.

2. List the components of a microcomputer.

3. Describe the functions of a microprocessor.

4. How many bits are in 1 byte?

Table 1-1
Typical Microprocessor Buses

| | Microprocessors | | | | | |
	8080A	6800	SC/MP	PACE	8086	Z8000
Data bus width (bits)	8	8	8	16	20	16
Address bus width (bits)	16	16	12 or 16	16	16	16

5. What is the parity of $0100\ 0001_2$? What value would the parity status flag have to indicate this parity?

ARITHMETIC AND LOGIC SECTION

The manipulation of data is carried out in the arithmetic and logic section of the microprocessor. This section consists of the ALU with its arithmetic registers. Working on one or two 8-bit words in parallel, the ALU performs addition, subtraction, logical operations, and complementing. Most microprocessors cannot multiply or divide without the help of external circuitry or the use of a computer program.

A typical arithmetic and logic section is shown in Fig. 1–5. The major sections are the ALU itself (which performs complementing, adding, and Boolean functions), a shift register, and a buffer register. There are two data inputs, a control input, and a single output. There is also a path for recirculating data from the shifter to the ALU. All registers and data paths are 8 bits wide.

The inputs for the operation, such as Boolean AND, are sent to the arithmetic and logic section prior to application of the control input. The control input commands the ALU to perform an ANDing of input A with input B. After the AND has been completed,

the answer passes through the shifter (unchanged) and into the buffer register, where it is available on the output lines. Other operations of the ALU are computed in a similar manner. (We will study computer arithmetic in more detail in Chaps. 2 and 6.) The shifter allows the programmer to shift the data left or right (see Chap. 8 for a full discussion).

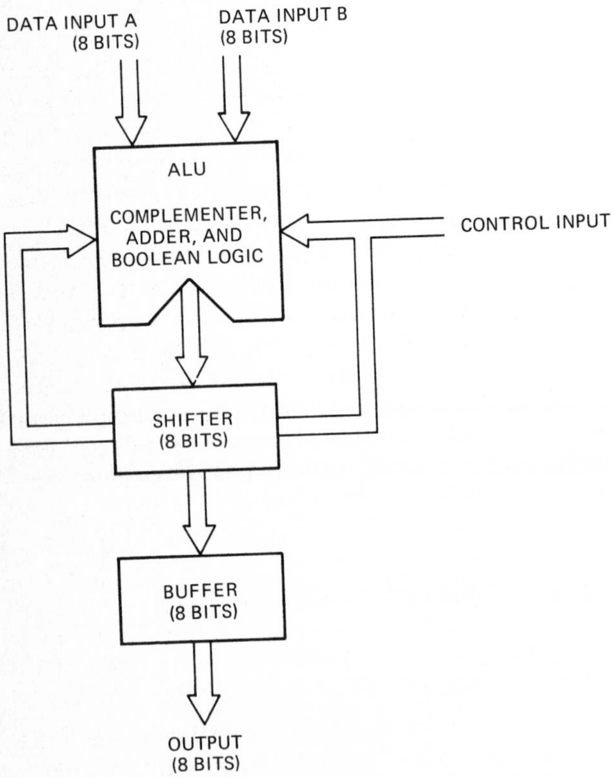

Arithmetic Section Review

1. List the components of the arithmetic and logic section.

2. Describe the purpose of the shifter.

3. How many inputs are required for an addition? For complementing?

4. Describe a possible use for the data path between the shifter and the ALU.

CONTROL SECTION

The control section maintains the correct timing and sequencing for the microcomputer. The crystal oscillator is the basis for timing, while sequencing is driven by the contents of the instruction register. Each instruction is actually a bit pattern that generates a series of enabling signals throughout the processor.

Each instruction requires one or more clock periods to complete execution. The timing pulses are generated by a crystal oscillator together with the clock logic, thus forming the master clock. The clock period in modern microprocessors is 100 ns to 1 μs. The clock logic may or may not be on the microprocessor chip. Figure 1-6 shows how two clock phases may be used for timing. The clock phases delineate the beginning or the end of each event within a single clock period.

Every instruction cycle consists of fetching and

DATA INPUT A
(8 BITS)

DATA INPUT B
(8 BITS)

ALU

COMPLEMENTER,
ADDER, AND
BOOLEAN LOGIC

CONTROL INPUT

SHIFTER
(8 BITS)

BUFFER
(8 BITS)

OUTPUT
(8 BITS)

Figure 1-5. Arithmetic Logic Unit.

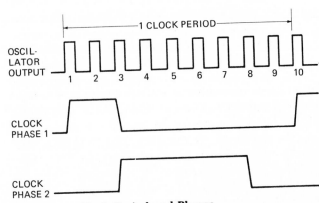

Figure 1-6. Clock Period and Phases.

Table 1-2
Instruction Fetching

Step 1.	The contents of the program counter are sent to memory
Step 2.	The contents of the memory cell are transferred to the data bus
Step 3.	The data moves into the instruction register
Step 4.	The program counter increments

executing the instruction. During the instruction fetch portion of the cycle, the instruction is read from memory. Table 1-2 lists the steps necessary to obtain the instruction. First, the contents of the program counter are transferred to memory. The word in that memory location (the instruction) is sent to the data bus and then to the instruction register. Finally, the program counter is incremented to be ready to fetch the next instruction. "Instruction execution" is another way of saying that the instruction is being decoded and the operation carried out. Instruction execution may require another memory reference to get the data, called the *operand,* to be processed, or alternatively, memory is referenced to write data back into some location.

Microprogramming

The instruction fetch sequence is an example of a *microprogram.* Each instruction in the computer instruction set, such as the one to complement the contents of the A register, requires a series of commands to move or operate on the data. The user need not be too concerned with the microprogram, as most microcomputers already have one developed for them. For special applications, a user can microprogram some models of MPUs, although this would be an unusual circumstance. Knowledge of the microprogram is quite useful in tracing a signal from within the processor, so an understanding of this concept will enhance your abilities to work with microcomputers.

Now consider the complement instruction. The microprogram steps necessary for its execution are illustrated in Fig. 1-7. All registers except for the program counter and A register were cleared prior to this sequence. The instruction fetch was also completed before execution of the microprogram begins, as shown in Fig. 1-7a. A brief review of the instruction fetching steps will explain the current contents of the registers. The program started at address $1000\ 0000\ 0000\ 0000_2$. This is the original value in the program counter that is sent to the

memory to obtain the instruction. The contents of cell $1000\ 0000\ 0000\ 0000_2$ were transferred to the instruction register and the program counter incremented to $1000\ 0000\ 0000\ 0001_2$.

The bits in the instruction are a coded message to control the start of the complementing microprogram. (The code $0010\ 1111_2$ means to complement the A register.) First, the contents of the A register are gated onto the internal bus and then into the ALU, where complementing takes place. Note that input B is not necessary for this instruction (Figs. 1-7b and d). The data is passed through the shifter and buffer, is then placed on the bus, and is finally returned to its complemented form to the A register (Figs. 1-7e and f). The complement of $1101\ 0001_2$ is $0010\ 1110_2$, as shown in Fig. 1-7.

Five microprogram steps were necessary to execute the instruction. On completion of the instruction execution the shifter and buffers registers still hold the result, but this data will be overwritten during the next operation. Because detailed knowledge of the signal and data flow within the processor is required, microprogramming a computer is a significant effort. Not every microprocessor can be microprogrammed by the user, but for those that can be, a microprogram development system is used.

Microprogram Development Systems

The microprogram must not be altered, so a ROM is used to store the control program. This memory is called a *control ROM* (CROM) to distinguish it from other ROMs used in the computer. Microprogramming consists of writing the microsequences for the control section. Development systems are available to make microprogramming easier. The monitor in Fig. 1-8 is an example of such a system.

Development systems usually consist of three parts: a microprogram controller, storage, and a display. The microprogram controller operates in the same manner as the control section of the microprocessor; that is, the microprogram controller *emulates* the control section. The microprogram being developed and tested is written and read into the storage device. The storage device is usually a read-write memory so that the program can be changed to correct errors; after the microprogram is completely debugged, it is copied into a ROM. The display unit permits the operator to read or write microcode in the storage unit, cause the controller to execute the microcode, and inspect the results of each microinstruction.

After the microprogram is checked out, prototype control ROMs are produced. These ROMs are exercised in the actual MPU to ensure that the micropro-

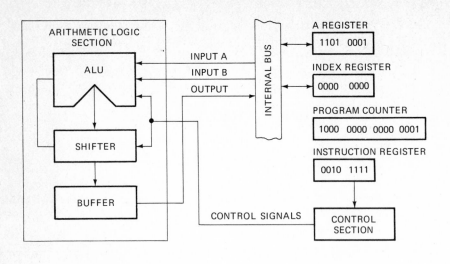

(a)

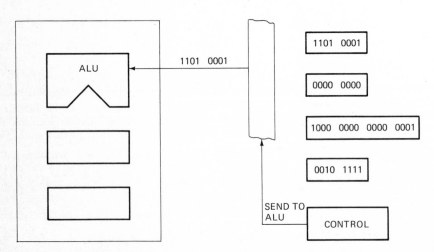

(b)

(c)

Figure 1-7. Microprogram for Complementing the Contents of the Accumulator.

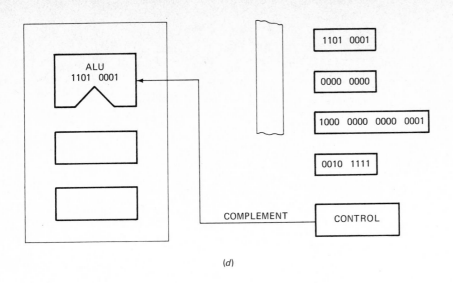

(d)

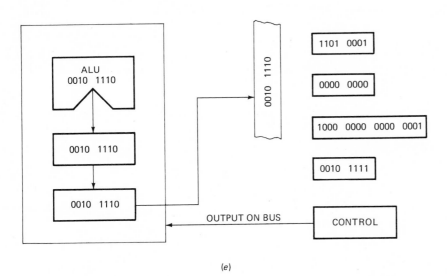

(e)

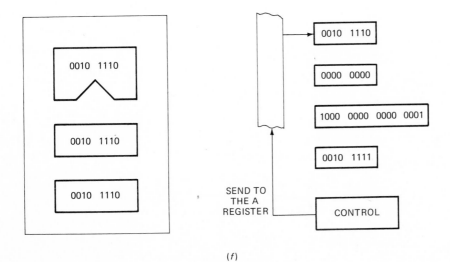

(f)

Figure 1-7. (Cont'd.)

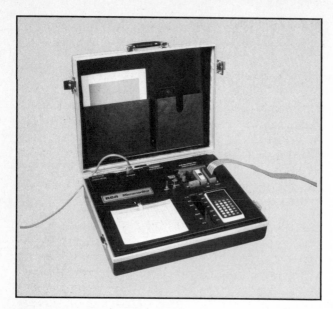

Figure 1-8. The COSMAC Micromonitor Helps Debug Prototype Microprograms *(RCA)*.

gram runs the same in the MPU as it did in the development system. On completion of this testing, the program is placed in production to generate as many CROMs as required.

Control Section Review

1. Describe the two parts of the instruction cycle.

2. List the events required to fetch the instruction.

3. Why must the program counter be incremented after fetching the instruction?

4. List the microprogram steps needed to complement the contents of the accumulator.

5. Describe the function of the internal bus in microprocessor operations.

MEMORY

Two types of memory are commonly used in microcomputers. Read-only memory is used to store programs and data which are not to be changed. (Do not confuse this use of ROM with the CROM; the CROM is read by the control section, while ROM is read by the MPU and contains the instructions needed for the microprocessor to perform its designated tasks.) Read-write memory stores data and programs which are frequently altered. Random-access memories are further divided into *static* or *dynamic* memories. Static memories must constantly receive power, while dynamic memories require only periodic refresh cycles. The memory area is often

partitioned into a ROM area and a RAM area. For example, a memory with 65,536 locations may have addresses 0000_{10} through 4095_{10} assigned to ROM and the remainder in RAM. Usually, the two types of memory are packaged in separate DIPs.

The size of memory is often indicated by a symbolic notation. The 65,536 memory mentioned above could also be written as 64K, where K means that the number to the left should be multiplied by 1024 to obtain the actual number of locations in the memory ($64 \times 1024 = 65,536$). The 8-bit word size can also be indicated as in 8K $\times$ 8 (bits). Rarely does the memory of a microprocessor exceed 64K; in fact, memories of 4K or 8K are more common.

Addressing

Memory capacity is always a power of 2. For example, the 64K memory is equal to 2^{16} ($2^{16} = 65,536$). The reason for this relationship is that memory must be addressed by use of the address bus. A given number of address bus lines (say, n) allow us to address 2^n different locations in memory. Each address line corresponds to 1 bit of the binary address.

Every memory location is capable of holding 1 byte of data. To find the total number of bits in a memory, simply multiply the memory capacity by the word length. Two examples are provided to illustrate these relationships.

☐ **EXAMPLE 1.** How many bits are there in an 8K $\times$ 8-bit memory?

$$8K = \begin{array}{ll} 8192 & \text{words} \\ \underline{\times\ 8} & \text{bits/word} \\ 65,536 & \text{total bits in memory} \end{array}$$

☐ **EXAMPLE 2.** A certain memory requires 10 address bits to specify the location of each word, and each word is 8 bits long. How many bits does the memory hold?

$$2^{10} = \begin{array}{ll} 1024 & \text{words} \\ \underline{\times\ 8} & \text{bits/word} \\ 8192 & \text{total bits in memory} \end{array}$$

Memory Map

A plan for laying out memory, called a *memory map,* must be prepared when a new microcomputer is being designed. Consider a case where 256 $\times$ 8 RAMs and ROMs are being used for the memory. Because each RAM or ROM contains 256 different locations, 8 address bits must be used to select the

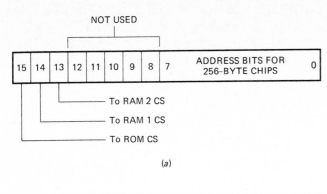

NOT USED

| 15 | 14 | 13 | 12 | 11 | 10 | 9 | 8 | 7 | ADDRESS BITS FOR 256–BYTE CHIPS | 0 |

To RAM 2 CS
To RAM 1 CS
To ROM CS

(a)

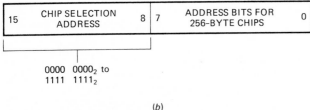

| 15 | CHIP SELECTION ADDRESS | 8 | 7 | ADDRESS BITS FOR 256–BYTE CHIPS | 0 |

0000 0000$_2$ to
1111 1111$_2$

(b)

Figure 1-9. Addressing Methods. (*a*) Linear Selection Addressing; (*b*) Fully Decoded Addressing.

correct location within each chip ($2^8 = 256$). In addition, we must design the memory to hold several of each type of chip.

If we want 1K of ROM and 3K of RAM, a total of 4 ROM chips and 12 RAM chips will be needed. Then the addressing process must select the correct chip in addition to the address bits within the chip. As we see later, the chip-select (CS) input to each RAM or ROM can be used to activate the correct memory IC. We also must designate whether the operation is to be read or write for the RAM chips.

LINEAR SELECTION ADDRESSING. If only a few chips are needed for the memory, linear selection addressing may be used. For a 256-word ROM or RAM, bits 0 through 7 can address the 256 locations in the chip. Now assume that our microcomputer uses one ROM and two RAMs and has a 16-bit address bus. Then we can let bit 15 of the address select the ROM, bit 14 select RAM 1, and bit 13 select RAM 2. By setting bit 15 to a 1, we mean that the

Table 1-3
Linear Selection Addressing Example

Address					Memory Selected
	0000	0000	0000	0000$_2$	None (illegal addresses)
to	0001	1111	1111	1111$_2$	
	0010	0000	0000	0000$_2$	RAM 2 (addresses above 0010 0000 1111 1111$_2$ are illegal)
to	0011	1111	1111	1111$_2$	
	↑ bit 13				
	0100	0000	0000	0000$_2$	RAM 1 (addresses above 0100 0000 1111 1111$_2$ are illegal)
to	0101	1111	1111	1111$_2$	
	↑ bit 14				
	0110	0000	0000	0000$_2$	RAM 1 and RAM 2 (illegal)
to	0111	1111	1111	1111$_2$	
	↑↑ bit 14 bit 13				
	1000	0000	0000	0000$_2$	ROM (addresses above 1000 0000 1111 1111$_2$ are illegal)
to	1001	1111	1111	1111$_2$	
	↑ bit 15				
	1010	0000	0000	0000$_2$	Combinations of ROM, RAM 1, and RAM 2 (illegal)
to	1111	1111	1111	1111$_2$	
	↑↑ bit 15 bit 14 bit 13				

address is in the ROM (see Fig. 1-9a). The consequences of this address assignment are listed in Table 1-3. Because an MSB of 1 selects the ROM, addressing conflicts can occur with careless programming, as shown in the last case in Table 1-3. Here bits 15, 14, and 13 are all set selecting all three memories; this programming is clearly wrong.

As Table 1-3 shows, a major shortcoming of linear selection is that some of addresses are unusable or "illegal." The total number of chips that can be addressed is limited, should you want to expand the memory. In this case the use of bits 8 through 15 limits the maximum number of memories to eight. However, the scheme, is simple, and no logic is required to decode the address of the memory chip selected; in fact, each is selected by a dedicated address bit. Small microcomputer memories are often designed to use linear selection addressing to minimize costs.

FULLY DECODED ADDRESSING. If the capability for addressing a 64K memory is to be provided, fully decoded addressing must be used. Each RAM or ROM is given a unique address corresponding with the binary number in bits 8 through 15. If we let those addresses be

```
ROM     0000  0000  XXXX  XXXX
RAM 1   0000  0001  XXXX  XXXX
RAM 2   0000  0010  XXXX  XXXX
```

we get for each memory chip the address range shown at the bottom of this page.

The remaining addresses available, but not used, will provide for an expansion to a total of 256 chips, each with 256 bytes (see Fig. 1-9b). Total memory size will be 64K $[(256 \times 256) = 65,536]$. Because consecutive addresses are used in this method, none is illegal; however, the cost of decoding the address is a disadvantage.

Decoding the address is simple in theory. Figure 1-10 shows a NAND gate used to decode the address for the ROM chip and then to select that chip. The

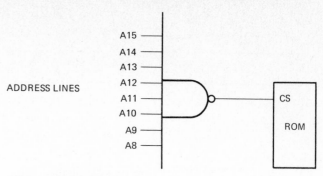

Figure 1-10. Simple Address Decoding.

CS input to the ROM will be set only if bits 8 through 15 on the address bus are all zero.

A more practical device that can be used for address decoding is the 74138 3-to-8 decoder. Three address lines connected to the inputs will set only one of the output lines (S0 through S7); the one corresponding to that address. If only 8 memory chips are used, one 74138 IC with address bus bits 8 through 10 as inputs will fully decode the address (see Fig. 1-11). If more than eight memory chips are used, several 74138 ICs can be combined to select the proper memory chip.

ADDRESSING DYNAMIC RAM. Dynamic RAM requires special addressing consideration. A typical $4K \times 1$ RAM will be used in the following discussion on addressing dynamic memories. In this case 12 address pins are required ($2^{12} = 4096$). Other pins are needed in this RAM as well; there are three needed for power (-5 V, $+5$ V, and $+12$ V), one for ground, one for the input, one for the output, one for chip selection, and one for read-write selection. The total number of pins needed is far in excess of the 16 available on the IC. How can this be?

In fact, there are not 12 address pins needed, but only 6 (A0 through A5). The pins are used twice in a *split addressing cycle*. To understand split-cycle addressing, first refer to Fig. 1-12, which presents

	Address Range							
	Low				**High**			
ROM	0000	0000	0000	0000	0000	0000	1111	1111
RAM 1	0000	0001	0000	0000	0000	0001	1111	1111
RAM 2	0000	0010	0000	0000	0000	0010	1111	1111

These bits designate the memory chip.   These bits address the 256 bits within each chip.   These bits designate the memory chip.   These bits address the 256 bits within each chip.

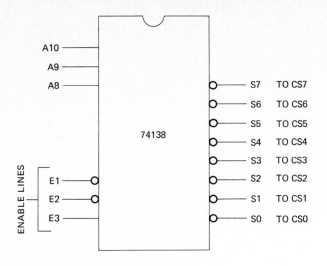

74138 FUNCTION TABLE			
INPUTS			OUTPUT HIGH
A10	A9	A8	S7
A10	A9	$\overline{A8}$	S6
A10	$\overline{A9}$	A8	S5
A10	A9	$\overline{A8}$	S4
$\overline{A10}$	A9	A8	S3
$\overline{A10}$	A9	$\overline{A8}$	S2
$\overline{A10}$	$\overline{A9}$	A8	S1
$\overline{A10}$	$\overline{A9}$	$\overline{A8}$	S0

Figure 1-11. Three-to-Eight Address Decoder.

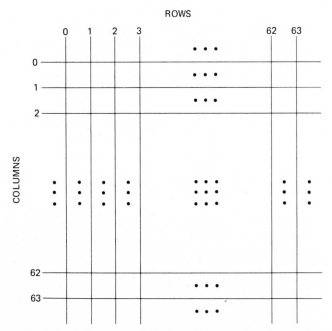

Figure 1-12. Row and Column Addresses in a Dynamic RAM.

a conceptual picture of the addressing arrangement. The memory is a matrix of 64 rows by 64 columns. At the intersection of each row and column is a memory address, so there are $(64 \times 64) = 4096$ addresses. Now each address for the RAM is divided into two groups of bits which are applied to the pins in two cycles. The 6-bit address for the row is first applied through an external multiplexer and a row-address strobe ($\overline{RAS}$) is set, which latches the row address into bits A0 through A5. Then the second group of address bits designating the column is applied, and the column-address strobe ($\overline{CAS}$) latches the column address into bits A6 to A11. By using a multiplexed addressing scheme, 6 address pins are made to do the job of 12.

All the pins on the RAM are identified in Fig. 1-13. The bars over some of the signals, $\overline{RAS}$ and $\overline{CAS}$, for example, indicate that the signal is true when it is low.

This memory has a word length of only a single bit, but our microprocessor requires 8 bits. To achieve

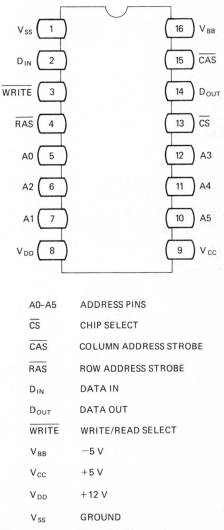

A0–A5	ADDRESS PINS
$\overline{CS}$	CHIP SELECT
$\overline{CAS}$	COLUMN ADDRESS STROBE
$\overline{RAS}$	ROW ADDRESS STROBE
D_{IN}	DATA IN
D_{OUT}	DATA OUT
$\overline{WRITE}$	WRITE/READ SELECT
V_{BB}	−5 V
V_{CC}	+5 V
V_{DD}	+12 V
V_{SS}	GROUND

Figure 1-13. 4K RAM Pin Assignments.

An Introduction to Microprocessors and Microcomputers **13**

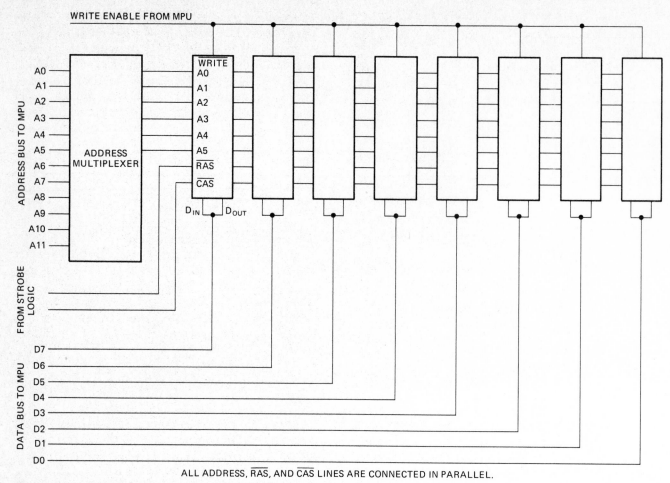

WRITE ENABLE FROM MPU

ADDRESS BUS TO MPU

A0
A1
A2
A3
A4
A5
A6
A7
A8
A9
A10
A11

ADDRESS MULTIPLEXER

WRITE
A0
A1
A2
A3
A4
A5
$\overline{RAS}$
$\overline{CAS}$

FROM STROBE LOGIC

D_{IN} D_{OUT}

DATA BUS TO MPU

D7
D6
D5
D4
D3
D2
D1
D0

ALL ADDRESS, $\overline{RAS}$, AND $\overline{CAS}$ LINES ARE CONNECTED IN PARALLEL.

Figure 1-14. 8-Bit Dynamic RAM Organization.

the desired word length, eight of the RAMS are used in parallel (Fig. 1-14). The address bits, $\overline{RAS}$, $\overline{CAS}$, and $\overline{WRITE}$, are paralleled to each RAM, while input data (Din) and output data (Dout) are connected to individual data lines from the microprocessor.

Because this RAM is dynamic, it must be refreshed, that is, periodically rewritten; otherwise, the data stored in the memory will be lost. Reading or writing of the memory is prohibited during the refresh cycle. To refresh the memory, bits A0 to A5 are set to the row address to be refreshed. Because it is necessary only to refresh the rows, a total of 64 cycles will take care of the entire 4K RAM. After each cycle, the row address is simply incremented by one until all rows have been refreshed.

Memory Review

1. Distinguish between the uses of ROM and RAM in microcomputers.

2. List the two types of read-write memories.

3. How many words are there in a 16K memory?

4. Explain why memory capacity is always some power of 2.

5. Discuss the advantages and disadvantages of linear selection and fully decoded addressing.

6. Describe how split-cycle addressing saves pins on a dynamic RAM integrated circuit.

BIT-SLICED MICROPROCESSOR ARCHITECTURE

There are some applications for which a general-purpose microprocessor is quite inefficient. In those cases, characterized by the need for a special purpose MPU and by high volume for cost-effectiveness, bit-sliced microprocessors can be used with success. These microprocessors differ in two ways from those that we have discussed to this point. First, they are available in 4-bit segments, thus allowing the designer to construct a microcomputer with word lengths of 4 to 32 bits or more. Second, the microprograms for these machines must be written by the

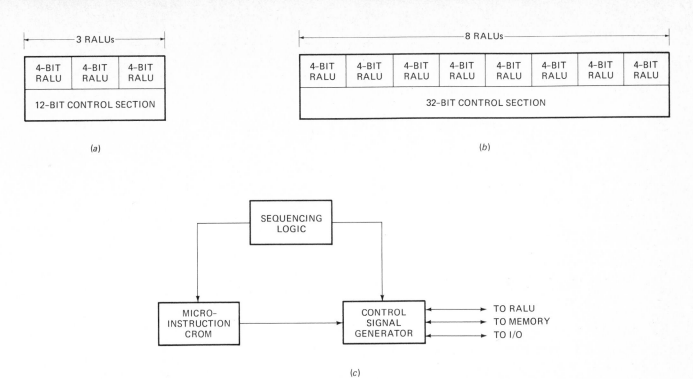

Figure 1-15. Bit-Sliced Microprocessors (*a*) 12-Bit Microprocessor; (*b*) 32-Bit Microprocessor; (*c*) Sequencer.

user, so the instruction set can be dedicated to the task.

This general nature of bit-sliced MPUs has a price, however, in that these MPUs are more difficult to use than are fixed-word-size devices. Designing the instruction set means that the control section must be uniquely tailored to each usage of the microprocessor. A great deal of effort and expense goes into producing the sequencing logic and microprogram of the control section.

A bit-sliced microprocessor provides all the registers, data paths, and ALU for the arithmetic section in segments which can be joined together. Earlier versions of these devices were available in 2-bit or 4-bit increments, but the 4-bit configuration is most common today. Figure 1-15 provides a conceptual view of how a 12-bit and a 32-bit microcomputer can be constructed from the bit-sliced *register arithmetic-logic units* (RALUs). Note that the control sections for the two microcomputers are different. Trying to expand the 12-bit control section to 32 bits would be difficult. Starting with a new 32-bit design would be more feasible.

The *sequencer* decides on the order for executing the microinstructions. The sequencer can step through the program consecutively, or it can jump from one program location to another. Sometimes the same series of microinstructions is to be repeated several times, so the sequencer must be able to maintain a count and decide when to terminate the repetitive series. In Fig. 1-15*c* we can see that the

sequencer contains three components. The CROM was already covered in the section on microprogramming. The *sequencing logic* interprets the microinstructions, decides the order for stepping through the microprogram, and orders the control signal generator to send commands to the other sections of the microcomputer.

The RALU is similar to the arithmetic section discussed earlier, except for the fact that the RALU is sliced into 4-bit segments. Figure 1-16 illustrates this concept. Data is received from the input data bus and is temporarily stored in a register file which is equivalent to 16 general registers. From the file, data can be sent either to the ALU, where the arithmetic, Boolean, and complement operations are performed, or to the shifter. A second shifter is in series with the data stream from the ALU, so a data word can be shifted in either of two shift registers. The buffer holds ALU results until they are placed back into the register file or on the output bus. All these components are 4 bits wide. The RALU can be joined together with another identical unit (Fig. 1-17). Here an 8-bit RALU has been formed by paralleling two slices. The ALU and all the registers and data paths now provide 8-bit parallel word handling.

The *control-signal generator* section must direct all the processing. Data must be routed along the paths at the correct time. The source registers for operands and the destination register for results must be designated. The input to the ALU and the opera-

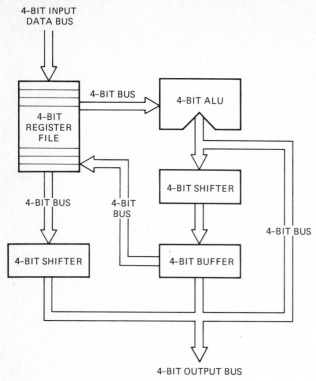

4-BIT INPUT
DATA BUS

4-BIT BUS

4-BIT ALU

4-BIT
REGISTER
FILE

4-BIT SHIFTER

4-BIT BUS

4-BIT
BUS

4-BIT BUS

4-BIT SHIFTER

4-BIT BUFFER

4-BIT OUTPUT BUS

Figure 1-16. 4-Bit Sliced RALU.

tion to be performed on them must be controlled, and a destination for ALU results must be specified. Even when control is considered from this simplified point of view, the complexity of designing that section of a microprocessor is obvious. Because of the work involved in using bit-sliced microprocessors, these devices are not as widely used as those with fixed word sizes.

Bit-Sliced Architecture Review

1. How many RALUs would be needed in a 24-bit microcomputer? How many control sections?

2. Describe the function of the sequencer and list its components.

3. How does the bit-sliced RALU differ from one with a fixed word size?

4. Discuss the operations that the control-signal generator section must direct.

INPUT/OUTPUT

There are three methods for exchanging information between the microcomputer and its outside environment. *Programmed I/O* transfers data under control of the computer instructions, so the external logic is commanded by the program. In contrast to pro-

gramed I/O are *interrupts* from the external logic which force an input data exchange although the processor was not expecting it. The most complex I/O logic is required for *direct memory access* which moves data to and from memory without involving the microprocessor in the data transfer. This section introduces I/O concepts which are more fully covered in Chaps. 11 and 12

Programmed I/O

Most commonly, microcomputer I/O uses serial data transfer. The serial data from the I/O is converted to parallel before the bits are placed on the system bus. Data from the processor must also be converted to serial. Most MPUs move data through some register in performing programmed I/O.

Interrupts

When a computer system is used in real-time operations, the processor must be notified of unscheduled events from the outside. Interrupt signals are used for this function. An interrupt request signal is transmitted to the processor by an external system-bus control line. The microprocessor, under program control, can accept or reject the interrupt. If the interrupt is accepted, the processor sets the interrupt acknowledge signal and enters an interrupt-handling program. When the external device senses the acknowledge signal, the device transfers the input data to the I/O port.

Remember that the interrupt was unscheduled, so the microprocessor must suspend whatever action it had been doing prior to servicing the interrupt. Table 1-4 lists the microprogram steps for interrupt processing. First, the processor and arithmetic registers must be saved in memory. Then the program counter and other registers are loaded with the address of the interrupt handling program. After that program has completed processing the interrupt, the registers are reloaded with their original contents

Table 1-4
Interrupt Servicing Program

Step 1.	Store the contents of the A register, program counter, and status flags (in some microcomputers memory is used for storage; alternatively, the stack can be employed)
Step 2.	Load the program counter with the address of interrupt handling program
Step 3.	Execute the interrupt handling program
Step 4.	Restore the contents of the A register, the program counter, and the status flags

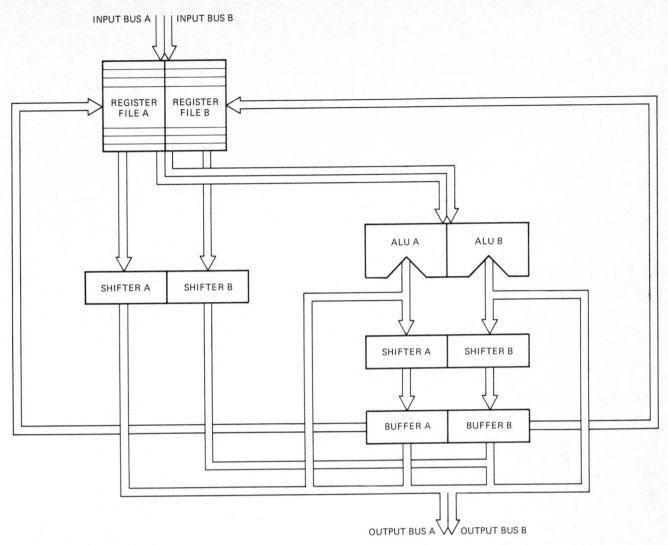

INPUT BUS A   INPUT BUS B

REGISTER FILE A   REGISTER FILE B

ALU A   ALU B

SHIFTER A   SHIFTER B

SHIFTER A   SHIFTER B

BUFFER A   BUFFER B

OUTPUT BUS A   OUTPUT BUS B

Figure 1-17. Joined RALUs.

so that the main program can resume executing at the same point where it left off.

Direct Memory Access

Using a direct access to memory, an external device can read or write data and bypass the microprocessor entirely. The advantage of direct memory access (DMA) is that the processor is not involved in I/O operations. As we see later, the disadvantages are the sophisticated I/O device necessary and the fact that instruction execution time may increase. Use of DMA is most commonly required when the processor would otherwise be overloaded in executing its program and managing I/O.

The scheme used to implement DMA is called *memory cycle stealing.* The external equipment sets a memory request signal high when it wants to access memory. The microprocessor logic responds with an acknowledge signal. The signal is an automatic

response by the microprogram and does not require execution of an I/O instruction by the processor. (Until the acknowledge signal becomes high, the requesting device must wait.) While the I/O device is referencing memory the processor can perform any operation except using memory; hence the term "cycle stealing." Some processors allow the device to continue to use memory for many cycles; others only allow a single memory reference before the processor regains control. Because only one user can reference memory at one time, the processor may have to wait for the peripheral equipment to finish. This delay in accessing memory could result in slowing down the speed of instruction execution.

Once the information transfer is complete, the I/O device drops the request, and the processor again can use memory. A device which employs DMA must have the same memory logic as the processor; that is, the device needs a counter to keep track of the number of words read or write, status register, I/O clock, and memory addressing and control logic.

Input/Output Review

1. List the I/O methods used by microprocessors.

2. List the sequence of events that an interrupt triggers if it arrives while the microprocessor is executing another program.

3. List the signals required to access memory directly.

MICROPROCESSOR PRODUCTS

Having covered microprocessor concepts in general, we now examine some specific devices. Figure 1-18 is a chart relating the characteristics of several microprocessors. It shows that microprocessors can be grouped by their word size, that is, 4, 8, 12, or 16 bits. They can also be classed as multichip MPUs, single-chip MPUs, or bit-sliced MPUs. The chart provides the genealogy for MPUs which grew from earlier versions. We can see how much the industry has advanced in just a few years from the fact that some microprocessor families have already produced three generations.

4-Bit Microprocessors

The earliest microprocessors had 4-bit word lengths instead of the more common 8 bits of the present microprocessors. This constraint was logical as the designers wanted to limit the risk in developing the large-scale integration (LSI) technology necessary for the microprocessor. As they gained

experience with the technology, the more cost-effective 8-bit device evolved.

The early 4-bit MPUs included the Intel 4004 and 4040 and the National Semiconductor IMP-4. Because these microprocessors were fabricated as multiple-chip devices, they can no longer compete economically with the 8-bit MPU. Single-chip 4-bit microprocessors still can provide a cost-effective approach to many applications, though.

The TMS 1000 series is just such a device. Actually, the TMS 1000 is practically a microcomputer on its own; a single package provides the MPU, ROM, RAM, and I/O logic. Its low cost makes the TMS 1000 a good choice for simple equipment items that are produced in a large quantity. Many consumer products are in this category.

Table 1-5 lists the members of the TMS 1000 family. The designer can choose from among ROM sizes of 1024 or 2048 bytes, RAMs of 64 or 128 4-bit words, and 11 to 16 control lines. All members of the family are fabricated by using PMOS technology and a single −15-V power supply. The instruction execution time is six clock periods, so if a clock period of 2.5 μs (which is minimum) is used, it takes 15 μs to complete each instruction. As might be expected, the instruction set for the TMS 1000 MPU is primitive.

8-Bit Microprocessors

The 8-bit microprocessor has become the industry standard today. The trend in this group of MPUs has been to decrease the number of chips and power

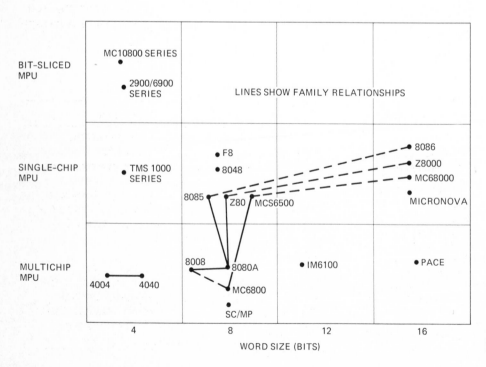

Figure 1-18. A Microprocessor Family Tree.

Table 1-5
TMS 1000 Family

Parameter	Device					
	TMS 1000	TMS 1200	TMS 1070	TMS 1100	TMS 1270	TMS 1300
Package pin count	28	40	28	28	40	40
ROM (bytes)	1024	1024	1024	2048	1024	2048
RAM (4-bit words)	64	64	64	128	64	128
Control-signal output lines	11	13	11	11	13	16
Output data lines	8	8	8	8	10	8
Power dissipation (mW)	90	90	90	90	90	90

supply voltages necessary to construct a micro-computer. This trend has grown to the point that manufacturers now produce single-chip micropro-cessors that need just one transistor transistor logic (TTL) compatible +5-V power supply.

THE 8080A. The 8080A is now being used in more different applications than any other microprocessor. Figure 1-19 shows an 8080A on a microcomputer card. The 8080A is both a descendant of and an improvement on the 8008 MPU. Of special interest to designers is the extensive range of supporting ICs available for use with the 8080A.

The 8080A is the basis for a three-chip micropro-cessor. In addition to the 8080A, an 8224 System Clock Generator, and the 8228 or 8238 System Controller ICs are necessary to provide all functions of a microprocessor. The 8224 is used to generate the timing signals for the 8080A MPU system from an external oscillator, and the 8228/8238 demulti-plexes the data lines of the 8080A. Chapter 4 provides a detailed description of the 8080A architecture.

The 8080A requires three power supplies of +5 V, +12 V, and −5 V. Using a 500-ns clock, the 8080A instruction execution times range from 2 to 9 μs. All signals are TTL-compatible.

The other devices in the 8080A family are listed in Table 1-6. The 8224, 8228, and 8238 were de-scribed above. The 8251 provides either synchronous or asynchronous data communications in a single IC. The μPD379 or μPD369 can also support these communications channels. The 8255 provides from one to three 8-bit I/O ports to the MPU. A multipurpose device, the 8212 I/O port can be used as an address buffer and decoder, a priority interrupt arbitrator, or an I/O peripheral interface. Direct memory access can be implemented by using the 8257 IC. Programmable delays or timed pulses can be created with the 8253.

Interrupt processing is facilitated by the 8259 or the 8214. The 8259 arbitrates priority among eight interrupts and initiates the software servicing rou-tine. The 8214 allows several simultaneous interrupt

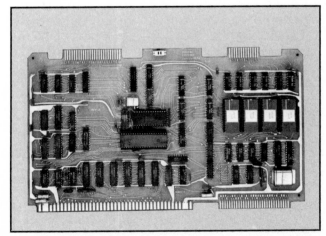

Figure 1-19. The DSC-80 Microcomputer Uses the 8080A *(Digital Microsystems).*

Table 1-6
8080A Support Devices

Device	Purpose
8224	System clock generator
8228/8328	System controller
8251	Serial I/O communications Interface
μPD379	Synchronous I/O interface
μPD369	Asynchronous I/O interface
8255/8255A	Programmable parallel I/O interface
8212	I/O port
8253	Programmable timer
8259	Priority interrupt controller
8214	Priority interrupt device
TMS 5501	Multifunction I/O controller
8205	Address buffer decoder
8216/8226	Bidirectional bus drivers

Table 1-7
Second Sources for the 8080A Family

Device	Intel	AMD	NEC	TI	NS
8080A	8080A	9080A	8080A	TMS 8080A	8080A
8205	8205	25LS138			
8212	8212	8212	8212	SM74S412	
8214	8214		8214		
8216/8226		8216/8226	8216		
8224	8224	8224	8224	SM74LS424	8224
8228/8238	8228/8238	8228/8238	8228/8238	SM74LS428	8228/8238
8251	8251	9551	8251		
8253	8253		8253		
8255	8255	9555	8255		8255
8259	8259				
μPD369			μPD369		
μPD379			μPD379		
TMS5501				TMS5501	

requests to be received and serviced by the software. Features of the TMS 5501 include two external interrupt request lines, an 8-bit input port, an 8-bit output port, one asynchronous serial I/O channel, and five programmable timers. The 8205 is a 1-of-8 decoder that can be used for memory selection. Proper signals on the bidirectional bus rely on such devices as the 8216 or the 8226. Except for those devices made by Intel Corporation, all 8080A and support ICs are manufactured by unauthorized second sources. Differences are often found between the Intel and second source parts. Table 1-7 lists the similar components made by Advanced Micro devices (AMD), NEC, Texas Instruments (TI), and National Semiconductor (NS).

THE MC6800. While Intel was developing the 8080A, Motorola produced the MC6800 as its answer to an improved 8008. The MC6800 is probably the

Table 1-8
MC6800 Support Devices

Device	Purpose
MC6802	MPU with RAM
MC6870A MC6871A MC6871B MC6875	Clock generator
MC6820	Peripheral interface adapter
MCS6850	Asynchronous communications interface adapter
XC6852	Synchronous serial data adapter
MC8507 (MC6828)	Priority interrupt controller

second most popular microprocessor family. There are considerable differences between the 8080A and MC6800, even though they may have a common ancestor. The MC6800 uses simpler timing signals and control signals than does the 8080A. The MC6800 does not multiplex the data bus, so no system controller (like the 8228) is required.

Only a single +5-V power supply is used. The MC6800 is fabricated by using N-channel silicon gate depletion MOS. Of course, the MC6800 has a different instruction repertoire; there are fewer basic instruction types than those provided by the 8080A. An off-chip clock device is required. The MC6800 uses a 1-μs clock and can execute instructions in 2 to 12 μs. (A faster instruction cycle is possible with the MC6800A, which uses a 750-ns clock, and the MC6800B, which uses a 500-ns clock.)

A family of support devices, listed in Table 1-8, is also available for the MC6800. The MC6802 provides 128 bytes of RAM with the MPU, but some pins and signals differ from those of the MC6800. The two-phase clock signals are generated by the MC6870 series clock chips, which contain both the crystal and the oscillator. General parallel I/O functions are supported by the MC6820, which provides two 8-bit I/O ports. For asynchronous serial data transfer and control, the MC6850 is used. The XC6852 performs synchronous serial I/O logic functions. The MC8507 priority interrupt controller has two part numbers because it is a bipolar component which is compatible with the NMOS MC6800 family.

THE F8. Although the 8080A is used in more different applications, the F8 is used in larger quantities than any other MPU. The F8 is an ideal microprocessor for consumer products because a simple micro-

Table 1-9
F8 Support Devices

Device	Purpose
3850	MPU
3851 3856 3857	Programmable storage unit
3852	Dynamic memory interface
3853	Static memory interface
3854	Direct memory access interface
3859	Single-chip microcomputer
3870	Single-chip microcomputer

computer can be constructed from just two ICs. The simplicity of the F8 results in an inefficient instruction set, but that is not a serious disadvantage in large-volume use.

The F8 uses +5-V and +12-V power supplies. The range of instruction times is 2 to 13 μs when a 500-ns clock is used. N-channel isoplanar MOS technology is used in the F8 fabrication.

There is a wide variety of devices in the F8 family (Table 1-9). The 3850 MPU also has two self-contained I/O ports. When the 3850 is used with the 3851 storage unit (which provides 1024 bytes of ROM, two additional I/O ports, interrupt request and priority logic, and a programmable timer), it can operate as a two-chip F8 system. The 3851 may be rendered obsolete by the 3856 and 3857 storage units, each of which provides twice as much ROM and a function similar to that of the 3851.

The 3852 can be used as an interface to either dynamic or static RAM, but the 3853 can interface to only static RAM. When the 3854 chip is used with the 3852 IC, it provides a DMA capability. The 3859 is a combination of the 3850 and the 3851 with 1024 bytes of ROM, 64 bytes of RAM, and four I/O ports. The 3870 differs in that it has twice the ROM space and needs only a single +5-V power supply.

THE SC/MP. There are two versions of the SC/MP. The original is a P-channel silicon gate MOS device which uses two power supplies (+5-V and −7-V). Instructions could be completed in 10 to 50 μs. The SC/MP II, built by N-channel technology, is twice as fast and requires only one-fourth as much power. It is powered by a single +5-V supply.

Consisting of one chip, the SC/MP provides an arithmetic and logic unit, a control unit, registers, and memory addressing logic. All its supporting devices are standard buffers, bidirectional drivers, ROMs, and RAMs. The SC/MP includes a serial-to-

parallel interface with access through two serial pins, one for input and the other for output. The on-chip clock oscillator is driven by an external capacitor, crystal, or TTL clock. The circuit has TTL-compatible inputs and outputs.

THE 8085. This MPU is Intel's next generation of the 8080A. A single chip replaces the three ICs needed in the earlier model. The 8085 package contains the ALU, the control unit, the accumulator and registers, and the clock logic. An external crystal or an RC network drives the clock logic. All bus interface logic is also provided by the 8085. Only a single +5-V power supply is needed by this N-channel silicon gate device. Its instruction set is almost identical to the 8080A.

In addition to being able to use many of the 8080A support devices, the 8085 also has some unique components (Table 1-10). The 8155 and 8156 were specifically designed for use with the 8085. They supply 256 bytes of static RAM, two or three (two 8-bit, and one 16-bit) parallel I/O ports, and a programmable timer. The 8355 has 2048 bytes of ROM with two 8-bit I/O ports. The only difference between the 8755 and the 8355 is that the former has erasable programmable read-only memory (EPROM).

THE 8048. The 8048 is a series of single-chip microprocessors. This family is at the low-capability end of microcomputers, designed for low-cost, high-volume applications. Only one +5-V power supply is used by any of the chips. All I/O is TTL-compatible. The user can select either a 2.5-μs or a 5-μs clock, and all these devices have a built-in timer. The members of the 8048 family are listed in Table 1-11.

Any of these processors can interface with the 8155, the 8355, or the 8755 chips developed for the 8085 MPU. In addition an I/O expander, the 8243, is unique to this series. The 8243 expands I/O port 2 into four individually addressable 4-bit ports. N-channel MOS is used in these 24-pin DIPs.

THE Z80. All 8080A instructions are a subset of the Z80 repertoire. The NMOS microprocessor is based

Table 1-10
8085 Support Devices

Device	Purpose
8155 8156	Static RAM with I/O ports and timer
8355 8755	ROM with I/O ports

Table 1-11
8048 Family

Designator	ROM bytes	EPROM bytes	RAM bytes	Clock Period μs	I/O Ports 8-bit
8035	0	0	64	2.5	3
8035–8	0	0	64	5	3
8048	1024	0	64	2.5	3
8748	0	1024	64	2.5	3
8748–8	0	1024	64	5	3

on the 8080A architecture, but it is not pin-for-pin compatible. The Z80 also has more registers and addressing modes than the 8080A has. Only one power supply is necessary, and clock logic is in the Z80. A novel feature of the MPU is automatic dynamic memory refresh. The popular TRS-80 microcomputer has a Z80 chip for its processor (Fig. 1-20).

All 8080A support devices except the 8259 priority interrupt control unit and the TMS5501 multifunction I/O device can be used with the Z80, although the 8155, the 8355, and the 8755 are not recommended. Other support ICs are listed in Table 1-12. The parallel I/O interface (PIO) is a functional equivalent to the 8255 of the 8080A support devices. It provides two 8-bit I/O ports. The clock timer circuit (CTC) is a programmable timer. It can serve as an internal timer or external event counter. There are four individual counters-timers within the circuit.

THE MCS6500 FAMILY. Although this family of NMOS microprocessors does not use the same instruction set or systems bus, it can be considered

a derivation of the MC6800. In some cases the clock logic is on the chip. These MPUs use a +5-V power supply. Instruction execution times vary between 2 and 12 μs with a 1-μs clock.

Table 1-13 lists the capabilities of the processors in the family. While the data bus is always 8 bits, the address bus ranges from 12 to 16 bits in length. Packaging is either 28- or 40-pin DIPs.

Two support devices are available (Table 1-14). The MCS6522 can be considered as an improved MC6820 with general-purpose parallel I/O logic, two 8-bit I/O ports, a counter-timer, and serial I/O logic. The MCS6530 provides 1024 bytes of ROM, 64 bytes of RAM, an internal timer, and interrupt servicing logic.

12-Bit Microprocessors

THE IM6100. This microprocessor is a copy of Digital Equipment Corporation's PDP-8E minicomputer. The unusual 12-bit word length of the IM6100 is the same as that of the PDP-8E. This MPU is also unusual in that it is CMOS technology. The IM6100 needs a power supply in the range +4 V to +11 V. Clock logic is on the chip, and instructions execute in 5 to 11 μs.

Supporting the IM6100 are two devices listed in Table 1-15. The IM6101 parallel interface unit must be used for system bus control. The IM6101 provides four flag outputs, four sense inputs, two write output strobes, and two read input strobes. A maximum of 31 IM6101 circuits can be used with a single microprocessor. The IM6402 is a universal asynchronous receiver transmitter (UART).

Figure 1-20. TRS-80 Microcomputer *(Radio Shack)*.

Table 1-12
Z80 Support Devices

Device	Purpose
PIO	Parallel I/O interface
CTC	Clock timer circuit

Table 1-13
MCS 6500 Family

MPU	Address Bus bits	Data Bus bits	Pins	Clock on-chip
6502	16	8	40	Yes
6503	12	8	28	Yes
6504	13	8	28	Yes
6505	12	8	28	Yes
6506	12	8	28	Yes
6512	16	8	40	No
6513	12	8	28	No
6514	12	8	28	No
6515	12	8	28	No

Table 1-14
MCS 6500 Support Devices

Device	Purpose
MCS6522	Peripheral interface adapter
MCS6530	Multifunction support logic device

Table 1-15
IM6100 Support Devices

Device	Purpose
IM6101	Parallel interface element
IM6102	UART

16-Bit Microprocessors

PACE (IPC-16A/520D). A 16-bit microprocessor, the PACE, is based on National Semiconductor's multi-chip minicomputer, IMP-16. Most of its signals are MOS levels rather than TTL levels. Power supplies for +5 V, +8 V, and −12 V are needed, but the +8 V can be derived fairly simply from +5 V, thus eliminating one. The PMOS processor executes instructions in 12 to 30 μs when a 750-ns clock is used. Data and address signals are multiplexed on the same bus.

Signals are translated from MOS to TTL levels by the bidirectional transceiver element (BTE). Each BTE is 8 bits wide, so two are used in the microcomputer. All timing signals are generated by the system timing element (STE). There are two identical

Table 1-16
PACE Support Devices

Device	Purpose
STE	System timing
BTE	Bidirectional transceiver element
MILE	Microprocessor interface latch element

sets of timing pulses, one at MOS levels for use by the microprocessor and the other at TTL levels for external logic. The microprocessor interface latch element (MILE) provides an 8-bit bidirectional latched interface between the PACE system bus and external devices.

THE MICRONOVA. Based on Data General's Nova minicomputer, the MicroNova is analogous to the Nova 3 central processing unit. (Another device, the 9440, is quite similar to the MicroNova.) Fabricated from NMOS, the MicroNova needs four power supplies: −4.25 V, +5 V, +10 V, and +14 V. The MicroNova has a 16-bit word and, as expected from its minicomputer derivation, extensive addressing modes. Instruction execution time is 2.4 to 10 μs (240-ns clock).

THE 8086. The 8086 extends the 8080A family into the 16-bit word microprocessors. Much of the 8080A/8085 software can be run on the 8086 after being translated by a special program. In addition to these features, the 8086 provides 16-bit arithmetic (including multiplication and division), string operations, and bit manipulation. Extremely sophisticated programming techniques such as reentrant routines, relocatable programs, and multiprocessing have been designed into this processor. The extended set of addressing modes allows the microprocessor to address 1 megabyte (10^6 bytes) of memory.

The 8086 is also considerably faster than its predecessors because it is fabricated from silicon gate HMOS. The reduced propagation delays allow a 5-MHz clock to be used. The instruction and memory efficiency allow the 8086 to run 12 times faster than the 8080A. The IC has 40 pins and uses a single power supply and two grounds.

The 8086 is supported by a large family of components. In addition to such devices as I/O ports and bus drivers like those we saw in other processors, this family also includes peripheral controllers: the 8251A programmable communications interface, the 8271 floppy disk controller, the 8275 CRT controller, and the 8278 keyboard interface.

THE Z8000. This 16-bit microprocessor is also in the category of competing with minicomputers in terms of the instruction set and speed. It is 5 to 10 times faster than the Z80A, with a 4-MHz clock rate. The processor instructions include 32-bit operations (including multiplication) as well as 16-bit operations. It, too, performs string manipulations and can run in a multiprocessor environment.

The Z8000 comes in two versions. The 40-pin nonsegmented version can directly access 64K bytes of memory, while the 48-pin segmented version can address 8 megabytes. The segmented version must be supported by the Z-MMU memory management unit for address translation and other memory overhead functions. The segmented version is upward compatible from the nonsegmented Z8000.

Other chips in the family include the Z-MBU microprocessor buffer unit, the Z-FIFO buffer memory, the Z-CIO and the Z-SIO I/O circuits, and the Z-UPC universal peripheral controller.

THE MC68000. A design goal of the MC68000 was to efficiently support high-level software languages by providing a suitable instruction set. This MPU, like the two previous ones, can run in a multiprocessor configuration.

Although the data bus is 16 bits wide, all registers within the MC68000 are 32 bits. Memory addresses of up to 16 megabytes can be reached by the 24-bit program counter. The processor is housed in a 64-pin DIP to provide a 16-bit data bus and a 23-bit address bus together with control and power pins. The 24th bit of the address bus is a combination (by external gating) of the address strobe with two data lines.

A +5-V power supply and two grounds are required. A single-phase TTL-level clock with a frequency of up to 8 MHz provides timing. Many of the existing MC6800 family support chips can be used with this processor.

Bit-Sliced Microprocessors

THE 2900 SERIES. The 2900 series microprocessor products (and the similar 6900 series) support a 4-bit sliced microprocessor architecture similar to that described earlier in this chapter. The processor is driven by a microprogram stored in ROM. Provided in the RALU 4-bit sections are the input and output buses, the ALU, complementer, shifter, register file, and buffer registers.

Table 1-17
MC10800 Support Devices

Device	Purpose
MC10801	Microprogram control unit
MC10802	Timing device
MC10803	Memory interface device

The 2909 microprogram sequencer creates the addresses for the proper microinstruction routines stored in ROM. Each microinstruction takes about 100 μs to execute. Operating directly on the ALU and buses, the microinstructions must specify the sources of data for each operation and the destination for the results of the operation. The microinstruction sequences will permit fetching instructions, moving data, performing arithmetic, carrying out Boolean algebra operations, complementing, and shifting.

THE MC10800 SERIES. More advanced than the 2900 family, the MC10800 series of bit-sliced devices is implemented in ECL technology. Characteristics of the devices are high-speed operation (5- to 5-μs microinstruction cycles) and high power consumption. The MC10800 ALU circuit provides a substantial portion of the processor and can be cascaded to any word size. The ALU is 4-bit sliced and used with a register file. Binary or binary-coded decimal (BCD) addition and subtraction, Boolean algebra

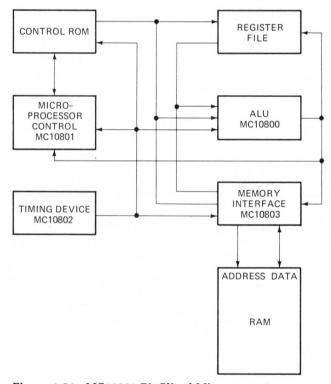

Figure 1-21. MC10801 Bit-Sliced Microcomputer.

functions, status signal generation, and shifting are performed by the MC10800.

Supporting ICs are listed in Table 1-17. The MC10801 control unit sequences through the microprogram stored in the control ROM. It contains a 4-bit slice of the total sequencer logic and can execute 16 different instruction codes. The MC10802 generates four timing signals, all under program control. Memory interfacing is the job of the MC10803, which performs all memory addressing for program and data in a 4-bit slice. The MC10803 is capable of sophisticated addressing modes, as it contains a small ALU to calculate the address needed for fetching the next instruction or reading and writing data.

The architecture of a microcomputer based on the MC10800 ALU is shown in Fig. 1-21. An external register file is used by the ALU for temporary data storage. Data from memory moves to the ALU and then to the register file in preparation for manipulation. After the operation, the destination of data from the ALU can be either the register file or memory.

CHAPTER SUMMARY

1. Digital computers receive, store, manipulate, and send binary data. Operations are directed by the instructions of the program. The computer is composed of control, arithmetic and logic, memory, and I/O sections.

2. Microcomputers are digital computers based on microprocessors. The microprocessor forms the control, the arithmetic and logic, and part of the I/O sections of the computer. Additional I/O logic, memory, an oscillator, and power supplies are used with the microprocessor in the microcomputer.

3. The microprocessors have data, address, and control buses to transmit and receive signals. Most of the buses use three-state logic.

4. Bits in computer words are numbered to facilitate referencing a specific bit. In this book the LSB is bit 0. The MSB is bit 7 in 8-bit words and bit 15 in 16-bit words.

5. The accumulator, or A register, is the primary arithmetic and logic register. The accumulator may also temporarily store memory and I/O data.

6. The index register is most frequently used for counting the number of times an operation is to be repeated. Some microprocessors com-bine the function of the accumulator and index register into a general register.

7. The instruction currently being executed is held in the instruction register for interpretation. The program counter contains the address of the next instruction.

8. Data can be pushed on top of the stack, and the item on top can be retrieved by popping. The stack pointer maintains an indication of the top location in the stack. In using the stack, errors of overflow or underflow must be prevented.

9. The result of the last arithmetic or logical operation is indicated by the flags of the status register. Most microprocessors provide carry, zero, sign, and parity flags.

10. The arithmetic and logic section is composed of an ALU, a shift register, and a buffer register. Arithmetic, Boolean algebra, and complement operations are capabilities of the ALU. The control input to this section specifies which function is selected.

11. Timing and sequencing are the responsibilities of the control section. Instruction cycles consist of fetching the instruction from memory and then executing the instruction. Fetching the instruction requires several steps.

12. The steps necessary to execute and fetch instructions are specified by the microprogram. Microprogram development systems are used to debug and verify and program before the CROM is fabricated.

13. Memory is often partitioned into ROM and RAM. Memory address bits specify an individual location. The memory map depicts the layout of the ROMs and RAMs in the memory. Both linear selection and fully decoded addressing have been used in microcomputer memories. Dynamic RAM uses split-cycle addressing to minimize pin count on the DIP.

14. Bit-sliced microprocessors allow designers to build computers with almost any word length and instruction set. Each such computer requires a unique control section.

15. Programmed I/O is the most commonly used data-exchange method for microcomputers. A peripheral device can signal its need for attention by sending the computer an interrupt. When large amounts of data must be transferred, DMA can be used.

Digital computer

Program

Microcomputer

Microprocessor (MPU)

Word size

Byte

Read-only memory (ROM)

Random-access memory (RAM)

Control section

Arithmetic and logic section

Input/output (I/O) section

Bidirectional bus

Three-state devices

Most significant bit (MSB)

Least significant bit (LSB)

Accumulator (A register)

Arithmetic-logic unit (ALU)

Index register

General register

Instruction register

Program counter

Stack and stack pointer

Pushing and popping

Status register and flags

Instruction cycle

Operand

Microprogramming and microinstructions

Microprogram development systems

Control ROM (CROM)

Static and dynamic RAM

Memory map

Linear selection addressing

Fully decoded addressing

Chip-select (CS) input

Split-cycle addressing of dynamic RAM

Refreshing dynamic RAM

Bit-sliced microprocessors

Register arithmetic-logic unit (RALU)

Programmed I/O

Interrupts

Direct memory access (DMA)

INTRODUCTION: The working of the experiments in each chapter of this book will increase your comprehension of microprocessor concepts more than any other method of study. The experiments use a minimum of equipment to reduce setup time but demonstrate the key points of hardware and software operation. After completing the experiment, you may wish to go further by trying variations on the programs. By all means do so, because the software will in no way damage the equipment—even if you make mistakes in your programs.

A microcomputer is, of course, required in each experiment. A wide range of 8080A-based computers is available, and any one would be satisfactory, provided that the data, address, and control buses can be accessed and the +5-V power supply can drive the few additional ICs used in the experiments. Figure 1-22 shows a typical microprocessor training laboratory.

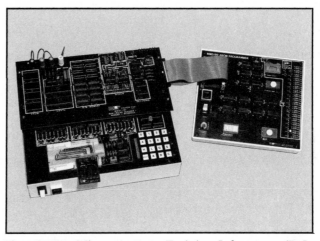

Figure 1-22. Microprocessor Training Laboratory *(E&L Instruments, Inc.).*

TOOLS AND TEST EQUIPMENT: Only common hand tools and a voltmeter are required for these experiments. The suggested items are:
Diagonal cutters
Needle-nose pliers
Knife
Wire stripper
Small screwdriver
Voltmeter [either volt-ohm-milliameter (VOM) or vacuum-tube voltmeter (VTVM)]

HINTS FOR WORKING WITH TTL:

1. All inputs to a TTL IC must be connected to either an input signal, the power supply, or ground. If they are allowed to float, the inputs will rise to a high-level input, thus producing incorrect outputs, and will also become excellent sources for introducing noise.

2. If you are not familiar with IC pin numbering, be extra careful to insert the chip with the indicating notch, (or the dot) toward the left. When the pins are pointing downward and the notch

(or the dot) is toward the left, pin 1 is in the left-hand bottom corner of the IC.

3. Use solderless breadboarding systems to build your circuits. Integrated circuits and other components snap in place on the board. Remove ICs gently by prying them up with a screwdriver, to avoid bending the pins.

4. Keep your wiring neat. Leads should be no longer than necessary to interconnect circuit components.

5. A complete description of the electrical and logical operations of each IC used in the experiments is briefly described in this book. More information can be found in the manufacturer's data books.

HINTS FOR USING CMOS: 1. Connect the power supply to the IC before you connect the inputs.

2. Store CMOS circuits on conductive foam or in conductive tubes to prevent damage. Place the circuits on aluminum foil during experiments.

COMPONENTS: A breadboard socket such as one of those shown in Fig. 1-23 is recommended for connecting the external circuitry. Almost any component can be used with the sockets. Leads must be short to reduce stray capacitance. Conventionally, the common ground line is placed on the bottom bus and the +5-V power on the top so that the board layout will correspond to most schematics.

Either TTL or CMOS ICs introduce current spikes when they switch. These spikes (or glitches) will pass through the power supply lines and false trigger other circuits. These problems can be avoided by using bypass capactiors.

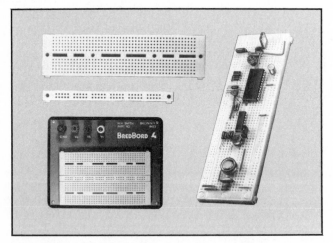

Figure 1-23. Breadboard Sockets *(H. H. Smith).*

2

NUMBER SYSTEMS AND CODES

A microcomputer works exclusively with numbers. To reduce costs and simplify the implementation, the binary number system is used instead of the more familiar decimal system. You saw binary numbers used in Chap. 1 to illustrate how data and addresses are routed in the computer. A good grasp of binary number systems and computer arithmetic is essential to anyone involved with microcomputers. In addition, knowledge of the codes used for representing information and for error detection and correction is necessary to understand the processing of textual data and the accurate transmitting of information over noisy data channels.

CHAPTER OBJECTIVES

Upon completion of this chapter, you should be able to:

1. Discuss the concept of positional number systems.
2. Convert numbers in the binary, octal, or hexadecimal systems to their decimal equivalents and vice versa.
3. Add, subtract, multiply, and divide binary, octal, or hexadecimal numbers.
4. Perform arithmetic operations using complement systems.
5. Define the requirements for double-precision arithmetic.
6. Encode or decode data using common digital coding methods.
7. Describe the techniques used for error detection and correction in digital communications systems.

POSITIONAL NUMBER SYSTEMS

You are so well acquainted with the decimal number system that you hardly think about it in counting or performing arithmetic. In elementary arithmetic courses you were taught rules for counting and adding, but these rules have been used so many times that you can perform the operations even though the basic principles are not explicitly recalled. When you start to use another number system, you will be required to remember these basic concepts until your aptitude with other systems becomes as good as it is with decimal.

All the number systems we are interested in use a *positional weighting* for each of the symbols, which are called *digits.* The quantity of digits in a number systems is equal to the *base* of that system. A positional number system can be represented in the form

$$(\cdots d_3 d_2 d_1 d_0 \cdot d_{-1} d_{-2} d_{-3} \cdots)_b \qquad (2\text{-}1)$$

where d_i is a digit and b is the base. Table 2-1 lists the base and digits for each of the number systems that we will be interested in. For the *binary* (or base 2) system there are two digits—0 and 1. In *octal* there are eight, *decimal* ten, and *hexadecimal* (or hex) sixteen. The hexadecimal system uses the letters A through F as symbols for the digits equal to the decimal numbers 10 through 15. In each number system the largest digit is always one less than the base. The largest decimal digit is 9 (10 − 1 = 9), while the largest octal digit is 7 (8 − 1 = 7).

Radix is another term with the same meaning as base. The two words are used interchangeably. You already know that a period separates the fractional part of a number from the integer in the decimal system. We call it a *decimal point.* In general, that mark is called a *radix point,* and it is used in the other bases as well.

The position a digit occupies in a number represents its *weight* in a positional number system. By using the representation of Eq. (2-1), we can express the weighting as

$$
\begin{aligned}
d_3 d_2 d_1 d_0 &\cdot d_{-1} d_{-2} d_{-3} \\
= d_3 b^3 &+ d_2 b^2 + d_1 b^1 + d_0 b^0 \\
&+ d_{-1} b^{-1} + d_{-2} b^{-2} + d_{-3} b^{-3} \qquad (2\text{-}2)
\end{aligned}
$$

Each digit's position represents the base raised to an appropriate power. In decimal, the first column to the left of the decimal point is weighted by 1 (10^0), the second column to the left by 10 (10^1), the third column to the left by 100 (10^2), and so on in positive powers of 10. To the right of the decimal point weighting is in negative powers of 10, that is, $1/10$ (10^{-1}), $1/100$ (10^{-2}), and so forth. We can portray this concept in the following manner.

			Decimal point ↓		
Decimal number	7	9	4.	8	0
Column weight	10^2	10^1	10^0	10^{-1}	10^{-2}

The same procedure is used in other bases. Again, the columns are weighted by increasing positive powers of the base to the left of the radix point and negative powers of the base to the right of the radix point. Examples in binary, octal, and hexadecimal follow.

			Radix point ↓			
Binary number	1	1	0.	0	0	1
Column weight	2^2	2^1	2^0	2^{-1}	2^{-2}	2^{-3}
Octal number	7	0	3.	4	2	
Column weight	8^2	8^1	8^0	8^{-1}	8^{-2}	
Hexadecimal number	F	2	B.	A	9	
Column weight	16^2	16^1	16^0	16^{-1}	16^{-2}	

To make the base of a number readily apparent, a subscript is appended to indicate the radix; otherwise, it might be impossible to distinguish between the values of numbers in different bases. For example, consider numbers composed of the same digits in several bases.

$$
\begin{aligned}
&11.101_2 &&\text{binary} \\
&11.101_8 &&\text{octal} \\
&11.101_{16} &&\text{hexadecimal}
\end{aligned}
$$

Positional Number Systems Review

1. Define the terms "base," "radix," and "radix point."

Table 2-1
Number Systems

Number System	Base	Digits
Binary	2	0,1
Octal	8	0, 1, 2, 3, 4, 5, 6, 7
Decimal	10	0, 1, 2, 3, 4, 5, 6, 7, 8, 9
Hexadecimal	16	0, 1, 2, 3, 4, 5, 6, 7, 8, 9, A, B, C, D, E, F

2. List all the digits in the base 16 number system.

3. What would be the largest admissible digit in a base 4 number system?

4. What does the subscript 8 on a number imply?

5. In the number $70.8F_{16}$, what are the column weights for each digit?

CONVERSION BETWEEN BASES

In our everyday business we use the decimal system, but when using digital computers the base 2 system will be of most importance to us. Converting between binary and decimal will become necessary in many cases to check answers, verify memory addresses, or decode data. Octal and hexadecimal numbers will also be encountered frequently because they are used to express binary numbers in a compact form.

Polynomial Expansion

The value of each digit in a number is determined by three factors: (1) the digit itself, (2) the number system base, and (3) the position of the digit in the number. The value of 159.8_{10} can be expanded by using these factors in a form similar to Eq. (2-2).

$$159.8_{10} = 1 \times 10^2 + 5 \times 10^1 + 9 \times 10^0 + 8 \times 10^{-1}$$

Writing a number in this way is called *polynomial expansion*. The same means of expansion can be used in any other base.

Polynomial expansion is the principle behind conversion from one number system to another. More efficient methods will be presented later in this chapter, but by understanding polynomial expansion you will gain insight into the conversion process. With the use of polynomial expansion, the number 111.01_2 can be converted to decimal by a series of multiplications and additions.

$$111.01_2 = 1 \times 2^2 + 1 \times 2^1 + 1 \times 2^0 + 0 \times 2^{-1} + 1 \times 2^{-2}$$
$$= 4 + 2 + 1 + 0 + 0.25$$
$$= 7.25_{10}$$

All the arithmetic operations needed to make the conversion are accomplished by using decimal numbers. Because the original base of the number was 2, the multiplications involved powers of 2.

By using the same approach but changing the multiplier to powers of the appropriate bases, octal and hexadecimal numbers can also be converted to decimal.

$$604.52_8 = 6 \times 8^2 + 0 \times 8^1 + 4 \times 8^0 + 5 \times 8^{-1} + 2 \times 8^{-2}$$
$$= 384 + 0 + 4 + 0.625 + 0.03125$$
$$= 388.65625_{10}$$

$$CFA.9_{16} = 12 \times 16^2 + 15 \times 16^1 + 10 \times 16^0 + 9 \times 16^{-1}$$
$$= 3072 + 240 + 10 + 0.5625$$
$$= 3322.5625_{10}$$

With hexadecimal numbers, you must change digits larger than 9 (that is, A through F) to their decimal equivalents before expanding the number.

Polynomial Expansion Review

1. List the three factors that determine the value of each digit of a number.

2. What is the weight of the digit 4 in the number 746.21_{16}?

3. What must be done to digits larger than 9 before expanding a hexadecimal number?

Conversion by Grouping

Octal and hexadecimal numbers are used because it is easy to convert from binary to either of those larger bases. The larger bases are a convenient, short way of writing long binary numbers because fewer digits are involved; for example:

$$101\ 001\ 110\ 101\ 011\ 000\ 111_2 = 5,165,307_8$$

It took only seven octal digits to represent the same quantity as 21 binary digits, so it is easier to write the number in octal rather than a long string of 1s and 0s. Simple mistakes such as inserting or deleting a digit can more easily be avoided by using the base 8 or 16 number systems.

A binary number can be converted to another base that is a power of 2 by properly grouping the bits to the right and the left of the radix point. In converting to octal, the binary number is arranged in groups of three digits.

$$1\ |\ 100\ |\ 111\ |\ 011\ |\ 010\ |\ 101\ |$$
$$111\ |\ 011.\ |\ 101\ |\ 110_2$$
$$= 001\ 100\ 111\ 011\ 010\ 101\ 111\ 011.\ 101\ 110_2$$

It may be necessary to insert leading and trailing zeros to form groups of exactly three digits. Next, the digits in each group are converted to their octal equivalents (which are listed in Table 2-2). The result for the number above is

$$= 14,732,573.56_8$$

Converting to hexadecimal requires that the groups be 4 bits long; for example:

$$1,111,100,101,011.011,01_2$$
$$= 1\ |\ 1111\ |\ 0010\ |\ 1011.\ |\ 0110\ |\ 1_2$$

Grouping and inserting leading and trailing zeros:

$$= 0001\ 1111\ 0010\ 1011.\ 0110\ 1000_2$$
$$= 1F2B.68_{16}$$

Obviously, the process can be reversed. It is possible to go from octal and hexadecimal numbers to binary by converting each digit in the higher base number to its direct binary equivalent.

$$65{,}231.4_8 = 110\ 101\ 010\ 011\ 001.\ 100_2$$
$$C01.A_{16} = 1100\ 0000\ 0001.\ 1010_2$$

It does not matter whether you use the octal or the hexadecimal system. Every binary number can be represented in either base. In this book we will concentrate on the hexadecimal system because it is easier to understand the manufacturer's literature for the microprocessor used in our experiments if we use that base. You should have knowledge of the octal system as well, because some equipment manufacturers use this system in their documentation.

Conversion by Grouping Review

1. Explain why the octal and hexadecimal number systems are often used in microcomputer documentation.

2. Describe the grouping process for converting from binary to octal and from hexadecimal to binary.

3. Discuss what you would do if the bits are not evenly divisible into groups of four digits when you are converting from binary to hexadecimal.

Conversion from Other Bases to Decimal

To convert to decimal from another base, an efficient method called "explosion" can be used. The explosion procedure consists of several steps, so it is more like a recipe than an equation. Mathematical descriptions of such processes are called *algorithms.* Algorithms are named after al-Khowârizmî, a ninth century Arabian mathematician who wrote a textbook on decimal arithmetic. Strictly speaking, an algorithm consists of the precise rules for transforming specified inputs into specified outputs in a finite number of steps. An example of converting from an octal number to decimal is used to illustrate this concept. The conversion method is called the "explosion algorithm."

INTEGER CONVERSION. If we want to convert the number 421.702_8 to decimal, we must first separate it into integer and fractional components. The reason for making the split is that the explosion algorithm uses one procedure for integers and another with fractions.

The first step in the algorithm is to write the old base (octal) as a decimal number, that is, 8_{10}. Next, the most significant digit (MSD) of the number to be converted is multiplied by the old base. The product is added to the next digit to the right. The multiplication and addition is repeated as many times as there are digits. The final sum is the answer.

The conversion process is shown below. The octal digits are "exploded" across the page to allow room for the multiplication and addition.

Start with the most significant digit

$$421_8 = 273_{10}$$

Explosion also works with hexadecimal. To convert CBA_{16} to decimal, the old base used as a multiplier is 16_{10}.

$$CBA_{16} = 3258_{10}$$

Each hexadecimal digit larger than 9 must first be converted to its decimal value by using Table 2-2.

Table 2-2
Decimal, Binary, Octal, and Hexadecimal Equivalents

Decimal	Binary	Octal	Hexadecimal
0	0000	0	0
1	0001	1	1
2	0010	2	2
3	0011	3	3
4	0100	4	4
5	0101	5	5
6	0110	6	6
7	0111	7	7
8	1000	10	8
9	1001	11	9
10	1010	12	A
11	1011	13	B
12	1100	14	C
13	1101	15	D
14	1110	16	E
15	1111	17	F

FRACTIONAL CONVERSION. Next we will convert the octal fraction to a decimal fraction. Recall that the number was 421.702_8. The process for fractional conversion uses division. First, the least-significant digit (LSD) of the fraction is divided by the original base expressed in decimal (8_{10}). The quotient is added to the next digit to the left, and the process repeated as many times as there are digits. The final quotient is the answer. Converting 0.702_8 to decimal:

Start with the least significant fractional digit

$$\frac{2}{8} = 0.25$$

Stop with the most significant fractional digit →

$$\frac{0 + 0.25}{8} = 0.03125$$

$$\frac{7 + 0.03125}{8} = 0.879$$

$$0.702_8 = 0.879_{10}$$

The original octal number can now be converted to decimal by adding the integer, found previously, to the fraction above.

$$421.702_8 = 273_{10} + 0.879_{10}$$
$$= 273.879_{10}$$

Hexadecimal fractions can be converted by using the same algorithm, but the divisor must be 16_{10}. Converting $0.C16_{16}$ to decimal:

$$\frac{6}{16} = 0.375$$

$$\frac{1 + 0.375}{16} = 0.0859$$

Before the next step remember to convert C_{16} to 12_{10}.

$$\frac{12 + 0.0859}{16} = 0.755$$

$$0.C16_{16} = 0.755_{10}$$

The accuracy of the conversion depends on the number of places to the right of the decimal point in each quotient. Often the conversion is carried to one greater than the desired number of places of accuracy and is then rounded. For example, to get a conversion that is accurate to two places past the decimal point, carry all arithmetic to three places and then round to two places as a final step.

ROUNDING. The rule for rounding a number in any base depends on whether the number is positive or negative. For positive numbers, add half the base

(5 for decimal, 4 for octal, and 8 for hexadecimal) in the position to the right of the final length. Then *truncate* the sum at that position; For example:

	Decimal	Octal	Hexadecimal
	Final length ↓	Final length ↓	Final length ↓
Add in third position	0.972_{10}	0.0756_8	$0.AFF_{16}$
	$+5$ ← Half the base	$+4$	$+8$
	$0.97\underline{7}$	$0.10\underline{16}$	$0.B0\underline{7}$
	Truncate		

Final results

0.97_{10}	0.10_8	$0.B0_{16}$

In the octal and hexadecimal cases, a carry was propagated into the higher-order positions, thus causing the final result to be *rounded up*.

For negative numbers, half the base is subtracted from the position to the right of the final length and the difference truncated; For example:

	Decimal	Octal	Hexadecimal
	Final length ↓	Final length ↓	Final length ↓
Subtract in third position	-0.6512_{10}	-0.076_8	$-0.CF2_{16}$
	-5 ← Half the base	-4	-8
	$-0.65\underline{62}$	$-0.10\underline{2}$	$-0.CF\underline{A}$

Final results

-0.65_{10}	-0.10_8	$-0.CF_{16}$

In the octal example, a carry was propagated to the higher-order positions, thus causing the number to be rounded up.

Conversion by Explosion Summary

The explosion algorithm for converting any base to decimal is summarized as follows:

EXPLOSION ALGORITHM

STEP 1. Separate integers and fractions.

STEP 2. Integer conversion.
   a. Express the original base as a decimal number.
   b. Multiply the MSD by the original base.
   c. Add the product to the next digit to the right.
   d. Multiply the sum by the original base. Repeat steps **c** and **d** as many times as there are digits. The final sum is the answer.

STEP 3. Fractional conversion.
a. Express the original base as a decimal number.
b. Divide the LSD by the original base.
c. Add the quotient to the next digit to the left.
d. Divide the sum by the original base. Repeat steps **c** and **d** as many times as there are digits remaining. The final quotient is the result.

Conversion from Decimal to Other Bases

The *digit-by-digit* conversion algorithm is used in converting from decimal to other bases. Here, too, mixed numbers must be separated into integer and fractional portions. Conversion of the integer is discussed first.

INTEGER CONVERSION. Integer conversion using the digit-by-digit algorithm requires that the number to be converted be divided by the new base expressed in decimal. The remainder is saved, and the residual quotient is again divided. The process is repeated until the quotient is zero. The MSD of the number is the last remainder generated. Find the octal equivalent of 75_{10} as follows:

Remainders

Divide by 8_{10}:

$$8\overline{)75} \quad 9$$
$$3 \leftarrow \text{LSD}$$

Residual quotient

$$8\overline{)9} \quad 1$$
$$1$$

$$8\overline{)1} \quad 0$$
$$1 \leftarrow \text{Last remainder is MSD}$$

$$75_{10} = 113_8$$

Converting 109_{10} to hexadecimal, we have

Remainders

$$16\overline{)109} \quad 6$$
$$13 = D \leftarrow \text{LSD}$$

$$16\overline{)6} \quad 0$$
$$6 \leftarrow \text{MSD}$$

$$109_{10} = 6D_{16}$$

FRACTIONAL CONVERSION. Fractional conversion by the digit-by-digit algorithm starts with the new base expressed as a decimal number. The fraction to be converted is multiplied by the new base, and the integer generated in the product is removed and saved. The process is repeated with the residual product until the desired number of significant digits has been generated. The first generated digit is the most significant.

Converting 0.896_{10} to octal (two places past the radix point), we have

Integers generated

$$0.896$$
$$\times 8$$
MSD 7 $\leftarrow \boxed{7}.\boxed{168}$
$$0.168 \leftarrow$$
$$\times 8$$
1 $\leftarrow \boxed{1}.\boxed{344}$
$$0.344 \leftarrow$$
$$\times 8$$
LSD 2 $\leftarrow \boxed{2}.752$

Rounding to two places, the result is 0.71.

$$0.896_{10} = 0.71_8$$

Converting 0.32_{10} to hexadecimal, we proceed in the same manner. We use 16 as the multiplier in that case.

$$0.32$$
$$\times 16$$
5 $\leftarrow \boxed{5}.\boxed{12}$
$$0.12 \leftarrow$$
$$\times 16$$
1 $\leftarrow \boxed{1}.\boxed{92}$
$$0.92 \leftarrow$$
$$\times 16$$
14 = E $\leftarrow \boxed{14}.72$

Rounding to two places gives 0.52, so

$$0.32_{10} = 0.52_{16}$$

Digit-by-Digit Conversion Summary

The digit-by-digit algorithm used to convert from decimal to any other base is summarized as follows:

DIGIT-BY-DIGIT ALGORITHM

STEP 1. Separate integers and fractions.

STEP 2. Integer conversion.
a. Express the new base as a decimal number.
b. Divide the number to be converted by the new base.
c. Collect the remainders.

DIGIT-BY-DIGIT ALGORITHM *(Continued)*

    d. Divide the remaining quotient by the new base. Repeat steps **c** and **d** until the quotient is 0. Collect the remainders in the reverse order in which they were generated to find the equivalent number.

STEP 3. Fractional conversion.
    a. Express the new base as a decimal number.
    b. Multiply the number to be converted by the new base.
    c. Collect the integer portion of the product and multiply the residue by the base. Repeat this step until the desired number of significant digits is obtained.

ARITHMETIC IN OTHER BASES

Checking of computer results can be accomplished most quickly by converting all numbers to decimal and using ordinary arithmetic. Because we are most experienced with decimal arithmetic, this manner of working will be the easiest to use. When it is necessary to perform arithmetic in other bases, possibly to follow step-by-step execution in the processor, we must use the arithmetic rules of the appropriate base.

Before looking at the rules in other bases, we will briefly review those for decimal. In addition, the *addend* is added by columns to the *augend* to calculate the *sum.* How do we know what the sum is? We use an addition table that we memorized long ago. Any column that adds up to more than 9 propagates a *carry* into the column to the left.

$$
\begin{array}{rl}
1 & \text{carry} \\
29 & \text{augend} \\
+37 & \text{addend} \\
\hline
66 & \text{sum}
\end{array}
$$

When we subtract, the *subtrahend* is subtracted in columns from the *minuend* using a subtraction table. The answer is called the *difference.* If a digit in the subtrahend is larger than that of the minuend in the same column, a *borrow* from the column to the left is required.

$$
\begin{array}{rl}
6 & \text{borrow} \\
\not73 & \text{minuend} \\
-18 & \text{subtrahend} \\
\hline
55 & \text{difference}
\end{array}
$$

If the subtrahend is larger than the minuend, the order of subtraction is inverted. A minus sign is placed on the difference, showing that the inversion was necessary.

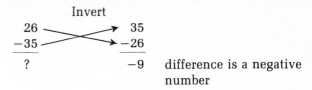

          -9   difference is a negative number

The rules for adding and subtracting in bases 2, 8, and 16 are the same, except we use new addition or subtraction tables. These sums and differences are listed in Tables 2-3 and 2-4.

Table 2-3*a*
Binary Addition

	Augend	
Addend	**0**	**1**
0	0	1
1	1	10

Table 2-3*b*
Octal Addition

	Augend							
Addend	**0**	**1**	**2**	**3**	**4**	**5**	**6**	**7**
0	0	1	2	3	4	5	6	7
1	1	2	3	4	5	6	7	10
2	2	3	4	5	6	7	10	11
3	3	4	5	6	7	10	11	12
4	4	5	6	7	10	11	12	13
5	5	6	7	10	11	12	13	14
6	6	7	10	11	12	13	14	15
7	7	10	11	12	13	14	15	16

Table 2-3*c*
Hexadecimal Addition

	Augend															
Addend	**0**	**1**	**2**	**3**	**4**	**5**	**6**	**7**	**8**	**9**	**A**	**B**	**C**	**D**	**E**	**F**
0	0	1	2	3	4	5	6	7	8	9	A	B	C	D	E	F
1	1	2	3	4	5	6	7	8	9	A	B	C	D	E	F	10
2	2	3	4	5	6	7	8	9	A	B	C	D	E	F	10	11
3	3	4	5	6	7	8	9	A	B	C	D	E	F	10	11	12
4	4	5	6	7	8	9	A	B	C	D	E	F	10	11	12	13
5	5	6	7	8	9	A	B	C	D	E	F	10	11	12	13	14
6	6	7	8	9	A	B	C	D	E	F	10	11	12	13	14	15
7	7	8	9	A	B	C	D	E	F	10	11	12	13	14	15	16
8	8	9	A	B	C	D	E	F	10	11	12	13	14	15	16	17
9	9	A	B	C	D	E	F	10	11	12	13	14	15	16	17	18
A	A	B	C	D	E	F	10	11	12	13	14	15	16	17	18	19
B	B	C	D	E	F	10	11	12	13	14	15	16	17	18	19	1A
C	C	D	E	F	10	11	12	13	14	15	16	17	18	19	1A	1B
D	D	E	F	10	11	12	13	14	15	16	17	18	19	1A	1B	1C
E	E	F	10	11	12	13	14	15	16	17	18	19	1A	1B	1C	1D
F	F	10	11	12	13	14	15	16	17	18	19	1A	1B	1C	1D	1E

Addition

We will use Table 2-3 to compute binary, octal, and hexadecimal sums. Remember that carrying is accomplished in these bases the same as in decimal, but the value carried into the next column is equal to the base.

$$
\begin{array}{r}
11 \leftarrow \text{carries} \\
01_2 \\
+11_2 \\
\hline
100_2
\end{array}
$$

$$
\begin{array}{r}
11 \leftarrow \text{carries} \\
2.7_8 \\
7.3_8 \\
+4.2_8 \\
\hline
16.4_8
\end{array}
$$

$$
\begin{array}{r}
1 \leftarrow \text{carry} \\
2A_{16} \\
+B_{16} \\
\hline
35_{16}
\end{array}
$$

Starting with the rightmost column in the binary addition example, we have $(1 + 1) = 10_2$ (from Table 2-3a). So we put down 0 in the first column and carry 1. In the next column we have $(1 + 0 + 1) = 10_2$, so again we put down 0 and carry. Finally, the last column has only a 1 in it, so we put down 1.

The octal and hexadecimal additions also rely on the tables. In the rightmost column of the hexadecimal example, we have $(A + B) = 15_{16}$, so we write the 5 in that column and carry 1. We next have $(1 + 2) = 3$. That sum is put down in the second column.

Subtraction

As in addition, we start with the two numbers vertically aligned on the radix point. (After the numbers are properly aligned, the operations of addition or subtraction ignore the radix point.) Direct subtraction is performed column by column in any base. First, the minuend is found along the top row of the subtraction table, and then the row of the subtrahend is located. The difference will be found

Table 2-4a
Binary Subtraction

		Minuend	
		0	**1**
Subtrahend	**0**	0	1
	1	−1	0

Table 2-4b
Octal Subtraction

		Minuend							
		0	**1**	**2**	**3**	**4**	**5**	**6**	**7**
Subtrahend	**0**	0	1	2	3	4	5	6	7
	1	−1	0	1	2	3	4	5	6
	2	−2	−1	0	1	2	3	4	5
	3	−3	−2	−1	0	1	2	3	4
	4	−4	−3	−2	−1	0	1	2	3
	5	−5	−4	−3	−2	−1	0	1	2
	6	−6	−5	−4	−3	−2	−1	0	1
	7	−7	−6	−5	−4	−3	−2	−1	0

Table 2-4c
Hexadecimal Subtraction

		Minuend															
		0	**1**	**2**	**3**	**4**	**5**	**6**	**7**	**8**	**9**	**A**	**B**	**C**	**D**	**E**	**F**
Subtrahend	**0**	0	1	2	3	4	5	6	7	8	9	A	B	C	D	E	F
	1	−1	0	1	2	3	4	5	6	7	8	9	A	B	C	D	E
	2	−2	−1	0	1	2	3	4	5	6	7	8	9	A	B	C	D
	3	−3	−2	−1	0	1	2	3	4	5	6	7	8	9	A	B	C
	4	−4	−3	−2	−1	0	1	2	3	4	5	6	7	8	9	A	B
	5	−5	−4	−3	−2	−1	0	1	2	3	4	5	6	7	8	9	A
	6	−6	−5	−4	−3	−2	−1	0	1	2	3	4	5	6	7	8	9
	7	−7	−6	−5	−4	−3	−2	−1	0	1	2	3	4	5	6	7	8
	8	−8	−7	−6	−5	−4	−3	−2	−1	0	1	2	3	4	5	6	7
	9	−9	−8	−7	−6	−5	−4	−3	−2	−1	0	1	2	3	4	5	6
	A	−A	−9	−8	−7	−6	−5	−4	−3	−2	−1	0	1	2	3	4	5
	B	−B	−A	−9	−8	−7	−6	−5	−4	−3	−2	−1	0	1	2	3	4
	C	−C	−B	−A	−9	−8	−7	−6	−5	−4	−3	−2	−1	0	1	2	3
	D	−D	−C	−B	−A	−9	−8	−7	−6	−5	−4	−3	−2	−1	0	1	2
	E	−E	−D	−C	−B	−A	−9	−8	−7	−6	−5	−4	−3	−2	−1	0	1
	F	−F	−E	−D	−C	−B	−A	−9	−8	−7	−6	−5	−4	−3	−2	−1	0

directly below the minuend, in the row of the subtrahend.

$$\begin{array}{r} 01 \leftarrow \text{borrows} \\ \cancel{1\cancel{0}0}_2 \\ -11_2 \\ \hline 001_2 \end{array}$$

If the digit in the minuend is smaller than that in the subtrahend, we must borrow from the next column to the left. Remember that in binary we are borrowing 2 from the next column. In octal the borrow is 8 and in hexadecimal, 16, of course. If the subtrahend is a larger number than the minuend, we simply invert the order of the subtraction and put a minus sign on the difference.

In this octal subtraction problem the subtrahend is larger than the minuend.

$$\begin{array}{r} 3 \leftarrow \text{borrows} \\ 27_8 \quad\quad \cancel{4}6 \\ -46_8 \qu\quad -27_8 \\ \hline ? \quad\quad -17_8 \end{array}$$

A similar procedure is followed in hexadecimal subtraction.

$$\begin{array}{r} 1 \leftarrow \text{borrows} \\ \cancel{2}.A_{16} \\ -1.F_{16} \\ \hline 0.B_{16} \end{array}$$

Multiplication

The multiplication tables in Table 2-5 provide the rules for this operation. Multiplication in other bases uses the same process as decimal. That is, each digit of the *multiplier* is multiplied by the *multiplicand*, and then the *partial products* are added. The position of the radix point in the *product* is found by adding the number of places in the multiplier and the multiplicand. An example of binary multiplication is

$$\begin{array}{r} 111\,001_2 \\ \times\,101_2 \\ \hline \end{array}$$

| 111 001 | multiplicand |
| 101 | multiplier |

$$\left.\begin{array}{r} 111\,001 \\ 0\,000\,00 \\ 11\,100\,1 \end{array}\right\} \text{partial products (move over one place for each row)}$$

$$100\,011\,101_2 \quad \text{product}$$

The octal multiplication below shows how the radix point position is found.

$$\left.\begin{array}{r} 7.45_8 \\ \times 2.1_8 \end{array}\right\} \text{3 radix places}$$
$$\begin{array}{r} 745 \\ 1712 \\ \hline 20.065_8 \leftarrow \end{array}$$

Similarly, in hexadecimal:

$$\begin{array}{r} B.E_{16} \\ \times 9_{16} \\ \hline 6A.E_{16} \end{array}$$

Table 2-5a
Binary Multiplication

		Multiplicand	
		0	**1**
Multiplier	**0**	0	0
	1	0	1

Table 2-5b
Octal Multiplication

		Multiplicand							
		0	**1**	**2**	**3**	**4**	**5**	**6**	**7**
Multiplier	**0**	0	0	0	0	0	0	0	0
	1	0	1	2	3	4	5	6	7
	2	0	2	4	6	10	12	14	16
	3	0	3	6	11	14	17	22	25
	4	0	4	10	14	20	24	30	34
	5	0	5	12	17	24	31	36	43
	6	0	6	14	22	30	36	44	52
	7	0	7	16	25	34	43	52	61

Table 2-5c
Hexadecimal Multiplication

		Multiplicand															
		0	**1**	**2**	**3**	**4**	**5**	**6**	**7**	**8**	**9**	**A**	**B**	**C**	**D**	**E**	**F**
Multiplier	**0**	0	0	0	0	0	0	0	0	0	0	0	0	0	0	0	0
	1	0	1	2	3	4	5	6	7	8	9	A	B	C	D	E	F
	2	0	2	4	6	8	A	C	E	10	12	14	16	18	1A	1C	1E
	3	0	3	6	9	C	F	12	15	18	1B	1E	21	24	27	2A	2D
	4	0	4	8	C	10	14	18	1C	20	24	28	2C	30	34	38	3C
	5	0	5	A	F	14	19	1E	23	28	2D	32	37	3C	41	46	4B
	6	0	6	C	12	18	1E	24	2A	30	36	3C	42	48	4E	54	5A
	7	0	7	E	15	1C	23	2A	31	38	3F	46	4D	54	5B	62	69
	8	0	8	10	18	20	28	30	38	40	48	50	58	60	68	70	78
	9	0	9	12	1B	24	2D	36	3F	48	51	5A	63	6C	75	7E	87
	A	0	A	14	1E	28	32	3C	46	50	5A	64	6E	78	82	8C	96
	B	0	B	16	21	2C	37	42	4D	58	63	6E	79	84	8F	9A	A5
	C	0	C	18	24	30	3C	48	54	60	6C	78	84	90	9C	A8	B4
	D	0	D	1A	27	34	41	4E	5B	68	75	82	8F	9C	A9	B6	C3
	E	0	E	1C	2A	38	46	54	62	70	7E	8C	9A	A8	B6	C4	D2
	F	0	F	1E	2D	3C	4B	5A	69	78	87	96	A5	B4	C3	D2	E1

Division

Straight division in other bases is quite difficult. Instead, a multiplication table is constructed for the problem to prevent error. An octal example using such a table and illustrating the general rules of division is given below. The easiest way of developing the multiplication table is by repeated addition of the divisor. Instead of multiplying 26_8 by each digit from 0 to 10, simply add 26_8 to the product above for each row in the table. As a check, the last addition should be the original number (26_8) with a 0 to the right (260_8).

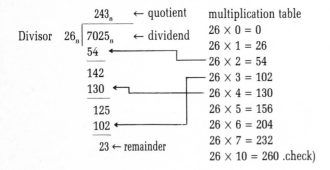

Divisor 26_8 | 7025_8 ← dividend, 243_8 ← quotient

```
multiplication table
26 × 0 = 0
26 × 1 = 26
26 × 2 = 54
26 × 3 = 102
26 × 4 = 130
26 × 5 = 156
26 × 6 = 204
26 × 7 = 232
26 × 10 = 260 (check)
```

23 ← remainder

Binary division is so simple that a multiplication table is unnecessary. If the divisor is less than or equal to the dividend, the quotient is 1 in that position; otherwise, the quotient is 0. In the following problem the radix points in the divisor and dividend are both moved two places to the right to properly align the quotient. The general rule for the radix is to move it as many places as necessary to have it appear at the extreme right of the divisor.

$$
\begin{array}{r}
1101.0_2 \\
10.01_2 \overline{) 11101.010_2} \\
1001 \\
\hline
1011 \\
1001 \\
\hline
100 \\
000 \\
\hline
1001 \\
1001 \\
\hline
0
\end{array}
$$

Hexadecimal division requires a multiplication table constructed in a manner similar to the one for octal division.

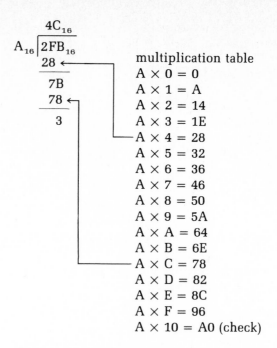

A_{16} | $2FB_{16}$, $4C_{16}$

```
28
7B
78
3
```

```
multiplication table
A × 0 = 0
A × 1 = A
A × 2 = 14
A × 3 = 1E
A × 4 = 28
A × 5 = 32
A × 6 = 36
A × 7 = 46
A × 8 = 50
A × 9 = 5A
A × A = 64
A × B = 6E
A × C = 78
A × D = 82
A × E = 8C
A × F = 96
A × 10 = A0 (check)
```

Arithmetic Review

1. Describe how a table is used for the addition rules in any positional number system.

2. How is the radix point handled in binary subtraction?

3. Discuss the position of the radix point in the product of hexadecimal multiplication.

4. Describe the purpose of the multiplication table constructed for division of octal numbers. What simple check can be made to ensure that the multiplication table is correct before using it to carry out the division?

COMPLEMENT SYSTEMS

Digital circuits that perform arithmetic must be able to represent both positive and negative quantities. Because the circuits do not provide an easy method of indicating plus and minus signs, another indication is used in their place. The most significant bit of a binary number is used to show whether it is positive or negative. Recall that the quantity of bits in a number is the word length, so the sign bit is the leftmost bit in a word.

Figure 2-1 shows the range of hexadecimal numbers for an 8-bit word. A 0 in the most significant bit position indicates a positive number, and a sign bit of 1 is a negative value. In Fig. 2-1 the positive numbers run from 00_{16} ($0000\ 0000_2$) to $7F_{16}$ ($0111\ 1111_2$). Negative numbers range from 80_{16} ($1000\ 0000_2$) through FF_{16} ($1111\ 1111_2$). We can distinguish a positive number from a negative by just

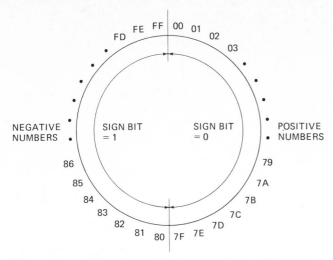

Figure 2-1. A Hexadecimal 8-Bit Complement System.

examining 1 bit. Arranging the numbers in a circle (as in Fig. 2-1) shows the cyclic nature of the numbers.

1's Complement

While not immediately obvious, there are two common ways of assigning the negative numbers to the quantities listed in Fig. 2-1. With either method, a complement system is used for negative numbers. One way that the negative numbers can be assigned is to convert each digit to its negative equivalent by binary subtraction in each column. Expressing the 8-bit number $-2A_{16}$ in this way, we start with the positive number $2A_{16} = 0010\ 1010_2$. Subtracting each bit from 1:

$$
\begin{array}{cccccccc}
1 & 1 & 1 & 1 & 1 & 1 & 1 & 1 \\
-0 & -0 & -1 & -0 & -1 & -0 & -1 & -0 \\
\hline
1 & 1 & 0 & 1 & 0 & 1 & 0 & 1
\end{array}
$$

$$= 1101\ 0101_2 = D5_{16}$$

The word length must be specified prior to converting the number to its negative equivalent, so we know where the sign bit is to appear.

This convention is called the *1's complement,* or the *radix minus 1* complement. Its properties are shown in Table 2-6. Table 2-6 shows that all positive numbers are not changed in value, but negative numbers must be converted in the manner used above. The conversion can also be carried out in hexadecimal by subtracting each digit from F_{16}.

The 1's complement system has an unusual property. There are both positive and negative representations for zero. Both 00_{16} and FF_{16} equal the same quantity. Proof of their equivalence is straightforward. The conversion process is accomplished

Table 2-6
Hexadecimal 8-Bit 1's Complements

Number	Representation	
+7F	7F	
+7E	7E	
+7D	7D	
.	.	
.	.	Positive numbers
.	.	
+02	02	
+01	01	
+00	00	
−00	FF	
−01	FE	
−02	FD	
−03	FC	
.	.	
.	.	Negative numbers
.	.	
−7D	82	
−7E	81	
−7F	80	

in hexadecimal this time. Converting FF_{16} to its positive equivalent, we subtract each digit from F_{16}.

$$
\begin{array}{cc}
F & F \\
-F & -F \\
\hline
0 & 0
\end{array}
$$

Thus the complement of FF_{16} is -00_{16}. (Of course, -0 is the same as $+0$.)

The negative zero in the 1's complement system makes counting clumsy. On the other hand, there are equal quantities of positive and negative numbers in the 1's complement system; that is, we can make a one-to-one match of positives and negatives.

Positive	Negative
7F	80
7E	81
7D	82
.	.
.	.
.	.
02	FD
01	FE
00	FF

2's Complement

Even more widely used than the 1's complement system is the 2's complement. Using 8-bit words, the 2's complement is found by first determining the 1's complement and then adding 1 to the number that results. We showed in the last section that the 1's complement of $-2A_{16}$ is $D5_{16}$. The 2's complement is simply

$$D5_{16} + 1 = D6_{16}$$

Thus $D6_{16} = -2A_{16}$ in the 2's complement system. You may wonder why more than one complement system is necessary. Only one of these two ways of indicating negative numbers is used in any given microprocessor. Although the 2's complement is most popular, some manufacturers have built machines that used the 1's complement.

We emphasize the use of the 2's complement in this book. Using this conversion method, several other examples of finding the 2's complement are worked below.

□ EXAMPLE 1.

What is the 2's complement of 35_{16}? First, obtain the 1's complement.

$$
\begin{array}{cc}
F & F \\
-3 & -5 \\
\hline
C & A \\
\end{array}
$$

Add 1:
$$
\begin{array}{cc}
+ & 1 \\
\hline
C & B \\
\end{array}
$$

$$CB_{16} = -35_{16}$$

□ EXAMPLE 2.

Find the 2's complement of -00_{16}.

$$
\begin{array}{cc}
F & F \\
-0 & -0 \\
\hline
F & F \\
+ & 1 \\
\end{array}
$$

Discard the MSD: ①0   0

$$-00_{16} = 00_{16}$$

There is only one representation for zero in this complement system.

□ EXAMPLE 3.

What is the 2's complement of $-FA_{16}$?

$$
\begin{array}{cc}
F & F \\
-F & -A \\
\hline
0 & 5 \\
+ & 1 \\
\hline
0 & 6 \\
\end{array}
$$

$$-FA_{16} = 06_{16}$$

The sign bit was set, and the minus sign precedes the number. The two negative signs cancel, thus giving a positive result.

Table 2-7
Hexadecimal 8-Bit 2's Complements

Number	Representation	
+7F	7F	
+7E	7E	
+7D	7D	
.	.	
.	.	Positive numbers
.	.	
+02	02	
+01	01	
+00	00	
−01	FF	
−02	FE	
−03	FD	
.	.	
.	.	Negative numbers
.	.	
−7E	82	
−7F	81	
−80	80	

Table 2-7 shows that there are two major differences between the 1's and the 2's complements. First, there is only a single value for zero in the 2's complement. Thus the counting properties of the 2's complement are better. Second, the 2's complement has more negative numbers than positive. The value -80_{16} is included in Table 2-7, but there is no corresponding positive value of $+80_{16}$. The difference in the quantity of positive and negative numbers is mostly of interest to programmers and has little electronic significance.

Subtraction Using Complements

The main reason for using complements in microprocessors is that they make it possible to subtract by means of addition, thus allowing the same circuitry to be used in the processor for both operations.

SUBTRACTING BY 1'S COMPLEMENT. If we want to subtract by 1's complement, the minuend of the problem is not changed, but the subtrahend is converted to its 1's complement. We then add the two numbers. If the last column generates a carry, a 1 is "ended around" and added to find the final answer. Using an 8-bit word, subtract 14_{16} from 53_{16}.

Direct subtraction		1's complement
53_{16}		53_{16}
-14_{16} → 1's complement →		$+EB_{16}$
$3F_{16}$	end around	①3E
		+ 1
identical results →		$3F_{16}$

SUBTRACTING BY 2'S COMPLEMENT. Subtraction can also be carried out in the 2's complement system, as you might expect. The subtrahend is converted to its 2's complement and the numbers added. In this case any carry generated from the last column is just discarded.

Direct subtraction		2's complement
53_{16}		53_{16}
-14_{16}	→ 2's complement →	$+EC_{16}$
$3F_{16}$	discard	(1)$3F_{16}$

↑ identical results ↑

Complement Systems Review

1. Distinguish between the 1's and the 2's complement systems. Why are both in use?
2. List some 8-bit octal numbers. Separate the list into positive and negative numbers and assign values to these numbers by using the 2's complement system.
3. Describe how subtraction can be performed by using addition with the 2's complement system.
4. What do you do if there is a carry out of the last column in the sum during 2's complement subtraction?

DOUBLE-PRECISION ARITHMETIC

A microprocessor word size limitation of 8 bits may seem to put some mathematical problems outside the reach of a small processor. Considering that the largest positive number is only $7F_{16}$ (127_{10}), how can the MPU be used in applications with numbers which extend beyond this range? Double-precision arithmetic is one way of overcoming this problem. As shown in Fig. 2-2, two 8-bit words can be joined to hold a larger number. A total of 15 bits for magnitude and the 16th bit for a sign will provide a range of numbers from $+32{,}767_{10}$ to $-32{,}768_{10}$ in the 2's complement. Even more capacity can be obtained by the use of triple-precision or longer multibyte word lengths, but microprocessors seldom need such precision.

The double-precision word consists of two half words called the *most* and *least significant halves* (MSH and LSH) or bytes. Addition and subtraction can easily be accomplished using complement arithmetic. The *double-precision addition algorithm* requires three steps:

1. Add the LSH of the augend to the LSH of the addend.
2. Add the carry from bit 7 of step 1 to the MSH of the augend.
3. Add the MSH of the augend and the MSH of the addend.

□ **EXAMPLE 1.** Add $07FA_{16}$ to $02AB_{16}$.

Add the LSH.

```
             AB
            +FA
Carry out  (1)A5 ← LSH sum
```

Add carry to the MSH of the augend.

```
 02
 +1
 03
```

Add the MSH of the augend and the addend.

```
 03
+07
 0A ← MSH sum
```

The double-precision sum is

$$0AA5_{16}$$

Check.

$$\begin{array}{r} 02AB_{16} \\ +07FA_{16} \\ \hline 0AA5_{16} \end{array}$$

□ **EXAMPLE 2.** Subtract 0726_{16} from $0B3C_{16}$. Convert the subtrahend to the 2's complement.

$$-0726_{16} = F8DA_{16}$$

Add the LSH.

$$\begin{array}{r} 3C_{16} \\ +DA_{16} \\ \hline 116_{16} \end{array}$$

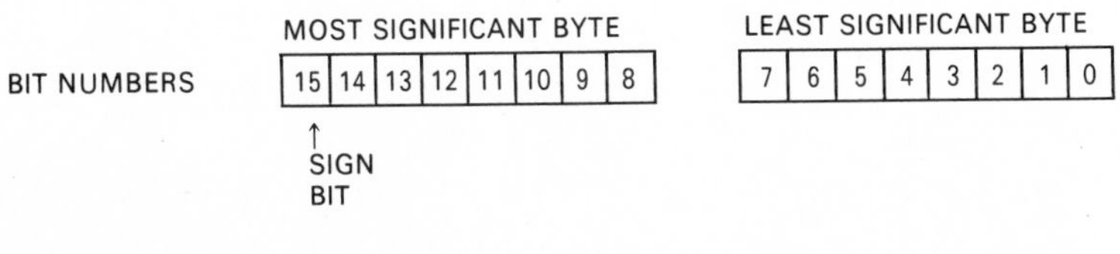
MOST SIGNIFICANT BYTE
LEAST SIGNIFICANT BYTE
BIT NUMBERS
15 14 13 12 11 10 9 8
7 6 5 4 3 2 1 0
SIGN BIT

Figure 2-2. Double Precision Word Format.

Add carry to the augend MSH.

$$0B_{16}$$
$$+1_{16}$$
$$\overline{0C_{16}}$$

Add the MSH of the augend and the addend.

$$0C_{16}$$
$$+F8_{16}$$
$$\overline{104_{16}}$$ discarding carry from last position
$$= 04_{16}$$

The double-precision sum is therefore

$$0416_{16}$$

As a check, we will carry out the subtraction in the normal manner.

$$0B3C_{16}$$
$$-0726_{16}$$
$$\overline{0416_{16}}$$

Double-Precision Arithmetic Review

1. Describe the word format for double-precision arithmetic.

2. List the steps for double-precision addition. Why can the same algorithm be used for subtraction?

3. How is the carry from bit 7 of the LSH of the sum handled?

4. Why was the final carry from bit 15 in the answer to Example 2 discarded?

CODES

Much of the data processed by computers is nonnumeric. Text characters, shaft angles, and control signals are only a few types of information that can be manipulated by the processor. Because microprocessors are limited to storing only 1s and 0s, many codes have been developed to translate other forms of data into binary numbers.

Binary Coded Decimal

Binary coded decimal (BCD) is commonly used by input/output devices. The keyboards of many pocket calculators encode data into BCD. The encoded data represents the decimal digits in the range of 0 through 9 as 4-bit quantities. Table 2-8 lists the coded value for each digit.

Table 2-8
Binary-coded Decimal

Decimal Digit	BCD Code
0	0000
1	0001
2	0010
3	0011
4	0100
5	0101
6	0110
7	0111
8	1000
9	1001

While BCD is a good way of representing the decimal values, the coded versions of the numbers will not give the correct answer if used in normal arithmetic. This problem can easily be seen in the following example.

Decimal	BCD
19_{10}	$0001\ 1001$
$+1$	$+\ 0001$
$20_{10} = 1\ 0100_2$	$0001\ 1010$

But $$1\ 0100_2 \neq 0001\ 1010$$

The problem arises because BCD cannot represent the true binary value of the sum. A correct solution results if the BCD is first converted to the true binary representation.

Decimal	BCD	Binary
$19_{10} =$	$0001\ 1001 =$	$1\ 0011_2$
$+1_{10} =$	$+\ 0001 =$	$+0001_2$
$20_{10} = 1\ 0100_2$	$= 1\ 0100_2$	$= 1\ 0100_2$

$= 1\ 0100_2$

Chap. 6 provides a detailed description of the use of BCD with microprocessors.

The American Standard Code for Information Interchange (ASCII)

The ASCII code is widely used by digital communications systems and computers. The code, shown in Table 2-9, is a 7-bit code. The characters, their coded values, and their meanings are listed in the table.

This code can be divided into subsets, if the application does not require all 128 characters. There are 64 of the codes (20_{16} to $5F_{16}$) used for uppercase letters, numbers, common punctuation marks, and the blank space (SP). Another 32 codes (60_{16} to $7F_{16}$) specify lowercase letters and less commonly used

Table 2-9
ASCII Code

Character	Code (hex)	Meaning	Character	Code (hex)	Meaning
NUL	00	All-zero character	9	39	9
SOH	01	Start of heading	:	3A	Colon
STX	02	Start of text	;	3B	Semicolon
ETX	03	End of text	<	3C	Less than
EOT	04	End of transmission	=	3D	Equal to
ENQ	05	Enquiry	>	3E	Greater than
ACK	06	Acknowledge	?	3F	Question mark
BEL	07	Bell	@	40	Commercial at
BS	08	Backspace	A	41	A
HT	09	Horizontal tabulation	B	42	B
LF	0A	Line feed	C	43	C
VT	0B	Vertical tabulation	D	44	D
FF	0C	Form feed	E	45	E
CR	0D	Carriage return	F	46	F
SO	0E	Shift out	G	47	G
SI	0F	Shift in	H	48	H
DLE	10	Data link escape	I	49	I
DC1	11	⎫	J	4A	J
DC2	12	⎬ Device controls	K	4B	K
DC3	13	⎭	L	4C	L
DC4	14		M	4D	M
NAK	15	Negative acknowledge	N	4E	N
SYN	16	Synchronous idle	O	4F	O
ETB	17	End of transmission block	P	50	P
CAN	18	Cancel	Q	51	Q
EM	19	End of medium	R	52	R
SUB	1A	Substitute	S	53	S
ESC	1B	Escape	T	54	T
FS	1C	File separator	U	55	U
GS	1D	Group separator	V	56	V
RS	1E	Record separator	W	57	W
US	1F	Unit separator	X	58	X
SP	20	Space	Y	59	Y
!	21	Exclamation point	Z	5A	Z
"	22	Quotation marks	[	5B	Opening bracket
	23	Number sign	\	5C	Reverse slant
$	24	Dollar sign	]	5D	Closing bracket
%	25	Percent	^	5E	Circumflex
&	26	Ampersand	—	5F	Underline
'	27	Apostrophe	`	60	Accent grave
(	28	Opening parenthesis	a	61	a
)	29	Closing parenthesis	b	62	b
*	2A	Asterisk	c	63	c
+	2B	Plus	d	64	d
,	2C	Comma	e	65	e
-	2D	Hyphen	f	66	f
.	2E	Period	g	67	g
/	2F	Slant	h	68	h
0	30	0	i	69	i
1	31	1	j	6A	j
2	32	2	k	6B	k
3	33	3	l	6C	l
4	34	4	m	6D	m
5	35	5	n	6E	n
6	36	6	o	6F	o
7	37	7	p	70	p
8	38	8	q	71	q

Table 2-9 *(Continued)*
ASCII Code

Character	Code (hex)	Meaning	Character	Code (hex)	Meaning
r	72	r	y	79	y
s	73	s	z	7A	z
t	74	t	{	7B	Opening brace
u	75	u	|	7C	Vertical line
v	76	v	}	7D	Closing brace
w	77	w		7E	Overline
x	78	x	DEL	7F	Delete

punctuation marks; these codes are not frequently encountered. The final 32 codes (00_{16} to $1F_{16}$) specify machine commands such as "line feed" (LF), "carriage return" (CR), and "ring the bell" (BEL). They do not appear in a message or in print, but they control the communications equipment from both ends of the line.

In practice, an eighth bit is usually appended to the MSB position. This bit can be used for error detection or may be always 0. The 8 bits of the complete code may be sent either serially (1 bit at a time) or in parallel (all 8 bits at once).

The meanings of all the control codes may not be obvious from Table 2-9. A brief description of each should clarify their use. The "start-of-heading" character is used to begin a character sequence which includes the address and routing information, called the *message heading*. The "start-of-text" character terminates the heading and signals the start of the message. The message ends with the "end-of-text" character. When an entire transmission is concluded, the "end-of-transmission" character is sent.

An "enquiry" is used to request a response from a remote station, such as identification or status. "Acknowledge" is sent by the receiver as an affirmative response to the sender; "NAK" is used for a negative response.

Many of the characters control the message-handling equipment. The "bell" character sounds an alarm or buzzer. Backspace, line feed, horizontal and vertical tabulation, form feed, and carriage return position the print head on the page. "Delete" is used to erase an unwanted character.

When one or more characters outside the standard ASCII set are to be sent, they are preceded by the "shift-out" control. "Shift in" is sent after those codes have been transmitted. "Data link escape" and "escape" provide supplementary controls in data communications networks to change the meaning of a limited number of characters which follow. The DLE and ESC characters are usually terminated by the "shift-in" character.

Device controls are used to switch teleprocessing devices on or off. "Synchronous idle" is used to provide a synchronism signal when there are no other characters to be sent. The "end of transmission block" allows blocking of data for communications purposes. The "cancel" character indicates that erroneous data has been sent and should be disregarded. "End of medium" indicates the conclusion of useful data. "Substitute" is used in place of a character that has been found to be invalid. File, group, record, and unit separators can divide data into segments.

Error Detection and Correction Codes

When data is transmitted from one place to another in a digital system, the receiver may question the validity of the data. Noise, crosstalk, or malfunction can introduce errors in the received bit stream. Through the use of error detection and correction (EDAC) codes, data can be checked for the possibility of error, and it can be modified to restore the original message if errors are found.

PARITY. The concept of parity was introduced in Chap. 1. Here we examine how parity can indicate inaccuracies in the data. Commonly an extra bit is appended to the ASCII code character to be used for a parity indicator. The *parity bit* is a form of redundancy that is part of the message. However, the redundancy has a price. By increasing the number of bits per character from 7 to 8, an overhead of 14 percent is incurred. The overhead of any error-detection code is a measure of its *efficiency*.

Continuing the discussion, we pick the capital letter E as the ASCII character to be transmitted. Referring to Table 2-9, the code 45_{16} is found to represent an uppercase E. The parity bit will occupy the MSB position. We have a choice of using even or odd parity, so both possibilities are investigated. Writing the code in binary $0100\ 0101_2$ shows that the parity is odd. By setting the parity bit ($1100\ 0101_2$), the overall parity for the 8 bits becomes even. Making the parity bit 0 is equivalent to giving the word odd parity.

Starting with the even parity situation, we look into the consequence of errors. Assume that the letter E is transmitted four times in a message: the first time, with no errors; the second time, bit 1 was read as a 1 because of noise on the line; the third time, bit 2 became a 0 and bit 4 became a 1; and the fourth time, bits 3, 4, and 5 were set erroneously. The received characters are summarized as follows:

		Binary Data Received	Received Parity
	Bit number	7 6 5 4 3 2 1 0	
Case 1		1 1 0 0 0 1 0 1	Even
Case 2		1 1 0 0 0 1 1 1	Odd
Case 3		1 1 0 1 0 0 0 1	Even
Case 4		1 1 1 1 1 1 0 1	Odd

In case 1 the received character had even parity, as was expected. In case 2 the word was received as having odd parity, but we know it was transmitted with even parity. Receiving a character which has improper parity implies that some bit changed state; either a 1 was reset to 0 or a 0 was set to 1 by noise. Case 3 has two errors, but the parity does not show any irregularity. Why? The reason is that even parity can only detect an odd number of bits in error. An even number of incorrect bits gives a seemingly correct indication of even parity. Case 4, with 3 bits in error, again shows the wrong parity, but we see that there is no way to distinguish between 1-bit and 3-bit errors. In fact, any odd number of incorrect bits will produce odd parity. While this parity code can detect an odd number of bit errors, it cannot indicate how many errors occurred or which bits are actually wrong.

Had we started with odd parity at the transmitter, the situation would be just the reverse. An odd number of bits in error (1,3,5, ...) would be received with even parity, but an even number (2,4,6, ...) would be seemingly correct at the receiving station. Using more bits for parity strengthens the detection of multiple errors and can even indicate which bit or bits are wrong. An elaborate theory for EDAC coding has been developed and can be used to assure reliable data communications.

CHECKSUMS. Sometimes we are not concerned with the correctness of one word, but with an entire block of data composed of many words. An efficient code for verifying data blocks is the *checksum* (also called *hash totals*). Generation of the checksum requires that the transmitting station add all the data codes and append the sum as a final word in the message. The receiving station also sums the data and compares its answer with the last word. If the data sums agree, there is a high probability that the data are correct.

You may wonder why the receiving station cannot be sure whether the data were correct if the checksums agree. First, there may be compensating errors in the data; that is, one word may have increased by the same amount that another decreased. Second, the addition is performed in an adder of finite length. In most microprocessors that could be 8 bits. That means that all carries from the MSB position are discarded, and errors may occur which are hidden by this loss of information.

The data block shown below will be used to demonstrate the checksum procedure. Each word in the block is 8 bits long. Adding the first two words gives 60_{16}, but when that partial sum is added to FF_{16}, the result is $15F_{16}$. Because we are limited to 8 bits, the MSB of 1 is lost and the resulting sum is $5F_{16}$. Finally, adding $0E_{16}$ gives $6D_{16}$.

a. Generating the checksum:

Data block   checksum development

$$
\begin{array}{l}
20 \\
40
\end{array}\Big] \quad + = 60
$$

$$
FF \longrightarrow \quad + = 15F \quad \text{(discarding carry from bit 7)}
$$

$$
0E \longrightarrow \quad + = 6D_{16}
$$

b. Transmission block:

$$
\left.\begin{array}{l}
20 \\
40 \\
FF \\
0E
\end{array}\right] \text{ data}
$$

$$
6D \leftarrow \text{checksum}
$$

c. Correctly received data:

$$
\left.\begin{array}{l}
20 \\
40 \\
FF \\
0E
\end{array}\right] \quad \text{calculated checksum} = 6D_{16}
$$

$$
6D \longleftarrow \text{match}
$$

d. Incorrectly received data:

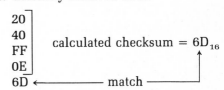

errors
$$
\left.\begin{array}{l}
21 \\
C0 \\
FF \\
0E
\end{array}\right] \quad \text{calculated checksum} = EE_{16}
$$

$$
6D \longleftarrow \text{no match}
$$

The data are blocked for transmission with the checksum in an extra word (not part of the data). In this case the checksum has an efficiency of 25 percent (1 code word/4 data words). If the data are received correctly, the checksum independently calculated by the receiver will match the last word in the block; however, bits that have changed will cause a different sum to be produced. No indication of which word has the error is provided, so the entire block must be retransmitted when a mistake is detected.

CYCLIC REDUNDANCY CHECK. Another code that can be used to provide error detection capability on blocks of data is the cyclic redundancy check (CRC). The CRC uses fewer bits than do parity codes and has been implemented in both hardware and software. There are ICs on the market which will automatically calculate the CRC bit pattern that is appended to the data block as an extra word, much like the checksum. Computer programs have also been written which can generate the same bit pattern. Almost all floppy disks and digital tape cassettes use the cyclic redundancy check when recording data.

The CRC is a bit pattern for a polynomial of degree 7. The pattern of the data words can be expressed as

$$D(x) = D_7x^7 + D_6x^6 + D_5x^5 + D_4x^4 \\ + D_3x^3 + D_2x^2 + D_1x^1 + D_0x^0 \qquad (2\text{-}3)$$

where x is a *dummy variable*.

A *generator polynomial* is used as the divisor of $D(x)$

$$\frac{D(x)}{G(x)} = Q(x) + R(x) \qquad (2\text{-}4)$$

where $G(x)$ is the generator polynomial, $Q(x)$ is the quotient, and $R(x)$ is the remainder. The purpose of the CRC, which is appended to the data, is to make the remainder in Eq. (2-4) become zero. By rewriting that equation, we can see how to accomplish this task.

$$D(x) - R(x) = Q(x)G(x) \qquad (2\text{-}5)$$

In other words, if the remainder is used for the CRC word, the generator polynomial will exactly divide the total data string.

The CRC transmitted in the last word in the block is thus the remainder of the generator division. When the receiving station divides by $G(x)$ and subtracts $R(x)$, it will find that there is a nonzero remainder if an error has occurred. If the remainder is zero, either the data have been correctly received or an undetectable error appears in the data stream.

A simplified example will illustrate the CRC concept more concretely. Let $D = 1000\ 0101_2$; then

$$D(x) = 1 \cdot x^7 + 0 \cdot x^6 + 0 \cdot x^5 + 0 \cdot x^4 + 0 \cdot x^3 \\ + 1 \cdot x^2 + 0 \cdot x^1 + 1 \cdot x^0$$
$$D(x) = x^7 + x^2 + 1$$

Use of $G(x) = x^2 + 1$ gives

$$\frac{D(x)}{G(x)} = x^5 - x^3 + x + 1$$

with a remainder of $-x$. Use of Eq. (2-5) to obtain an exact dividend gives

$$D(x) - R(x) = x^7 + x^2 + 1 - (-x)$$
$$= x^7 + x^2 + x + 1$$

Thus $-x$ corresponds to the CRC bits. Because x is a dummy variable, we can arbitrarily assign the value of 1 to x. That assignment would make the CRC bits FF_{16} in an 8-bit, 2's complement.

Codes Review

1. List the reasons for the use of codes in digital communications.

2. When would use of BCD instead of binary cause an incorrect result?

3. List the ASCII codes for the characters T, ?, $, and 7.

4. What are the meanings of the control characters DLE, SOH, ENQ, and LF?

5. Why does a single parity bit, used to check ASCII codes, for instance, seem correct when there are two received errors in the code?

6. Compare the efficiency of parity bits with checksums. Which would be more efficient for a 1000-word data block?

7. How do CRC bits make the bit pattern $D(x)$ exactly divisible by the generator polynomial?

CHAPTER SUMMARY

1. The place occupied by a digit in a positional number system signifies its weight in terms of the base raised to an appropriate power. Examples of positional number systems are binary, octal, decimal, and hexadecimal systems.

2. The quantity of symbols, or digits, in a positional number system is always equal to the base.

3. The radix point separates the integer and the fraction in a number. A subscript indicates its base.

4. Polynomial expansion allows us to convert between bases by considering the digits, the radix, and the weight of each digit.

5. Conversion from binary to another base that is a power of 2, such as octal or hexadecimal, is most easily accomplished by grouping.

6. The explosion algorithm is used to convert from other bases to decimal, and the digit-by-digit algorithm is used for conversion in the opposite direction.

7. Arithmetic in other bases employs addition and multiplication tables similar to those used in decimal. The rules of arithmetic in binary, octal, and hexadecimal are identical to those used in base 10 operations.

8. Complement systems make it possible to use the same circuitry for addition and subtraction. Both 1's and 2's complements are frequently encountered in microprocessor ALUs.

9. Because many microprocessors do 8-bit arithmetic, double precision is often necessary to prevent overflow.

10. Codes are employed to represent numbers and letters in binary form. Common codes include BCD and ASCII. Alternatively, coding may be used to provide error detection and correction of data transmitted over some digital communications network. Parity, checksums, and CRCs are examples of the latter types of codes.

KEY TERMS AND CONCEPTS

Positional number systems	Rounding	1's complement
Positional weighting	Truncation	2's complement
Base	Digit-by-digit algorithm	Double-precision arithmetic
Digits	Arithmetic in other bases	Codes
Binary	Augend, addend, and sum	Binary-coded decimal (BCD)
Octal	Carry	American Standard Code for Information Interchange (ASCII)
Hexadecimal (hex)	Minuend, subtrahend, and difference	
Radix		Error detection and correction (EDAC) codes
Radix point	Borrow	
Polynomial expansion	Multiplicand, multiplier, and product	Parity
Conversion by grouping		Checksum
Explosion algorithm	Divisor, dividend, quotient, and remainder	Cyclic redundancy check (CRC)

PROBLEMS

2-1 Convert the following numbers to decimal by use of polynomial expansion.

  a. 1276_8
  b. $011\ 110\ 010\ 000_2$
  c. $F7D_{16}$

2-2 Convert to decimal. All fractions should have accuracy to two places past the radix point.

  a. 47_8 **b.** $A9_{16}$
  c. $1\ 000\ 111_2$ **d.** 563.22_8
  e. $A.F12_{16}$

2-3 Convert the following numbers from decimal to octal. Compute all fractional values to two places past the radix point.

a. 802_{10} **b.** 9999_{10}
c. 0.75_{10} **d.** 196.017_{10}

2-4 Find the hexadecimal equivalents to the following decimal numbers with two-place accuracy for all fractions.

a. 999_{10} **b.** $42,769_{10}$
c. 295.156_{10} **d.** 13.86_{10}

2-5 Perform the indicated arithmetic operations using the binary number system.

a. $110\ 011\ 011_2$ **b.** $001\ 110\ 111_2$
$+1\ 011\ 111_2$ $-010\ 000\ 000_2$

c. $110\ 011_2$ **d.** $101\ 111\ 010_2$
$\times1\ 101_2$ $\overline{1\ 110_2}$

2-6 Perform the indicated octal arithmetic operations.

a. 37_8 **b.** 432_8 **c.** 21.76_8 **d.** $76,532_8$
$+26_8$ -264_8 $\times3.2_8$ $\overline{33_8}$

2-7 Perform the following arithmetic operations using the hexadecimal number system.

a. $B73_{16}$ **b.** $B64_{16}$ **c.** $3.1F_{16}$ **d.** $\overline{715.C_{16}}$
$+2FD_{16}$ $-DC1_{16}$ $\times2.05_{16}$ 2.17_{16}

2-8 Convert these binary numbers to their octal and hexadecimal equivalents by grouping.

a. $101\ 111\ 011\ 010\ 001_2$
b. $1\ 000\ 010.110\ 100_2$
c. $110.001\ 000\ 1_2$
d. $10\ 111.110\ 01_2$

2-9 Convert the octal and hexadecimal numbers below to their binary equivalents.

a. $67,014_8$ **b.** $F,C75_{16}$
c. 216.425_8 **d.** $5B2.6175_{16}$

2-10 Find the parity of the following numbers.

a. $1\ 110\ 111_2$ **b.** 37_8
c. $12F_{16}$ **d.** 7776_8

2-11 Is the parity of these ASCII characters even or odd?

a. A **b.** f **c.** ? **d.** 2

2-12 What is the checksum for the data block below? (An 8-bit adder is to be used in computing the sum.)

200_8
177_8
126_8
515_8

2-13 Using the same generating function given in the text, give the values of R(x) and Q(x) if D $= 1000\ 1001_2$.

2-14 Instead of using a single parity bit with an ASCII character, two are used in a 9-bit word. Bit 7 is set or cleared to make the parity of bits 1 through 7 even. Bit 8 is chosen to make the parity of bits 1 through 8 odd. What should the value of these bits be for the ASCII character %?

2-15 If the character transmitted in Prob. 2-14 were received with odd parity over bits 1 through 7 and even parity over bits 1 through 8, what could be concluded?

EXPERIMENT 2 _____

PURPOSE: To gain familiarity with microprocessors.

PARTS LIST:

Item	Quantity
Microcomputer	1
7400	1
LED	1
330-Ω resistor	1
900-Ω resistor	1
SPDT slide switch (spring return)	1
Voltmeter	1

IC DIAGRAMS:

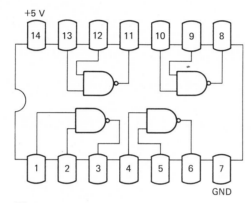

Figure 2-3. 7400.

PROCEDURE: Your instructor will introduce you to the microcomputer that you will be using in the experiments. In almost every experiment you will be required to place data and instructions in memory, examine registers, and use the power supply.

STEP 1. Record the voltages from each output terminal of the power supply.

STEP 2. Record the range of memory addresses (upper and lower limits) for your computer in both hexadecimal and decimal.

STEP 3. Record the I/O port addresses and indicate the purpose of each port.

STEP 4. Record the procedures for changing and inspecting the contents of a memory cell.

STEP 5. Explain how the value of any programmable register may be examined or replaced and how a program is executed.

STEP 6. **Light-emitting diode (LED) indicator.** Wire the circuit shown in Fig. 2-4. Attach the probe to the 5-V power supply output. Is the LED on or off? Now touch the probe to ground. What does the LED do? Explain your results.

Figure 2-4. Logic Probe.

STEP 7. **Pulser.** Using the 7400 IC, construct the circuit shown in Fig. 2-5. Connect the LED indicator to each output and record the voltage level at Pin 3 and Pin 6. Now close the switch and repeat the readings for Pin 3 and Pin 6. How could this pulser be used to produce signals that swing between high and low levels?

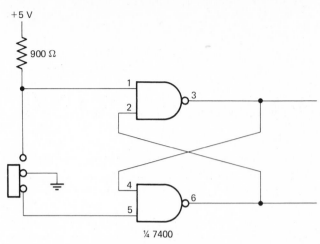

Figure 2-5. Logic Pulser.

PROGRAMMING

A digital computer differs from every other electronic device in one important aspect—the computer can do no useful work without its program. This combination of hardware and software forms the processing entity which is useful in solving a wide range of problems. The hardware-software interactions often result in situations where it is difficult to decide if a failure was caused by the electronics or by the program. Everyone intending to work with computers must, therefore, have some knowledge of software. With programming skills you will be able to develop simple software routines to help in assessing the cause of problems and in localizing faulty circuits. In addition to assisting in isolating problems, some elementary programming background will improve your ability to communicate with programmers.

CHAPTER OBJECTIVES

Upon completion of this chapter, you should be able to:

1. List the steps necessary to write a program.
2. Draw flowcharts using the proper American National Standards Institute (ANSI) symbols.
3. Describe the use of test cases, tracing, and simulation in debugging.
4. Debug programs by manually checking them before running them on the computer.

THE PROGRAMMING PROCESS

A *program* is a logical sequence of instructions and data which can be understood by a computer and which produces a specified result after execution. As such, the program might be considered to be an overall plan for the solution to a problem. Programs of any length are divided into several *routines*. A routine is a set of instructions within a larger program. This set of instructions is properly arranged to cause the computer to carry out frequently needed tasks. A further subdivision, the *subroutine*, is a short sequence of instructions designed to solve a specific part of the problem; usually subroutines have application to more than one routine.

For example, consider a simplified navigation problem on a coast-to-coast airline route. The program must be capable of calculating the course and speed changes necessary for travel between any two points on the earth. One of the routines in this program will be able to find the distance between those points. To measure this quantity, the distance routine may require a square root function to calculate the distance between given Cartesian coordinates

$$d = \sqrt{(x_2 - x_1)^2 + (y_2 - y_1)^2} \qquad (3\text{-}1)$$

where
$$d = \text{distance}$$
$$x_1, x_2 = x \text{ coordinates of the two points}$$
$$y_1, y_2 = y \text{ coordinates of the two points}$$

The square root function can be written as a subroutine to be used not only by the distance routine, but perhaps by the speed routine as well. Figure 3-1 shows the relationship among the routines, the subroutines, and the data in a computer program.

The computer program written to solve a problem must completely specify what to do and how to do it and what data are involved. Should any of these questions be ignored or erroneously answered, the program will contain an error, or *bug*. To be sure that all necessary details have been covered, the programmer will generally follow a systematized series of steps. For small programs, the outcome of this process may simply be a mental discipline, but on large software projects each step will be formally documented. The process described in this section is the *top-down approach*, which is frequently used in structured programming.

Problem Statement

The first step required of the programmer or analyst is to write a clear, complete statement of the problem. Many times the person who will use the program is not exactly sure what the program is to do. For this reason, it is especially important for the programmer and user to mutually define the limits and capabilities of the program.

The problem statement for a computer must be much more comprehensive than instructions to another person would be. For instance, the system to be used in running the program must be described. In addition to designating the computer, the description must list the *peripheral equipment* (such as paper tape readers, printers, display terminals, and floppy disks) to be used.

A full summary of the data to be manipulated and the formats for input and output must be provided. Input parameters might include the source of the data, the format of the data (such as binary, BCD, ASCII), the range of numbers to be handled, and the rate at which the information arrives. Important output parameters are the desired format, the accuracy requirements, the distribution of the output reports, and the *media* (magnetic disks, printer paper, CRT display) for the output. Furthermore, restrictions concerning compatibility with other programs, memory space available, and time available to run the program must be known.

Analysis

Once the problem has been fully defined, the programmer begins to analyze it. The analysis will

NAVIGATION PROGRAM

SQUARE ROOT SUBROUTINE

ARCTANGENT SUBROUTINE

SPEED ROUTINE

DISTANCE ROUTINE

COURSE ROUTINE

DATA SECTION

Figure 3-1. Program Structure.

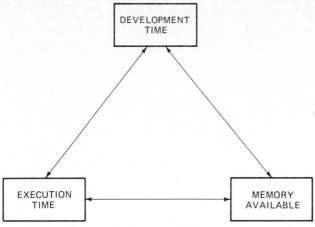

Figure 3-2. Programming Trade-Offs.

survey the methods of solution available. For common problems, the programmer may already know the methods and be able to immediately reference the proper manuals. Otherwise, an in-depth study of the programming literature and consultation with experts in the field may be necessary. Usually a wide variety of solutions will be found.

The ultimate result of the analysis phase is to select the one solution that best suits the problem. One of the considerations that enters into this decision is the amount of memory space needed to hold the program and data. Another consideration is the time available to develop the program. Any sizable program involves a large amount of time to write and test it. A simple solution can produce significant savings here. A third consideration is how much computer time is allocated to executing the program. If the program is to be run frequently, it may be less costly to select a solution which minimizes the run time. As Fig. 3-2 shows, these three aspects of the program are not independent. Production of a program which runs very fast will require more time to be spent in refining the program; hence the development time increases, and the written program may occupy more memory. Production time almost always increases when memory conservation is emphasized; as memory constraints become quite stringent, the development time can increase markedly.

When the solution is selected, the programmer will review it to assure that accuracy requirements, compatibility with other programs, and other restrictions in the problem statement are satisfied.

Problem Model

The formulas and the equations that will be used in the computer solution become a model of the actual situation. In selecting a mathematical representation, many variables are excluded from consideration. For example, if Newton's laws of motion are used as a model for automobile acceleration, such factors as temperature, humidity, type of rubber in the tires, and altitude cannot affect the computed solution, but they may be significant to automotive performance.

Not all programs require a model. Business programs may be of such a nature that only simple arithmetic is necessary. Complicated scientific programs, such as sending a rocket to the moon, almost always require a sophisticated model. The model is derived from the solution selected during analysis. The model will guide the programmer during the development of a step-by-step procedure for solution.

Before a model has been selected, it is not uncommon for the programmer to have uncovered some facets of the problem statement that are incomplete or incompatible. A complication may arise that changes the initial conclusion derived from the analysis. If so, the results of the earlier steps must be reconsidered and revised. This method of going back and forth among these steps in a repeated fashion shows the iterative nature of programming. The final program may be the outcome of many cycles of problem statement, analysis, and modeling.

Flowcharts

The next step of programming involves construction of a graphic representation of the logic to be used in the problem solution. The graphic technique most frequently used is the flowchart. The following section will describe the specifics of flowcharts in more detail. Here it is sufficient to note that a flowchart is constructed by using symbols and notations to further communications between programmers, analysts, and users. The flowcharts often form part of the permanent documentation of the program.

Coding

Many people who are not familiar with programming (and, unfortunately, too many inexperienced programmers) are surprised to find that coding is the fifth step of the effort. The actual instructions for the computer are prepared at this time. Using the flowcharts or other graphic aids as a guide, the programmer writes the instruction sequence. Usually a special coding sheet is used, so the instructions are in the proper format for computer data entry.

There is a large number of programming languages to choose from. One special language must be selected from the general category of machine codes, assemblers, or compilers. Most microcomputer manufacturers provide only a limited number of languages, so this choice may be dictated more by the languages that are available than by desirability. All these options mean that programmers are frequently required to learn new languages for microcomputers, languages which they have not previously used.

Debugging

Any type of program error may be called a "bug." The error may have been caused by faulty logic, failure to follow the coding language rules, or simply a data entry mistake. Regardless of the cause, *debugging* is the method used in an attempt to eliminate all program problems.

Debugging begins with a manual check by the programmer, who reads through the *listing* of instructions and data. The first time through the listing, typographical errors, misspellings, and format errors are eliminated. Next, the listing is compared to the flowchart. There should be a corresponding area of code for each flowchart symbol. Finally, the programmer *simulates* the computer processing by stepping through the program, instruction by instruction. All operations such as data transfers, mathematical processes, and input/output are checked.

In spite of a careful desk check, the program is rarely bug-free at completion of the manual checking. The program generation and execution processes will usually uncover additional errors. The testing of a large program to eliminate bugs can easily consume half the development effort. Normally, the programmer will be expected to test small programs. Test data are prepared to verify that the program can handle the full range of data values, including positive and negative numbers. It is important to realize that debugging cannot prove that all errors have been eliminated. Only those which have been detected can be corrected. Examples of debugging are provided later in this chapter, but you will probably gain more experience in this art as you perform the experiments.

Documentation

The final and possibly most important step of the programming process is documentation. Documentation is not as interesting to most programmers as are coding and debugging, so it is too often slighted. The operator's description of how to use the program and the permanent record of program structure necessary for future error correction or changes are as needed as the object code itself.

There is no standard method for documentation, but three levels of program description are commonly used: design documents, operator manuals, and descriptive documents. Design documents are the result of the problem statement, the analysis, and the model. They are guides on how the program is expected to perform. Operator manuals specify all procedures necessary for use of the program. Every control, switch, readout, and display affected by the program should be covered in sufficient detail for an untrained operator to learn how to use the system from the manual. Descriptive documents are written after the fact to describe the software for those who must maintain it. Complete details, in programmer's terms, describe the code and data of each program. Flowcharts are frequently included in these documents. Programs of any size at all will require several additional documents. Typically, these would include test plans and procedures, descriptions of the *interfaces* between the hardware and the software (how the two will communicate with each other), and reports on specific project areas.

Programming Process Review

1. List the steps of programming in their proper order.

2. List what should be included in the problem statement.

3. Describe what is accomplished during the program model step.

4. Define the term "bug."

5. How is debugging accomplished?

6. Why is documentation important?

FLOWCHART PREPARATION

Before coding a program, the programmer must analyze the problem and break it into well-defined segments. Graphic aids provide a visual representation of the problem which makes it easier to understand the component parts. By using graphic aids as a blueprint, the programmer is able to grasp the overall picture as well as details of a particular element.

Flowcharts are diagrams consisting of symbols and statements that represent computer operations. Data transfers, arithmetic and logical functions, and the flow of program logic can all be depicted on a flowchart. The symbols indicate the type of operation to be performed, and the lines connecting the symbols show the sequencing that the computer is to carry out. American National Standards Institute symbols are used in this book, but other flowcharting standards exist.

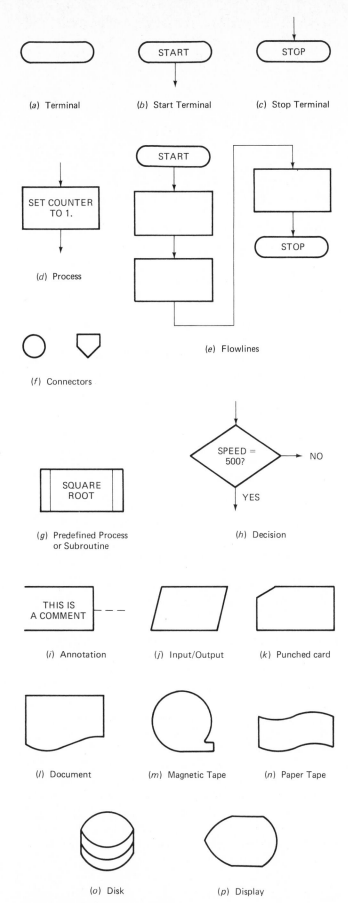

(a) Terminal   (b) Start Terminal   (c) Stop Terminal

(d) Process

(e) Flowlines

(f) Connectors

(g) Predefined Process or Subroutine

(h) Decision

(i) Annotation   (j) Input/Output   (k) Punched card

(l) Document   (m) Magnetic Tape   (n) Paper Tape

(o) Disk   (p) Display

Figure 3-3. Flowchart Symbols.

Terminals

The terminal shown in Fig. 3-3a designates starting, stopping, delay, or interrupt points in the normal flow of a program. Every flowchart begins with a terminal. Every program has a single starting point, although the program may have as many delay, interrupt, or stop terminals as desired. The start terminal, (see Fig. 3-3b) has an arrow leading out, thus indicating that the flow of logic begins from that point. The word "start" or the name of the program or routine is usually written in the symbol. The stop terminal (see Fig. 3-3c) depicts a stop, a delay, or an interrupt point, depending on what is written in the symbol.

Processes

A process is indicated by a rectangle, as shown in Fig. 3-3d. The process box means that some action is to be taken which will change the value of some data unit. In this example a counter is to be set to the value of 1. Only one input and one output are permitted by the process (denoted by a single arrow leading in and out of the symbol).

Flowlines

The arrows are called *flowlines.* They are used to show operational sequence and data flow directions. Arrowheads show the direction of movement. The lines are always drawn either vertically or horizontally and never cross one another. If arrows are not provided on the flowlines, the presumed flow direction is from top to bottom for vertical lines and from left to right for horizontal ones. Normally, no more than two 90° bends are allowed in a flowline (see Fig. 3-3e).

Connectors

There are two symbols used for connectors (see Fig. 3-3f). The circle is used to show continuation to or from another part of the flowchart on the same page. The pentagon shows connections from or to another page. Letters, numbers, or a combination of these are used to identify matching continuation points. Connector symbols can be used in pairs to replace long flowlines or to prevent flowlines from crossing.

Predefined Processes

A subroutine, or *predefined process,* is a named operation consisting of a series of program steps specified in another flowchart. Any widely used routine can be formed into a predefined process. The symbol for a subroutine is shown in Fig. 3-3g. The subroutine can be inserted into another program any time that function is to be used. When a subroutine is referenced, or "called," the predefined operation will be executed.

Decisions

The decision diamond (see Fig. 3-3h) indicates that a choice must be made to decide which of two output paths will be taken. If the answer to the question in the diamond is "yes," then the flowline labeled "yes" indicates the next step; otherwise, the "no" direction is followed.

Other Symbols

When further explanation than will fit into one of the flowchart symbols is needed, additional descrip-

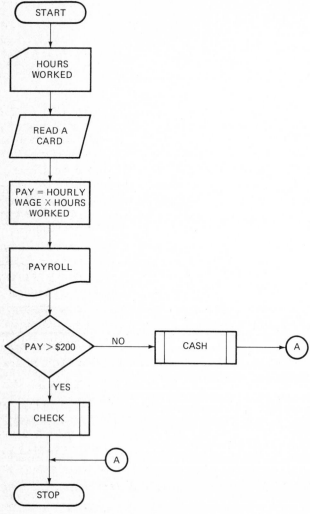

Figure 3-4. Flowchart Example.

tive comments can be placed in an annotation box (see Fig. 3-3i). The annotation should help to clarify a difficult portion of the flowchart. The I/O symbol shows that data are entering or leaving the computer at that point. The I/O medium can also be indicated by using an appropriate symbol. Input/output media symbols are shown in Figs. 3-3j through 3-3p. Identification of the I/O data can be written in the symbol.

Example Flowchart

A flowchart presenting samples of the use of these symbols is shown in Fig. 3-4. This program reads a punched card containing an employee's time clock information and records it on the master payroll tape. If the pay exceeds $200, a check is prepared in addition to recording the data.

Flowcharts Review

1. List the primary uses for a terminal.

2. Describe the two types of connectors.

3. How many right angles are allowed in flowlines?

4. How many exits does a decision symbol have? A subroutine?

5. List the I/O media symbols available for flowcharting.

DEBUGGING TECHNIQUES

As surprising as it seems, the time a programmer spends in debugging and testing a program will be almost twice as long as the time spent in initially coding the program. Because the computer interprets every instruction literally, nothing can be left to chance. Every possible situation must be visualized and accounted for prior to releasing a program to the user. As you have undoubtedly heard stories of program bugs which resulted in employees receiving million-dollar paychecks or, more common, credit card customers being billed for merchandise they had already paid for, it should not be surprising to find that debugging is very difficult. In fact, software testing cannot accomplish what we actually want, that is, to prove that the program is bug-free. Instead, as testing uncovers errors, it shows the presence of bugs, not their absence. This limitation usually results in testing until the developer is reasonably confident that all serious bugs have been found. Then the user assumes the risk of undiscovered bugs interfering with daily operations.

As an example of how bugs can creep into a program, consider the square root routine flowchart shown in Fig. 3-5. This routine uses the *Newton-Rhapson algorithm* for extracting a square root, which provides a faster solution by computer than the more familiar method you learned in your mathematics courses. Explanation of the algorithm will be clearest by means of an example. The algorithm finds the nearest integer square root of any positive number; that is, there is no decimal point in the answer. The nearest integer square root of 12 is 3 because 9 is the largest square less than 12.

The lack of a decimal point in the answer is not really a shortcoming, as the number could be multiplied by 100 or 10,000 prior to finding the root. This multiplication, also called *scaling*, would produce a root correct to one or two fractional positions, respectively. In this example the nearest integer square roots would be:

Number	Scale Factor	Nearest Integer Square Root
12	1	3
1200	100	34
120,000	10,000	346

The square root of 12 to two decimal places is 3.46. By first multiplying by 10,000 and then placing the decimal point in the proper position in the answer, the Newton-Rhapson algorithm can be used to find the root quite accurately.

Now let's return to the flowchart and follow the example through the process. Let the number be 12. (Each step in the flowchart is numbered, so we can easily refer to them.) In process 1 the number is reduced to 11. Then "guess old" is set to 100. (If we had forgotten to *initialize* "guess old" in this manner, it would have had a zero value in the computer. Then step 3 would involve a division by 0, which is clearly the wrong approach.) The number is divided by "guess old" in process 3 and the answer is saved in a variable called "quotient"; carrying out this division gives us 0 for an answer [(11/100) = 0 because no fractional numbers are used by the algorithm]. Process 4 will then yield

$$\frac{0 + 100 + 1}{2} = 50$$

for a value of "guess new." The decision in box 5 is answered negatively, so we return to process 3 after replacing "guess old" by "guess new." The iterative or *looping* process continues until "guess old" is equal to "guess new." At that time the root has been found and the process terminates. You should continue to follow the flowchart for the case

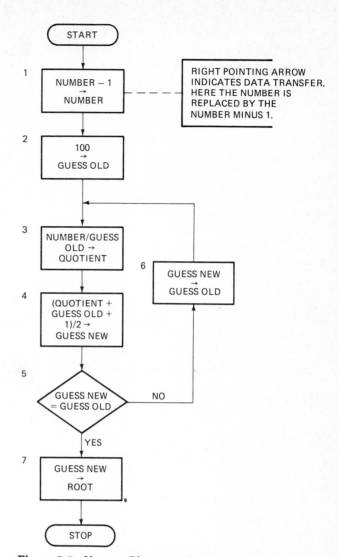

Figure 3-5. Newton-Rhapson Algorithm

where the original number is 12 to convince yourself that the correct answer is produced. Table 3-1 summarizes partial results at key points of each iteration.

Although the algorithm worked in this case, there are actually two bugs in the flowchart as given. One way to find bugs prior to running on a computer is to use test cases as we started above. The computer action is traced as we execute each step. We simulate

Table 3-1
Newton-Rhapson Algorithm Partial Results

Iteration	Guess old	Quotient	Guess new
1	100	0	50
2	50	0	25
3	25	0	13
4	13	0	7
5	7	1	4
6	4	2	3
7	3	3	3 stop

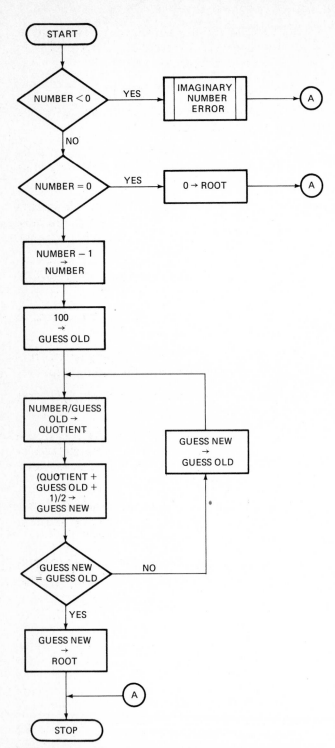

Figure 3-6. Corrected Newton-Rhapson Algorithm.

use 0 as an input, we see that step 1 results in a negative number. The answer will no longer converge to the root if the number becomes negative at this point. (In fact, division by 0 occurs in the ninth iteration, as you can prove by following the flowchart.) This error can be prevented by placing a decision at the beginning of the algorithm to check for a 0 input.

The second bug is slightly harder to detect, but a knowledge of arithmetic should lead the programmer to it. The error is that the square root of negative numbers is imaginary. We only want to use real numbers in our navigation routine, so this case must also be eliminated by a second decision at the beginning to prevent negative inputs. The corrected flowchart is shown in Fig. 3-6.

Having seen one example of debugging, let's consider one more. You will also have ample opportunity to practice your debugging skills in the experiments, as your programs will often not run correctly the first time you try them. This algorithm (see Fig. 3-7), computes the factorial of the input by using the equation

$$n! = (n)(n-1)(n-2) \cdots (1) \qquad (3\text{-}2)$$

where n is the input number. First, check the algorithm by using 6 as an input. If you found that 6! is 720, you correctly traced the program operation. What bugs can you discover? Does the algorithm

the computer by not taking fractional quotients, for example. Obviously, every possible number could not be tested in this way because there is not enough time to make that many manual checks. Instead, a selected set of numbers is chosen. A good rule of thumb is to use the minimum and the maximum values an algorithm can accept, a value of 0, and a few values between these extreme cases. If we

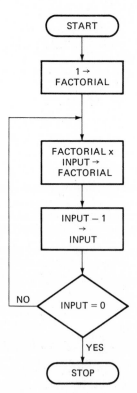

Figure 3-7. Factorial Algorithm.

work for 0? With large positive numbers? With negative numbers? The answers to the first and third questions are "no." In the case of either a 0 input or a negative input, the process will not terminate because the input will never decrement to 0 in the third process box. Checks at the beginning for a 0 input and setting the output to 1 (0! equals 1 by definition) and giving an error indication for a negative input should be inserted in the flowchart.

Debugging Review

1. What does a right-pointing arrow in a process box mean?

2. Describe the use of tracing, test cases, and simulation to debug programs prior to running them on a computer.

3. What values should you use in test cases for an algorithm that allows a range of inputs of -100 to $+200$?

CHAPTER SUMMARY

1. A computer program is a logical sequence of instructions and data which produce a specified result after computer execution.

2. Routines are sets of instructions (portions of a larger program) which cause the computer to carry out frequently needed tasks.

3. A subroutine is a short instruction sequence which provides a solution to frequently encountered problems.

4. A bug is an error in a program.

5. A top-down approach to programming follows a disciplined series of actions.

6. The problem statement establishes exactly what the program is to do and what data are to be used in the operations.

7. After problem definition, the analysis surveys all methods of solution and selects the most suitable one in terms of development time, execution time, and memory available.

8. A problem model is a mathematical description of the program to be written.

9. Flowcharts graphically depict the process to be used in the computer solution.

10. Converting the flowchart to computer instructions takes place during the coding step.

11. Debugging a complicated program often takes more time than coding it.

12. Documentation is needed by the user to understand how to operate the program and by programmers who must maintain the software after delivery.

13. The American National Standards Institute has established a set of symbols to be used in flowcharting computer programs.

14. Debugging can start prior to running the program on a computer by using test cases, tracing, and simulation.

KEY TERMS AND CONCEPTS

Program	Problem model	Connector
Routine	Flowcharting	Flowlines
Subroutine	Coding	Predefined process
Bug	Listing	Decision
Problem statement	Documentation	Annotation
Peripheral equipment	Terminal	Input/Output
Analysis	Process	Test cases, tracing, and simulation

PROBLEMS

3-1 Prepare a written statement of the problem, the analysis, and the model for a program which finds the roots to the second-degree quadratic equation

$$Ax^2 + Bx + C = 0$$

where the input parameters are A, B, and C. Use the formula

$$x = \frac{-B \pm \sqrt{B^2 - 4AC}}{2A}$$

3-2 Prepare a flowchart for the computer program of Prob. 3-1. Use the algorithm given below. Assume that all named subroutines have previously been programmed. (No flowcharts of those subroutines are to be drawn.)

STEP 1. Compute the value $B^2 - 4AC$, and if the result is negative, perform a subroutine called PROCESS IMAGINARY and then exit.

STEP 2. If $B^2 - 4AC$ is positive and A and B are 0, perform a predefined process called PROCESS TRIVIAL and then exit.

STEP 3. If $A = 0$ and $B \neq 0$, compute $-C/B$ and place the answer in variables called ROOT1 and ROOT2. Exit from the routine.

STEP 4. If $B^2 - 4AC$ is positive and A is not 0, send $B^2 - 4AC$ to a variable called SQUARE ROOT INPUT. Then perform the SQUARE ROOT subroutine.

STEP 5. Following Step 4, compute the value $-B$ + SQUARE ROOT OUTPUT. Divide this sum by $2A$ and place the result in ROOT1. Compute $-B$ - SQUARE ROOT OUTPUT and divide the difference by $2A$. Transfer the result to ROOT2 and then exit from the routine.

3-3 Prepare a flowchart of the following routine.

PROBLEM STATEMENT: This program is to compute the absolute values of the sums of the items in two lists and place these resulting values into corresponding positions in a third list.

INPUTS: List A and list B, each containing eight combinations of positive or negative numbers.

OUTPUT: List C, eight items long. Each item is equal to the absolute value of the sum of the two corresponding items in lists A and B.

ANALYSIS: The absolute value of a number is the magnitude of that number, regardless of the sign. This value is obtained in the computer by checking the number to see if it is negative or positive. If it is positive, then it is its own absolute value. If it is negative, then its 2's complement is the absolute value.

$$|A_i + B_i| \rightarrow C_i$$

where the symbol | | stands for absolute value.

PROBLEM MODEL: **1.** Compute the sum A + B.
2. Complement the sum if it is negative.

3-4 Using the Newton-Rhapson algorithm, compute the nearest-integer square root of 26. Show partial results in a format similar to Table 3-1.

3-5 Repeat Prob. 3-4, computing the answer to two places to the right of the decimal point.

3-6 Change the flowchart shown in Fig. 3-7 to eliminate all bugs and to compute factorial values of positive integers greater than or equal to 0 and less than 1000π (where $\pi = 3.1415926$).

3-7 Prepare a problem model and a flowchart for this problem.

STATEMENT: Convert a 16-digit binary fraction into the BCD codes equivalents of four decimal fractional digits and pack these codes into an answer cell from right to left in reverse order of significance.

ANALYSIS: Use the explosion fractional base conversion algorithm.

INPUT: bit numbers 15   0

| .XXXX | XXXX | XXXX | XXXX |

↑
radix point

OUTPUT: 15   11   7   3   0

| 4th BCD code | 3rd BCD code | 2nd BCD code | 1st BCD code |

4 bits each

(*Note*: The rightmost BCD code is the most significant digit and the first generated. It will represent the decimal fractional digit next to the radix point.)

3-8 Given two lists of cordinates, each 10 items long, a program must be written to find the distance between each set of two points. The table layout is shown below.

List 1				List 2		
Item 1	x_a	y_a		Item 1	x_b	y_b
2	x_a	y_a		2	x_b	y_b
⋮	⋮	⋮		⋮	⋮	⋮
10	x_a	y_a		10	x_b	y_b

Using the information from this chapter, draw a flowchart for the distance routine. The distance routine may use Fig. 3-6 as a subroutine.

3-9 The answer below is calculated to a specific precision by using scale factors. Complete the table to show the effects of scaling.

Input		Operation	Result
Name	Value		
A	3.14	Scale up by 10^2	314
B	271828	Scale down by 10^3	271.828
D	0.107	$A - D \to A$	
—	—	$AB/0.22 \to B$	
—	—	Scale A by 10^{-2}	
—	—	Scale B by 10^{-3}	

3-10 Provide a flowchart for the following problem. Given three tables called table C, table D, and table T, each of which is 100 items long: table C starts at address CREDIT and contains 100 numbers. Table D starts at address DEBIT and contains 100 numbers. Table T starts at address TOTAL and contains 100 items that all are intially cleared to 0.

Add the first value of table C to the first value in table D and place the sum in the first empty item in table T. Now add the second value from table C to the second value of table D and the first item you just placed in table T, and place this sum (subtotal) in the second item of table T. Continue in this fashion until all the items have been processed or until the subtotal in table T goes negative. Perform a subroutine called BANKRUPT and exit the routine if table T does go negative. If all items are processed and the subtotal never became negative, execute a predefined process called SUCCESS and exit the routine. (If the process SUCCESS were ever executed, table T would contain 100 values, and the last value would be the grand total of debits and credits.) For example:

Table C	Table D	Table T
4	−2	2
6	−3	5
2	−5	2
4	−4	2
⋮	⋮	⋮

EXPERIMENT 3

PURPOSE: To investigate hexadecimal addition and subtraction.

PROCEDURE: In this experiment input values will be stored in two memory cells. The answer is provided at an I/O port. In this experiment and the ones to follow, memory addressing always starts with 0000_{16} for the first instruction in a program. Your microcomputer will no doubt not allow you to enter programs at that address. The only change necessary is to modify the upper address of any instruction that must reference memory.

The part of the instruction to be changed will be indicated by *italic* type. Only those cells need be different if you load your program starting at an address with a lower half of 00_{16}.

For example, for the first program below, the beginning instruction is

Address	Op Code
0000	21
0001	21
0002	*00*

Assume that you want to start the program at address 3300_{16}. The value in cell 0002 must be changed to 33 to correspond to the upper two digits of the new address.

Similarly, all I/O ports in the programs are assigned device addresses which may not agree with yours. These device addresses are also set in italics, so you can change them to insert the device codes appropriate for your machine. In this experiment the device code is in cell 0008_{16}.

STEP 1. Place the first value in cell 0020_{16} and the second value in cell 0021_{16} for each run of the program. The answer will be found at the output of the I/O port.

STEP 2. Enter the program.

Mnemonic	Address	Instruction
LHLD	0000	2A
21	0001	21
00	0002	*00*
LDA	0003	3A
20	0004	20
00	0005	*00*
ADD M	0006	86
OUT 0	0007	D3
	0008	*00*
HLT	0009	76

STEP 3. Enter these values into the appropriate input cells, run the program, and record the resulting sum.

Location 0020_{16}	Location 0021_{16}	Sum
14	3B	
56	21	
82	45	
F2	E4	

STEP 4. Change cell 0006 to a subtraction with the instruction

SUB   96

Rerun the program with the inputs below and record your answers.

Location 0020_{16}	Location 0021_{16}	Difference
41	3A	
3A	2D	
28	85	
EA	FB	

STEP 5. Prove that the results in Steps 3 and 4 are correct by carrying out the arithmetic operations.

4

8080A MICROPROCESSOR ARCHITECTURE

Now we will begin a detailed examination of a specific microprocessor, the 8080A, and its supporting devices. As was stated earlier, the 8080A is used in more applications than is any other microprocessor; in fact, it is the heart of at least 20 microcomputers. When microprocessors that are upward-compatible with the 8080A are included (that is, the 8085 and Z80), then over half the microcomputers commercially available today are based on this same architecture and instruction set. Furthermore, the 16-bit 8086 shares some features with the 8080A. So by learning about this microprocessor, you will actually be covering the essential characteristics of a significant number of other microprocessors. You already know that the 8080A microprocessor usually is combined with two other integrated circuits (ICs), the 8224 clock generator and driver, which provides the timing signals of the microprocessor system; and the 8228 system controller, which demultiplexes data lines and sends control or status signals. Other devices in the 8080A family used for input/output and timing control are covered in later chapters.

CHAPTER OBJECTIVES

Upon completion of this chapter, you should be able to:

1. List the functions of the 8080A, 8224, and 8228 integrated circuits.
2. Describe the programmable registers and stack of the 8080A.
3. Discuss the functions of the ALU.
4. Explain the control and timing of the 8080A by use of timing diagrams.
5. Describe the interface between the 8080A and either ROM or RAM and the methods of address mapping.
6. Define the purpose of bidirectional bus drivers in a microcomputer system.
7. List the types of instructions used in the 8080A and explain timing diagrams of the instructions.

THE 8080A MICROPROCESSOR INTEGRATED CIRCUIT

The 8080A is characterized by its performance of all the MPU functions needed in a computer system, including arithmetic and logic, control and timing, and programmable registers. The microprocessor provides and accepts TTL-compatible signals. Three power supply voltages are necessary to drive the chip: +5 V, +12 V, and −5 V. There are several manufacturers of the 8080A, and slight functional differences are found among the several versions of the 8080A. If such differences are significant to our study, they are noted. Variations in maximum clock frequency, environmental conditions, and electrical parameters are characteristic of these differences. Because the particular 8080A model must suit the intended operating conditions, always consult the data sheets to assure proper performance of that model in your application.

Data and Address Lines

Figure 4-1 is the pin assignment for the 8080A. As you can see, the 8080A is housed in a 40-pin DIP. The purpose of each pin is described in Table 4-1. The address lines (A0 through A15) make up the *three-state address bus.* Addresses set on these lines indicate the binary location in memory of data to be read or written. The address lines also designate a particular I/O device to be used in data transfers external to the microcomputer. The address bus, which consists of three-state lines, can *float* (switch to the high-impedance state) to allow other users on the bus to exchange data without confusing the MPU.

The bidirectional data lines form the *internal data bus* for the 8 bits of information being sent or received by the microprocessor. Input/output data to or from the processor is transferred by means of this bus.

Timing Signals

Not every device can run as fast as the 8080A. When some peripheral cannot respond within the MPU-dictated timing constraints, the peripheral can request that the MPU extend the interval. To request the delay, the peripheral sets the READY input low. This signal causes the 8080A to enter the wait state. The microprocessor signals this condition by setting the WAIT output high. All MPU operations are suspended while waiting, but the address on the address bus remains stable.

The microprocessor can also be stopped between the completion of one instruction and the start of the next. Setting the HOLD input high accomplishes this result, which could be used for program debugging or computer maintenance. Another use for the hold state is to coordinate direct memory access, which is discussed in Chap. 11. On receipt of the high HOLD signal, the processor floats both the data and address buses, thus allowing external logic to use the buses at will. The 8080A also sets HLDA high to acknowledge the input signal. This output signal is used by an external device to identify the beginning of the time that the buses are floated.

If the RESET input is held high for at least three clock periods, the microprocessor will zero all its registers (except the status register, which remains unchanged). Because the program counter register has been zeroed, the computer will start by executing the instruction in cell 0000_{16}.

Data Bus Status

Two signals are provided to indicate the situation on the data bus. A high level for DBIN means that data from the addressed memory location or the I/O device must immediately be placed on the data bus. This signal is a convenient input strobe for external logic. (Incidentally, remember that input and output are always relative to the processor. An input com-

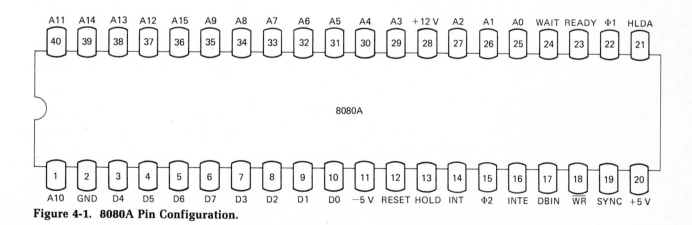

Figure 4-1. 8080A Pin Configuration.

Table 4-1
8080A Signals

Signal Name	Purpose	Type of Data	Other Characteristics
A0–A15	Address lines	Output	Three-state system bus
D0–D7	Data lines	Bidirectional	Internal three-state bus
DBIN	Data input strobe	Output	System bus
HOLD	Hold state request	Input	System bus
HLDA	Hold acknowledge	Output	System bus
INT	Interrupt request	Input	System bus
INTE	Interrupt acknowledge	Output	System bus
READY	Data input stable	Input	System bus
RESET	Reset MPU	Input	System bus
SYNC	Machine cycle synchronizer	Output	
WAIT	MPU in wait state	Output	System bus
$\overline{\text{WR}}$	Data output strobe	Output	System bus
Φ1, Φ2	Clock signals	Input	

PROGRAM STATUS WORD   PRIMARY ACCUMULATOR

SOMETIMES TREATED AS 16-BIT REGISTERS

PSW	A
B	C
D	E
H	L

SECONDARY ACCUMULATORS/ ADDRESS COUNTERS

SP

STACK POINTER

PC

PROGRAM COUNTER

Figure 4-2. Programmable Registers.

mand to a peripheral unit means that the device is to send data to the computer.)

The processor signals memory or other users that output data on the data bus is stable with the $\overline{\text{WR}}$ line. (The bar over the name of any signal means that the signal is true when it is low.) When $\overline{\text{WR}}$ is low, the receiving device should sample the data. This status line is usually used as the output, or write, strobe.

Interrupt Control

Two status lines are used to coordinate exchange of interrupt status. The INT line is set high by the external logic. The processor uses INTE as a reply to indicate that the interrupt has been acknowledged (see Chap. 11).

Programmable Registers

There are 10 registers in the 8080A which are used by the programmer and controlled by use of processor instructions (see Fig. 4-2). The purpose of these registers is similar to those discussed in Chap. 1. A brief comment on each serves as a review.

The A register is the 8-bit primary accumulator. It is most commonly used in arithmetic, logical, and data transfer instructions. Certain aspects of arithmetic or logical results are shown by flag bits in the status register. The meaning of each bit in the status register is shown in Fig. 4-3. The sign, zero, parity, and carry flags were discussed previously. The auxiliary carry is a new feature, though. This flag operates the same as the carry indicator, but the A_C bit reflects carries out of bit position 3 into position 4 of the 8-bit sum. This status flag is often used in BCD operations (see Chap. 6). In some cases the A register is combined with the status register to form a 16-bit unit.

There are six secondary accumulators: B, C, D, E, H, and L. Each is an 8-bit register which can, in many cases, be used in the same manner as the

BIT NUMBER   7 6 5 4 3 2 1 0

S	Z	—	A_C	—	P	—	C

Figure 4-3. Status Register.

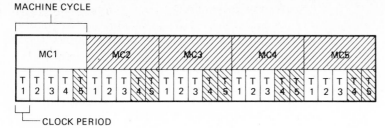

Figure 4-4. 8080A Timing.

MACHINE CYCLE WHICH MAY BE OMITTED

CLOCK PERIOD WHICH MAY BE OMITTED

A register. In addition, these registers can be linked to be 16-bit address counters. When used in this manner, they are referred to as the BC, DE, or HL registers. The HL register is used as the primary address counter. The use of the address counters is discussed in detail in Chap. 5.

You already know how the stack pointer (SP) is set to show the address for the top of the stack. The 8080A uses memory as the stack, so the programmer can have a stack 64K locations long if desired. Normally, much shorter stack lengths are called for. When the stack is popped, the content of the memory cell on top of the stack, as addressed by the SP register, is obtained. New data are pushed on the stack also by using the address given in the pointer register.

The final register in the 8080A of interest to programmers is the program counter (PC). The program counter holds the address of the next instruction to be executed. Recall that this register is incremented during the instruction fetching, so that it always shows the proper memory location.

8080A Integrated Circuit Review

1. List the microprocessor functions performed by the 8080A.

2. Describe the purpose and type of signal applied to or sent by each pin of the 8080A.

3. Why are the data lines and address lines three-state buses? Why are only the data lines bidirectional?

4. How does the DBIN signal indicate to a peripheral device the proper time to send data to the processor? What signal does the processor use to indicate that output data is stable?

5. Describe the use of the 10 programmable registers in the 8080A.

CONTROL

The control section of the 8080A executes instructions as timed by a sequence of machine cycles (MC),

which are further subdivided into clock periods (T). An instruction may require from one to five machine cycles to complete its execution. Each of these machine cycles will be made up of three, four, or five periods (except MC1, which always is four or five periods in duration). Figure 4-4 summarizes the timing sequences. Specific instructions are studied in this and following chapters to further illustrate how the processor timing is controlled by the machine cycles and the clock periods.

Clock Phases

Two clock phases, Φ1 and Φ2, are used by the microprocessor to delineate the clock periods T shown in Fig. 4-4. These periods are derived from the two phases as shown in Fig. 4-5. The beginning of each period is indicated by the leading edge of Φ1.

A separate SYNC pulse is produced to identify T1 during every machine cycle. The SYNC signal rises on the leading edge of the first Φ2 pulse during each machine cycle and falls on the leading edge of the second Φ2 pulse. Arrows on the timing diagram show this cause and effect. As Φ2 goes high the first time, it causes SYNC to switch to the high state. On the second Φ2 transition, SYNC returns to the original low level. While synchronizing clocking signals can be quite involved, they are easily generated if the 8224 clock signal generator is used.

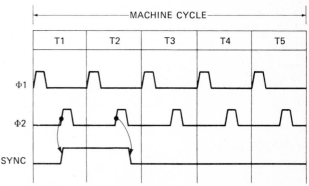

Figure 4-5. Clock Phases.

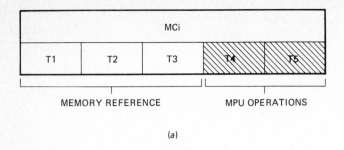

(a)

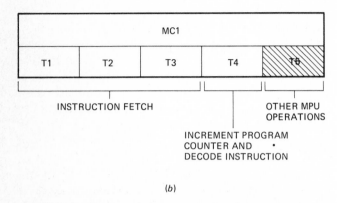

(b)

NOTE: CROSSHATCHED CLOCK PERIODS MAY BE OMITTED.

Figure 4-6. Machine Cycles. (a) Other than MC1; (b) MC1.

Instruction Execution Timing

During any machine cycle, clock periods T1 through T3 are reserved from memory references. The use of these clock periods is illustrated in Fig. 4-6a. The remaining time in the machine cycle, T4 and T5, is available for MPU functions not involving memory or for use by external logic to complete its operations.

In addition, there is a special meaning of MC1 for any instruction; it is during this machine cycle

that the instruction is fetched. As Fig. 4-6b shows, T1, T2, and T3 are used to obtain the instruction. This timing is a special case of the basic rule that memory is referenced during the first three clock periods. It is in the T4 interval that the program counter will increment and the instruction be decoded. The remaining period T5 is optional; that is, for some instructions the MPU can use this time for other operations. Otherwise, T5 is canceled.

IDENTIFYING OPERATIONS. With all the different tasks accomplished by the 8080A, how can external devices keep track of what is happening? Actually, this seemingly complex problem is solved quite simply. During T2 of every machine cycle the processor signals the operation to be performed on the data bus. A code on the 8-bit data bus informs all devices of what is to take place.

A timing diagram of these signals is shown in Fig. 4-7a. The status signals are stable when both $\Phi 1$ and SYNC are high. From this fact the simple circuit (see Fig. 4-7b), can be constructed to trigger an external device to sample the data lines at the proper time. The "read status strobe" goes high only during the proper interval of T2.

The meaning of each bit in the status message is listed in Table 4-2. As you can see, each data bit (D0 to D7) is assigned a unique meaning in the status code. For example, if D1 is low, the instruction will use the data bus to transmit information to memory or to an external device.

Each microinstruction sequence usually requires more than one operation. Several status bits are set to provide a complete indication of the operations to be performed. As Table 4-3 shows, the code on the data lines uniquely identifies every microinstruction sequence. Consider the instruction fetch with its code of $A2_{16}$. Status bits 7, 5, and 1 are

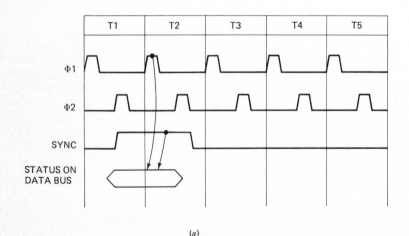

(a)

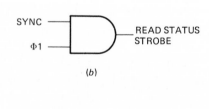

(b)

Figure 4-7. Read Strobe (a) Timing Diagram; (b) Circuit.

Table 4-2
Status Bits Set During T2

Data Bus Bit	Status Indication	Meaning
D0	INTA	Acknowledge signal for interrupt request.
D1	$\overline{WO}$	The data bus will be used for a write operation to either memory or an external device.
D2	STACK	The address bus now represents the stack pointer address.
D3	HLTA	Acknowledge signal for the halt instruction.
D4	OUT	The address bus now indicates the output device that should accept data when $\overline{WR}$ is low.
D5	M1	The MPU is in the fetch cycle of the first byte of an instruction.
D6	INP	The address bus now indicates the input device that should place data on the bus when DBIN goes high.
D7	MEMR	The data bus will be used for reading from memory.

set. Referring back to Table 4-2, we see that these bits indicate memory reading, fetching the first byte of an instruction, and *not* writing. (Remember that $\overline{WO}$ must be low to be true.) These three operations are just those you would expect for fetching an instruction.

To aid the hardware designer in the use of the status bits during T2, the 8228 system controller was developed. This IC automatically handles these status signals and converts them to command lines on the control bus.

INSTRUCTION FETCHING. Let's analyze the instruction fetching microprogram in more detail to gain a further understanding of the timing relationships in the MPU. The sequence of events is specified in Table 4-4. A timing diagram showing each period of MC1 is shown in Fig. 4-8. During T1 the clock phases and SYNC pulse indicate the start of a machine cycle. The WAIT line is low, thus allowing the processor to proceed without delay. Because this is a read operation, $\overline{WR}$ is held high.

At about this same time, the processor sets the status code for instruction fetching on the data lines ($A2_{16}$ from Table 4-3). The memory address of the instruction is placed on the address lines. (The instruction address was obtained from the program counter.) In the next clock period the memory can anticipate an input operation by ANDing $\Phi1$ with SYNC to generate a "status read strobe." DBIN goes high thus indicating that the data bus is ready to receive data; the processor floats the bus in preparation for the data transfer. At the beginning of T3, memory data must be stable on the lines so that the processor can move the instruction into the

instruction register. The data bus is floated by the memory after $\Phi2$ of the third period to make it available to other users. During T4 the processor counts up the program counter and also floats the address bus. The next period, T5, is an optional period in the machine cycle that may or may not be used depending on the instruction.

READING MEMORY DATA. The microprogram for reading memory uses practically the same procedures as does the instruction fetching sequence. There are only two changes. First, some machine cycle other than MC1 would be used. Second, the status code set on the data lines during T1 would be 82_{16} because the M1 status bit (D5) is 0. Of course, every memory read operation adds one machine cycle to the instruction execution time.

Table 4-3
Status Codes for the Microinstructions

Type of Microinstruction	Address Bus Status Code (Hexadecimal)
Instruction fetch	A2
Memory read	82
Memory write	00
Stack read	86
Stack write	04
Input read	42
Output write	10
Interrupt acknowledge	23
Halt acknowledge	8A or 0A
Interrupt acknowledge while halted	2B or 23

Table 4-4
Single-byte Instruction Fetching

T1: 1. Leading edge of Φ2 causes SYNC to rise, thus marking the period of T1.
2. WAIT is low, so the MPU is not in the wait state.
3. $\overline{WR}$ is high; data are to be read (not written) from memory.
4. Data bits are set with the status code
$\overline{WO}$ (D1) high: the MPU is expecting an input
M1 (D5) high: the instruction is in the fetch cycle
MEMR (D7) high: input from memory
5. The appropriate memory address is set on the address lines (A0 to A15).

T2: 1. Memory uses Φ1 ANDed with SYNC to read status from the data bus.
2. DBIN high causes the data bus to be ready to receive input (the signal stays high until the rising edge of Φ2 during T3).

T3: 1. The MPU stores the instruction in the instruction register where the control section will interpret it.
2. The data bus is floated during T3, thus making it available to external logic

T4: 1. The data and address buses are floated during T4.
2. The program counter is incremented.

WRITING MEMORY DATA. The operations for sending a byte of data from the processor to memory have many similarities to those required for reading. The sequence is listed in Table 4-5 and a timing diagram provided in Fig. 4-9. The first difference occurs during Step 4 of T1. The status code on the data lines is all 0. With $\overline{WO}$ low, we know that this will be a write operation. During T2 the processor sets the data to be placed in memory on the data lines. (The memory already has the address available on the address bus.) When $\overline{WR}$ goes low during T3, the memory accepts the data.

The Wait State

When an external device (for example, a slow memory) wants the MPU to provide more time for an input data transfer, the device signals its request by setting the READY signal low. As Fig. 4-10 shows, the wait state occurs between T2 and T3. If the READY signal remains low at Φ2 of T2, the MPU enters the wait mode. Here the processor can be held for any number of clock periods until the peripheral device raises the READY line. The MPU indicates that no operations are being performed by setting the WAIT signal high; however, all output signals such as data and address lines remain constant. When the device finally sets READY high, the processor detects the condition on the first Φ2 pulse after READY is high. The MPU then continues execution of the instruction at T3.

The Hold State

Be careful to distinguish the wait state from the 8080A hold state. During the wait state the processor is held up in the middle of executing an instruction, but in the hold state the MPU is between instructions.

Another important difference is that during the hold state the system buses are floated, so that external logic can use them. (Output signals other than data and addresses are held constant.) Any number of clock periods may elapse between the machine cycles from the end of one instruction and the beginning of the next. Figure 4-11b shows the hold state situation which should be compared with the wait state shown in Fig. 4-11a.

The hold state basically allows the external logic to stop the MPU. The hold sequence is listed in Table 4-6. If the HOLD signal is detected high during T1, the microprocessor responds by setting the acknowledge, HLDA, high. If the current instruction was to read memory ($\overline{WO}$ high during T2), then HLDA goes high at the leading edge of Φ1 during T3. Had the current instruction been a write operation ($\overline{WO}$ is low during T2), the HLDA is set high on the leading edge of Φ1 of T4. Timing diagrams of these two situations are shown in Figs. 4-12a

Table 4-5
Writing Data in Memory

T1: 1. Leading edge of Φ2 causes SYNC to rise, thus marking the period as T.
2. WAIT is low, so the MPU is not in the wait state.
3. $\overline{WR}$ is high until it is time to write.
4. All data bits are 0.
5. The appropriate memory address is set on the address lines (A0–A15).

T2: 1. Memory uses Φ1 ANDed with SYNC to read status from the data bus.
2. DBIN remains low.

T3: 1. $\overline{WR}$ goes low.
2. The data are transferred from the processor to the data bus and then to memory.

T4: 1. The data and address buses are floated during T4.
2. The program counter is incremented.

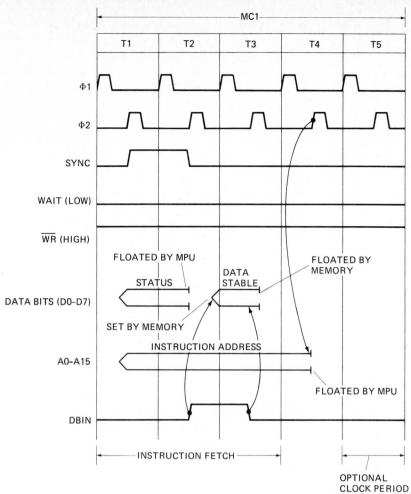

Figure 4-8. Memory Reading.

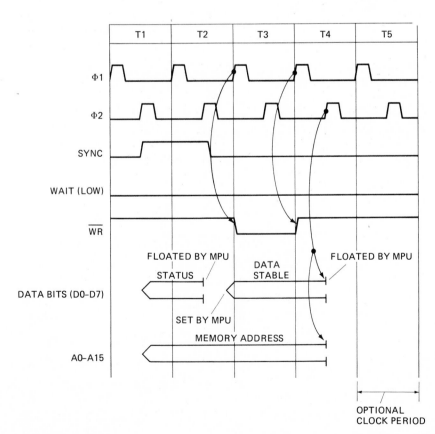

Figure 4-9. Memory Writing.

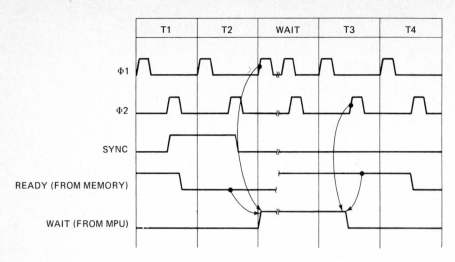

Figure 4-10. WAIT Timing Diagram.

and 4-12*b*. When the external device drops HOLD, it is sensed on the leading edge of either clock phase by the processor, thus terminating the hold state. The hold state always ends at Φ1 of the next machine cycle, that is, during the next available T1 period. At that time the 8080A resets HLDA.

The Halt State

The programmer can cause the 8080A to stop by executing a halt instruction. The processor stops all operations and pauses with nothing to do until it is restarted. None of the system buses is floated in the halt state. Almost every program written for

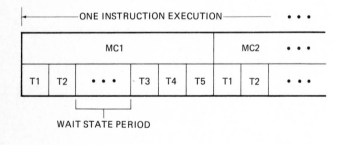

(a)

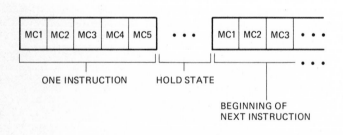

(b)

Figure 4-11. HOLD Timing Diagram (*a*) WAIT State; (*b*) HOLD State.

the microprocessor will contain at least one halt instruction. When the 8080A stops, the programmer knows that the program has been completed.

The RESET Signal

The RESET signal is frequently used to restart the processor after a halt. When RESET goes high, the processor clears registers as was previously explained. As long as RESET is high, the 8080A is in a suspended state; no operations are performed. When RESET falls, instruction execution begins with T1 at the next Φ1 pulse. Because the program counter is 0, the instruction in memory location 0000_{16} is selected. When the 8080A is initially powered up, it must be reset. Otherwise, all the registers, including the program counter, will contain random data. Program execution would then erroneously start at some meaningless memory address.

Table 4-6
Hold Sequence

1. The hold state is initiated by the HOLD input signal.
2. The MPU responds with HLDA high.
   a. If the hold was requested during a read operation, then HLDA is set high at the leading edge of Φ1 of T3.
   b. If the hold was requested during a write operation, the HLDA is set high at the leading edge of Φ1 of T4.
3. HOLD low is sensed at the leading edge of Φ1 or Φ2. The hold state is terminated at the starting Φ1 of the next machine cycle.
4. HLDA is reset by the processor.

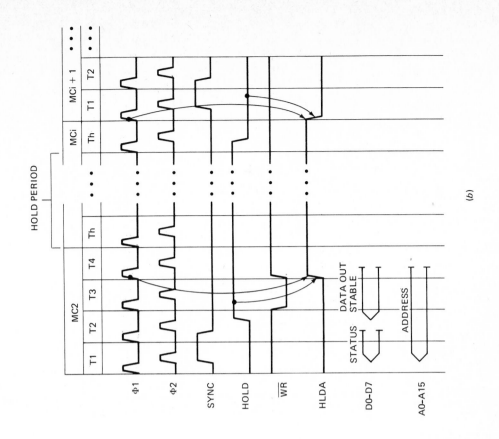

(b)

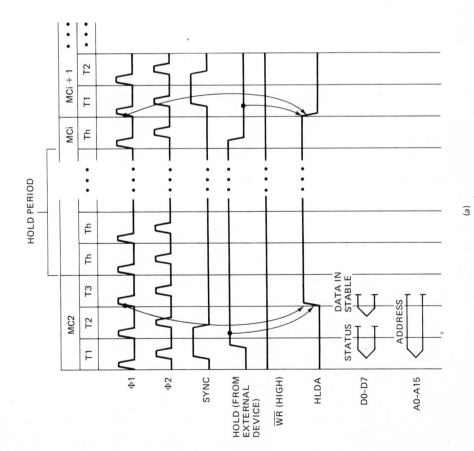

(a)

Figure 4-12. HOLD During (*a*) Read and (*b*) Write.

Control Review

1. Distinguish between machine cycles, clock periods, and clock phases.

2. What is the purpose of T1 through T3 in any machine cycle? What is T4 used for during MC1?

3. In which clock period is an instruction fetched? When is it decoded so that the processor knows the action to complete?

4. How does the processor use the data bus during T2 to tell other devices what the operation is to be?

5. Describe the use of the status bits in specifying the operations which comprise the microinstruction. How are the status bits converted to control bus commands?

6. List the sequence of signals used during MC1 to fetch an instruction. How does fetching data from memory differ?

7. Discuss the differences between control signals used to write and to read memory data.

8. How does an external device request more time for a reply? What signal does the 8080A use to acknowledge that the request is granted?

9. Contrast the hold state with the halt state.

10. Why does the processor execute the instruction in memory location 0000_{16} after the RESET line goes low after being held high?

THE 8224 CLOCK GENERATOR DRIVER

The 8224 provides the 8080A with its $\Phi1$ and $\Phi2$ clock phases. This IC also creates READY and RESET inputs properly synchronized with $\Phi2$ as required

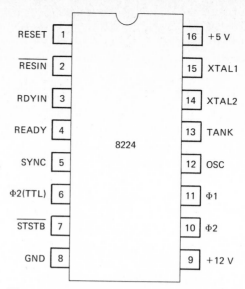

Figure 4-13. 8224 Clock Generator and Driver.

by the MPU. The pin arrangement of the 8224 is shown in Fig. 4-13, and the signals are described in Table 4-7.

The XTAL and TANK inputs are associated with the crystal that must be used to generate the clock phases. The 8224 produces the nonoverlapping $\Phi1$ and $\Phi2$ pulses which swing between 11 V and 0.3 V. Because these voltages are not TTL-compatible, separate TTL-level outputs of $\Phi2$ (TTL) and OSC are provided. An equivalent circuit to the 8224 is shown in Fig. 4-14. Tracing the operations of the 8224 on that figure will make it easier to follow the discussion of its functions.

Timing Signals

The clock frequency of the 8224, and thus of the 8080A, depends on a crystal oscillator. The crystal frequency must be exactly nine times the required clock period. The standard clock period (and the

Table 4-7
8224 Signals

Name	Purpose	Type
OSC	Crystal oscillator waveform	Output
RDYIN	Ready signal	Input
READY	Control signal to 8080A	Output
RESET	Control signal to 8080A	Output
RESIN	Reset signal	Input
STSTB	Synchronization signal	Output
SYNC	Control signal	Input
XTAL1, XTAL2, TANK	External crystal connections	Input
$\Phi1$, $\Phi2$	Clock signals	Output
$\Phi2$ (TTL)	TTL-compatible clock	Output

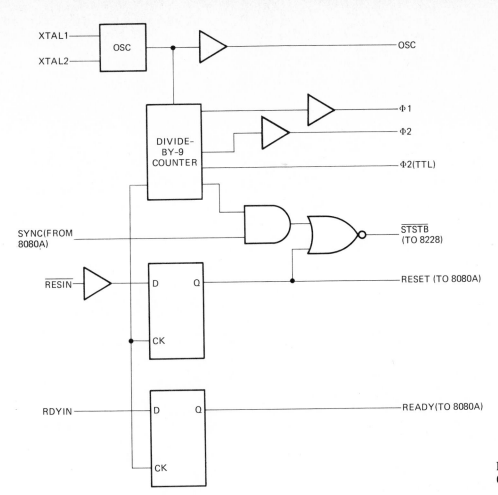

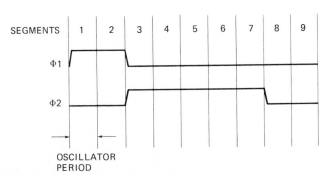

Figure 4-14. 8224 Equivalent Circuit.

one used in this book) for the 8080A is 500 ns, thus indicating that the crystal frequency should be 18 MHz. Each clock period is divided into nine segments (see Fig. 4-15). Each segment is then equal to one crystal oscillation period. If a supporting LC network is used with an overtone mode crystal, the TANK input to the 8224 is used.

Referring to the equivalent circuit, we see that the divide-by-9 counter is used to convert the higher crystal frequency to the slower clock phase frequency. A buffered output of the oscillator signal and a TTL-level duplicate of Φ2 are produced by the counter for general use throughout the microcomputer system.

Control Signals

There are two sets of corresponding control signals handled by the 8224. The external-logic-supplied $\overline{RESIN}$ is converted to a synchronized RESET to be sent to the 8080A. Similarly, RDYIN from another device is translated to READY by the 8224. In addition, the 8224 sends a signal to the 8228.

RESET. It would be difficult for external logic to synchronize the reset signal input with Φ2, so the 8224 provides that service for the system. Furthermore, the 8224 converts a slowly varying input of $\overline{RESIN}$ to a crisp reset output by the use of an internal Schmitt trigger. The output goes to the high level in synchronism with Φ2 when $\overline{RESIN}$ falls below a threshold value (see Fig. 4-16).

It is common to use a manual switch to provide $\overline{RESIN}$, but it may be desirable to reset after a power failure or initial startup as well. Figure 4-17 shows

Figure 4-15. Generating the Clock Phases.

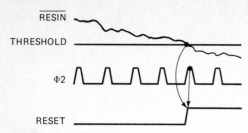

Figure 4-16. RESET Signals.

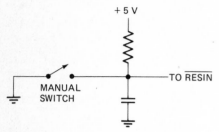

Figure 4-17. RESET Switch Circuit.

a simple circuit which accomplishes all these functions.

READY. The 8224 will accept an asynchronous RDYIN signal also. As the timing diagram of Fig. 4-18 shows, RDYIN can arrive at any point in the interval between successive Φ2 pulses. The 8224 will generate a ready signal to the 8080A to coincide with the leading edge of the next Φ2 pulse.

STSTB. A status strobe signal is sent from the 8224 to the 8228 system controller. This signal is produced as a result of the SYNC input from the 8080A. As long as the three ICs are being used to form the microprocessor, this signal is of little interest to the user.

8224 Review

1. Describe the purpose of each pin on the 8224.

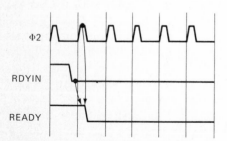

Figure 4-18. READY Timing Diagram.

2. How does the 8224 convert the external oscillator frequency to Φ1 and Φ2 clock pulses?

3. What is the purpose of the Schmitt trigger in the 8224?

4. Explain the conversion of RDYIN to a signal in synchronization with the leading edge of a Φ2 pulse.

THE 8228 SYSTEM CONTROLLER AND BUS DRIVER

This IC performs most of the bus handling in the 8080A-based microcomputer. The 8228 is a bidirectional bus driver combined with signal-generation logic. The almost identical 8238 provides longer delays in memory signals so that more time is allowed for slow memory circuits. The pin configuration of this 28-pin DIP is shown in Fig. 4-19. Many of the signals are those provided by the 8080A or the 8224, which have already been described. The signals are summarized in Table 4-8. As we will

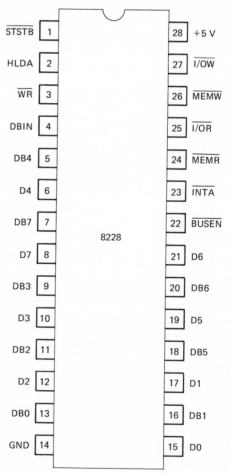

Figure 4-19. 8228 System Controller and Bus Driver.

Table 4-8
8228 Signals

Name	Purpose	Type
$\overline{\text{BUSEN}}$	Data bus float/enable control	Input
DBIN	Data input strobe	Input
D0–D7	Microprocessor data bus	Bidirectional
DB0–DB7	System data bus	Bidirectional
HLDA	Hold acknowledge	Input
$\overline{\text{I/OR}}$	I/O read control	Output
$\overline{\text{I/OW}}$	I/O write control	Output
$\overline{\text{INTA}}$	Interrupt acknowledge	Output
$\overline{\text{MEMR}}$	Memory read control	Output
$\overline{\text{MEMW}}$	Memory write control	Output
$\overline{\text{STSTB}}$	Status strobe	Input
$\overline{\text{WR}}$	Data output strobe	Input

see, the 8228 was developed to overcome the pin-count limitation on the 8080A. Because the number of pins must be minimized, control and data signals are multiplexed on the 8080A data bus. The 8228 basically acts as a demultiplexer for those signals as the equivalent circuit in Fig. 4-20 shows.

Data Signals

The 8228 provides a bidirectional buffer for data moving between the 8080A and the system data bus. The 8080A internal microprocessor bus signals are designated D0 through D7. These bidirectional sig-

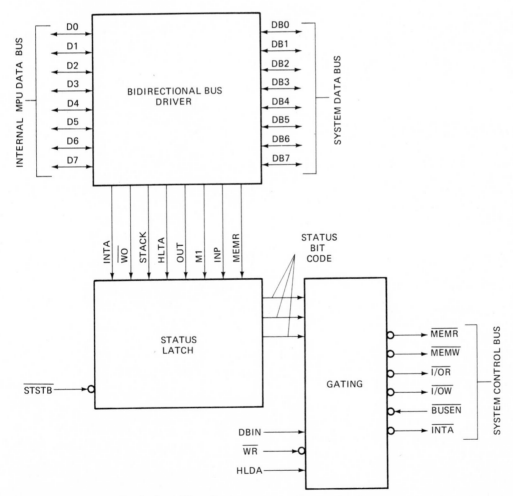

Figure 4-20. 8228 Equivalent Circuit.

nals are passed through the bus driver to become the data on the system bus used by external logic. The corresponding system data bus lines are labeled DB0 through DB7.

Control Signals

The 8228 combines various combinations of three 8080A control signals ($\overline{WR}$, DBIN, and HLDA) with status codes on the microprocessor data lines during T2 to generate the system control bus signals.

These signals are generated by combinatorial logic, as shown in Table 4-9. Note that all system bus signals use negative logic; that is, $\overline{MEMR}$, $\overline{MEMW}$, $\overline{I/OR}$, $\overline{I/OW}$, and $\overline{INTA}$ are all true when low. The 8228 produces $\overline{MEMR}$ by ANDing MEMR (which is bit D7 on the data bus during T1) with DBIN from the 8080A. Other system bus signals are also derived from 8080A signals.

An example of the 8228 signals used for fetching an instruction from memory followed by writing

Table 4-9
System Control Bus Signals

Inputs	System Control Bus Output
MEMR (D7) AND DBIN	$\overline{MEMR}$
OUT (D4) AND WR	$\overline{MEMW}$
OUT (D4) AND $\overline{WR}$	$\overline{I/OW}$
INP (D6) AND DBIN	$\overline{I/OR}$
INTA (D0)	$\overline{INTA}$

into memory is shown in the timing diagram of Fig. 4-21. The signal to read, $\overline{MEMR}$, results from the MEMR bit being set in the status code during T1 of MC1 and from DBIN going high during T2. (The 8228 must latch the status codes so that they will be available during T2.) The $\overline{MEMR}$ signal is synchronized with the input $\overline{STSTB}$ (from the 8224). The true state of $\overline{MEMR}$ is a read strobe for memory which places the data on the system data bus lines which the 8228 relays to the processor on the internal

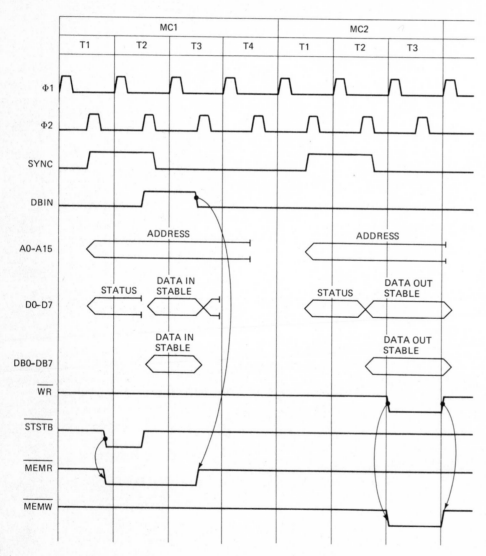

Figure 4-21. Control Signal Timing Diagram.

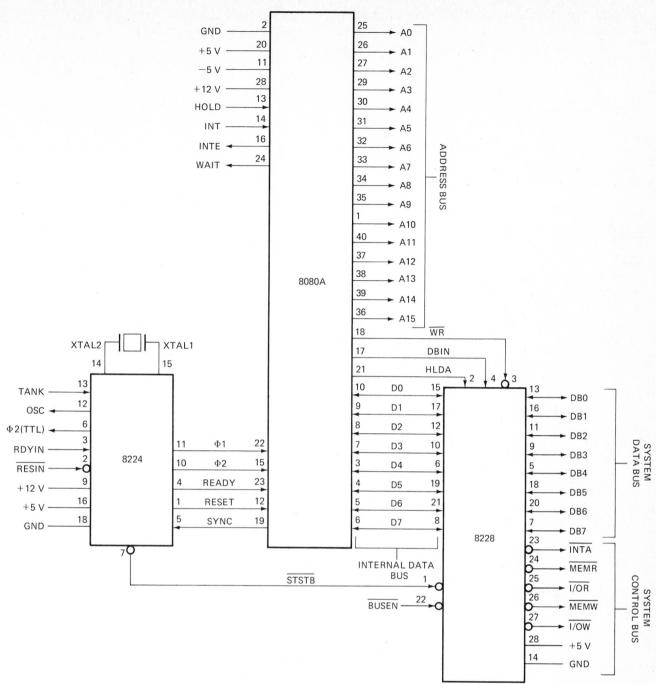

Figure 4-22. 8080A Microprocessor System.

data bus during T2 and T3 until $\overline{\text{MEMR}}$ goes high again. The writing of memory takes place in MC2. Then $\overline{\text{WR}}$ causes $\overline{\text{MEMW}}$ to become true (low), and memory accepts the data at the location specified by the address bus.

A system diagram for a complete microprocessor composed of three ICs is shown in Fig. 4-22. The address bus, the internal and system data buses, and the system control bus are shown in the diagram. Three power supplies are used by the 8080A, while the 8224 shares two of them, and the 8228 requires

only 5 V. A common ground is also necessary for the three ICs.

8228 Review

1. Distinguish between pins D0 through D7 and pins DB0 through DB7 on the 8228.

2. Explain why the 8228 must demultiplex signals sent on the internal microprocessor data bus.

3. What combination of signals cause $\overline{\text{MEMW}}$ to become true?

4. Describe the use of $\overline{\text{STSTB}}$ in causing $\overline{\text{MEMR}}$ to become true.

MEMORY

There are so many memory locations available for use with the 8080A that it may be difficult to grasp the overall organization. The *memory map* as shown in Fig. 4-23 is an effective way of picturing the memory space in the computer. The 64K memory is shown in 1K *blocks.* (The notation "1K" actually means 1024 memory locations.) There is no requirement to equip the microcomputer with the entire 64K cells, so some of the blocks may be missing for a particular implementation. Eight blocks form a *memory bank.*

Furthermore, the memory in each block may be either ROM or RAM. Recall from Chap. 1 that the capacity of each memory IC will be the deciding factor in how many ICs are required in the total memory. For example, if 256 × 8 ROMs are used, four ROM ICs (a total of 1024 × 8) comprise one block. On the other hand, it would take eight 1K × 1 RAMs to form a block because there are 8 bits in each word.

A memory address does not depend on the type of memory used. The designer assigns the addresses in memory by laying out the memory configuration. Any address can be used for either ROM or RAM. In addition, it makes no difference whether the ROM is mask programmed by the manufacturer or is a programmable fusible link ROM (PROM) or ultraviolet erasable ROM (EPROM).

The address bits designate the bank and memory block as indicated in Fig. 4-23. The process of selecting the correct block is a result of *address decoding.* For instance, let the address be $06BC_{16}$. Converting the hexadecimal address to binary, we see that bits A15, A14, and A13 are all 0s, thus causing bank 0 to be selected. The column of the block on the map depends on bits A12, A11, and A10, which are 001_2, respectively. The intersection of the bank 0 row and the 001_2 column is block 1, which contains addresses in the range of 0400_{16} to $07FF_{16}$. The remaining address bits (A0 through A9) select the specific cell within the memory block.

A decoding circuit that uses the 8205 decoder is shown in Fig. 4-24. The pin diagram and the logic table for the 8205 1-of-8 decoder are shown in Fig. 4-25. The 8205 has three address input pins (A0, A1, and A2) and three enabling pins ($\overline{\text{E1}}$, $\overline{\text{E2}}$, and E3). There are eight outputs, only one of which can be low at any time. When E3 is high and the

		ADDRESS BITS A12, A11, AND A10							
		000	001	010	011	100	101	110	111
000 BANK 0		BLOCK 0 0000–03FF	BLOCK 1 0400–07FF	BLOCK 2 0800–0BFF	BLOCK 3 0C00–0FFF	BLOCK 4 1000–13FF	BLOCK 5 1400–17FF	BLOCK 6 1800–1BFF	BLOCK 7 1C00–1FFF
001 BANK 1		BLOCK 8 2000–23FF	BLOCK 9 2400–27FF	BLOCK 10 2800–2BFF	BLOCK 11 2C00–2FFF	BLOCK 12 3000–33FF	BLOCK 13 3400–37FF	BLOCK 14 3800–3BFF	BLOCK 15 3C00–3FFF
010 BANK 2		BLOCK 16 4000–43FF	BLOCK 17 4400–47FF	BLOCK 18 4800–4BFF	BLOCK 19 4C00–4FFF	BLOCK 20 5000–53FF	BLOCK 21 5400–57FF	BLOCK 22 5800–5BFF	BLOCK 23 5C00–5FFF
011 BANK 3		BLOCK 24 6000–63FF	BLOCK 25 6400–67FF	BLOCK 26 6800–6BFF	BLOCK 27 6C00–6FFF	BLOCK 28 7000–73FF	BLOCK 29 7400–77FF	BLOCK 30 7800–7BFF	BLOCK 31 7C00–7FFF
100 BANK 4		BLOCK 32 8000–83FF	BLOCK 33 8400–87FF	BLOCK 34 8800–8BFF	BLOCK 35 8C00–8FFF	BLOCK 36 9000–93FF	BLOCK 37 9400–97FF	BLOCK 38 9800–9BFF	BLOCK 39 9C00–9FFF
101 BANK 5		BLOCK 40 A000–A3FF	BLOCK 41 A400–A7FF	BLOCK 42 A800–ABFF	BLOCK 43 AC00–AFFF	BLOCK 44 B000–B3FF	BLOCK 45 B400–B7FF	BLOCK 46 B800–BBFF	BLOCK 47 BC00–BFFF
110 BANK 6		BLOCK 48 C000–C3FF	BLOCK 49 C400–C7FF	BLOCK 50 C800–CBFF	BLOCK 51 CC00–CFFF	BLOCK 52 D000–D3FF	BLOCK 53 D400–D7FF	BLOCK 54 D800–DBFF	BLOCK 55 DC00–DFFF
111 BANK 7		BLOCK 56 E000–E3FF	BLOCK 57 E400–E7FF	BLOCK 58 E800–EBFF	BLOCK 59 EC00–EFFF	BLOCK 60 F000–F3FF	BLOCK 61 F300–F7FF	BLOCK 62 F800–FBFF	BLOCK 63 FC00–FFFF

ADDRESS BITS A15, A14, AND A13

Figure 4-23. 6K Memory Map.

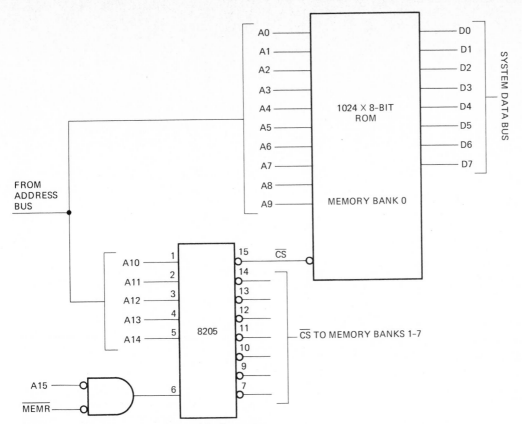

Figure 4-24. Address Decoding with the 8205.

other enable inputs low, the level of the output line corresponding to the binary value on the address lines is low and all others high. For example, when levels A2 through A0 are low, high, and low, respectively (010_2), output line 2 is driven to its low state; all other outputs stay high.

Returning to Fig. 4-24, we see that the enable lines can be used to extend the addressing range of the 8205. Address bit 15 is ANDed with $\overline{\text{MEMR}}$ to synchronize the addressing of memory with the true state of the latter signal. (The inverters on the AND gate inputs produce an output of the correct level to enable E3 when both inputs are low.) Bits A14 through A10 are properly connected to select the eight blocks of memory bank 0. (The entire 64K memory will require eight 8205 decoders in all.) When all inputs to the 8205 are low, pin 15 (output 0) goes low, thus making chip select ($\overline{\text{CS}}$) true for bank 0. The remaining bits on the address bus (A0 through A9), are applied to the 10 address pins on the ROM to read one of its 1024 memory cells. The data is available on the ROM output lines (D0 through D7), which place the data on the system bus.

Sequencing and timing signals used to read the ROM are shown in Fig. 4-26. The microprocessor ensures that the address is stable on the address bus at the same time that $\overline{\text{MEMR}}$ is set low. The 8205 decodes the upper 6 bits of the address, thus

causing $\overline{\text{CS}}$ to go low for one memory bank. Data is unstable on the output lines during ROM access time, but eventually the information levels stabilize and the data can be read.

Accessing RAM is accomplished in much the same manner as is accessing ROM, except another control line must be provided to store data. Figure 4-27 shows another example of address decoding using 1K × 1 RAMs. Of course, the 8205 could also have been used with RAMs. Here instead the upper 6 bits for each block are decoded by a NAND gate for addresses in the range $FC00_{16}$ to $FFFF_{16}$. In all, 64 gates would be needed for a full 64K memory. Appropriate inverters on the NAND perform the decoding function (0 bits in the address must be inverted). For example, if bits A15 through A10 for the address block to be selected were $110\ 101_2$, address lines A13 and A11 must be inverted on the NAND inputs. Then the output of the gate ($\overline{\text{CS}}$) would be low only when the input was $110\ 101_2$, and the proper memory block would be selected.

Each RAM in Fig. 4-27 provides 1 bit of the output data, so all 8 must be enabled by the same low $\overline{\text{CS}}$ signal. The RAM knows whether to read or write data from the settings of $\overline{\text{MEMW}}$ and $\overline{\text{MEMR}}$. The timing diagram for reading RAM is quite similar to that for ROM (see Fig. 4-28), but there are two differences in writing data into memory (see Fig.

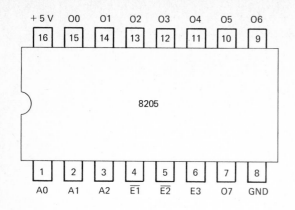

INPUTS						OUTPUTS							
ADDRESS			ENABLE										
A2	A1	A0	E3	E̅2̅	E̅1̅	7	6	5	4	3	2	1	0
L	L	L	H	L	L	H	H	H	H	H	H	H	L
L	L	H	H	L	L	H	H	H	H	H	H	L	H
L	H	L	H	L	L	H	H	H	H	H	L	H	H
L	H	H	H	L	L	H	H	H	H	L	H	H	H
H	L	L	H	L	L	H	H	H	L	H	H	H	H
H	L	H	H	L	L	H	H	L	H	H	H	H	H
H	H	L	H	L	L	H	L	H	H	H	H	H	H
H	H	H	H	L	L	L	H	H	H	H	H	H	H
X	X	X	L	L	L	H	H	H	H	H	H	H	H
X	X	X	L	L	H	H	H	H	H	H	H	H	H
X	X	X	L	H	L	H	H	H	H	H	H	H	H
X	X	X	L	H	H	H	H	H	H	H	H	H	H
X	X	X	H	L	H	H	H	H	H	H	H	H	H
X	X	X	H	H	L	H	H	H	H	H	H	H	H
X	X	X	H	H	H	H	H	H	H	H	H	H	H

Figure 4-25. 8205 1-of-8 Decoder.

result in the two drivers for a single bus line attempting to pull the level in opposite directions; that is, a high in one case and a low in the other. Those two drivers become almost a short for 5 V to ground, which sends a sharp pulse, or *glitch*, to other devices on the bus. The glitch, in turn, can produce random data errors or incorrect state changes.

Some new memories are providing a means for avoiding this problem. Two pins are used in place of a single $\overline{CS}$ input. A timing diagram of these signals is shown in Fig. 4-30. The chip enable ($\overline{CE}$) pin is used to enable the memory device when the address is decoded and a particular memory IC is selected. The output enable ($\overline{OE}$) input is used to strobe the data onto the output bus. The $\overline{OE}$ signal to the memory is the $\overline{MEMR}$ signal supplied by the microprocessor. The narrower $\overline{OE}$ strobe eliminates the possibility of causing contention when the information is placed on the bus.

Charge-Coupled Device (CCD) Memory

New memory technologies offer the user larger capacity than semiconductor RAMs can provide. One of these technologies is charge-coupled-device memories which, having higher density than RAM, can pack more bits in a smaller area. The higher density comes about because only 30 percent of the CCD chip area needs to be dedicated to overhead circuitry, such as address decoding, while 50 percent of a RAM chip is needed for this purpose.

The CCD memories are inherently slower than RAM because of their internal structure. Actually, the CCD is a serial shift register, and data is continuously circulating through the device. In contrast to the random access of RAM, a CCD lends itself

4-29). First, the processor supplies the data which is placed on the system data bus. Second, the $\overline{MEMW}$ signal is set low as a command for the memory action to be performed.

Bus Contention

Because of the uncertainty in the time that data is stable on the system bus when reading ROM or RAM, bus contention can occur. In both Figs. 4-26 and 4-28 the output data is unstable when first strobed onto the output bus by the $\overline{CS}$ signal. During the memory access delay, information may be placed on the shared bus too early, and some other source may also be using the bus. This contention may

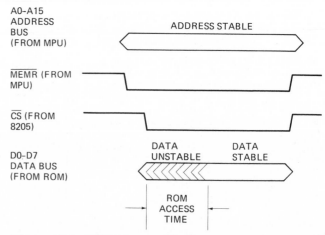

Figure 4-26. ROM Memory Timing.

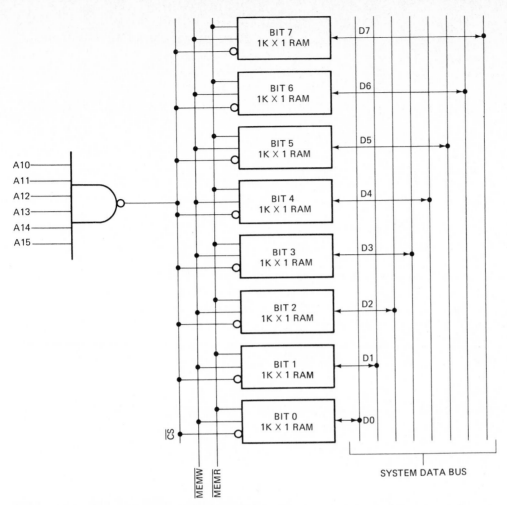

Figure 4-27. Address Decoding with a NAND Gate.

to block-oriented access in which data is read serially in large quantities. Transfer speed of 5 megabits per second can be achieved when data is properly organized. Table 4-10 lists the parameters of some typical 64K memories. One characteristic that CCD memories share with RAM is their *volatility;* that is, memory content is lost when power is turned off.

Bubble Memory Devices

Bubble memory devices (BMDs) are IC packages containing all the components needed for storing data in the form of magnetic domains. The bubble memory chip, two magnetic field coils, and two permanent magnets are the components of the device. Using magnetic circuits, cylindrical magnetic

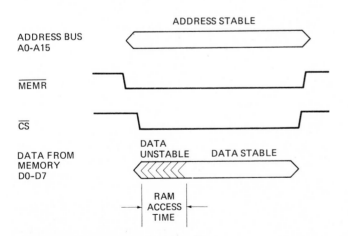

Figure 4-28. RAM Timing (Read).

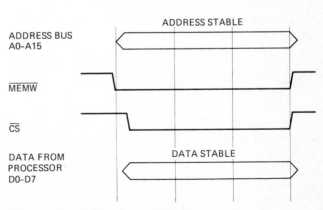

Figure 4-29. RAM Timing (Write).

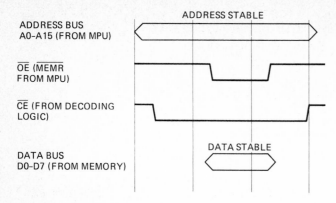

ADDRESS BUS
A0–A15 (FROM MPU)

ADDRESS STABLE

OE (MEMR
FROM MPU)

CE (FROM DECODING
LOGIC)

DATA BUS
D0–D7 (FROM MEMORY)

DATA STABLE

Figure 4-30. Improved Memory Read Timing.

domains, or "bubbles," can be formed. The magnetic domains can point up or down, so binary data can be represented by the bubble orientation. Bubbles are 2 to 20 microns in diameter, although manufacturers are working to reduce that size. The bubbles are circulated through the device by a magnetic field in the field coils.

Rotating magnetic fields generated by the coils (which are arranged at right angles to each other) cause the bubbles to move through the chip in a serial manner—much like a serial shift register. The permanent magnets stabilize the bubbles and make the memory nonvolatile, so no data is lost when power is removed.

Table 4-11 lists the characteristics of two memories. The data input and output lines are TTL-compatible. In addition to nonvolatility, the bubble memories each have a large capacity and are very rugged. They appear to be attractive replacements for floppy disks as storage devices. As compared with RAMs, the bubble memories have a slower data rate and require more complex interfacing circuitry.

Memory Review

1. List the types of information displayed on a memory map.

2. What bank contains address $92AB_{16}$ in a 32K memory? Which block is that address in?

3. Describe the address decoding process.

4. Explain the use of an 8205 decoder in a microcomputer memory.

5. How can a NAND gate be used to perform a similar decoding function?

6. Describe the use of $\overline{CE}$ and $\overline{OE}$ memory signals in preventing bus contention.

BIDIRECTIONAL BUS DRIVERS

Most microprocessor ICs can drive only limited loads, so bus drivers are used to guarantee sufficient capacity. A three-state bus driver, such as the 8216 shown in Fig. 4-31 consists of two separate buffers; each is used to transmit data in its respective direction. The output of one buffer is tied to the input

Table 4-10
Typical 64K CCDs

Manufacturer	Fairchild	Texas Instruments	Intel
Part number	CCD 464	TMS 3064JL	2464
Access time	500 μs	820 μs	256 μs
Bit transfer rate	1.5 MHz	1.5 MHz	250 kHz to 2.5 MHz
Power (Operate/standby)	400 mW/70 mW	260 mW/500 mW	400/60 mW

Table 4-11
Magnetic Bubble Memories

Manufacturer	Texas Instruments	Rockwell International
Model	TIB0203	RBM256
Capacity (bits)	92,304	266,500
Architecture	Major loop, 144 minor loops	282 loops
Data rate (kHz)	50	150
First bit access time (ms)	4	4
Package	14-pin DIP	18-pin DIP
Size (in²/cm²)	1.25/8	1.4/9.3
Power (mW)	700	820

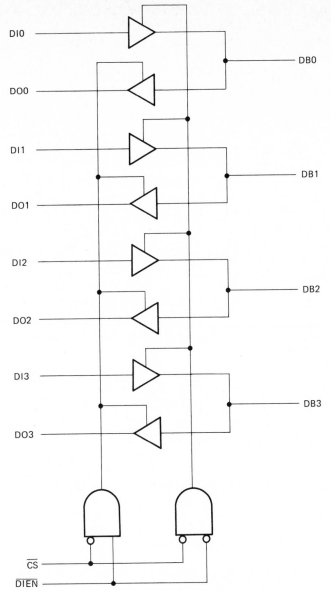

DI0

DO0

DB0

DI1

DB1

DO1

DI2

DB2

DO2

DI3

DB3

DO3

$\overline{CS}$

$\overline{DIEN}$

Figure 4-31. 8216 Three-State Bidirectional Bus Driver.

of the other, thus forming a system bus. For an 8-bit bus, two 8216 ICs would be used.

There are two control inputs to the driver. Chip selection is controlled by $\overline{CS}$ in the same way that we saw being used with memories. The direction of flow is determined by $\overline{DIEN}$. When this signal is low, data flows from the inputs (DI0 through DI3) to the system bus interface (DB0 through DB3). When $\overline{DIEN}$ is high, data flow is in the opposite direction (from DB0 through DB3 to DO0 through DO3).

INTRODUCTION TO 8080A PROGRAMMING

Having studied the components of the microcomputer, let's now see how the processor can be pro-

grammed to perform calculations and process information. Instructions for the 8080A can be grouped into six functional areas:

> Data transfer
> Arithmetic
> Logical
> Branching
> Input/Output
> Miscellaneous

Data transfer operations are those which involve moving data between the processor registers and memory. Arithmetic instructions allow us to add and subtract, and logical instructions execute Boolean functions such as ANDing and ORing. When a program is to do one of two things based on the outcome of a decision, one or more branching instructions are used in making that choice. All data is sent or received by means of input and output instructions. The remaining instructions are used for stack operations and control, such as halting the processor.

Instructions can also be categorized by format. One, two, or three memory words may be used for an instruction (see Fig. 4-32). Single-byte instructions consist only of the *operation code* (op code). The op code is an 8-bit number that tells the processor what to do, such as data transfer, halt, input data, or perform addition. Every instruction, regardless of length, has the op code in its first byte.

The second word of a 2-byte instruction is used for either data or a device code. If the second byte is data, it is used as the *operand* of the instruction. For example, the data can be a number to be added to the accumulator. The 8 bits can be used for coded data as well as for numbers if the programmer desires. The data could represent two BCD digits or an ASCII code for an alphanumeric character. The processor

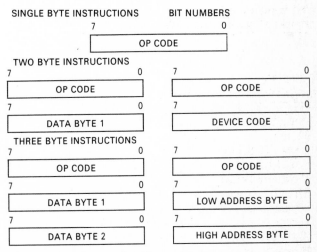

Figure 4-32. Instruction Formats.

can operate on decimal numbers or text in their coded form, as well as on binary digits. The device code is used only for I/O instructions. The code specifies the input or output equipment to be used in the operation. The 8 bits of the device code provide the capability for addressing 256 ($2^8 = 256$) different input devices and the same number of output devices. If a peripheral device is used for both input and output, such as a cassette tape unit, then both input and output device codes must be assigned.

There are also two formats for the 3-byte instructions. One format provides for 2 data bytes. This type of instruction allows the processor to work on data as 16-bit words. The other uses words 2 and 3 of the 3-byte instruction to indicate the memory address of the operand. Word 2 is called the *low address byte*—the least significant 8 bits (bits A0 through A7) of the address. The *high address byte*, of course, provides the most significant 8 bits of the address (bits A8 through A15).

Some Instructions

The instructions necessary to write a simple program are provided in this section. Aspects of the instructions that do not affect the outcome of this program will not be covered in this first exposure to programming. In the following chapters the full details of these instructions, together with the rest of the 8080A repertoire, will be discussed.

The description of each instruction will include the *mnemonic* code and the hexadecimal, or *machine,* code for the instruction. The instruction is also listed in binary form with data bytes, device codes, or address bytes indicated. A timing diagram for each instruction is provided, showing the number of machine cycles and clock periods for execution. An explanation of the changes that the instruction causes in the registers and on the system buses completes the description.

HALT INSTRUCTION. The halt instruction causes the processor to increment the instruction counter and enter the halt state. No further processor activity takes place until some external actions occur. Timing is shown in Fig. 4-33. Seven clock periods are used in execution. During the first three periods of MC1 the instruction is fetched from memory. The instruction is interpreted in T4 of MC1. By this time the address bus is floating. During MC2 the READY control line goes low and the WAIT line high, at which point the processor has entered the halt state.

Mnemonic code HLT
HLT Machine code 76_{16}

	bit number							
	7	6	5	4	3	2	1	0
word 1	0	1	1	1	0	1	1	0

Most computer programs use the halt instruction to stop after all the data has been processed.

□ **EXAMPLE.** Stop the processor.

Mnemonic	Address$_{16}$	Machine code$_{16}$
HLT	0501	76

Before execution	After execution
Program counter [0501]	Program counter [0502]

MOVE IMMEDIATE TO ACCUMULATOR. The data *immediately* following the op code is stored in the primary accumulator. Timing is shown in Fig. 4-34. In a manner similar to the previous instruction, MC1 is used to fetch and interpret the instruction. The address for byte 2 of the instruction is set on the bus on the rising edge of Φ2 for T1 of MC2. The data is read and stored in the A register in the following two clock periods.

Mnemonic code MVI A
Machine code $3E_{16}$

	bit number							
	7	6	5	4	3	2	1	0
word 1	0	0	1	1	1	1	1	0
word 2				data byte				

□ **EXAMPLE.** Set the A register to 1.

Mnemonic	Operand	Address$_{16}$	Machine code$_{16}$
MVI A	01	1000	E
		1001	01

Before execution	After execution
Program counter [1000]	Program counter [1002]
A register [F2]	A register [01]

The original content of the accumulator (which could have been any value) is changed to 1 and the program counter is set to the address of the next instruction.

ADD IMMEDIATE TO ACCUMULATOR. The data byte is added to the contents of the accumulator by using 2's complement arithmetic. The timing for this instruction is the same as that for MVI A shown in Fig. 4-34.

Mnemonic code ADI
Machine code $C6_{16}$

	bit number							
	7	6	5	4	3	2	1	0
word 1	1	1	0	0	0	1	1	0
word 2				data byte				

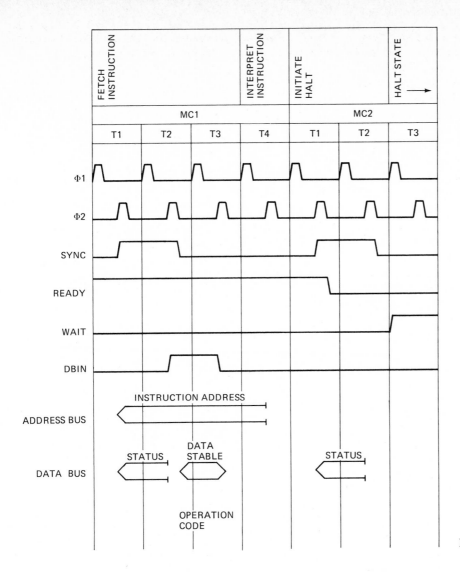

Figure 4-33. Halt Instruction Timing.

□ **EXAMPLE.** Add 22_{16} to the accumulator.

Mnemonic	Operand	Address$_{16}$	Machine code$_{16}$
ADI	22	FF01	C6
		FF02	22

Before execution		**After execution**	
Program counter	FF01	Program counter	FF03
A register	04	A register	26

STORE ACCUMULATOR DIRECT. The contents of the accumulator are placed in the memory location given by the high and low address bytes. The timing for this instruction is shown in Fig. 4-35. Three accesses to memory are needed to read the instruction and the 2 address bytes. A fourth memory access is used to write the data. Altogether, four machine cycles, totaling 13 clock periods, are consumed by this instruction.

Mnemonic code   STA
Machine code 32_{16}

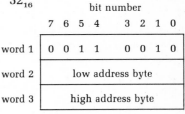

	bit number	
	7 6 5 4 3 2 1 0	
word 1	0 0 1 1 0 0 1 0	
word 2	low address byte	
word 3	high address byte	

□ **EXAMPLE.** Store the number in the A register in memory location $03FD_{16}$.

Mnemonic	Operand	Address$_{16}$	Machine code$_{16}$
STA	03FD	DB01	32
		DB02	FD
		DB03	03

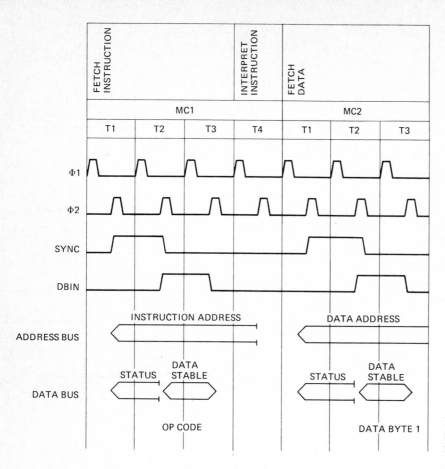

Figure 4-34. Move Immediate to Accumulator and Add Immediate to Accumulator Instruction Timing.

Before execution

Program counter	DB01
A register	A0
Memory	03FD 03

After execution

Program counter	DB04
A register	A0
Memory	03FD A0

Do not get confused between the address of the instruction (DB01) and the destination address for the accumulator contents (03FD). Note that the accumulator is unchanged after execution.

OUTPUT. The contents of the accumulator are sent to the output device designated by the device code. The output instruction timing is shown in Fig. 4-36. The first two machine cycles are identical to those for previous instructions. The first is used to fetch and interpret the instruction, and the second is used to obtain the device code. Data is transmitted over the data lines during MC3. The devices on the system bus can determine which is to receive the data by decoding the address bus and comparing that device address with their own.

Mnemonic code   OUT
Machine code $D3_{16}$

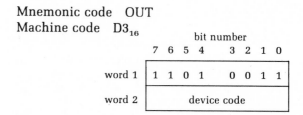

□ **EXAMPLE.** Send the A register contents to output device 7.

Mnemonic	Operand	Address$_{16}$	Machine code$_{16}$
OUT	07	200F	D3
		2010	07

Before execution

Program counter	200F
A register	B7

After execution

Program counter	2011
A register	B7

A Simple Program

Now that you know a few of the instructions, let's put them to use in a simple program. The program

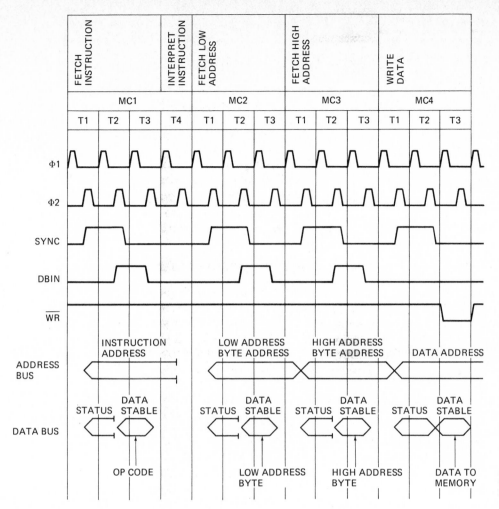

Figure 4-35. Store Accumulator Direct Timing.

will execute the following procedure:

1. Clear memory cell 0200_{16}.

2. Add 20_{16} to the accumulator.

3. Send the sum in the accumulator to output device 1.

4. Stop.

The first step will have to be split into two actions, so that we can use the instructions to carry it out. First, the accumulator must be cleared, and then it will be stored in address 0200_{16}. The program is given below.

Mnemonic	Operand	Address$_{16}$	Machine Code$_{16}$	Comments
MVI A	0	0150	3E	Clear A
		0151	00	Data byte
STA	0200	0152	32	Store A
		0153	00	Low address byte
		0154	02	High address byte
ADI	20	0155	C6	Add to A
		0156	20	Address byte
OUT	01	0157	D3	Output
		0158	01	Device code
HLT		0159	76	Stop

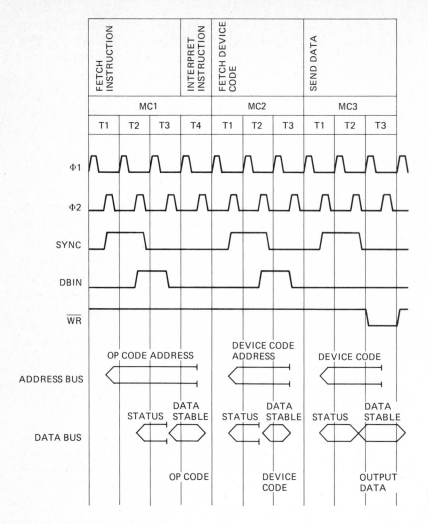

Figure 4-36. Output Instruction Timing.

Go over the program line by line to be sure that you understand what each instruction is doing. Note how the values which represent the op code are almost impossible to decipher without the mnemonics and comments. Remember this problem when you are documenting your own programs.

8080A Programming Introduction Review

1. List the six functional groups of 8080A instructions.

2. Describe the instruction formats used in the 8080A.

3. How are two 8-bit words used to represent a 16-bit address?

4. Why are four machine cycles required in the STA instruction when ADI only needs two?

CHAPTER SUMMARY

1. The 8080A microprocessor usually is used together with the 8224 system clock generator and the 8228 system controller.

2. The 8080A is a 40-pin DIP with three power supply inputs, one ground, 16 address lines, and eight data lines. The remaining pins are used for control signals. The address and data buses use three-state logic.

3. A device can request the processor to wait for a data exchange by driving the ready input low. The 8080A then enters the wait state and sets the wait signal high.

4. A high input on the HOLD line causes the processor to stop between instructions. The data and address buses are floated by the microprocessor, which indicates this action by setting the HLDA signal high.

5. A high reset input clears the microprocessor registers and causes the instruction in cell 0000_{16} to be executed.

6. The situation on the data bus is signaled by DBIN, the read strobe, and by $\overline{WR}$, the write strobe.

7. There are 10 programmable registers in the 8080A. The A register is the primary accumulator. The status register provides flags of the results from the last operation. The six secondary accumulators can also be linked into 16-bit address counters. The stack pointer contains the top address on the stack. The program counter contains the address of the next instruction.

8. Timing for control of the microprocessor is based on a sequence of machine cycles which are subdivided into clock periods. The two clock phases, Φ1 and Φ2, establish the boundaries of clock periods. The SYNC pulse marks T1 during each machine cycle. The 8224 clock signal generator produces these synchronized clock signals.

9. All memory references take place in T1 through T3 of any machine cycle. During MC1, T1 through T3 are used for instruction fetching and T4 for instruction interpretation.

10. The data bus status code during T2 informs all devices on the bus which operation will be performed. Because each microinstruction consists of a series of operations, usually the status code will have 2 or more bits set. The 8228 system controller handles the status signals and converts them to commands on the control bus.

11. The wait state permits external devices to request additional time in which to reply. The hold state causes the processor to pause between instructions.

12. On restart the 8080A can be initialized in a known state by use of the reset signal.

13. The 8224 converts the external oscillator frequency to clock signals for the 8080A. The 8224 also processes control signals for the microprocessor IC and the 8228.

14. The 8228 demultiplexes status and data signals from the 8080A data bus and converts them to system data and control bus signals.

15. A memory map shows the organization of computer storage into banks and blocks. Address decoding logic in the memory selects the bank and block to be referenced. Address bits A13 through A15 designate the bank and bits A10 through A12, the block within the bank.

16. Charge-coupled device and bubble memories offer higher density, but slower speeds, than semiconductor RAM.

17. Bidirectional bus drivers can produce sufficient current to provide reliable three-state signal levels. The driver is actually a matched set of buffers, one for each signal direction.

18. The instruction set of the 8080A provides for data transfer, arithmetic, Boolean logic, branching, and I/O. Instruction formats use one, two, or three words.

KEY TERMS AND CONCEPTS

Microprocessor

Data bus

Address bus

Programmable registers (A, B, C, D, E, H, L, PSW, SP, PC)

Status flags (S, Z, A_c, P, C)

Secondary accumulators

Address counters (BC, DE, HL)

Machine cycles

Clock periods

Clock phases (Φ1 and Φ2)

Reading and writing memory data

Hold, wait, and halt states

Reset

Crystal oscillator

Demultiplexing the internal data bus

Memory map

Memory organization

Memory banks and blocks

Address decoding

Memory timing diagrams

Bus contention

Charge-coupled device (CCD) memories

Bubble memory devices (BMD)

Bidirectional bus drivers

Instruction formats

Operation code (op code)

Operand

Device code

High and low address bytes

PROBLEMS

4-1 How many memory banks are needed in a 24K memory? What is the range of addresses in the memory?

4-2 Draw a 16K memory map for a memory organized as follows.

Device	Address
256 × 8 ROM	2000-20FF
8 each 1K × 1 RAMs	3C00-3FFF
8 each 1K × 1 RAMs	3400-37FF
256 × 8 ROM	2200-22FF
8 each 1K × 1 RAMs	2C00-2FFF
1K × 8 ROM	3000-33FF
256 × 8 ROM	2300-23FF
8 each 1K × 1 RAMs	3800-3BFF
8 each 1K × 1 RAMs	2400-27FF
256 × 8 ROM	2100-21FF
1K × 8 ROM	0000-03FF

Indicate the type of memory used in each block. (Some blocks will be empty.)

4-3 Draw a circuit diagram using the 8205 decoder shown in Fig. 4-25 to decode addresses in memory bank 5. (Total memory capacity is 64K.) Your diagram will differ from Fig. 4-24 primarily in the possible use of inverters on pins 1 through 6.

4-4 Draw the circuit diagram for a NAND gate decoder, similar to that of Fig. 4-27, for addresses in the same block as $AC17_{16}$.

4-5 What memory block is referenced by the following instructions to obtain the operands?

a.
Address$_{16}$	Machine Code$_{16}$
1010	32
1011	A1
1012	B2

b.
Address$_{16}$	Machine Code$_{16}$
AC01	C6
AC02	0A

4-6 Show the changes in the registers and memory locations after the given program has been executed.

Address$_{16}$	Instruction
C716	MVI A
C717	10
C718	STA
C719	17
C71A	27
C71B	ADI
C71C	2
C71D	HLT

PC [C716] A [4F]

Memory

1727	FF
2717	00
C71A	27

4-7 The following machine code program has run to completion. What value is in the accumulator?

Address$_{16}$	Machine Code$_{16}$
5020	C6
5021	71
5022	3E
5023	12
5024	76
5025	D3

4-8 After the execution of the program below, what number is left in the A register?

Address$_{16}$	Instruction
7777	MVI A
7778	80
7779	ADI
777A	20
777B	ADI
777C	92
777D	HLT

4-9 What changes in memory are produced by this program?

Address	Instruction
F000	OUT
F001	03
F002	MVI A

F003	04
F004	STA
F005	FF
F006	08
F007	ADI
F008	A1
F009	ADI
F00A	F0
F00B	STA
F00C	0C
F00D	AA
F00E	HLT

4-10 Write a program, using only the instructions given in this chapter, that will do the following:

1. Zero memory cell $BB7D_{16}$.

2. Transmit the number $2E_{16}$ to device number 18_{10}.

3. Set the A register to 76_{16}.

4. Halt.

EXPERIMENT 4

PURPOSE: To investigate bus monitors and single stepping the processor.

PARTS LIST:

Item	Quantity
74LS47	1
5082-7340 hexadecimal display	2
Pulser	1

IC DIAGRAMS:

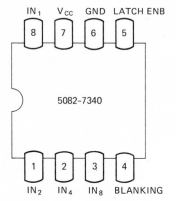

NOTE: Pin 1 is indicated by a dot underneath. This is the *top* view.

Figure 4-37. 5082-7340.

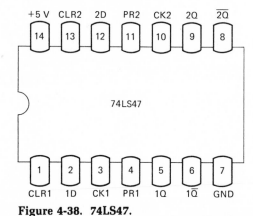

Figure 4-38. 74LS47.

PROCEDURE

STEP 1. Wire the circuit shown in Fig. 4-39. Connect the strobe input to ground after attaching the data inputs to the data bus lines. Record the value displayed.

STEP 2. Enter the program below, but do not run the computer. After the strobe has been attached to $\overline{\text{OUT}}$, what do the displays read?

STEP 3. Now run the program. How does this affect the displays?

STEP 4. Repeat the process after first changing the contents of cell 0001_{16} to any number you like. How is the output changed?

STEP 5. Now change the output port address in cell 0003_{16} to any not used by your computer. What effect does running the program have on the display? What can

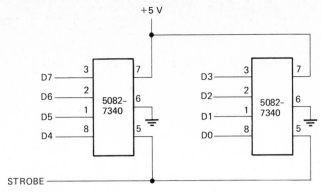

Figure 4-39. Bus Monitor.

you conclude about this circuit? You will find the bus monitor to be very useful in troubleshooting future experiments and also in debugging your program.

STEP 6. Leave the previous circuit in place. Add the components and wiring shown in Fig. 4-40. Ground pin 4 of the 74LS47 and rerun the program. Do you detect any changes? (The answer should be "no.")

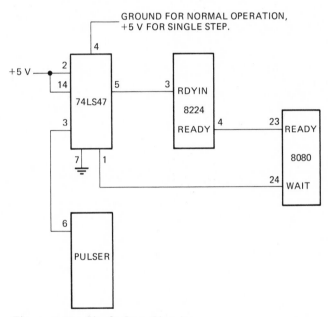

Figure 4-40. Single Step Circuit.

STEP 7. Attach pin 4 of the 74LS47 to 5 V. Repeat Step 6. What happens? You execute only a single instruction each time you pulse the circuit. The single-step mode of operation allows you to examine the bus operation in great detail. You will be able to verify the timing for the circuit by combining the single-step circuit with the bus monitor.

Mnemonic	Operand	Address	Machine Code
MVI	A,01	0000	3E
		0001	01
OUT	2	0002	D3
		0003	02
JMP	0000	0004	C3
		0005	00
		0006	00

5

INTRODUCTION TO THE INSTRUCTION REPERTOIRE

Having studied the registers, data paths, and control timing of a microprocessor, we can now proceed to a more detailed look at the instructions. The 8080A MPU can perform a total of 78 instructions. By use of these instructions, the programmer can move data between memory locations and registers, perform arithmetic and logical operations, control the program sequence, and communicate by using input and output transactions.

CHAPTER OBJECTIVES

Upon completion of this chapter, you should be able to:

1. List the instruction notation used for working registers and memory.
2. Describe the three methods of addressing memory.
3. Distinguish between register, immediate, and direct addressing modes.
4. Encode and decode instructions by properly interpreting the operation code and operand fields.
5. Describe the operations performed by the 8080A data transfer instructions.
6. Control computer operations which involve the program counter register and stopping computer operations.

MEMORY, REGISTER, AND I/O DEVICE NOTATION

The 8080A is a *stored program* computer. By this term, we mean that all the instructions and data are stored in memory. The program informs the processor which cells are to be treated as containing instructions and which cells hold the information to be manipulated. Remember that every memory location simply represents an 8-bit number to the processor. The number $2A_{16}$ could indicate the necessity to execute a particular operation; on the other hand, it could be just a hexadecimal quantity or even the ASCII code for an asterisk. The processor treats that number precisely as the program dictates. This literal nature of the computer, which is incapable of such a simple act as distinguishing between data and instructions, can easily lead to a *bug* (mistake) in the program if the operator is careless.

Working Registers

Recall from Chap. 4 that there are seven working registers in the 8080A MPU: the accumulator and six *scratch-pad* registers. Each register is 1 byte in length. The registers were referred to as the A (accumulator), B, C, D, E, H, and L registers. When these registers are used in carrying out some processor action, the MPU must be told which register to use. The registers are assigned numbers (listed in Table 5-1) which inform the processor that a particular register is involved in the instruction. For example, an instruction which is to move data to the accumulator provides the number 7 to specify the destination for the data. As you know, an operation may alternatively involve a memory cell rather than a register. The number 6 has been reserved for this purpose, as Table 5-1 shows. (The particular memory cell to be addressed must be indicated as well. The method used is described in the following section.)

Table 5-1
Working Registers and Memory Designation

Register	Numerical Designation
B	0
C	1
D	2
E	3
H	4
L	5
M (memory)	6
A	7

Table 5-2
Register Pair Designation

Register Pair	Single-letter Designation	Numerical Designation
BC	B	0
DE	D	1
HL	H	2
PSW/A or SP	—	3

Register Pairs

Perhaps you recall from Chap. 4 that the registers could be linked to form a 16-bit-capacity register. When the registers are linked, there are three ways to refer to them. Table 5-2 lists these options. The double-length BC register, (see Fig. 5-1a) has its least significant 8 bits in the C register and most significant in the B register. The register pair is also referenced by the most significant register alone in some instruction manuals, that is the, "B register pair." As Table 5-2 indicates, the DE pair is also known as the "D" or "1" pair and HL as just "H" or "2."

The last row in Table 5-2 requires a little more explanation. When the program status word is linked to the accumulator, the two registers are designated as the number "3" register pair in an instruction. The stack pointer is also sometimes given the same designator. Could the assignment of the same number cause confusion in the processor? The answer is no because only instructions dealing with stack addressing refer to the stack pointer. Other instructions will involve only the PSW and the A register. (Even though the processor will not be confused by the assignment of the same designator to two register pairs, programmers may be. In the explanations to follow, carefully note which pair is specified in the descriptions for each instruction.)

Memory Designation

The program can read the contents of any memory cell and write in any location in RAM. The contents of an ROM location cannot be altered by program

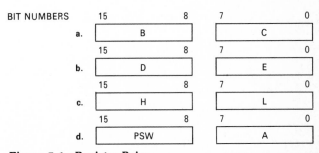

Figure 5-1. Register Pairs.

action, but a bug will result if writing into ROM is attempted. Let's consider an example. Say that a programmer meant to store the results of a calculation at memory location 1400_{16}, which is an RAM cell. By mistake the address of the storage location in the program was altered to 0400_{16}, a ROM location. (Such an error could result from a bad input from the peripheral device which read the program, from human error, or from a malfunction in the I/O circuitry.) When that instruction is executed, the processor will attempt to store data at memory location 0400_{16}. As a result, *no* error indication is generated, but three errors have been committed:

1. The contents of cell 0400_{16} do not change in spite of the store action.

2. Cell 1400_{16} does not contain the correct value.

3. The answer of the calculation is lost.

Obviously, in programming, writing into ROM must be avoided.

The entire memory address range of 65,536 cells (0000_{16} through $FFFF_{16}$) can be reached by the instructions. Another memory-addressing error that can occur is referencing of a nonexistent location. If the computer is not supplied with a full 64K memory, some locations are illegal. If the memory is actually only 32K in length (0000_{16} through $7FFF_{16}$), attempts to read location 8000_{16} or above would be wrong. Again the processor does not give

any indication of this mistake, so it is the responsibility of the programmer to prevent it.

Memory-addressing Procedures

There are three ways of providing the processor with the 16-bit address of a memory cell. The memory address may be specified by 2 bytes of an instruction, the contents of a register pair, or the stack pointer.

ADDRESS SPECIFICATION BY INSTRUCTION.

Many instructions supply the address explicitly and require 3 bytes to indicate the operation as well as the data address. Figure 5-2a shows the 3-byte format, which we briefly studied in Chap. 4. The operation code can be placed in any memory cell, say, memory cell 2020_{16}. The least-significant address byte must be located at location 2021_{16}. The upper byte of the address then occupies cell 2022_{16}. (This somewhat cumbersome address designation is a carry-over from the 8008 design. The designers wanted to maintain some downward compatibility between the 8080A and its predecessor.)

ADDRESS SPECIFICATION BY REGISTER PAIR.

The main purpose for linking registers into pairs is to allow them to hold a 2-byte address as shown in Fig. 5-2b. The HL pair is most frequently used, but the BC or DE pairs are also employed in some cases. The first register of the pair always holds

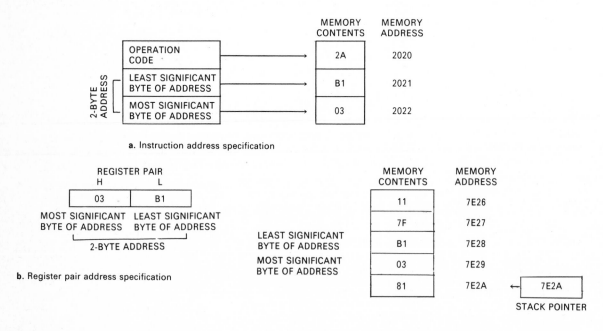

a. Instruction address specification

b. Register pair address specification

c. Stack pointer address specification

Figure 5-2. Memory Cell Addressing.

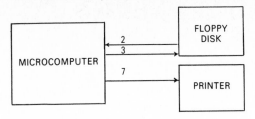

Figure 5-3. Input/Output Port Example.

the most significant address byte, as was shown in Fig. 5-1.

ADDRESS SPECIFICATION BY STACK POINTER.

The 16-bit stack pointer can also provide the address. Only two instructions permit us to use the stack pointer in this manner: PUSH and POP. Figure 5-2c shows the use of the stack pointer. If the contents of the stack pointer is $7E2A_{16}$, the most-significant byte of the specified address is in the stack at location $7E29_{16}$, and the least significant is at $7E28_{16}$. The use of the stack pointer will be fully discussed in Chap. 10.

I/O Devices

The 8080A can specify up to 256 independent input devices and the same number of output devices. The input ports are numbered 00_{16} through FF_{16}. The output ports are identically designated. To demonstrate the use of I/O port designators, consider the peripheral equipment configuration shown in Fig. 5-3.

If the program were to send an output on port 3, the information would be written on the floppy

disk. An output command to port 7 would cause a printer action. If only one input port is provided, port 3 can be used to read from the disk.

All other port numbers are invalid, but no error indication is generated by the processor if a program attempts to use them.

Memory, Register, and I/O Device Review

1. List the 8080A microprocessor working registers and their respective numerical designations.

2. What does the register designation "6" signify?

3. Which register pair has a numerical designation of 2? What is the single letter for the pair?

4. Which registers would the processor use if an instruction specifies register pair 3?

5. What happens if the processor attempts to store data in ROM?

6. Distinguish between instruction address specification and register-pair address specification.

7. Why does the floppy disk in Fig. 5-3 require two address ports?

ADDRESSING MODES

Now that we know how memory addresses are indicated, let's see how the address may be used. The mode of addressing depends on the instruction

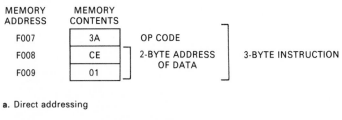

a. Direct addressing

b. Register addressing

c. Immediate addressing

Figure 5-4. Addressing Modes.

format of each instruction. The addressing mode we select must be either a direct address, a register, or an immediate address. Figure 5-4 illustrates each of the addressing modes. Every instruction is limited to use of only one of these three modes. As you read the descriptions below, note whether the instruction provides the data immediately or just points to the data by means of an address.

Direct Addressing

Direct addressing is used by instructions which transfer data from memory to a particular register or to write data from a register into memory. The instruction supplies the specific address to be used. When the direct addressing mode is used, the instruction always occupies 3 memory bytes (refer to Fig. 5-2a). The address is in the two memory cells following the operation code.

Register Addressing

Some instructions involve only the data in a single register, such as adding data to a register. Others use a register pair to hold an address. If a single register is involved, the number of the register (see Table 5-1) will be included in the instruction. Other instructions specify the register pair which contains the address. Instructions which use two registers (moving data from one to the other, for example) must specify the register sending the information and the one receiving. The former is the *source register* and the latter, the *destination register.*

Immediate Addressing

The instruction may include the value to be used in the operation. In the immediate addressing mode the byte following the op code is the quantity that will be used in executing the command. The data is obtained in conjunction with fetching the instruction.

Addressing Modes Review

1. Define the terms "direct addressing" and "immediate addressing."

2. Why are 3 bytes required for the instruction in Fig. 5-4a and only one for that in fig. 5-4b?

3. How is the register pair designated in the instruction of Fig. 5-4b?

ENCODING AND DECODING INSTRUCTIONS

Before we begin our study of specific instructions, we will consider the coded method used in writing an instruction. Because we are using machine code, every instruction will be an 8-bit binary string. We will write the code in hexadecimal for compactness. Every instruction must include two parts, or *fields.*

Operation Code Field

The operation code (or op code) field uniquely identifies the machine function to be performed as we have seen. In addition to the numerical op code, each instruction has a *mnemonic* associated with it. A mnemonic is a three- or four-letter abbreviation for the instruction intended to help the programmer remember the operation and document the program, but the computer cannot interpret the mnemonic. Examples of mnemonics are ADD for addition and LDA for load accumulator direct. If an assembler is used to generate programs, the mnemonics can be used as inputs to the assembler directly. In this book, mnemonics are used only to document the routines.

Operand Field

The second part of the instruction is the operand field. The operand field designates the data to be manipulated as a result of the computer decoding the operation and executing the instruction. The operand field may specify that data is:

1. Immediate (part of the instruction)

2. Contained in some register

3. Contained in the memory cell indicated by a 16-bit memory address

4. Contained in the address indicated by a register pair

5. Contained in the address indicated by the stack pointer

The operand can be any value represented by binary numbers. Examples of operands include hexadecimal values, hexadecimal I/O device codes, hexadecimal addresses, ASCII codes, and BCD codes.

Label Field

The programmer can simplify the coding process by assigning optional names to certain addresses in the program. These names, called *symbolic ad-*

Label Field	Mnemonic	Memory Address	Operation Code Field	Operand Field	
START	LDA	2000	3A	—	}First instruction
		2001	—	00	
		2002	—	10	
STOP	HLT	2003	76	—	Second instruction

dresses, are useful only to human beings. They appear on the coding sheet but are not meaningful to the computer. They help some one reading the program keep track of what is happening. Examples of two instructions, with all the fields described in this section, are given above. The first instruction requires 3 bytes; 1 byte for the op code and 2 bytes to specify the address of the operand (memory location 1000_{16}). The second instruction uses only 1 byte because the halt operation does not need any data. Memory location 2000_{16} is given the label START, and cell 2003_{16} is labeled STOP. The mnemonics remind us that the first instruction means to load the accumulator using the direct addressing mode and that the second halts the processor.

Encoding and Decoding Instructions Review

1. What is the purpose of the operation code field?

2. Define the term "mnemonic." How does the use of mnemonics help the programmer?

3. List the locations that the operand field can designate as the source of data.

4. Which of the following cannot be operands for a computer instruction: I/O device codes, BCD codes, letters, binary numbers, and decimal numbers?

5. What is the purpose of the label field?

INTRODUCTION TO 8080A INSTRUCTIONS

This section presents 14 instructions which will allow you to transfer data from one location to another and to control the instruction sequence. The explanation for each instruction code will describe what the instruction does and the addressing mode it uses, the execution time (assuming that a 2-MHz clock is used with the 8080A), and the effect on the status register. A complete discussion of the status register is provided in Chap. 6 where it is more appropriate, as none of the instructions explained here have any effect on the status flags.

Examples of how the instruction might be used follow the description.

No Operation

The "no operation" instruction is the simplest one in the 8080A repertoire. It does just what the name says—nothing. One of its purposes is to fill unused memory cells, which are being reserved for adding instructions at a later time. The no operation can also be used to create a time delay, as its execution takes four clock periods. Use of the standard 2-MHz clock results in a 2-μs instruction execution cycle. The instruction uses a single-byte format.

Operation code	00
Mnemonic	NOP
Addressing mode	none
Effect on status bits	none
Clock periods	4
Execution time	2 μs
Format	

bit number

	7	6	5	4	3	2	1	0
Memory cell m	0	0	0	0	0	0	0	0

☐ **EXAMPLE**

Before execution	After execution
Program counter 3000	Program counter 3001
Memory 3000 00	Memory 3000 00

The only change apparent as a result of executing the instruction is that the program counter has been incremented.

Load Instruction

There are four instructions for loading registers, that is for moving information from memory to one of the working registers. The loading operation is usually a preliminary to a longer sequence, such as an arithmetic function or establishing the operand address.

LOAD ACCUMULATOR DIRECT. This instruction moves 1 byte from the memory cell specified by the direct address and places the value in the A register. The previous content of the register is lost.

Operation code	3A
Mnemonic	LDA
Addressing mode	direct
Effect on status bits	none
Clock periods	13
Execution time	6.5 μs

Format

bit number
7 6 5 4   3 2 1 0

Memory cell	m	0 0 1 1 1 0 1 0
	m + 1	low address byte
	m + 2	high address byte

☐ **EXAMPLE**

Before execution			After execution		
Program counter		1050	Program counter		1053
A register		47	A register		BB
Memory	1050	3A	Memory	1050	3A
	1051	26		1051	26
	1052	17		1052	17
	1726	BB		1726	BB

This instruction is frequently used to set the accumulator to the value of a constant stored in memory.

LOAD ACCUMULATOR REGISTER. The value in the memory cell, specified by the contents of a register pair, replaces the number in the accumulator on completion of the instruction. The register pair can be either BC or DE. The address in the register pair is unchanged after instruction execution. Bit 4 of the operation code selects the register pair; if that bit is 0, BC is designated, but setting the bit to 1 results in the use of DE.

Operation codes	0A	1A
Mnemonic	LDAX B	LDAX D
Addressing mode	register	
Effect on status bits	none	
Clock periods	7	
Execution time	3.5 μs	

Format

bit number
7 6 5 4   3 2 1 0

Memory cell	m	0 0 0 r 1 0 1 0

If r = 0, use register pair BC
If r = 1, use register pair DE

☐ **EXAMPLE 1**

Before execution			After execution		
Program counter		B0C1	Program counter		B0C2
A register		14	A register		00
B register		26	B register		26
C register		01	C register		01
D register		00	D register		00
E register		14	E register		14
Memory	0014	FF	Memory	0014	FF
	2601	00		2601	00
	B0C1	0A		B0C1	0A

The instruction at location B0C1$_{16}$ (indicated by the program counter) specifies that register pair BC points to the address of the data which will replace the present value in the accumulator. The memory cell (2601$_{16}$) value is 0, so the accumulator is cleared after the instruction has been completed.

☐ **EXAMPLE 2**

Before execution			After execution		
Program counter		30C0	Program counter		30C1
A register		14	A register		FF
B register		26	B register		26
C register		01	C register		01
D register		00	D register		00
E register		14	E register		14
Memory	0014	FF	Memory	0014	FF
	2601	00		2601	00
	30C0	1A		30C0	1A

The instruction at 30C0$_{16}$ causes the value in cell 0014$_{16}$ (DE register pair indicates the address) to be transferred to the accumulator. The program counter increments to reference the next instruction.

LOAD H AND L REGISTER PAIR DIRECT. The H and L register pair can be loaded with the information in two consecutive memory locations with a single instruction. The usual reason for this operation is

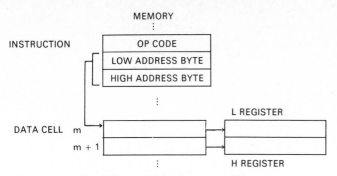

INSTRUCTION

MEMORY

OP CODE

LOW ADDRESS BYTE

HIGH ADDRESS BYTE

L REGISTER

DATA CELL m

m + 1

H REGISTER

Figure 5-5. Load H and L Register Pair Direct.

to set up an address in HL to be used by another instruction. The byte in the memory cell addressed is transferred to the L register; the byte in the next successive memory cell goes to the H register. Figure 5-5 depicts the instruction operation.

Operation code	2A
Mnemonic	LHLD
Effect on status bits	none
Clock periods	16
Execution time	8 μs
Format	

bit number
7 6 5 4   3 2 1 0

Memory cell	m	0 0 1 0 1 0 1 0
	m + 1	low address byte
	m + 2	high address byte

□ **EXAMPLE**

Before execution			**After execution**		
Program counter		4000	Program counter		4003
A register		77	A register		77
H register		01	H register		6D
L register		00	L register		21
Memory	4000	2A	Memory	4000	2A
	4001	07		4001	07
	4002	AB		4002	AB
	AB07	21		AB07	21
	AB08	6D		AB08	6D

The direct address in the instruction is $AB07_{16}$, which holds the value 21_{16}. The L register is, therefore, set equal to 21_{16}. The next cell ($AB08_{16}$) has $6D_{16}$ in it. This number is transferred to the H register. After execution, the contents of two

memory cells have been moved to fill the register pair.

LOAD REGISTER PAIR IMMEDIATE. There are several similarities between this instruction and LHLD. The instruction requires 3 bytes, but in this case the op code is followed by 2 bytes of immediate data. The instruction is illustrated by Fig. 5-6. Byte 2 of the instruction is moved to the second register of the specified pair, and the third byte to the first register of the pair. (There is an exception in the case of the stack pointer, where byte 2 fills the least significant byte of the pointer and byte 3, the most significant byte.

Operation codes	01	11	21	31
Mnemonics	LXI B	LXI D	LXI H	LXI SP
Addressing mode	immediate			
Effect on status bits	none			
Clock periods	10			
Execution time	5 μs			
Format				

bit number
7 6 5 4   3 2 1 0

Memory cell	m	0 0 r r 0 0 0 1
	m + 1	data byte 1
	m + 2	data byte 2

rr	Register pair
00	BC
01	DE
10	HL
11	SP

□ **EXAMPLE 1**

Before execution			**After execution**		
Program counter		5110	Program counter		5113
H register		76	H register		AF
L register		00	L register		02
Stack pointer		1658	Stack pointer		1658
Memory	5110	21	Memory	5110	21
	5111	02		5111	02
	5112	AF		5112	AF

Here the value of rr was 2, so HL is the register pair. The immediate data byte 1 (02_{16}) is sent to L and data byte 2 (AF_{16}), to the H register.

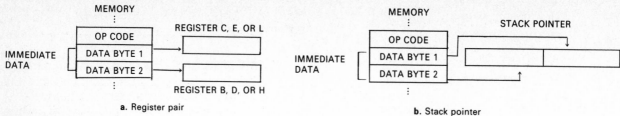

a. Register pair   **b.** Stack pointer

Figure 5-6. Load Register Pair Immediate.

□ EXAMPLE 2

Before execution		After execution	
Program counter	65BC	Program counter	65BF
H register	76	H register	76
L register	32	L register	32
Stack pointer	1658	Stack pointer	2211

Memory			Memory		
	65BC	31		65BC	31
	65BD	11		65BD	11
	65BE	22		65BE	22

Changing rr to 3 specifies the stack pointer as the data destination. The pointer's lower byte is obtained from immediate data byte 1, and the upper byte of the pointer is found in immediate data byte 2.

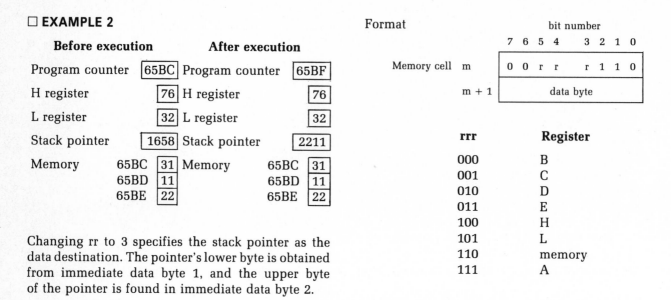

Format

bit number

7 6 5 4   3 2 1 0

Memory cell m   0 0 r r   r 1 1 0

m + 1   data byte

rrr	Register
000	B
001	C
010	D
011	E
100	H
101	L
110	memory
111	A

Move Instructions

Move instructions are a lot like the load instructions, except data can be moved to memory locations as well as to registers. There are two types of move instruction in the 8080A repertoire.

MOVE IMMEDIATE. One byte of immediate data is transferred to either a register or a memory location. The memory location's address must first be placed in the linked HL registers. Figure 5-7 shows the operation.

□ EXAMPLE 1

Before execution		After execution	
Program counter	1700	Program counter	1702
A register	42	A register	0F
H register	00	H register	00
L register	CB	L register	CB

Memory			Memory		
	1700	3E		1700	3E
	1701	0F		1701	0F
	00CB	AA		00CB	AA

With op code $3E_{16}$, the register bits, rrr, are 7 so the A register will be set to the value of the immediate data byte.

Operation codes	06	0E	16	1E	26	2E	36	3E
Mnemonic	MVI B	MVI C	MVI D	MVI E	MVI H	MVI L	MVI M	MVI A
Addressing mode	immediate							
Effect on status bits	none							
Clock periods	7							
Execution time	3.5 μs							

□ EXAMPLE 2

Before execution			After execution		
Program counter		1800	Program counter		1802
A register		42	A register		42
H register		00	H register		00
L register		CB	L register		CB
Memory	1800	36	Memory	1800	26
	1801	0F		1801	0F
	00CB	AA		00CB	0F

Now with rrr of 6, a memory location will receive the data. The value of the HL pair is examined, and it is found that the contents of cell $00CB_{16}$ will be changed to equal the immediate data byte.

TRANSFER DATA. When a programmer wants to move 1 byte from a source register or memory location to a destination register or location, the transfer instruction can be used. The source and destination are indicated by using the standard number code for registers and memory. If memory is specified as either source or destination, the location is the contents of register pair HL. When the source and destination registers are the same, the instruction is essentially the same as a no operation. (A memory cell cannot be both source and destination.)

Mnemonic	MOV d, s
where	d = A, B, C, D, E, H, L, or M
	s = A, B, C, D, E, H, L, or M
Addressing mode	register
Effect on status bits	none
Clock periods	5 (7 if memory is used)
Execution time	2.5 μs (3.5 μs)

Table 5-3
Transfer Op Codes

		Source							
		B	**C**	**D**	**E**	**H**	**L**	**M**	**A**
Destination	**B**	40	41	42	43	44	45	46	47
	C	48	49	4A	4B	4C	4D	4E	4F
	D	50	51	52	53	54	55	56	57
	E	58	59	5A	5B	5C	5D	5E	5F
	H	60	61	62	63	64	65	66	67
	L	68	69	6A	6B	6C	6D	6E	6F
	M	70	71	72	73	74	75	*	77
	A	78	79	7A	7B	7C	7D	7E	7F

*Op code 76 is reserved for the halt instruction.

Format

bit number

7 6 5 4　3 2 1 0

Memory cell　m　| 0 1 d d | d s s s |

ddd	sss	Register
000	000	B
001	001	C
010	010	D
011	011	E
100	100	H
101	101	L
110	110	Memory
111	111	A

□ EXAMPLE 1

Before execution			After execution		
Program counter		2000	Program counter		2001
A register		00	A register		FF
B register		FF	B register		FF
Memory	2000	78	Memory	2000	78

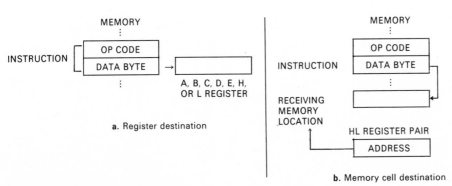

a. Register destination

b. Memory cell destination

Figure 5-7. Move Immediate.

The source is the B register. Its contents are moved to the destination, the A register.

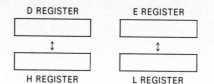

Figure 5-8. Exchange.

The 16 bits which were in HL are now in DE and vice versa.

□ EXAMPLE 2

Before execution		After execution	
Program counter	3500	Program counter	3501
A register	00	A register	00
H register	10	H register	10
L register	00	L register	00
Memory 1000	B0	Memory 1000	00
3500	77	3500	77

The contents of the A register (source) clear memory cell 1000_{16}. The address for the memory cell was found in register pair HL.

Exchange Instruction

One instruction allows us to swap the values in the DE and HL register pairs. The 8 bits from the H and the D registers are interchanged, as are the 8 bits from the L and the E registers. Figure 5-8 shows the operation.

Operation code	EB
Mnemonic	XCHG
Addressing mode	none
Effect on status bits	none
Clock periods	4
Execution time	2 µs
Format	

bit number
7 6 5 4   3 2 1 0
Memory cell   m | 1 1 1 0 | 1 0 1 1 |

□ EXAMPLE

Before execution		After execution	
Program counter	7600	Program counter	7600
D register	11	D register	33
E register	22	E register	44
H register	33	H register	11
L register	44	L register	22
Memory 7600	EB	Memory 7600	EB

Store Instructions

The store instructions are reverse operations to the load commands. Data is transferred from a register to memory. There is no change in the originating register contents when the data is written into memory. The 8080A provides three store instructions.

STORE ACCUMULATOR DIRECT. The value in the A register is moved to the memory cell addressed by the immediate data address bytes. The most-significant byte of the memory address is data byte 2 and the least-significant byte, data byte 1.

Operation code	32
Mnemonic	STA
Addressing mode	direct
Effect on status bits	none
Clock periods	13
Execution time	6.5 µs
Format	

bit number
7 6 5 4   3 2 1 0
Memory cell	m	0 0 1 1 0 0 1 0
	m + 1	low address byte
	m + 2	high address byte

□ EXAMPLE

Before execution		After execution	
Program counter	7700	Program counter	7703
A register	EE	A register	EE
Memory 7700	32	Memory 7700	32
7701	00	7701	00
7702	FE	7702	FE
FE00	00	FE00	EE

The number in the accumulator has been stored in the directly addressed memory location.

STORE ACCUMULATOR. This instruction is identical to the previous one, except that the address is specified by either the BC or the DE register pairs.

Operation codes	02	12
Mnemonics	STAX B	STAX D
Addressing mode	register	
Effect on status bits	none	
Clock periods	7	
Execution time	3.5 μs	

Format

```
                            bit number
                    7 6 5 4   3 2 1 0
                   ┌─────────────────┐
Memory cell   m    │ 0 0 0 r   0 0 1 0 │
                   └─────────────────┘
```

If r = 0, BC holds the address
If r = 1, DE holds the address

□ **EXAMPLE**

Before execution		After execution	
Program counter	8100	Program counter	8101
A register	1F	A register	1F
B register	F0	B register	F0
C register	FB	C register	FB
Memory 8100	02	Memory 8100	02
F0FB	00	F0FB	1F

The address is to be found in register pair BC because the r field in the op code is 0. The contents of the A register are written into memory cell F0FB.

STORE H AND L DIRECT. This instruction stores the L register contents in the directly addressed memory cell. The result of executing the instruction is shown in Fig. 5-9. The L register is stored at the cell addressed by data bytes 1 and 2, while the H register is stored in the next-higher memory location.

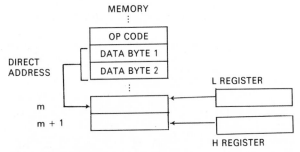

Figure 5-9. Store H and L Direct.

Operation code	22
Mnemonic	SHLD
Addressing mode	direct
Effect on status bits	none
Clock periods	16
Execution time	8 μs

Format

```
                                  bit number
                          7 6 5 4   3 2 1 0
                         ┌─────────────────┐
Memory cell   m          │ 0 0 1 1   0 0 1 1 │
                         ├─────────────────┤
              m + 1      │   low address byte │
                         ├─────────────────┤
              m + 2      │  high address byte │
                         └─────────────────┘
```

□ **EXAMPLE**

Before execution		After execution	
Program counter	2900	Program counter	2903
H register	46	H register	46
L register	00	L register	00
Memory 2900	22	Memory 2900	22
2901	03	2901	03
2902	29	2902	29
2903	FA	2903	00
2904	BE	2904	46

Jump Instructions

When a series of instructions has been completed, a change to a different sequence is sometimes required. Instead of selecting the next consecutive instruction, the microprocessor must transfer control to the instruction in a memory address far removed from the current one. This transfer of control is accomplished with some form of *jump* command. In this section we will investigate two types of jumps. Other jump options will be considered in Chap. 7.

JUMP. This instruction causes program control to transfer to the direct address in the 2 data bytes. Program execution continues from that memory address. In effect, the jump instruction changes the value of the program counter.

Operation code	C3
Mnemonic	JMP
Addressing mode	direct
Effect on status bits	none
Clock periods	10

Execution time   5 μs

Format

                                   bit number
                              7 6 5 4   3 2 1 0

Memory cell   m | 1 1 0 0   0 0 1 1 |
                    | |
             m + 1 | low address byte |
                    | |
             m + 2 | high address byte |

□ EXAMPLE

Before execution   **After execution**

Program counter [5027]   Program counter [4400]

Memory   5027 [C3]   Memory   5027 [C3]
          5028 [00]   5028 [00]
          5029 [44]   5029 [44]

Normally, the program counter would be set to $502A_{16}$ after executing the 3-byte instruction, but the JMP instruction forces the program counter to select the next instruction from cell 4400.

LOAD PROGRAM COUNTER. The effect of this instruction is similar to that of the JMP instruction, except that the source of the address is the HL register pair. The H register holds the high address byte and the L register, the low address byte. The value in the HL pair is transferred to the program counter, and program execution continues from that address.

Operation code   E9

Mnemonic   PCHL

Addressing mode   register

Effect on status bits none

Clock periods   5

Execution time   2.5 μs

Format

                                   bit number
                              7 6 5 4   3 2 1 0

Memory cell   m | 1 1 1 0   1 0 0 1 |

□ EXAMPLE

Before execution   **After execution**

Program counter [3000]   Program counter [0014]

H register   [00]   H register   [00]

L register   [14]   L register   [14]

Memory   3000 [E9]   Memory   3000 [E9]

The address in the program counter is forced to 0014_{16}, the content of the HL register pair.

Halt Instruction

After a program has run to completion, the computer must be stopped. The halt instruction brings this action about. Before stopping, the processor increments the program counter to the next sequential instruction. The MPU is halted until an interrupt arrives. (An interrupt is a break in the normal signal flow. Chapter 11 provides a full description of interrupts and their effects on the microcomputer.)

Operation code   76

Mnemonic   HLT

Addressing mode   none

Effect on status bits none

Clock periods   7

Execution time   3.5 μs

Format

                                   bit number
                              7 6 5 4   3 2 1 0

Memory cell   m | 0 1 1 1   0 1 1 0 |

□ EXAMPLE

Before execution   **After execution**

Program counter [1050]   Program counter [1051]

Memory   1050 [76]   Memory   1050 [76]

After completing the instruction and incrementing the program counter, the processor stops executing the program.

Instruction Summary

The instructions described in this chapter are summarized in Table 5-4. For each instruction, the mnemonic, operation code, number of bytes in length, and execution time are listed. None of these instructions changes the status bit settings.

PROGRAMMING EFFICIENCY

Even with the limited number of instructions you know, it may seem that several instructions do the same thing. This apparent redundancy of op codes is actually misleading. It is rather an indication of the flexibility that a large repertoire can offer.

We will examine four rather similar instructions to show how they differ and the way that choosing an instruction can affect the program execution time and memory requirements. The instructions we are interested in are listed in Table 5-5. As you can see just by selecting one instruction or the other,

Table 5-4
Instruction Summary

Mnemonic	Op Code	Bytes	Execution Time, µs
HLT	76	1	3.5
JMP	C3	3	5
LDA	3A	3	6.5
LDAX	0A, 1A	1	3.5
LHLD	2A	3	8
LXI	01, 11, 21, 31	3	5
MVI	06, 0E, 16, 0E, 26, 2E, 36, 3E	2	3.5
MOV	See Table 5-3	1	2.5/3.5
NOP	00	1	2
PCHL	E9	1	2.5
SHLD	22	3	8
STA	32	3	6.5
STAX	02, 12	1	3.5
XCHG	EB	1	2

we can seemingly get execution times ranging from 2.5 to 6.5 µs and use 1 to 3 bytes of memory. These obvious differences are not the whole effect, though, because instructions are never used in isolation. They must be combined to do a certain task. Let us assume that the job we want to do is to clear the accumulator. We will write programs using each of the instructions in Table 5-5 to accomplish this function.

Program 1

Memory address	Machine Code	Comments
1000	3E	MVI A
1001	00	Data

Program 2

Memory address	Machine Code	Comments
1000	2A	LHLD (Load HL with memory address)
1001	05	Address of data
1002	10	
1003	7E	MOV A,M
1004	00	Data
1005	04	Address of
1006	10	data

Program 3

Memory address	Machine Code	Comments
1000	3A	LDA
1001	03	Address of data
1002	10	
1003	00	Data

Program 4

Memory address	Machine Code	Comments
1000	01	LXI B (Load BC with memory address)
1001	04	Address of data
1002	10	
1003	0A	LDAX B
1004	00	Data

Now we will tabulate the time and the memory needed for each program. The results are shown in Table 5-6.

It is more obvious now that proper selection of instructions can significantly decrease both the execution time and the memory space needed for a program. There are no general rules for instruction selection, but as you become more familiar with

Table 5-5
Instruction Comparison

Mnemonic	Execution Time, µs	Bytes
MVI	3.5	2
MOV	2.5/3.5	1
LDA	6.5	3
LDAX	3.5	1

Table 5-6
Time and Memory Comparison

Instruction	Time, µs	Memory, Bytes
MVI	3.5	2
MOV	11.5	5
LDA	6.5	4
LDAX	8.5	5

the repertoire, finding the most appropriate instruction will get easier.

Some Problems to Avoid

The experiments in this book require that you enter some short programs into the computer. The program listing will always be provided, but sometimes you may find that it does not run properly. This failure is often the result of just not entering the program as written. Simple mistakes are easy to make, while the use of machine language instructions is a new experience. If your program does not run correctly, you must debug it to find the error. Inspecting memory contents and comparing them to the program listing is a good way to proceed. The results of two common errors are described so that you will have an idea of the problems that seemingly trivial mistakes can cause.

JUMPING TO A DATA CELL. A partial listing is provided in Table 5-7. The computer is to clear the accumulator and jump to the halt. By mistake, the program has a jump address of 1000_{16} instead of 0100_{16}. (The single-bit oversight in entering the program caused the error.) The program will clear the accumulator and then jump to cell 1000_{16}, where it will treat the data as an instruction. This data will be interpreted as a command to load the program counter with whatever value is in the HL register pair, because the data is the op code for a PCHL instruction. Now the processor is completely out of control and will randomly execute instructions in a manner not intended by the operator. The lesson is that even a single-bit mistake can totally disrupt a program. On the other hand, no real harm was done; it is impossible to damage a processor by putting in a bad program. That means that the price of experimentation is quite reasonable, because no hardware can be destroyed.

Table 5-7
Erroneous Jump

Location	Machine Code	Comments
0100	76	HLT
⋮		
1000	E9	Data
⋮		
10AE	3E	MVI A (clear A)
10AF	00	Data
10B0	C3	JMP
10B1	00	Incorrect address
10B2	10	

Table 5-8
Instruction Length Error

Location	Machine Code	Comments
0700	3A	LDA
0701	FF	Data (high address byte was omitted)
0702	EB	XCHG

INCORRECT INSTRUCTION LENGTH. Another easy trap to fall into is to put in an instruction with the wrong length. The purpose of the program given in Table 5-8 is to set the A register value to the number in memory cell $07FF_{16}$ and then exchange the contents of the DE and HL register pairs. When the processor executes cell 0700_{16}, it must take the contents of the next two locations as an address. The result is that the accumulator is loaded with the contents of cell $EBFF_{16}$ and the register pair exchange never takes place. Another simple omission has produced two incorrect actions. The impact of these actions will depend on the remainder of the program.

This section has provided just a small sample of the various things that can go wrong because of software errors. Remember that the computer is a very literal device—it cannot differentiate between a correct and an incorrect program. Only the human being doing the programming can.

Programming Efficiency Review

1. Why are the memory lengths in Table 5-5 misleading for evaluating efficiency?

2. Which instruction made the MOV execution time results in Table 5-6 so much longer than the other instruction sequences?

3. After the program in Table 5-7 is corrected, what is the value in the program counter when the processor stops?

CHAPTER SUMMARY

1. The working registers and the memory to be used in many instructions are indicated by a 3-bit code.

2. Register pairs are referred to by a single letter in many instruction manuals and by a 2-bit designator in some instructions.

3. Any memory address can be either written or read. It is the programmer's responsibility to prevent attempts of writing in ROM or of reading nonexistent locations.

4. A memory address for an instruction can be supplied by the data in an instruction, a register pair, or the stack pointer.

5. A maximum of 256 independent input and output ports is available. The user must avoid referencing nonexistent ports because no error notification is provided by the processor.

6. Three addressing modes are used by the 8080A. Direct addressing supplies the location as part of the 3-byte instruction. When a register pair holds the address, or when only a single register is involved in the instruction, the register addressing mode is used. Immediate addressing uses a format which includes data with the instruction.

7. The no operation instruction occupies a memory cell but does not cause any change in microprocessor state, except for incrementing the program counter.

8. Load instructions move data into the working registers or the stack pointer.

9. Move instructions are quite similar to the load instruction, but memory can be the destination, as well as registers.

10. The exchange instruction completely replaces the HL register pair content with the DE pair and then replaces the original DE value with that of HL. The result is an interchange of the register contents.

11. Store instructions write data into memory.

12. Jumps allow the programmer to change the sequence of instruction execution from the normal, consecutive order.

13. The halt instruction stops the execution of the program.

14. Proper choice of instructions can minimize the amount of time needed to run the program or the number of memory cells needed to store it. Usually only one of these two goals can be achieved; running time can be reduced only at the expense of more memory and conversely.

KEY TERMS AND CONCEPTS

Register notation	Mnemonic	Source and destination registers and memory
Direct addressing	Label field	
Register addressing	No operation	Exchange
Immediate addressing	Load	Store
Operation (op) code field	Move	Jumps
Operand field		Halt

PROBLEMS

The initial conditions for the following problems in this chapter are stated below; that is, the register and memory locations are set to the given values before the instructions in each problem are executed. For each case record, only the *changes* in any register or memory location *after* the instructions are executed.

Program counter 4090   **Stack pointer** 2000

Registers		Memory	
A	0F	0000	00
B	00	0001	50
C	01	0002	AA
D	02	0003	7B
E	A0	02A0	00
H	0F	0B0F	50
L	0B	A002	20
		0F0B	00
		0F0C	07

5-1

Location	Contents
4090	3A
4091	02
4092	00
4093	76

5-2

Location	Contents
4090	2A
4091	01
4092	00
4093	EB
4094	76

5-3

Location	Contents
4090	21
4091	95
4092	40
4093	E9
4094	76
4095	EB
4096	76

5-4

Location	Contents
4090	0A
4091	32
4092	00
4093	00
4094	00
4095	76

5-5

Location	Contents
4090	06
4091	FF
4092	32
4093	0B
4094	0F
4095	76

5-6

Location	Contents
4090	66
4091	00
4092	2A
4093	0B
4094	0F
4095	76

5-7

Location	Contents
4090	22
4091	02
4092	00
4093	32
4094	03
4095	00
4096	76

5-8

Location	Contents
4090	02
4091	2A
4092	01
4093	00
4094	00
4095	76
4096	00
4097	1A

5-9

Location	Contents
4090	C3
4091	94
4092	40
4093	76
4094	0A
4095	75
4096	00
4097	C3
4098	93
4099	40
409A	76

5-10 What is the bug in the following program? (Do not record changes in memory or registers.)

Location	Contents
4090	3A
4091	03
4092	00
4093	00
4094	31
4095	76
4096	76
4097	C3
4098	90
4099	40
409A	76

EXPERIMENT 5 _____

PURPOSE: To write and execute the first program.

PROCEDURE: You are to prepare a program to perform the operations listed below. Follow the steps for top-down design. Only the instructions introduced in this chapter are necessary for the program.

STEP 1. Set L to the value in memory cell 0030_{16} and H to the value in 0031_{16}.

STEP 2. Set A to the value in 0032_{16}.

STEP 3. Move the contents of A to D.

STEP 4. Move the contents of cell 0033_{16} to A.

STEP 5. Move A to E.

STEP 6. The value in H is to be exchanged with D, and the contents of L are to be exchanged with E.

STEP 7. Store L in 0034_{16} and H in 0035_{16}.

The initial values in memory are to be set to:

Location	Value
0030	06
0031	0F
0032	0B
0033	05

Your answer in cells 0034 and 0035 should be:

0034	05
0035	0B

STEP 8. Analyze this program by use of a flowchart.

6

ARITHMETIC AND LOGIC

Most people think of a computer as a fast arithmetic processor. In fact, computers were invented primarily to perform mathematical computations that would have taken years to do by hand. The ENIAC computer built in 1946 took only 2 hours to do calculations that took 100 engineers a full year. The ENIAC computer filled an entire building, yet today's microprocessors, like the 8080A, can do all that and more. In this chapter we will concentrate on the arithmetic and Boolean instructions of the microprocessor. Our study will require a detailed examination of the status register and how the operations change the flag bits to signify various conditions.

CHAPTER OBJECTIVES

Upon completion of this chapter, you should be able to:

1. Describe the meaning and application of the status indicators.
2. List two ways for directly controlling the carry status bit.
3. Explain how registers and memory cells can be incremented or decremented.
4. Describe how to complement the accumulator.
5. Distinguish among the various addition and subtraction instructions in the 8080A repertoire.
6. Describe the effects of Boolean AND, OR, and exclusive OR operations.
7. Demonstrate the use of Boolean instructions for masking specific bits in a register or memory.
8. Show how the 8080A can perform direct BCD additions.
9. Explain the use of compare instructions to determine the relative magnitudes of memory cell or register contents.
10. Describe the differences in arithmetic operations as performed by 8080A microprocessors built by different manufacturers.

THE STATUS REGISTER IN DETAIL

The status register was briefly discussed in Chap. 4. Remember that the flag bits in the status register show the conditions met by the data in the accumulator. The settings of all status flags (except the auxiliary carry) can be tested by computer instructions. The instructions used to test these bits are described in Chaps. 7 and 10. Here we are mainly interested in the meaning of the status bits and how they are set or cleared. Almost every arithmetic and logical instruction will have some effect on the status register. In the descriptions to follow, note which bits are changed by the instructions and whether these bit conditions can influence the operation of the processor.

Carry Bit (C)

The carry bit can be changed by addition, subtraction, shifting, and logical instructions. When adding, a carry from the high-order bit will set the carry status to 1. If no carry out is generated, the bit will be reset (that is, set to 0). Although it may seem a little strange, subtraction reverses the process. If a carry out is produced, it means that no borrow was required from the most-significant bit (MSB); therefore, it makes sense to reset the carry status for that case. Details are provided in the instruction explanations to clarify how the carry status is used for each one. Before beginning those explanations, let us look at some examples of how the carry status works.

□ **EXAMPLE 1.** Addition with no carry.

$$
\begin{array}{r}
2A_{16} = 0010\ \ 1010_2 \\
+\ 56_{16} = +0101\ \ 0110_2 \\
\hline
80_{16} = \boxed{0}1000\ \ 0000_2 \\
\uparrow \\
\text{No carry}
\end{array}
$$

Because the carry out is 0, the status bit will be reset.

□ **EXAMPLE 2.** Addition with carry.

$$
\begin{array}{r}
E7_{16} = 1110\ \ 0111_2 \\
+\ 7C_{16} = +0111\ \ 1100_2 \\
\hline
163_{16} = \boxed{1}0110\ \ 0011_2 \\
\uparrow \\
\text{Carry}
\end{array}
$$

There is a carry from the MSB position, so the status bit will be set.

□ **EXAMPLE 3.** Subtraction with no borrow.

$$
\begin{array}{r}
04_{16} = 0000\ \ 0100_2 \\
-\ 02_{16} = +1111\ \ 1110_2 \leftarrow \text{2's complement} \\
\hline
02_{16} \quad \boxed{1}0000\ \ 0010_2 \\
\uparrow
\end{array}
$$

Carry indicates no borrow

The MSB did not require a borrow, so the carry status will be reset.

□ **EXAMPLE 4.** Carry with borrow.

$$
\begin{array}{r}
04_{16} = 0000\ \ 0100_2 \\
-\ 07_{16} = 1111\ \ 1001_2 \\
\hline
-\ 03_{16} \quad \boxed{0}1111\ \ 1101_2 \\
\uparrow
\end{array}
$$

No carry

The MSB produces no carry, thus indicating that a borrow was necessary (the negative difference shows this borrow also); the carry status will be set.

Auxiliary Carry Bit (A_c)

The purpose of this status bit is to allow one instruction (decimal adjust accumulator) to perform its function. The use of this bit will be explained with that instruction description. For the time being, we will just examine situations which cause the bit to be set or cleared.

Any operation which produces a carry from the bit position 3 while adding, subtracting, incrementing, decrementing, or comparing will set the bit; otherwise, it will be reset.

□ **EXAMPLE**

Carry from MSB → $\boxed{0}$ $\boxed{1}$ ← Carry from position 3

$$
\begin{array}{r}
2A_{16} = 0010\ \ 1010_2 \\
+\ 56_{16} = 0101\ \ 0110_2 \\
\hline
80_{16} \quad 1000\ \ 0000_2
\end{array}
$$

The auxiliary carry will be set to 1 because bit position 3 generated a carry. The carry status bit (explained above) is independent of the auxiliary carry. In this case there is no carry from the MSB, so the carry status bit is reset.

Sign Bit (S)

Bit 7 of the accumulator always represents the sign of the number in that register. At the completion of arithmetic and logical operations, the sign status is set equal to bit 7.

□ **EXAMPLE**

Sign bit
↓

A register $92_{16} = 1\ 0\ 0\ 1\quad 0\ 0\ 1\ 0_2$

The sign status flag will be set to 1, meaning that the number is negative.

Zero Bit (Z)

If the accumulator value is 0 as the result of certain operations, this status flag is set. A nonzero number causes the flag to be reset. A special situation can result if the answer overflows the A register, and although the answer is not 0, the portion remaining in the accumulator is 0.

□ **EXAMPLE**

$\boxed{1}$ ← Carry
↑

$$\begin{array}{r} A7_{16} = 1\ 0\ 1\ 0\quad 0\ 1\ 1\ 1_2 \\ +\ 59_{16} = 0\ 1\ 0\ 1\quad 1\ 0\ 0\ 1_2 \\ \hline 100_{16}\quad \boxed{0\ 0\ 0\ 0\quad 0\ 0\ 0\ 0_2} \end{array}$$
←Final accumulator value

The A register can only hold the 8 least significant bits (LSBs). (Bit 9 is 1, but it will not fit into the register.) As a result the Z bit is set to indicate that the accumulator contents are 0. (In this example, the carry bit will also be set.)

Parity Bit (P)

The quantity of set bits (1s) in the accumulator are counted. Should this count be an odd number, the parity bit is cleared; if even, the bit is set.

□ **EXAMPLE**

$96_{16} = 1\ 0\ 0\ 1\quad 0\ 1\ 1\ 0_2$

4 bits are set (even): parity bit = 1

$BF_{16} = 1\ 0\ 1\ 1\quad 1\ 1\ 1\ 1_2$

7 bits are set (odd): parity bit = 0

Status Register Configuration

The bit assignments for the status register were described in Chap. 4. It would be appropriate to review those assignments and note a few details, not previously covered, before discussing the use of the status register in instructions. As was previously explained, bits 1, 3, and 5 have no meaning

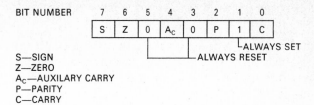

BIT NUMBER	7	6	5	4	3	2	1	0
	S	Z	0	Ac	0	P	1	C

ALWAYS SET
ALWAYS RESET

S—SIGN
Z—ZERO
Ac—AUXILARY CARRY
P—PARITY
C—CARRY

Figure 6-1. Status Register Bit Assignments.

attached to their condition, so their states are "don't care" values. Should you ever examine the register, however, knowledge of those bit states will avoid confusion. As Fig. 6-1 shows, bit 1 is always set and bits 3 and 5 are always reset. (The NEC 8080A uses one of these bits for a different purpose, as will be explained in the final section of this chapter.) Figure 6-1 also shows the positions for the parity, carry, auxiliary carry, zero, and sign bits.

Status Register Review

1. List the conditions that set the carry bit as a result of addition or subtraction.

2. Compare the auxiliary carry and carry bits. How are they similar? In what ways do they differ?

3. If the number in the accumulator is $C2_{16}$, is the sign bit set or cleared?

4. Given that the status register contains the value 83_{16}, what can you conclude about the parity of the accumulator value? Is the number nonzero?

CARRY BIT MODIFICATION

Two instructions in the repertoire directly affect the condition of the status register carry bit. The use of these instructions in computer arithmetic will be demonstrated in later chapters.

Set Carry Bit

The carry bit can unconditionally be set to 1 with this operation. None of the other status bits is changed after a set carry bit instruction. If the carry bit had been set before this instruction is executed, the effect is the same as a no-operation instruction.

Operation code	37
Mnemonic	STC
Addressing mode	none
Effect on status bits	carry bit set
Clock periods	4

Execution time | 2.0 μs

Format

```
                    bit number
              7 6 5 4   3 2 1 0
                ┌─────────────────┐
Memory cell   m │ 0 0 1 1   0 1 1 1 │
                └─────────────────┘
```

□ EXAMPLE

Before execution		After execution	
Program counter	5780	Program counter	5781
Status register	82	Status register	83
Memory 5780	37	Memory 5780	37

The carry bit is set. The previously set sign bit (bit 7) and the don't care bit (bit 1) are not altered.

Complement Carry Bit

The state of the carry bit can be inverted with this instruction. If the bit was previously 1, it becomes 0, and if 0, the bit will be set to 1. Again, no bits other than the carry condition bit will be modified.

Operation code	3F
Mnemonic	CMC
Addressing mode	none
Effect on status bits	carry bit complemented
Clock periods	4
Execution time	2.0 μs

Format

```
                    bit number
              7 6 5 4   3 2 1 0
                ┌─────────────────┐
Memory cell   m │ 0 0 1 1   1 1 1 1 │
                └─────────────────┘
```

□ EXAMPLE 1

Before execution		After execution	
Program counter	3300	Program counter	3301
Status register	02	Status register	03
Memory 3300	3F	Memory 3300	3F

The carry bit (bit 0) was changed from the 0 condition to a 1.

□ EXAMPLE 2

Before execution		After execution	
Program counter	4CF0	Program counter	4CF1
Status register	83	Status register	82
Memory 4CF0	3F	Memory 4CF0	3F

Because the carry bit was set, it becomes 0 after the complement instruction has been executed.

Carry Bit Modification Review

1. Describe the action of the STC instruction when the carry bit was clear prior to execution. When was it set prior to execution?

2. When is the set carry bit instruction equivalent to a no operation?

3. Explain the result of complementing the carry bit depending on its initial condition.

REGISTER INSTRUCTIONS

Several instructions are provided in the repertoire to assist in counting and in altering the values of registers or memory. This group of commands is especially useful for incrementing or decrementing a value which is used as an index.

Increment Register or Memory

A very straightforward command, the increment instruction increases the count contained in the designated register or memory cell by 1. The register is indicated by means of the standard numerical designator. If a memory cell is to be incremented, the address must have been entered in the HL register pair beforehand, as shown in Fig. 6-2.

Operation Code	Mnemonic
04	INR B
0C	INR C
14	INR D
1C	INR E
24	INR H
2C	INR L
34	INR M
3C	INR A

Addressing mode	register
Status bits affected	zero, sign, parity, and auxiliary carry
Clock periods	5 (10 for memory reference)
Execution time	2.5 μs (5 μs for memory reference)

Format

```
                    bit number
              7 6 5 4   3 2 1 0
                ┌─────────────────┐
Memory cell   m │ 0 0 r r   r 1 0 0 │
                └─────────────────┘
```

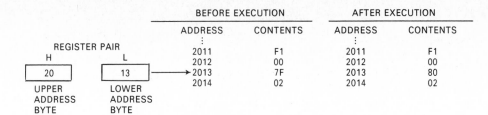

	BEFORE EXECUTION		AFTER EXECUTION	
	ADDRESS	CONTENTS	ADDRESS	CONTENTS
	2011	F1	2011	F1
	2012	00	2012	00
	2013	7F	2013	80
	2014	02	2014	02

Figure 6-2. Increment Memory.

rrr	Register
000	B
001	C
010	D
011	E
100	H
101	L
110	memory
111	A

□ **EXAMPLE**

Before execution   **After execution**

Program counter 4010   Program counter 4011

B register 03   B register 04

Memory 4010 04   Memory 4010 04

To see how the instruction may be combined with others you have studied, consider the task of saving the E register in two memory cells (10FE$_{16}$ and 10FF$_{16}$) for later use. The program below will accomplish the required storage.

Address	Machine Code	Instruction	Comments
0100	21	LXI H, 10FE	Load
0101	FE		HL register pair with first address
0102	10		
0103	73	MOV M,E	Store contents of E in 10FE
0104	2C	INR L	Increment lower half of destination address (new address will be 10FF)
0105	73	MOV M,E	Store contents of E in 10FF

After the address has been established in HL, it would be a simple matter to store the E register in several consecutive memory locations by using the same technique.

Increment Register Pair

In the short program above, what changes would be necessary if the addresses to be used for storage ranged from 10FE through 1104? After examination,

we conclude that the H register must be increased, as well as the L register, in going from 10FF to 1100. Although we could have carried the operation out using an INR instruction, the increment register pair command is much more practical. In this case the register pair is treated as a 16-bit quantity. If a carry is produced when the lower 8 bits (contained in the least significant register) are incremented, then the most significant byte is also incremented.

Operation Code	Mnemonic	Register Pair
03	INX B	BC
13	INX D	DE
23	INX H	HL
33	INX SP	Stack pointer

Addressing mode	Register
Status bits affected	none
Clock periods	5
Execution time	2.5 μs

Format			bit number		
			7 6 5 4	3 2 1 0	
Memory cell	m		0 0 r r	0 0 1 1	

rr	Register pair
00	BC
01	DE
10	HL
11	SP

Before execution		After execution	
Program counter	0250	Program counter	0251
D register	00	D register	01
E register	FF	E register	00
Memory 0250	13	Memory 0250	13

The previous program used with the INR instruction would perform as well if the instruction in cell 0104_{16} were changed to 23_{16}. The only effect is that the HL register pair would be incremented as a 2-byte quantity. The results would be identical.

Decrement Register or Memory

This instruction is a direct analog to INR. The two differ only in that this instruction decreases the register or memory value by 1. Two's complement arithmetic is used in the subtraction. As we have seen before, the linked H and L registers provide the address if a memory cell is involved.

Operation Code	Mnemonic
05	DCR B
0D	DCR C
15	DCR D
1D	DCR E
25	DCR H
2D	DCR L
35	DCR M
3D	DCR A

Addressing mode	register
Status bits affected	zero, sign, parity, auxiliary carry
Clock periods	5 (10 for memory reference)
Execution time	2.5 μs (5 μs for memory reference)

Format

bit number

7 6 5 4 3 2 1 0

Memory cell m 0 0 r r r 1 0 1

rrr	Register
000	B
001	C
010	D
011	E
100	H
101	L
110	memory
111	A

Before execution		After execution	
Program counter	35D3	Program counter	35D4
H register	20	H register	20
L register	14	L register	14
Memory 2014	00	Memory 2014	FF
35D3	35	35D3	35

The op code indicates that a memory cell is to be decremented. The address from the HL pair is 2014_{16}. By use of 2's complement subtraction, the original contents (00_{16}) are reduced by 1 to FF_{16} (-1).

Decrement Register Pair

Another instruction that is closely related to the previous register pair command is the decrement register pair. This operation decreases the quantity but otherwise works like the INX series of op codes. The register pair as a 16-bit number and is reduced in value by 1. The result is expressed in 2's complement terms.

Operation Code	Mnemonic	Register Pair
0B	DCX B	BC
1B	DCX D	DE
2B	DCX H	HL
3B	DCX SP	Stack pointer

Addressing mode	register
Status bits affected	none
Clock periods	5
Execution time	2.5 μ

Format

bit number

7 6 5 4 3 2 1 0

Memory cell m 0 0 r r 1 0 1 1

rr	Register Pair
00	BC
01	DE
10	HL
11	SP

Before execution		After execution	
Program counter	D100	Program counter	D101
B register	FF	B register	FD
C register	00	C register	FF
Memory D100	0B	Memory D100	0B

The value in the two registers is FE00$_{16}$. Subtracting one produces a difference of FDFF$_{16}$.

Complement Accumulator

The 8080A normally employs 2's complement arithmetic, but 1's complement may be needed for special purposes. This instruction supplies that capability. Execution of the instruction will cause each bit of the accumulation to reverse its state.

Operation code	2F
Mnemonic	CMA
Addressing mode	none
Status bits affected	none
Clock periods	4
Execution time	2.0 μs

Format   bit number

	7	6	5	4	3	2	1	0
Memory cell m	0	0	1	0	1	1	1	1

□ EXAMPLE

Before execution	After execution
Program counter AA01	After execution AA02
A register 00	A register FF
Memory AA01 2F	Memory AA01 2F

The original value of 00$_{16}$ in the accumulator has been changed to its 1's complement equivalent. (In 1's complement, FF$_{16}$ is negative 0.)

Register Instruction Review

1. Explain how the register affected in the INR instruction is indicated by the op code. Where is the address found if a memory cell is to be incremented?

2. Why is the INX instruction needed in addition to the INR instruction? When can INR be substituted for INX?

3. If the E register containing 7F$_{16}$ is incremented, the value becomes a negative number. Explain this contradiction.

4. Distinguish between the effects that the DCR and the DCX instructions have on the condition of the status flags.

5. Explain how 1's complement numbers can be introduced into the 8080A, which normal processes only 2's complements.

ADDITION

This section and the following one on subtraction introduce arithmetic processing within the 8080A. The capabilities of the microprocessor to calculate mathematical results depend not only on the basic arithmetic instructions, but also on instructions that can sense the outcome of these processes. By combining several instructions into a routine, the processor can handle multibyte arithmetic and even multiply and divide. Some of these routines will be covered in Chaps. 7 and 8. In this chapter the discussion will concentrate on basic functions.

Add Register or Memory to Accumulator

The byte, specified by the register designator, will be added to the present contents of the accumulator using 2's complement arithmetic. The resulting sum is placed in the accumulator, thus destroying the initial value. If memory is the origin for the byte to be added, the address is established by the HL register pair.

Operation Code	Mnemonic
80	ADD B
81	ADD C
82	ADD D
83	ADD E
84	ADD H
85	ADD L
86	ADD M
87	ADD A

Addressing mode	register
Status bits affected	carry, sign, zero, parity, auxiliary carry
Clock periods	4 (7 for memory reference)
Execution time	2.0 μs (3.5 μs for memory reference)

Format   bit number

	7	6	5	4	3	2	1	0
Memory cell m	1	0	0	0	0	r	r	r

rrr	Register
000	B
001	C
010	D
011	E
100	H
101	L
110	memory
111	A

□ **EXAMPLE 1.** Add $3E_{16}$ to $7B_{16}$

Before execution		After execution	
Program counter	5030	Program counter	5031
A register	7B	A register	B9
H register	10	H register	10
L register	00	L register	00
Status register	02	Status register	92
Memory 1000	3E	Memory 1000	3E
5030	87	5030	87

Binary Addition

No
$\boxed{0}$ carry $\boxed{1}$ Carry out of bit 3

$$\begin{aligned} 3E_{16} &= 0011\ \ 1110_2 \\ +\ 7B_{16} &= 0111\ \ 1011_2 \\ \hline B9_{16} &\quad\ 1011\ \ 1001_2 \end{aligned}$$

Several effects of this addition are worth noting. First, the A register value is changed to the resulting sum. The sum is negative and a carry was produced from bit position 3, so the sign and the auxiliary carry bits are set. The result is nonzero with odd parity, and no carry was generated from the MSB, so those respective status bits are reset. By examining the augend and addend, we see that they were both positive (sign bit is 0), but the sum is negative. How could addition of two positive numbers produce a negative sum? The answer to this puzzle is that the accumulator overflowed. Bit 7 is actually the MSB of the sum, but the computer interprets it as a negative number. All further computer operations on that value will treat it as a 2's complement negative number (-47_{16} in this case). Overflowing an 8-bit register is an easy mistake to make; the only way to prevent it is to be sure that the range of numbers to be added will not cause overflow. If larger numbers must be added, multibyte addition (also called *double precision*) will be needed.

□ **EXAMPLE 2.** Doubling the accumulator

Before execution		After execution	
Program counter	20B0	Program counter	20B1
A register	04	A register	08
Status register	02	Status register	02
Memory 20B0	87	Memory 20B0	87

By use of the ADD A (op code 87_{16}) instruction, the contents of the accumulator can be doubled.

In this case, final conditions of the status flags are the same as the initial ones because there was no change in sign, zero status, or carry, and the parity of both the initial and the final values is odd.

Add Immediate

The immediate data byte is added to the accumulator, and then the sum is placed in the accumulator. Other than the fact that the instruction uses immediate data, the 2's complement addition carried out by an add immediate is the same as that of the add instruction.

Operation code	C6
Mnemonic	ADI
Addressing mode	immediate
Status bits affected	carry, sign, zero, parity, auxiliary carry
Clock periods	7
Execution time	3.5 μs
Format	

bit number

7 6 5 4　3 2 1 0

Memory cell m	1 1 0 0　0 1 1 0
m + 1	immediate data byte

□ **EXAMPLE**

Before execution		After execution	
Program counter	0730	Program counter	0732
A register	D2	A register	8E
Status register	87	Status register	87
Memory 0730	C6	Memory 0730	C6
0731	BC	0731	BC

Binary Addition

$\boxed{1}$ Carry $\boxed{0}$ No carry

$$\begin{aligned} D2_{16} &= 1101\ \ 0010_2 \\ +\ BC_{16} &= 1011\ \ 1100_2 \\ \hline \boxed{1}8E_{16} &\quad\ 1000\ \ 1110_2 \end{aligned}$$

Although there was a carry out of the MSB, no overflow occurred in this problem. The sum is negative as expected from adding two negative numbers. By converting to 2's complement, we can verify that the final A register value is correct.

$$D2_{16} = -2E_{16}$$
$$BC_{16} = -44_{16}$$
$$\overline{-72_{16} = 8E_{16}}$$

Remember that a carry out in the case of subtraction (or addition of a negative number) means that no borrow was needed from the high-order bit. In this problem the carry status will be set because an add instruction is used. (Compare this result with that of the subtraction instruction.) The sign status and the parity bits remain set. No carry was produced from bit 3, so auxiliary carry status is 0.

Add Register or Memory to Accumulator with Carry

This instruction differs from a normal add in that the value of the carry status bit is added to the sum. The addition uses 2's complement arithmetic. If referenced, the memory address must be placed in the HL pair prior to executing the instruction.

Operation Code	Mnemonic
88	ADC B
89	ADC C
8A	ADC D
8B	ADC E
8C	ADC H
8D	ADC L
8E	ADC M
8F	ADC A

Addressing mode	register
Status bits affected	carry, sign, zero, parity, auxiliary carry
Clock periods	4 (7 for memory reference)
Execution time	2.0 µs (3.5 µs for memory reference)

Format

bit number

7 6 5 4   3 2 1 0

Memory cell   m | 1 0 0 0   0 r r r |

rrr	Register
000	B
001	C
010	D
011	E
100	H
101	L
110	memory
111	A

□ **EXAMPLE**

Before execution		After execution	
Program counter	1150	Program counter	1151
A register	17	A register	50
B register	38	B register	38
Status register	07	Status register	12
Memory 1150	88	Memory 1150	88

Binary Addition

$$
\begin{array}{llll}
17_{16} = & 0001 & 0111_2 \\
+\ 38_{16} = & 0011 & 1000_2 \\
\hline
4F & 0100 & 1111_2
\end{array}
$$

No
| 0 | carry | 1 | Carry

4F   0100   1111$_2$
Carry status +1   +1
$$\overline{50_{16} \quad 0101 \quad 0000_2}$$

The original carry bit was set, so 1 is added to the sum of the A and B register contents, and the final addition caused a carry from bit 3, so the auxiliary carry is set.

Add Immediate with Carry

This instruction is a simple extension of the add immediate instruction. The carry status existing prior to execution is added to the sum of the accumulator and the immediate data in computing the result.

Operation code	CE
Mnemonic	ACI
Addressing mode	immediate
Status bits affected	carry, sign, zero, parity, auxiliary carry
Clock periods	7
Execution time	3.5 µs

Format

bit number

7 6 5 4   3 2 1 0

Memory cell   m | 1 1 0 0   1 1 1 0 |

m + 1 | immediate data byte |

□ EXAMPLE

Before execution		After execution	
Program counter	0910	Program counter	0912
A register	0D	A register	00
Status register	03	Status register	57
Memory 0910	CE	Memory 0910	CE
0911	F2	0911	F2

Binary Addition

$$
\begin{array}{ll}
0D_{16} & 0000 \quad 1101_2 \\
+ F2_{16} & 1111 \quad 0010_2 \\
\end{array}
$$

$\boxed{1}$ Carry $\boxed{1}$ Carry

$$
\begin{array}{ll}
FF_{16} & 1111 \quad 1111_2 \\
\text{Carry status} + 1 & \qquad\quad + 1 \\
\hline
\boxed{1}00_{16} & 0000 \quad 0000_2 \\
\end{array}
$$

The 0 sum sets the zero and even parity flags. As a result of carries from bits 3 and 7, both carry status bits are set as well.

Double Add

The double byte in a register pair on the stack pointer can be added to the contents of the HL register pair by using the double add instruction. The addition is done in 2's complement form, and the final sum is placed in the HL pair.

Op Code	Mnemonic	Register Pair
09	DAD B	BC
19	DAD D	DE
29	DAD H	HL
39	DAD SP	SP

Addressing mode	register
Affected status bits	carry
Clock periods	4
Execution time	2.0 μs

Format

bit number

		7	6	5	4	3	2	1	
Memory cell	m	0	0	r	r	1	0	0	1

rr	Register Pair
00	BC
01	DE
10	HL
11	SP

□ EXAMPLE

Before execution		After execution	
Program counter	0778	Program counter	0779
B register	3F	B register	3F
C register	BA	C register	BA
H register	02	H register	42
L register	46	L register	00
Status register	17	Status register	16
Memory 0778	09	Memory 0778	09

Binary Addition

$\boxed{0}$ No carry

$$
\begin{array}{ll}
3FBA_{16} = & 0011 \; 1111 \; 1011 \; 1010_2 \\
+ 0246_{16} = & +0000 \; 0010 \; 0100 \; 0110_2 \\
\hline
4200_{16} & 0100 \; 0010 \; 0000 \; 0000_2 \\
\end{array}
$$

The double-byte sum is stored in the HL register pair. The carry bit is reset because there was no carry from the MSB. Other status bits are unchanged. The double add instruction op code 29_{16} doubles the value in the HL register.

Addition Review

1. Explain the reason for the final value of each bit in the status register resulting from example 1 of the add instruction.

2. Distinguish between the ADD and ADC operations.

3. How was the overflow in example 1 of the ADD instruction detected?

4. Explain the significance of the carry bit being set in the ADI example.

5. List the register pairs that can be summed by using the double add instruction.

SUBTRACTION

The subtraction instructions have a one-to-one correspondence with the addition instructions just discussed. That is, subtraction operands can be in registers, memory cells, or immediate data bytes. There is, however, no double register subtraction instruction. A subtle difference between addition and subtraction to watch for is the setting of the carry bit. As was explained earlier in this chapter, a carry from the MSB sets the bit for addition. A carry from that bit in subtraction means that a borrow did not occur, so the bit is *reset*. The examples in this section will provide more insight into the meaning of that status flag.

Subtract Register or Memory from the Accumulator

This instruction subtracts the designated byte from the A register using 2's complement. The difference is placed in the accumulator. If memory cell contents are the operand, the address must be put into the HL register pair.

Operation Code	Mnemonic
90	SUB B
91	SUB C
92	SUB D
93	SUB E
94	SUB H
95	SUB L
96	SUB M
97	SUB A

Addressing mode	register
Status bits affected	carry, sign, zero, parity, auxiliary carry
Clock periods	4 (7 for memory reference)
Execution time	2.0 μs (3.5 μs for memory reference)

Format

bit number

		7 6 5 4	3 2 1 0
Memory cell	m	1 0 0 1	0 r r r

rrr	Register
000	B
001	C
010	D
011	E
100	H
101	L
110	memory
111	A

□ **EXAMPLE.** Clear the accumulator and reset the carry bit.

Before execution		After execution	
Program counter	6700	Program counter	6701
A register	7B	A register	00
Status register	06	Status register	56
Memory 6700	97	Memory 6700	97

In this example we are subtracting the accumulator from itself.

Binary Subtraction

$$
\begin{array}{rcl}
 & \boxed{1}\,\text{Carry} & \boxed{1}\,\text{Carry} \\
 & \uparrow & \uparrow \\
7B_{16} = & 0\,1\,1\,1 & 1\,0\,1\,1_2 \\
-\,7B_{16} = & +1\,0\,0\,0 & 0\,1\,0\,1_2 \text{ (2's complement} \\
\hline
00_{16} & 0\,0\,0\,0 & 0\,0\,0\,0_2 \text{ is added)}
\end{array}
$$

Because the rules for subtraction are used, the carry from bit 7 will reset the carry status bit. Because of the carry from bit 3, the auxiliary carry bit is set. The parity and zero bits will also be set. Thus the subtract accumulator instruction will zero that register and the carry status bit.

Subtract Immediate from Accumulator

Using the accumulator value as the minuend and the immediate data as the subtrahend, a 2's complement difference is generated and sent to the accumulator. The example for this instruction uses the same values as the add immediate in the previous section. The treatment of the carry bit for the two operations is compared below.

Operation code	D6
Mnemonic	SUI
Addressing mode	immediate
Status bits affected	carry, sign, zero, parity, auxiliary carry
Clock periods	7
Execution time	3.5 μs

Format

bit number

		7 6 5 4	3 2 1 0
Memory cell	m	1 1 0 1	0 1 1 0
	m + 1	immediate data byte	

Before execution	After execution

Program counter $\boxed{0730}$ Program counter $\boxed{0732}$

A register $\boxed{\text{D2}}$ A register $\boxed{\text{8E}}$

Status register $\boxed{87}$ Status register $\boxed{82}$

Memory 0730 $\boxed{\text{D6}}$ Memory 0730 $\boxed{\text{D6}}$

0731 $\boxed{44}$ 0731 $\boxed{44}$

The immediate data is 44_{16} (which is the 2's complement of BC_{16} in the previous add immediate example).

Binary Subtraction

$\boxed{1}$ Carry $\boxed{0}$ No carry

$$D2_{16} = \quad 1\ 1\ 0\ 1 \quad 0\ 0\ 1\ 0_2$$
$$-44_{16} = \quad +1\ 0\ 1\ 1 \quad 1\ 1\ 0\ 0_2 \text{ (2's complement}$$
$$8E_{16} \quad \overline{1\ 0\ 0\ 0 \quad 1\ 1\ 1\ 0_2} \text{ is added)}$$

The difference is identical to that of the former example. Although the carry from bit 7 took place in both cases, this time the carry status is reset. Table 6-1 summarizes the way in which the carry status and the auxiliary carry status are used in addition and subtraction.

Subtract Register or Memory from Accumulator with Borrow

The primary purpose for this instruction is multibyte subtraction, which is explained in Chap. 7. Here we will show the single-byte use of the instruction. The subtract with borrow instruction first adds the carry status bit value to the contents of the appropriate memory cell or register. Then that sum is subtracted from the accumulator. The results are put into the A register. Two's complement arithmetic is used. As usual with memory operands, the memory address corresponds to the HL register value.

Operation Code	Mnemonic
98	SBB B
99	SBB C
9A	SBB D
9B	SBB E
9C	SBB H
9D	SBB L
9E	SBB M
9F	SBB A

Addressing mode	register
Status bit affected	carry, sign, zero, parity, auxiliary carry
Clock periods	4 (7 for memory reference)
Execution time	2.0 μs (3.5 μs for memory reference)
Format	bit number

```
              7 6 5 4   3 2 1 0
Memory cell  m | 1 0 0 1   1 r r r |
```

rrr	Register
000	B
001	C
010	D
011	E
100	H
101	L
110	memory
111	A

Table 6-1
Carry Status Bits

| Operation | Carry | | Auxiliary Carry | |
	Condition	Meaning	Condition	Meaning
Addition	Set	Carry from MSB	Set	Carry from bit 3
	Reset	No carry from MSB	Reset	No carry from bit 3
Subtraction	Set	Borrow to MSB	Same as addition	Same as addition
	Reset	No borrow to MSB	Same as addition	Same as addition

□ EXAMPLE

Before execution		After execution	
Program counter	1805	Program counter	1806
A register	2C	A register	FC
C register	30	C register	30
Status register	02	Status register	87
Memory 1805	99	Memory 1805	99

STEPS IN EXECUTION

STEP 1. Adding the carry status to the subtrahend.

$$\begin{array}{ll} \text{C register} & 30_{16} \\ \text{Carry} & +\ 0_{16} \\ \hline & 30_{16} \end{array}$$

STEP 2. Binary subtraction.

$$\begin{array}{lll} & \boxed{0}\ \overset{\text{No}}{\text{carry}} & \boxed{0}\ \overset{\text{No}}{\text{carry}} \\ 2C_{16} = & 0\ 0\ 1\ 0 & 1\ 1\ 0\ 0_2 \\ -30_{16} = & +1\ 1\ 0\ 1 & 0\ 0\ 0\ 0 \quad \text{(2's complement} \\ \hline -\ 4_{16} & 1\ 1\ 1\ 1 & 1\ 1\ 0\ 0_2 = FC_{16} \quad \text{is added)} \end{array}$$

The 2's complement of the binary difference ($1111\ 1100_2 = FC_{16}$) is -4_{16}; thus the result is correct. There was no carry from the MSB, so the carry status bit will be set. The sign and parity bits will be set as well.

Subtract Immediate with Borrow

The immediate data byte is added to the carry status bit. That result is subtracted from the accumulator, and the difference replaces the initial accumulator quantity.

Operation code	DE
Mnemonic	SBI
Addressing mode	immediate
Status bits affected	carry, zero, parity, auxiliary carry
Clock periods	7
Execution time	3.5 μs
Format	

bit number

		7 6 5 4	3 2 1 0
Memory cell	m	1 1 0 1	1 1 1 0
	m + 1	immediate data byte	

□ EXAMPLE

Before execution		After execution	
Program counter	1220	Program counter	1222
A register	20	A register	11
Status register	03	Status register	06
Memory 1220	DE	Memory 1220	DE
1221	0E	1221	0E

STEPS IN EXECUTION

STEP 1. Adding the carry status to the subtrahend.

$$\begin{array}{ll} \text{Immediate data} & 0E_{16} \\ \text{Carry status} & +\ 1 \\ \hline & 0F_{16} \end{array}$$

STEP 2. Binary subtraction.

$$\begin{array}{lll} & \boxed{1}\ \text{Carry} & \boxed{0}\ \text{No carry} \\ 20_{16} = & 0\ 0\ 1\ 0 & 0\ 0\ 0\ 0_2 \\ -\ 0F_{16} = & +1\ 1\ 1\ 1 & 0\ 0\ 0\ 1_2 \quad \text{(2's complement} \\ \hline 11_{16} & 0\ 0\ 0\ 1 & 0\ 0\ 0\ 1_2 \quad \text{is added)} \end{array}$$

The 2's complement addition is straightforward. The carry status will be reset. Parity is even.

Subtraction Review

1. Explain how to clear the carry status flag and the accumulator using a single instruction.

2. Compare the way in which the carry bit is set or cleared in subtraction with the handling of that bit in addition.

3. List the two steps required to execute a SBB E instruction.

4. What effect does the group of subtraction instructions have on the auxiliary carry?

Boolean Operations

The MPU can perform logical AND, OR, and exclusive OR operations. You are probably well acquainted with these functions from your experience with combinatorial circuits. Tables 6-2 through 6-4 are a tabulation of the Boolean truth tables for these operators. The logical combination of the two 8-bit inputs is done on a bit-by-bit basis. The example in Figure 6-3 shows how.

A frequently used capability provided by logical instructions is *masking* of certain bits in a word. By using a suitable mask together with the proper instruction, a single bit can be read, set, cleared,

Table 6-2
AND Truth Table

Inputs Bits		
A	B	Result
0	0	0
0	1	0
1	0	0
1	1	1

Table 6-3
OR Truth Table

Inputs Bits		
A	B	Result
0	0	0
0	1	1
1	0	1
1	1	1

Table 6-4
Exclusive OR Truth Table

Input Bits		
A	B	Result
0	0	0
0	1	1
1	0	1
1	1	0

Addressing mode	register
Status bits affected	carry, zero, sign, parity
Clock periods	4 (7 for memory reference)
Execution time	2.0 μs (3.5 μs for memory reference)

Format

bit number

7 6 5 4   3 2 1 0

Memory cell   m | 1 0 1 0   0 r r r |

rrr	Register
000	B
001	C
010	D
011	E
100	H
101	L
110	memory
111	A

or complemented. This example of Boolean instruction usage will be demonstrated later in this section.

AND Register or Memory with Accumulator

The specified byte from the register or memory cell is bit-by-bit ANDed with the accumulator. The carry bit is always reset. The result will replace the original A register contents. The HL register pair represents the memory cell address if the operand is located in memory.

Operation Code	Mnemonic
A0	ANA B
A1	ANA C
A2	ANA D
A3	ANA E
A4	ANA H
A5	ANA L
A6	ANA M
A7	ANA A

□ **EXAMPLE**

Before execution		After execution	
Program counter	2AE0	Program counter	2AE1
A register	B7	A register	25
L register	65	L register	65
Status register	97	Status register	12
Memory 2AE0	A5	Memory 2AE0	A5

Binary AND

$$B7_{16} = 1011\ 0111_2$$
$$65_{16} = 0110\ 0101_2$$
$$25_{16} = 0010\ 0101_2$$

The sign of the result is positive and parity is odd, so those condition bits are reset. The auxiliary carry, which was set prior to execution, remains unchanged.

AND Immediate

This instruction is directly analogous to the previous one, except that the operand is immediate data. The carry bit is always reset at the completion of the operation.

Operation code	E6
Mnemonic	ANI

BYTE X	x_7	x_6	x_5	x_4	x_3	x_2	x_1	x_0
BYTE Y	y_7	y_6	y_5	y_4	y_3	y_2	y_1	y_0
RESULT	r_7	r_6	r_5	r_4	r_3	r_2	r_1	r_0

WHERE
$r_0 = x_0$ AND y_0 $r_4 = x_4$ AND y_4
$r_1 = x_1$ AND y_1 $r_5 = x_5$ AND y_5
$r_2 = x_2$ AND y_2 $r_6 = x_6$ AND y_6
$r_3 = x_3$ AND y_3 $r_7 = x_7$ AND y_7

Figure 6-3. Bit-by-Bit AND Example.

Addressing mode	immediate
Status bits affected	carry, zero, sign, parity
Clock periods	7
Execution time	3.5 μs

Format

bit number

Memory cell	m	7 6 5 4	3 2 1 0
		1 1 1 0	0 1 1 0
	m + 1	Immediate Data Byte	

□ **EXAMPLE**

Before execution		**After execution**	
Program counter	0672	Program counter	0674
A register	6D	A register	01
Status register	02	Status register	02
Memory	0672 E6	Memory	0672 E6
	0673 81		0673 81

Binary AND

$$6D_{16} = 0110\ 1101_2$$
$$81_{16} = 1000\ 0001_2$$
$$01_{16}\quad 0000\ 0001_2$$

OR Register or Memory with Accumulator

The selected byte will be ORed with the accumulator and the results placed in the latter register. Memory cell addressing is accomplished by means of the HL pair. The carry status is always reset.

Operation Code	Mnemonic
B0	ORA B
B1	ORA C
B2	ORA D
B3	ORA E
B4	ORA H
B5	ORA L
B6	ORA M
B7	ORA A

Addressing mode	register
Status bits affected	carry, zero, sign, parity
Clock periods	4 (7 for memory reference)
Execution time	2.0 μs (3.5 μs for memory reference)

Format

bit number

Memory cell	m	7 6 5 4	3 2 1 0
		1 0 1 1	0 r r r

rrr	Register
000	B
001	C
010	D
011	E
100	H
101	L
110	memory
111	A

□ **EXAMPLE**

Before execution		**After execution**	
Program counter	01A0	Program counter	01A1
A register	E3	A register	F3
H register	32	H register	32
Status register	87	Status register	82
Memory	01A0 B4	Memory	01A0 B4

Binary OR

$$E3_{16} = 1110\ 0011_2$$
$$32_{16} = 0011\ 0010_2$$
$$F3_{16}\quad 1111\ 0011_2$$

Carry, parity, and zero bits are reset to 0. The sign bit remains set.

OR Immediate

The immediate byte is ORed with the accumulator. Carry status is always reset.

Operation code	F6
Mnemonic	ORI
Addressing mode	immediate
Status bits affected	carry, zero, sign, parity
Clock periods	7
Execution time	3.5 μs

Format

bit number

Memory cell	m	7 6 5 4	3 2 1 0
		1 1 1 1	0 1 1 0
	m + 1	immediate data byte	

Before execution		After execution	
Program counter	0336	Program counter	0338
A register	00	A register	58
Status register	46	Status register	02
Memory 0336	F6	Memory 0336	F6
0337	58	0337	58

Binary OR

$$00_{16} = 0000\ 0000_2$$
$$58_{16} = 0101\ 1000_2$$
$$58_{16}\quad 0101\ 1000_2$$

Exclusive OR Register or Memory with Accumulator

An 8-bit quantity obtained from a register or a memory location is exclusive ORed with the accumulator. The acculator holds the final result. If a memory cell is to be referenced, the address must be in HL. The carry bit will be reset. The exclusive OR can be used to zero the accumulator, to set the accumulator to the 1's complement of any register or memory cell, and to test for a change in the value of any memory location. Examples of these applications are given below.

Operation Code	Mnemonic
A8	XRA B
A9	XRA C
AA	XRA D
AB	XRA E
AC	XRA H
AD	XRA L
AE	XRA M
AF	XRA A

Addressing mode	register
Status bits affected	carry, zero, sign, parity
Clock periods	4 (7 for memory reference)
Execution time	2.0 μs (3.5 μs for memory reference)
Format	

bit number

7 6 5 4   3 2 1 0

Memory cell   m | 1 0 1 0   1 r r r |

rrr	Register
000	B
001	C
010	D
011	E
100	H
101	L
110	memory
111	A

☐ **EXAMPLE 1.** Zero the accumulator.

Before execution		After execution	
Program counter	0200	Program counter	0201
A register	FF	A register	00
Status register	86	Status register	46
Memory 0200	AF	Memory 0200	AF

Binary Exclusive OR

$$FF_{16} = 1111\ 1111_2$$
$$FF_{16} = 1111\ 1111_2$$
$$00_{16}\quad 0000\ 0000_2$$

The carry status bit is also reset as a result of this instruction.

☐ **EXAMPLE 2.** Obtaining the 1's complement of a memory cell.

Before execution		After execution	
Program counter	0200	Program counter	0201
A register	FF	A register	4C
H register	05	H register	05
L register	00	L register	00
Status register	86	Status register	02
Memory 0200	AF	Memory 0200	AF
0500	B3	0500	B3

Binary Exclusive OR

$$FF_{16} = 1111\ 1111_2$$
$$B3_{16} = 1011\ 0011_2$$
$$4C_{16}\quad 0100\ 1100_2$$

The 1's complement of $B3_{16}$ is $4C_{16}$. The A register contains that value.

☐ **EXAMPLE 3.** Test for change in value. Assume that the initial value of a variable was stored in memory cell 0100_{16} and that the present value is in the accumulator.

Before execution		After execution	
Program counter	0200	Program counter	0201
A register	47	A register	11
H register	01	H register	01
L register	00	L register	00
Status register	06	Status register	06
Memory 0100	56	Memory 0100	56
0200	AE	0200	AE

Binary Exclusive OR

$$
\begin{array}{lll}
\text{New value} & 47_{16} = & 0\ 1\ 0\ 0\ \ 0\ 1\ 1\ 1_2 \\
\text{Original value} & 56_{16} = & 0\ 1\ 0\ 1\ \ 0\ 1\ 1\ 0_2 \\
& 11_{16} & 0\ 0\ 0\ 1\ \ 0\ 0\ 0\ 1_2
\end{array}
$$

Bit positions that changed in value

Two bits have changed in the variable. Bit 0 has gone from a 0 to a 1, and bit 4 has gone from a 1 to a 0. The 2-bit positions that have been altered are indicated by 1s in the result.

Exclusive OR Immediate

This instruction produces the exclusive OR of the immediate data byte and the accumulator; the result resides in the accumulator. The carry bit is always reset.

Operation code	EE
Mnemonic	XRI
Addressing mode	immediate
Clock periods	7
Execution time	3.5 μs

Format

bit number

		7 6 5 4	3 2 1 0
Memory cell	m	1 1 1 0	1 1 1 0
	m + 1	immediate data byte	

□ EXAMPLE

Before execution		After execution	
Program counter	00A3	Program counter	00A5
A register	00	A register	C2
Status register	46	Status register	02
Memory 00A3	EE	Memory 00A3	EE
00A4	C2	00A4	C2

Binary Exclusive OR

$$
\begin{array}{ll}
00_{16} = & 0\ 0\ 0\ 0\ \ 0\ 0\ 0\ 0_2 \\
C2_{16} = & 1\ 1\ 0\ 0\ \ 0\ 0\ 1\ 0_2 \\
C2_{16} & 1\ 1\ 0\ 0\ \ 0\ 0\ 1\ 0_2
\end{array}
$$

Masking

Often data is packed into *fields* of memory cells to conserve space. A field is a grouping of bits used to hold one item of information. As an example, consider Fig. 6-4. Field 1 (bits 3 through 7) represent the size of a family residing in a house. Field 2 is set if the occupant is a renter, but if the bit is clear, the occupant is a home owner. Bits 0 and 1 are unused but are always set. Assume that the contents of that memory cell has been placed in the accumulator, and on different occasions the information is to be retrieved or altered. The use of masking to satisfy those requirements is shown below.

READING A FIELD. The following example will demonstrate how only the family size can be read. Remember that the packed data word has already been fetched from memory and is in the A register.

□ EXAMPLE

A register	37
Instruction	ANI F8

Result of ANDing   These bits are to be read

$$
\begin{array}{ll}
\text{A register} & 37_{16} = 0\ 1\ 1\ 0\ \ 0\ 1\ 1\ 1_2 \\
\text{Immediate data (mask)} & F8_{16} = 1\ 1\ 1\ 1\ \ 1\ 0\ 0\ 0_2 \\
& \quad\quad\ \ 0\ 0\ 1\ 1\ \ 0\ 0\ 0\ 0
\end{array}
$$

Family size = 6

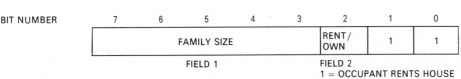

BIT NUMBER	7	6	5	4	3	2	1	0
	FAMILY SIZE					RENT/OWN	1	1
	FIELD 1					FIELD 2		

FIELD 2
1 = OCCUPANT RENTS HOUSE
0 = OCCUPANT OWNS HOUSE

Figure 6-4. Packed Data.

The immediate data byte is the mask. The ones in that byte correspond to the bits in the data to be read.

SELECTIVELY CLEARING BITS IN A FIELD.
New data has arrived which says the home is now owned by the occupant. Alter field 2 to reflect this change.

□ **EXAMPLE**

A register   37

Instruction   ANI FB

Result of ANDing   This bit will be cleared

$$\downarrow$$

Immediate data (mask) $FB_{16} = 1111 \quad 1011_2$
A register $37_{16} = 0011 \quad 0111_2$
                          $0011 \quad 0\boxed{0}11$

$$\uparrow$$

Rent/own code is now zero

SELECTIVELY COMPLEMENTING BITS IN A FIELD.
If we had known that the previous value of the rent/own field was 1, we could have changed the bit status with a complement operation instead. The result would be identical to selectively clearing the field.

□ **EXAMPLE**

A register   37

Instruction   XRI 04

Result of exclusive ORing   This bit will be complemented

$$\downarrow$$

Immediate data (mask) $04_{16} = 0000 \quad 0100_2$
A register $37_{16} = 0011 \quad 0111_2$
                          $1111 \quad 0\boxed{0}11$

$$\uparrow$$

Rent/own status has been complemented

SELECTIVELY SETTING BITS IN A FIELD.
The family size has increased to seven members. The contents of field 1 must be updated to the new number.

□ **EXAMPLE**

A register   37

Instruction   ORI 38

Result of ORing   These bits will be set

$$\downarrow\downarrow \quad\; \downarrow$$

Immediate data (mask) $38_{16} = 0011 \quad 1000_2$
A register $37_{16} = 0011 \quad 0111_2$

New family size is 7 → $\boxed{0011 \quad 1}111$

$$\uparrow\uparrow\uparrow$$

These bits are unaltered

Boolean Operations Review

1. What can be said about the carry status bit state at the completion of any Boolean instruction?

2. Explain why bit 4 of the status register remains set after instruction execution in the example for the ANA command.

3. What would be the result of an ORI instruction if the accumulator contained 72_{16} and the immediate data were 83_{16}?

4. List three applications for the XRA instruction. Can the XRI instruction be used for the same purposes?

5. Explain how masking can be used to read, set, clear, or complement selected bits in a memory word.

INTRODUCTION TO BCD ARITHMETIC

The 8080A will support BCD as well as binary arithmetic. This section presents the general concepts and explains the key instruction used for the operation. Chapter 7 completes the explanation for using the microprocessor for BCD addition and subtraction.

The problem of adding BCD numbers may not be immediately obvious. Let us examine the situation by looking at some specific cases. In some situations BCD addition is the same as binary addition.

□ **EXAMPLE 1.** Add the BCD quantities 62 and 13.

Decimal Addition	BCD Equivalent	Binary Addition
62_{10}	→	0110 0010
$+13_{10}$	→	0001 0011
75_{10}	→	0111 0101 = 75 BCD

A problem arises, however, when the sum of the least-significant BCD digit (LSD) is greater than 9.

□ **EXAMPLE 2.** Add the BCD quantities 28 and 36.

Decimal Addition	BCD Equivalent	Binary Addition
28_{10}	→	0010 1000
+ 36_{10}	→	0011 0110
64_{10}	?	0101 1110

The result of the binary addition has no BCD equivalent. This problem can be resolved, however, by use of an algorithm.

BCD ADDITION ALGORITHM

STEP 1. Add the numbers by use of binary arithmetic.

STEP 2. If the least-significant digit is less than 9, (1001_2), the BCD equivalent of the binary sum is the answer; otherwise, go to Step 3.

STEP 3. Add 6 to the LSD, thus generating a carry of 1 into the most-significant digit position. The binary sum is now the BCD equivalent.

Our examples above illustrated both possibilities of the algorithm. Example 1 has an LSD of 5, which is less than 9. The BCD code for the binary sum is the answer. Example 2 requires that we go to algorithm Step 3. We will continue that example by following the procedure of the algorithm as Step 3.

□ **EXAMPLE 2. (cont.)**

Decimal Addition	Binary Addition
28_{10}	0010 1000
+ 36_{10}	0011 0110
64_{10}	[1] Carry
	0101 [1 1 1 0] Greater than 9,
	+ 0110 so add 6
	0110 0100 = 64 BCD

Now the sum does represent the proper BCD result. The following instruction implements this BCD addition algorithm.

Decimal Adjust Accumulator

The decimal adjust accumulator command is used only for BCD arithmetic. It is unique in that this is the only instruction in the 8080A repertoire that is affected by the condition of the auxiliary carry bit. The method used to implement the BCD addition

algorithm is as follows. The accumulator is adjusted to form a proper two-digit BCD sum by

1. Testing the least-significant BCD digit in the accumulator.
   a. If the LSD is greater than 9 or if A_C is set, the accumulator is incremented by 6. If this addition generates a carry from bit position 3, the auxiliary carry bit is set; otherwise, it is reset.
   b. If the LSD is less than or equal to 9 and A_C is 0, there is no incrementing.

2. Testing the most significant digit.
   a. If the MSD is now greater than 9 or if the carry bit is set, the MSD of the accumulator is incremented by 6. If a carry is generated from bit position 7, the carry status is set; otherwise, it is reset.
   b. If the MSD is less than or equal to 9 and the carry bit is 0, there is no incrementing.

3. The proper sum is now held in the accumulator.

Before studying the instruction itself, we will trace the instruction execution through examples.

□ **EXAMPLE 3.** Add 19_{10} to 62_{10}.

Decimal Addition   Binary Addition

		No [0] carry	No [0] carry
62_{10}		0110	0010_2
+19_{10}		0001	1001_2
81_{10}		0111	1011_2

STEP 1a. $A_C = 0$ but LSD > 9. Add 6 to LSD.

No [0] carry   [1] Carry

0111 1011_2
       0110
1000 0001_2 = 81 BCD

STEP 2b. C = 0 and MSD ≤ 9. No incrementing.

Final result: A = 81, A_C = 1, C = 0 (carry status)

□ **EXAMPLE 4.** Add 19_{10} to 82_{10}.

Decimal Addition   Binary Addition

		No [0] carry	No [0] carry
82_{10}		1000	0010_2
+19_{10}		0001	1001_2
101_{10}		1001	1011_2

STEP 1a. LSD > 9. Add 6 to LSD.

No
$\boxed{0}$ carry $\boxed{1}$ Carry

$$
\begin{array}{cc}
1\,0\,0\,1 & 1\,0\,1\,1_2 \\
 & 0\,1\,1\,0 \\
\hline
1\,0\,1\,0 & 0\,0\,0\,1_2
\end{array}
$$

STEP 2a. MSD > 9. Add 6 to MSD.

$\boxed{1}$ Carry

$$
\begin{array}{cc}
1\,0\,1\,0 & 0\,0\,0\,1_2 \\
0\,1\,1\,0 & \\
\hline
0\,0\,0\,0 & 0\,0\,0\,1_2
\end{array}
$$

Final result: $A = 01$. $A_C = 1$. $C = 1$ (carry status)

The 9-bit sum is too large for the 8-bit register. The set carry status bit is an indication of this error. When the numbers are longer than two BCD digits, multibyte arithmetic is required, as the next example shows.

MULTIBYTE BCD ADDITION PROCEDURES

A series of 8080A instructions can be used for multibyte BCD arithmetic. (The specifics of the technique are provided in Chap. 7.) Repeated use of the decimal adjust accumulator provides the microprocessor with the capacity to handle the longer numbers.

☐ **EXAMPLE 5.** Add 5625_{10} to 1498_{10}.

Decimal Addition

$$
\begin{array}{r}
5625_{10} \\
+1498_{10} \\
\hline
7123_{10}
\end{array}
$$

STEP 1. Clear the carry bit.

STEP 2. Add the two lower-order digits.

$\boxed{0}$ $\boxed{0}$

$$
\begin{array}{rcc}
25 \rightarrow & 0\,0\,1\,0 & 0\,1\,0\,1 \\
+98 \rightarrow & 1\,0\,0\,1 & 1\,0\,0\,0 \\
\hline
& 1\,0\,0\,1 & 1\,1\,0\,1
\end{array}
$$

Status bits
$C = 0$
$A_C = 0$

STEP 3. Decimal adjust.

STEP 3a. The LSD is greater than 9, so increment by 6.

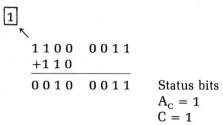

$\boxed{0}$ $\boxed{1}$

$$
\begin{array}{cc}
1\,0\,1\,1 & 1\,1\,0\,1 \\
 & +1\,1\,0 \\
\hline
1\,1\,0\,0 & 0\,0\,1\,1
\end{array}
$$

Status bits
$C = 0$
$A_C = 0$

STEP 3b. The MSD is greater than 9, so increment by 6.

$\boxed{1}$

$$
\begin{array}{cc}
1\,1\,0\,0 & 0\,0\,1\,1 \\
+1\,1\,0 & \\
\hline
0\,0\,1\,0 & 0\,0\,1\,1
\end{array}
$$

Status bits
$A_C = 1$
$C = 1$

Result = 23

STEP 4. Store lower-order digits.

STEP 5. Add two higher-order digits with the carry status.

$\boxed{0}$ $\boxed{0}$

$$
\begin{array}{rcc}
56 \rightarrow & 0\,1\,0\,1 & 0\,1\,1\,0 \\
14 \rightarrow & 0\,0\,0\,1 & 0\,1\,0\,0 \\
\text{Carry} \rightarrow & & +1 \\
\hline
& 0\,1\,1\,0 & 1\,0\,1\,1
\end{array}
$$

Status bits
$A_C = 0$
$C = 0$

STEP 6. Decimal adjust.

STEP 6a. The LSD is greater than 9, so increment

$\boxed{0}$ $\boxed{1}$

$$
\begin{array}{cc}
0\,1\,1\,1 & 1\,0\,1\,1 \\
 & +1\,1\,0 \\
\hline
0\,1\,1\,1 & 0\,0\,0\,1
\end{array}
$$

STEP 6b. The MSD is equal to or less than 9, so do not increment.
Result: $A = 71$ $A_C = 1$ $C = 0$

STEP 7. Store higher-order digits.

Final sum   ⌊71⌋ ⌊23⌋

High-order digits   Low-order digits

See Chap. 7 for the program listing specific instructions for this multibyte BCD addition. Next we will look at the instruction format.

Operation code	27
Mnemonic	DAA

Addressing mode	none	
Status bits affected	zero, sign, parity, carry, auxiliary carry	
Clock periods	4	
Execution time	2.0 µs	
Format		bit number

```
                        7 6 5 4   3 2 1 0
Memory cell   m    | 0 0 1 0   0 1 1 1 |
```

□ EXAMPLE

Before execution		After execution	
Program counter	0230	Program counter	0231
A register	3C	A register	42
Status register	02	Status register	16
Memory 0230	27	Memory 0230	27

BCD Arithmetic Review

1. List the steps in the BCD addition algorithm.

2. When does binary addition produce a correct BCD result?

3. Explain how the decimal adjust accumulator implements the algorithm.

4. What is the meaning of the carry bit condition at the completion of Example 4?

5. How is the carry bit generated in Step 3 of Example 5 used? What error would have resulted had that carry been ignored?

COMPARE INSTRUCTIONS

There are many occasions when the relative magnitudes of two numbers are important. Knowing if two numbers are equal, or which is the larger, allows the processor to make decisions based on the relationships between variables. Two instructions in the 8080A compare quantities and set the status bits to indicate the outcome of that comparison.

Compare Register or Memory with Accumulator

The byte in the specified register or memory cell is compared with the accumulator value. (Actually an internal subtraction is performed, but the final contents of the accumulator are the same as the initial values.) The results control the zero and carry status bits as shown in Table 6-5. The use of parentheses in Table 6-5 means that it is the *contents* of that register or cell which are being compared. As Table 6-5 shows for unequal values, the interpretation of the status bits depends on whether the accumulator and the register (or memory cell) being compared have the same sign. As we have seen before, the HL register pair contains the memory address.

Operation Code	Mnemonic
B8	CMP B
B9	CMP C
BA	CMP D
BB	CMP E
BC	CMP H
BD	CMP L
BE	CMP M
BF	CMP A

Addressing mode	register	
Status bits affected	carry, zero, sign, parity, auxiliary carry	
Clock periods	4 (7 for memory reference)	
Execution time	2.0 µs (3.5 µs for memory reference)	
Format		bit number

```
                        7 6 5 4   3 2 1 0
Memory cell   m    | 1 0 1 1   1 r r r |
```

Table 6-5
Compare Status Bit Conditions

Condition	Status Bits		Meaning*
	Zero	Carry	
Equality	1	X	(A) = (Register)
Accumulator and register have the same sign	0 0	1 0	(A) < (Register) (A) > (Register)
Accumulator and register have opposite signs	0 0	1 0	(A) > (Register) (A) < (Register)

X is a don't care setting.
*Parentheses refer to the contents of the register or memory cell.

rrr	Register
000	B
001	C
010	D
011	E
100	H
101	L
110	memory
111	A

Addressing mode	immediate
Status bits affected	carry, zero, sign, parity, auxiliary carry
Clock periods	7
Execution time	3.5 μs
Format	

bit number

7 6 5 4   3 2 1 0

Memory cell   m | 1 1 1 1   1 1 1 0 |

m + 1 | immediate data byte |

□ EXAMPLE

Before execution		After execution	
Program counter	0245	Program counter	0245
A register	38	A register	38
C register	72	C register	72
Status register	06	Status register	13
Memory 0245	B9	Memory 0245	B9

The zero status bit is reset and the carry is set. The quantities are unequal and have the same sign. From Table 6-5 we see that the set carry bit indicates that the accumulator value is less than that of the C register.

Compare Immediate

The immediate data byte is compared with the contents of the accumulator (by means of an internal subtraction). The final value in the A register is the same as the initial value. If the quantities are equal, the zero status bit is set. If they are not equal, the carry status bit indicates the larger by its setting. The meaning of the carry bit depends on whether the accumulator and the immediate data have the same or opposite signs as shown in Table 6-6.

Operation code	FE
Mnemonic	CPI

□ EXAMPLE

Before execution		After execution	
Program counter	0083	Program counter	0085
A register	73	A register	73
Status register	02	Status register	12
Memory 0083	FE	Memory 0083	FE
0084	5A	0084	5A

The quantities are unequal, so the zero bit is cleared. The A register value is the larger, as indicated by a resetting of the carry bit. Note that the auxiliary carry and parity bits reflect the value of the difference resulting from the internal subtraction; these bits should be ignored.

Compare Review

1. Explain how the compare instructions permit the programmer to decide the relative magnitudes of numbers in the accumulator and a memory cell.

2. What does the resetting of the zero bit, after the comparison, mean?

Table 6-6
Compare Immediate Status Bit Conditions

Condition	Status Bits		Meaning*
	Zero	**Carry**	
Equality	1	X	(A) = (data byte)
Accumulator and data byte have the same sign	0	1	(A) < (data byte)
	0	0	(A) > (data byte)
Accumulator and data byte have opposite signs	0	1	(A) > (data byte)
	0	0	(A) < (data byte)

X is a don't care setting.
*Parentheses refer to the contents of the register or memory cell.

3. What other information is needed, in addition to the zero and carry bit settings, to determine which quantity is greater after a compare instruction is examined?

4. Discuss the meaning of the parity and the auxiliary carry conditions following a compare instruction.

8080A MODEL DIFFERENCES

The manufacturers of 8080A microprocessors have not all provided identical arithmetic and logical instruction execution; these differences are slight, but they may lead to misunderstandings if you are using a second-source processor.

The NEC 8080A differs in three ways from the description given earlier in this chapter. First, the carry bit is not cleared on Boolean instructions; thus its condition should be ignored after one of the logical operations. Second, the auxiliary carry bit is not affected by logical instructions or the increment and decrement commands. Finally, there is another status bit provided by the microprocessor. An auxiliary borrow bit, which corresponds in operation to the auxiliary carry, is affected by subtraction. The auxiliary borrow occupies bit position 5 of the status register.

The AMD 8080A changes the execution of Boolean instructions in a minor way. In this microprocessor the auxiliary carry is always reset following those instructions.

Although these variations may seem minor, they

Table 6-7
Arithmetic and Logical Instructions

Mnemonic	Op Code	Bytes	Execution Time, µs	Status*				
				C	AC	Z	S	P
ACI	CE	2	3.5	X	X	X	X	X
ADC	88, 89, 8A, 8B, 8C, 8D, 8E, 8F	1	2.0/3.5	X	X	X	X	X
ADD	80, 81, 82, 83, 84, 85, 86, 87	1	2.0/3.5	X	X	X	X	X
ADI	C6	2	3.5	X	X	X	X	X
ANA	A0, A1, A2, A3, A4, A5, A6, A7	1	2.0/3.5	0	X	X	X	X
ANI	E6	2	3.5	0	X	X	X	X
CMA	2F	1	2.0					
CMC	3F	1	2.0	X				
CMP	B8, B9, BA, BB, BC, BD, BE, BF	1	2.0/3.5	X	X	X	X	X
CPI	FE	2	3.5	X	X	X	X	X
DAA	27	1	2.0	X	X	X	X	X
DAD	09, 19, 29, 39	1	5.0	X				
DCR	05, 0D, 15, 1D, 25, 2D, 35, 3D	1	2.5/5		X	X	X	X
DCX	0B, 1B, 2B, 3B	1	2.5					
INR	04, 0C, 14, 1C, 24, 2C, 34, 3C	1	2.5/5		X	X	X	X
INX	03, 13, 23, 33	1	2.5					
ORA	B0, B1, B2, B3, B4, B5, B6, B7	1	2.0/3.5	0	X	X	X	X
ORI	F6	2	3.5	0	0	X	X	X
SBB	98, 99, 9A, 9B, 9C, 9D, 9E, 9F	1	2.0/3.5	X	X	X	X	X
SBI	DE	2	3.5	X	X	X	X	X
STC	37	1	2.0	1				
SUB	90, 91, 92, 93, 94, 95, 96, 97	1	2.0/3.5	X	X	X	X	X
SUI	D6	2	3.5	X	X	X	X	X
XRA	A8, A9, AA, AB, AC, AD, AE, AF	1	2.0/3.5	0	X	X	X	X
XRI	EE	2	3.5	0	0	X	X	X

*Code: X indicates that bit is changed; 1 indicates that bit is always set; 0 indicates that bit is always cleared.

are significant enough to cause an arithmetic sequence to produce different results in two MPU models if the programmer carelessly ignores them. Proper programming will avoid this problem and eliminate the possibility of a bug which is model-dependent. Software that can be transferred from one model processor to another is called *transportable.* Programs that are transportable often save money because they can be run on more than a single-model MPU.

CHAPTER SUMMARY

1. The instructions discussed in this chapter are listed in Table 6-7. Operation code, length, execution time, and effect on the status bits are given for each.

2. The status register bits reflect the results calculated in arithmetic and logical operations. The carry bit indicates a carry from the MSB in addition or a borrow from that bit in subtraction. The auxiliary carry is set whenever there is a carry from bit position 3. The sign bit of the accumulator and the sign status bit are always equal. The zero condition bit is set to 1 if the accumulator contains a 0 value. The parity bit is cleared for odd parity and is set for even.

3. The carry bit can be set or complemented directly by microprocessor instructions.

4. Memory cells and registers can be incremented or decremented on command. Register pairs can also be incremented or decremented as 16-bit values.

5. A 1's complement can be introduced by means of the complement accumulator instruction.

6. Addition and subtraction instructions perform the basic arithmetic operations in the 8080A. More complex arithmetic requires instruction sequences.

7. The Boolean operations of AND, OR, and exclusive OR are provided in the logical instructions group.

8. Use of the decimal adjust accumulator instruction, in a routine, implements the BCD addition algorithm.

9. The relative magnitude of the accumulator value and that of a register or a memory cell can be determined by use of the compare instructions. The outcome can be found from the settings of the zero and carry bits.

10. Different manufacturers of 8080A microprocessors may change the instruction operations slightly. Always consult the repertoire section of the specification sheet when you begin to use a new model MPU to find these variations.

KEY TERMS AND CONCEPTS

Status register	Increment	Fields
Carry (C) bit	Decrement	Selective read
Auxiliary carry (A_C) bit	Complement accumulator	Selective set
Sign (S) bit	Addition	Selective complement
Zero (Z) bit	Subtraction	Selective clear
Parity (P) bit	Boolean (logical) instruction	BCD arithmetic
Setting and complementing the carry bit	Masking	Multibyte BCD addition
		Compare

6-1 The accumulator is set to 56_{16} and the status register to 17_{16}. Write a single instruction which will clear the carry bit without altering the accumulator.

6-2 Data is stored in memory cells $21FF_{16}$ and 2200_{16} in packed form. Supply the missing instructions in the following program to clear the field in bits 2 and 3 of each word.

2010	01 ⎤	Load register pair
2011	00 ⎬	BC with address
2012	22 ⎦	
2013	0A	Move first data word to A
2014	[Instruction 1]	Clear the field
2015	02	Store new data word
2016	[Instruction 2]	Decrement address
2017	0A	Move second data word to A
2018	[Instruction 3]	Clear the field
2019	02	Store new data word

6-3 The accumulator is set to $F9_{16}$ and the L register to 27_{16}. Write an instruction to add the two registers. What are the final values in the A, L, and status registers?

6-4 Assume that the accumulator contains 27_{16}. Subtract 40_{16} from that register with one instruction. What is the final accumulator and status register configuration?

6-5 Initial register and memory contents are:

Program counter	1412
Registers	A 46
	B 20
	C B1
	D 02
	E 14
Status register	02

Memory				
	1412	81	1415	32
	1413	C6	1416	12
	1414	02	1417	14
			1418	76

What will the values be after the program has run to completion?

6-6 What changes are produced in these registers and memory cells after the program given below halts?

Program counter	2007
Registers	A 00
	H F0
	L 47
Status register	47

Memory	2007	DE
	2008	00
	2009	29
	2010	00
	2011	76

6-7 Write a two-instruction sequence which will result in the 1's complement of memory location 2000_{16} being placed in the accumulator. The accumulator and carry status have starting values of 0.

6-8 When the microcomputer was first started, the status register contents were obtained and stored in memory cell $701A_{16}$. The latest value of the status register is stored at $02FB_{16}$. Write an instruction sequence which will show if the parity status bit differs between the two stored values.

6-9 What will the changes in the register contents below be after the program halts?

Program counter	1130
Registers	A 29
	C 1F
	L 39

Memory	1130	85
	1131	27
	1132	00
	1133	76
	1134	80

6-10 What are the final values in the registers below when the computer halts after executing the program?

Registers

Program counter ⟨1200⟩

Registers   A   ⟨F0⟩

           B   ⟨20⟩

           C   ⟨14⟩

           D   ⟨6F⟩

E   ⟨BA⟩

H   ⟨0E⟩

L   ⟨99⟩

Status register   ⟨02⟩

Memory		Memory	
1200	99	1206	87
1201	00	1207	B9
1202	C3	1208	76
1203	07	1209	C3
1204	12	120A	00
1205	83	120B	12

EXPERIMENT 6 _____

PURPOSE: To investigate arithmetic and logical instructions.

PROCEDURE: A series of programs will be executed by using data stored in cells 0050_{16} and 0051_{16}. The answer will always be found in 0052_{16}.

STEP 1. Enter the addition program and data set 1.

Addition Program

Instruction	Address	Machine Code
LDA 0050	0000	3A
	0001	50
	0002	*00*
STC	0003	37
LXI H, 0051	0004	21
	0005	51
	0006	*00*
ADD M	0007	86
INR L	0008	2C
MOV M,A	0009	77
HLT	000A	76

Data Set	0050	0051
1	37	46
2	2E	A3
3	89	BC

STEP 2. After execution, record the sum.

STEP 3. Repeat the addition with data sets 2 and 3. Record the results after each run.

STEP 4. Explain your results.

STEP 5. Change the instruction in address 0007_{16} to an add with carry:

ADC M   8E

Repeat the experiment with the following data:

Data Set	0050	0051
4	37	46
5	74	62

How does the sum of data set 4 compare with that of data set 1?

STEP 6. Change location 0007_{16} to a subtract instruction.

SUB M   96

Use the following data to run your program:

Data Set	0050	0051
6	7D	66
7	31	5B
8	FC	89

Explain the results.

STEP 7. Change the instruction in location 0007_{16} to subtract with borrow.

SBB M   9E

Use this data to run the program:

Data Set	0050	0051
9	7D	66
10	D2	C8

STEP 8. Change the instruction in 0007_{16} to AND:

ANA M   A6

Using the data shown, prove that the results you get from the program are correct.

Data Set	0050	0051
11	AA	96
12	21	E7
13	A5	5A

STEP 9. Repeat Step 8 for an OR instruction.

ORA M   B6

Use this data:

Data Set	0050	0051
14	73	4C
15	F7	30

STEP 10. Repeat Step 8 for an exclusive OR instruction.

XRA M   AE

Data Set	0050	0051
16	A5	5A
17	73	4C
18	17	17

7
JUMPS

Most of the processor decision-making capability involves the use of instructions which can choose between two alternatives. In a program, those alternatives will be characterized by two instruction strings. By using jump commands, the execution of the program can be diverted from the next successive address to a completely different sequence. This chapter presents the unconditional and conditional jump instructions of the 8080A and demonstrates how the instructions allow the processor to make decisions.

CHAPTER OBJECTIVES

Upon completion of this chapter, you should be able to:

1. Distinguish between conditional and unconditional jumps.
2. Describe the operation of all 8080A jump instructions.
3. Explain how conditional jumps are used to implement multibyte addition and subtraction algorithms.
4. Write multibyte BCD addition or subtraction routines for the 8080A.

UNCONDITIONAL AND CONDITIONAL JUMPS

The purpose of a jump instruction is to alter the normal sequence of operations in the processor. Rather than allowing the program counter to increment in a normal manner, a jump forces the counter to a particular value. Once that value has been entered in the program counter, the next instruction will be obtained from that address.

An *unconditional jump* always causes the program counter value to change. The JMP and PCHL instructions described in Chap. 5 were examples of unconditional jumps. In contrast, the *conditional jump* instruction transfers control only when a specified condition is true. If false, the jump is not taken; instead, the next sequential instruction is executed. Thus a conditional jump is like a decision block on a flowchart. (Examples of such conditions include a zero sum after addition or odd parity resulting from a Boolean instruction.) Figure 7-1 depicts the operation of the two types of jumps.

Even though the conditional jump instructions can sense the value of a status condition, no jump instruction can alter the status register. In the examples that follow, you will see some of the techniques used to properly set the status bits prior to an executing conditional jump instruction.

Unconditional and Conditional Jumps Review

1. Define the term "conditional jump."

2. Under what conditions is a conditional jump the same as an unconditional jump? When would a conditional jump be the same as a no operation instruction?

3. How does the setting of the status bits affect the conditional jump decision?

4. Which status bits can be changed by unconditional jumps?

Review of Unconditional Jump Instructions

The two instructions previously covered are briefly listed below for completeness. Refer to the earlier chapter for examples and more details.

JUMP. Unconditional transfer to a memory address.

Operation code	C3
Mnemonic	JMP
Addressing mode	direct
Effect on status bits	none
Clock periods	10
Execution time	5 µs

Format

		bit number
		7 6 5 4 3 2 1 0
Memory cell	m	1 1 0 0 0 0 1 1
	m + 1	low address byte
	m + 2	high address byte

LOAD PROGRAM COUNTER. Load the program counter with the value in the HL register pair. The H register contains the high-order address byte.

Operation code	E9
Mnemonic	PCHL
Addressing mode	none
Effect on status bits	none
Clock periods	5
Execution time	2.5 µs

Format

		bit number
		7 6 5 4 3 2 1 0
Memory cell	m	1 1 1 0 1 0 0 1

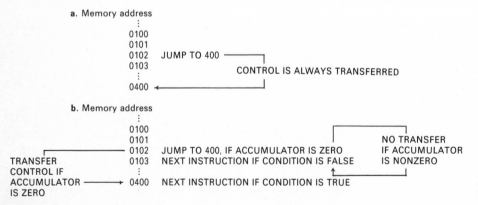

Figure 7-1. Jumps (*a*) Unconditional (*b*) Conditional.

CONDITIONAL JUMP INSTRUCTIONS

Each of the instructions that follow will decide the next address based on the setting of a status bit. The carry, parity, zero, or sign bit can be used as the deciding factor. (The auxiliary carry status is excluded from the conditions that can be tested.)

Jump if Carry

If the carry bit is set, the immediate address following the op code is placed into the program counter. The program sequence continues from that point. Should the carry bit be reset, however, this instruction is essentially a no operation. The next sequential instruction will be selected in the latter case.

Operation code	DA
Mnemonic	JC
Addressing mode	direct
Status bits affected	none
Clock periods	10
Execution time	5 μs
Format	

bit number
7 6 5 4   3 2 1 0

Memory cell	m	1 1 0 1 1 0 1 0
	m + 1	low address byte
	m + 2	high address byte

□ **EXAMPLE**

Before execution		After execution	
Program counter	0420	Program counter	0501
Status register	83	Status register	83
Memory	0420 DA	Memory	0402 DA
	0421 01		0421 01
	0422 05		0422 05

The carry status (bit 0) is set, so the jump condition is true. The program counter is set equal to the immediate address contained in memory cells 0421_{16} and 0422_{16}. In this example the next address will be 0501_{16}.

Jump if No Carry

This instruction performs a comparison which is the converse of the previous one. If the carry bit is 0, the jump is taken. Otherwise, the next instruction in the normal order will be executed.

Operation code	D2
Mnemonic	JNC
Addressing mode	direct
Status bits affected	none
Clock periods	10
Execution time	5 μs
Format	

bit number
7 6 5 4   3 2 1 0

Memory cell	m	1 1 0 0 0 0 1 0
	m + 1	low address byte
	m + 2	high address byte

□ **EXAMPLE**

Before execution		After execution	
Program counter	1040	Program counter	1043
Status register	03	Status register	03
Memory	1040 D2	Memory	1040 D2
	1041 11		1041 11
	1042 66		1042 66

The status register shows that the carry bit is set, so the jump is not taken. The program counter is set to fetch the next instruction of the original sequence.

Jump if Zero

The zero status bit controls the decision for this jump. If the bit is set (indicating that the accumulator contains a 0), the jump is selected.

Operation code	CA
Mnemonic	JZ
Addressing mode	direct
Status bits affected	none
Clock periods	10
Execution time	5 μs
Format	

bit number
7 6 5 4   3 2 1 0

Memory cell	m	1 1 0 0 1 0 1 0
	m + 1	low address byte
	m + 2	high address byte

Before execution	After execution
Program counter 0560	Program counter 0700
Status register 47	Status register 47
Memory 0560 CA	Memory 0560 CA
0561 00	0561 00
0562 07	0562 07

Bit 6 in the status register is set, so the A register value is 0. The jump is activated.

Jump if Not Zero

If the zero status bit is 0 (meaning that the A register is nonzero), the next instruction will be executed at the direct address location. Should the status bit be set, the jump is ignored.

Operation code	C2
Mnemonic	JNZ
Addressing mode	direct
Status bits affected	none
Clock periods	10
Execution time	5 μs
Format	

bit number

7 6 5 4   3 2 1 0

Memory cell	m	1 1 0 0 0 0 1 0
	m + 1	low address byte
	m + 2	high address byte

□ EXAMPLE

Before execution	After execution
Program counter 0250	Program counter 0253
Status register 42	Status register 42
Memory 0250 C2	Memory 0250 C2
0251 08	0251 08
0252 06	0252 06

The zero condition bit is set, so there is no jump.

Jump if Minus

If the accumulator value is negative, the processor will take the jump. The sign bit being set indicates this condition. If the sign bit is clear, there will be no jump.

Operation code	FA
Mnemonic	JM
Addressing mode	direct
Clock periods	10
Execution time	5 μs
Format	

bit number

7 6 5 4   3 2 1 0

Memory cell	m	1 1 1 1 1 0 1 0
	m + 1	low address byte
	m + 2	high address byte

□ EXAMPLE

Before execution	After execution
Program counter 0110	Program counter 0630
Status register 83	Status register 83
Memory 1010 FA	Memory 1010 FA
1011 30	1011 30
1012 06	1012 06

The number in the A register is negative, so the jump address is placed into the program counter.

So far in this discussion of the conditional jumps, we have not concerned ourselves with how the status bits become set. Before any of these tests are made, a deliberate effort is required to set the status bits to reflect the present value in the accumulator. The arithmetic and logical instructions cause the status bits to change, so generally an instruction from that group must precede a comparison by means of a conditional jump. Two examples which will cause the sign bit to be changed in preparation for a jump on minus condition are presented below.

□ **EXAMPLE 1.** Checking the results of addition.

Address	Machine Code	Comments
1000	86	Add memory contents to A.
1001	FA	Jump to 0200_{16} if the sign bit is set.
1002	00	
1003	02	

□ **EXAMPLE 2.** Testing a memory cell for a negative number.

Address	Machine Code	Comments
0500	7E	Move the memory contents to A.
0501	E6	AND immediate, to mask only sign bit into A. (Set all status bits except carry.)
0502	80	
0503	FA	Jump to 0200_{16} if the sign bit is set.
0504	00	
0505	02	

An alternate, equally effective sequence for the conditional jump in Example 2 would be:

0503	C2	Jump if A is not zero. (If the sign bit were set by the masking, the register would contain a nonzero quantity.)
0504	00	
0505	02	

Jump if Plus

With this instruction we can test for a positive result in the accumulator. The processor will jump only if the sign status bit is zero (positive).

Operation code	F2
Mnemonic	JP
Addressing mode	direct
Status bits affected	none
Clock periods	10
Execution time	5 μs

Format

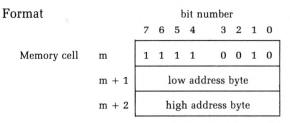

□ **EXAMPLE**

Before execution		After execution	
Program counter	0025	Program counter	0028
Status register	86	Status register	86
Memory 0025	F2	Memory 0025	F2
0026	80	0025	80
0027	06	0027	06

The sign is negative, so there will be no jump.

Jump if Parity Even

The parity status bit is used to decide the conditional jump selection. If the bit is 1, for even parity, the jump will happen. If the bit is 0 there is no jump.

Operation code	EA
Mnemonic	JPE
Addressing mode	direct
Status bits affected	none
Clock periods	10
Execution time	5 μs

Format

bit number

Memory cell	m	7 6 5 4 3 2 1 0
		1 1 1 0 1 0 1 0
	m + 1	low address byte
	m + 2	high address byte

□ **EXAMPLE**

Before execution		After execution	
Program counter	00E0	Program counter	0A10
Status register	07	Status register	07
Memory 00E0	EA	Memory 0050	EA
00E1	10	00E1	10
00E2	0A	00E2	0A

Because the parity is even (bit 2 is set), the jump occurs.

Jump if Parity Odd

On odd parity, that is, with the status bit zero, this instruction will cause a jump. If parity is even, there will be no jump.

Operation code	E2
Mnemonic	JPO
Addressing mode	direct
Status bits affected	none
Clock periods	10
Execution time	5 μs

Format

bit number

Memory cell	m	7 6 5 4 3 2 1 0
		1 1 1 0 0 0 1 0
	m + 1	low address byte
	m + 2	high address byte

□ **EXAMPLE**

Before execution		After execution	
Program counter	04B0	Program counter	14B3
Status register	87	Status register	87
Memory 04B0	E2	Memory 04B0	E2
04B1	00	04B1	00
04B2	0D	04B2	0D

No jump is executed because the parity status is set, thus indicating even parity.

Conditional Jump Instructions Review

1. If the condition is true, where is the new address (that is the address to jump to) found?

2. How can you be sure that the status register properly reflects the condition being tested? Give an example.

3. If you wanted to write a program that checks the result of a Boolean operation, which two instructions would you use to jump to address 0140_{16} if the answer were zero and to 0150_{16} if the answer had odd parity? Does it matter which test is performed first?

MULTIBYTE ADDITION

Earlier chapters have given examples of overflow caused by arithmetic operations that used too short a word length for the quantities included. This section will show how the conditional jumps, together with other instructions, can provide a multibyte addition capability. If the number length selected is 2 bytes, the operation is called *double-precision arithmetic;* 3 bytes is *triple-precision,* and so on. The method discussed here allows the arithmetic to be carried out to whatever level of precision is desired.

Multibyte Addition Algorithm

The technique for multibyte arithmetic is based on the algorithm below. Two indices, or subscripts, are used by the algorithm. One index, i, indicates the number of bytes of precision in the operation. (That index is set to 2 for double precision, for example.) The other index, j, is used to fetch data and to store results. The numbers to be added are designated x and y. Bytes are numbered by subscript, with byte 0 being least significant. The sum will replace the initial value for x.

MULTIBYTE ADDITION ALGORITHM

STEP 1. Clear the carry status bit.

STEP 2. Set index i to the number of bytes. Set the address into index j.

STEP 3. Add *with carry* byte x_j to byte y_j.

STEP 4. Store results in x_j.

STEP 5. Decrement index i, increment index j.

STEP 6. Is i = 0? If so, stop.

STEP 7. If not, go to Step 3.

We will use the algorithm for a triple-precision addition to show how it works.

□ **EXAMPLE.** Triple-precision addition. Use the algorithm for the problem below.

$$x = 28\ EB\ 9C_{16}$$
$$y = 79\ BA\ DF_{16}$$
$$sum = A2\ A6\ 7B_{16}$$

FIRST ITERATION

STEP 1. Clear the carry bit.

STEP 2. Set i to 3, j to 0.

STEP 3. Byte 0 addition with carry

Byte x_0	9C
Byte y_0	DF
Carry	0

[1] 7B
└ new carry

STEP 4. Store 7B in place of byte x_0.

STEP 5. i = 2, j = 1.

STEP 6. i is not zero.

STEP 7. Go to Step 3 (second iteration).

SECOND ITERATION

STEP 3. Byte 1 addition with carry.

Byte x_1	EB
Byte y_1	BA
Carry	1

[1] A6
└ new carry

STEP 4. Store A6 in place of byte x_1.

STEP 5. i = 1, j = 2.

LABEL	ADDRESS	CONTENTS	NOTES
NUMBX	0200	9C	BYTE x_0 ⟵
	0201	EB	BYTE x_1 ⟵ LOCATION OF SUM AFTER EXECUTING THE PROGRAM
	0202	28	BYTE x_2 ⟵
	⋮		
NUMBY	0210	DF	BYTE y_0
	0211	BA	BYTE y_1
	0212	79	BYTE y_2

Figure 7-2. Memory Map for Multibyte Addition.

STEP 6. i is not zero.

STEP 7. Go to Step 3 (third iteration).

THIRD ITERATION _____

STEP 3. Byte 2 addition with carry.

$$
\begin{array}{rl}
\text{Byte } x_2 & 28 \\
\text{Byte } y_2 & 79 \\
\text{Carry} & 1 \\
\hline
\boxed{0}\,& \!\!\overline{A2} \\
\end{array}
$$
└─new carry

STEP 4. Store A2 in place of byte x_2.

STEP 5. i = 0, j = 3.

STEP 6. i does equal zero, so stop.

The sum that was generated in this example is A2 A6 7B$_{16}$, which is the correct answer. The sum has replaced the bytes of x.

Multibyte Addition Routine

Next we will consider a program that performs the steps of the multibyte addition algorithm. The C register is used as index i; it must be set to the number of bytes desired for the final sum. The DE and HL register pairs operate as the j index. The numbers x and y are stored from the low-order byte to the high-order byte starting at memory locations labeled NUMBX and NUMBY, respectively. The sum is stored, in the same order, starting at address NUMBX. Figure 7-2 is a memory map of the situation. A flowchart of the program is shown in Fig. 7-3.

Multibyte Addition Review

1. Define the term "double-precision arithmetic."

2. Why must the add with carry instruction be used in Step 3 of the algorithm rather than just simple addition?

Multibyte Addition Routine

Label	Mnemonic	Operand	Address	Machine Code	Comments
	LXI D	NUMBX	0300	11	NUMBX address →
			0301	00	register pair DE
			0302	02	
	LXI H	NUMBY	0303	21	NUMBY address →
			0304	10	register pair HL
			0305	02	
	XRA	A	0306	AF	Clear carry (XOR A register with itself)
AGAIN	LDAX	D	0307	1A	Byte x_j → A
	ADC	M	0308	8E	Add byte y_j with carry (HL contains address)
	STAX	D	0309	12	Sum$_j$ → memory location x_j
	DCR	C	030A	0D	Decrement i
	JZ	STOP	030B	CA	If i = 0, jump
			030C	13	
			030D	03	
	INX	D	030E	13	Otherwise, increment address in DE in preparation for fetching next byte of x
	INX	H	030F	23	Increment address in HL in preparation for fetching next byte of y
	JMP	AGAIN	0310	C3	Go to next iteration
			0311	07	
			0312	03	
STOP	HLT		0313	76	Stop

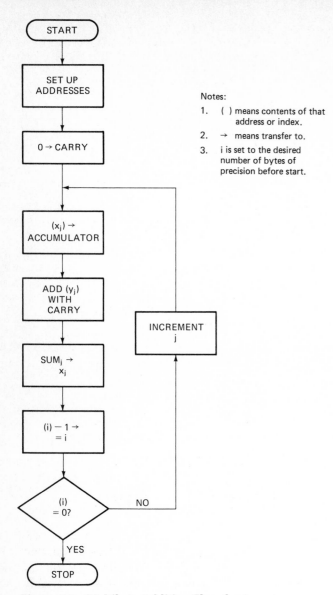

Figure 7-3. Multibyte Addition Flowchart.

Notes:
1. ( ) means contents of that address or index.
2. → means transfer to.
3. i is set to the desired number of bytes of precision before start.

3. What is the purpose of the two indices used in the algorithm?

4. Draw a memory map similar to Fig. 7-2 for the situation after the program has run to completion.

5. What is the purpose of the instructions at locations $030B_{16}$ and 0310_{16} in the program?

MULTIBYTE SUBTRACTION

There is, of course, a multibyte subtraction algorithm corresponding to one in the previous section for addition. Only a minor change to the addition algorithm is needed for this operation. At Step 3 we substitute a subtract with borrow operation for the addition. The algorithm and an example of its use are given below.

MULTIBYTE SUBTRACTION ALGORITHM

STEP 1. Clear carry bit.

STEP 2. Set index i to number of bytes. Set address into index j.

STEP 3. Subtract byte y_j from byte x_j *with borrow.*

STEP 4. Store results in x_j.

STEP 5. Decrement index i, increment index j.

STEP 6. Is i = 0? If so, stop.

STEP 7. If not, jump to Step 3.

☐ **EXAMPLE.** Double-precision subtraction.

$$x = 3807_{16}$$
$$y = \underline{15AD_{16}}$$
$$\text{difference} = 225A$$

FIRST ITERATION

STEP 1. Clear carry bit.

STEP 2. Set i = 2, j = 0.

STEP 3. Subtract byte y_0 from byte x_0 with borrow.

```
                               ┌──── new borrow
Byte x₀        │1│   07
Byte y₀            −AD
Borrow            −  0
                  ─────
                     5A
```

STEP 4. Store difference in x_0.

STEP 5. i = 1, j = 1.

STEP 6. i is not zero.

STEP 7. Go to Step 3 (second iteration).

SECOND ITERATION

STEP 3. Subtract byte y_1 from byte x_1 with borrow.

```
                               ┌──── new borrow
Byte x₁        │0│   38
Byte y₁            −15
Borrow            −  1
                  ─────
                     22
```

STEP 4. Store difference in x_1.

STEP 5. i = 0, j = 2.

STEP 6. i is equal to zero, so stop.

Multibyte Subtraction Routine

Label	Mnemonic	Operand	Address	Machine Code	Comments
	LXI D	NUMBX	0300	11	NUMBX address → DE
			0301	00	
			0302	02	
	LXI H	NUMBY	0303	21	NUMBY address → HL
			0304	10	
			0305	02	
	XRA	A	0306	AF	Clear carry
AGAIN	LDAX	D	0307	1A	Byte x_j → A
	SBB	M	0308	9E	Subtract byte y_j with borrow
	STAX	D	0309	12	Difference j → memory location x_j
	DCR	C	030A	0D	Decrement i
	JZ	STOP	030B	CA	If i = 0, jump to stop
			030C	13	
			030D	03	
	INX	D	030E	13	Otherwise, increment address in DE
	INX	H	030F	23	Increment address in HL
	JMP	AGAIN	0310	C3	Go to next iteration
			0311	07	
			0312	03	
STOP	HLT		0313	76	Stop

The final difference is $225A_{16}$. A program for this algorithm is listed below. All registers and memory allocations correspond to those of the addition program.

Multibyte Subtraction Review

1. Explain how a modification of the addition algorithm converts it to a multibyte subtraction algorithm.

2. Why is it necessary to clear the carry bit in Step 1 if we are doing subtraction?

3. Where is the difference stored?

MULTIBYTE BCD ADDITION

The algorithm for multibyte BCD addition was presented in Chap. 6. As you recall, the DAA instruction is the key element in providing that function in the 8080A. Because the algorithm was thoroughly discussed before, only the listing for the routine is given here. You may wish to review the earlier material to better understand the instruction sequence. It is identical to the previous multibyte addition program, except a DAA instruction is inserted after the add with carry.

Multibyte BCD Addition Routine

Label	Mnemonic	Operand	Address	Machine Code	Comments
	LXI D	NUMBX	0300	11	NUMBX address → DE
			0301	00	
			0302	02	
	LXI H	NUMBY	0303	21	NUMBY address → HL
			0304	10	
			0305	02	
	XRA	A	0306	AF	Clear carry

Multibye BCD Addition Routine (Continued)

Label	Mnemonic	Operand	Address	Machine Code	Comments
AGAIN	LDAX	D	0307	1A	Byte $x_j \to A$
	ADC	M	0308	8E	Add byte y_i with carry
	DAA		0309	27	Decimal adjust accumulator
	STAX	D	030A	12	$Sum_j \to$ memory location x_j
	DCR	C	030B	0D	Decrement j
	JZ	STOP	030C	CA	If j = 0, jump to stop
			030D	14	
			030E	03	
	INX	D	030F	13	Increment DE
	INX	H	0310	23	Increment HL
	JMP	AGAIN	0311	C3	Go to next iteration
			0312	07	
			0313	03	
	HLT		0314	76	Stop

MULTIBYTE BCD SUBTRACTION

The final algorithm in this chapter combines our previous knowledge of arithmetic and conditional jumps with a new concept to perform a BCD subtraction. We will be using the 9's complement of a decimal number, which corresponds to the 1's complement in binary. The reason for using the 9's complement is to properly adjust the auxiliary carry status bit setting prior to using the DAA instruction. (You may recall that the NEC 8080A had the extra subtraction status bit as was noted in Chap. 6. This bit is supplied just to eliminate the need for the 9's complement in BCD subtraction. Because most 8080A models do not offer this feature, we will demonstrate the use of the 9's complement technique.) The BCD subtraction algorithm is followed by an example.

BCD SUBTRACTION ALGORITHM

STEP 1. Set the carry bit. (This will simulate no borrow for the first iteration.)

STEP 2. Set the accumulator to 99 (the 9's complement of zero).

STEP 3. Add zero to the accumulator with carry. (The sum will be either 99_{16} or $9A_{16}$.)

STEP 4. Subtract the subtrahend byte from the accumulator.

STEP 5. Add the minuend byte to the accumulator.

STEP 6. Use DAA to obtain the BCD format and properly set the carry status (1 = no borrow, 0 = borrow). Store the difference byte.

STEP 7. If there are more bytes, go to Step 2; otherwise, stop.

☐ **EXAMPLE.** Multibyte BCD subtraction.

$$\begin{array}{lr} \text{Minuend} & 5829_{16} \\ \text{Subtrahend} & -3289_{16} \\ \hline & 2540_{16} \end{array}$$

FIRST ITERATION

STEP 1. Set carry = 1.

STEP 2. Set A to 99_{16}.

STEP 3. Add zero to A with carry.

$$\begin{array}{r} 99 \\ +0 \\ +1 \leftarrow \text{carry} \\ \hline 9A \end{array}$$

STEP 4. Subtract subtrahend least-significant byte.

Auxiliary carry

☐1 Carry ☐0

$$\begin{array}{rll} 9A_{16} = & 1001 & 1010 \\ -89_{16} = & +0111 & 0111 \quad \text{(2's complement)} \\ \hline 11_{16} = & 0001 & 0001 \end{array}$$

STEP 5. Add minuend least-significant byte.

☐0   ☐0

$$\begin{array}{rll} 11_{16} = & 0001 & 0001_2 \\ +29_{16} = & +0010 & 1001_2 \\ \hline 3A_{16} = & 0011 & 1010_2 \end{array}$$

STEP 6. Decimal adjust

☐0   ☐1

$$\begin{array}{rll} 3A_{16} = & 0011 & 1010 \\ +6_{16} = & + & 0110_2 \\ \hline 40_{16} = & 0100 & 0000_2 \end{array}$$

STEP 7. Store least-significant byte of difference. There are more bytes, so go to Step 2 (second iteration).

SECOND ITERATION

STEP 2. Set A to 99_{16}.

STEP 3. Add zero with carry.

$$
\begin{array}{l}
99 \\
+0 \\
\underline{+0} \leftarrow \text{Carry from Step 6 of first iteration} \\
99
\end{array}
$$

STEP 4. Subtract subtrahend most-significant byte.

$$
\begin{array}{rll}
\boxed{1} & \boxed{1} & \\
99_{16} = & 1001 & 1001_2 \\
-32_{16} = & \underline{+1100} & 1110_2 \text{ (2's complement)} \\
67_{16} = & 0110 & 0111_2
\end{array}
$$

STEP 5. Add minuend most-significant byte.

$$
\begin{array}{rll}
\boxed{0} & \boxed{0} & \\
67_{16} = & 0110 & 0111_2 \\
+58_{16} = & \underline{+0101} & 1000_2 \\
BF_{16} & 1011 & 1111_2
\end{array}
$$

STEP 6. Decimal adjust

$$
\begin{array}{rll}
\boxed{0} & \boxed{1} & \\
BF_{16} = & 1011 & 1111_2 \\
+6_{16} = & \underline{+} & 0110_2 \\
C5_{16} = & 1100 & 0101_2 \\
& \boxed{1} & \\
C5_{16} = & 1100 & 0101_2 \\
+60_{16} = & \underline{+0110} & 0000_2 \\
25_{16} = & 0010 & 0101_2
\end{array}
$$

STEP 7. Store most-significant byte of difference. There are no more bytes, so stop.

Multibyte BCD Subtraction Routine

The program below performs BCD subtraction on numbers of arbitrary length. The minuend is stored least significant byte first, starting at the address labeled MINU. The subtrahend is similarly stored, starting at address SBTRA. The bytes of the difference will replace the corresponding bytes in the minuend. Figure 7-4 is a memory map for this situation. A flowchart for the program is given in Fig. 7-5. Before program execution, the C register must be set equal to the number of bytes in the numbers.

Multibyte BCD Subtraction Routine

Label	Mnemonic	Operand	Address	Machine Code	Comments
	LXI D	MINU	0500	11	Minuend address → register pair DE
			0501	00	
			0502	02	
	LXI H	SBTRA	0503	21	Subtrahend address →
			0504	10	register pair HL
			0505	02	
	STC		0506	37	Set carry bit
AGAIN	MVI A	99	0507	3E	99_{16} → A (1's complement of zero)
			0508	99	
	ACI	0	0509	CE	
			050A	00	
	SUB	M	050B	96	Subtract subtrahend byte
	XCHG		050C	EB	Interchange contents of DE and HL
	ADD	M	050D	86	Add minuend byte
	DAA		050E	27	Decimal adjust accumulator
	MOV	M,A	050F	77	Store difference byte
	DCR	C	0510	0D	Decrement counter
	JZ	STOP	0511	CA	Jump if zero to stop
			0512	1A	
			0513	05	
	XCHG		0514	EB	Interchange contents of DE and HL
	INX	D	0515	13	Increment address of minuend byte
	INX	H	0516	23	Increment address of subtrahend byte
	JMP	AGAIN	0517	C3	Jump to next iteration
			0518	07	
			0519	05	
STOP	HLT		051A	76	Stop

LABEL	ADDRESS	CONTENTS	NOTES	
MINU	0200	29	MINUEND BYTE 0	← LOCATION OF DIFFERENCE AFTER
	0201	58	MINUEND BYTE 1	← EXECUTING THE PROGRAM
	⋮			
SBTRA	0210	89	SUBTRAHEND BYTE 0	
	0211	32	SUBTRAHEND BYTE 1	

Figure 7-4. Multibyte BCD Subtraction Memory Map.

A few comments on this routine will clarify some steps that may seem obscure. The routine relies on register addressing for the arithmetic instruction (addresses $050B_{16}$ and $050D_{16}$). Therefore, the operand address must be in the HL register pair prior to the arithmetic operation. The address of the subtrahend is initially in HL, but the exchange instruction at $050C_{16}$ swaps that for the address of the minuend. The second exchange, at 0514_{16}, restores the original order for the next iteration. The C register is used as the index for the size of the numbers. When it decrements to zero, all bytes have been processed.

Multibyte BCD Subtraction Review

1. Explain why the 9's complement must be used for BCD subtraction.

2. What is the purpose of Step 6 in the BCD subtraction algorithm?

3. Distinguish between the operations performed in iterations 1 and 2 for Step 6, Example 5.

4. How are the addresses specified by the memory map for the minuend, the subtrahend, and the difference initialized in the BCD subtraction routine?

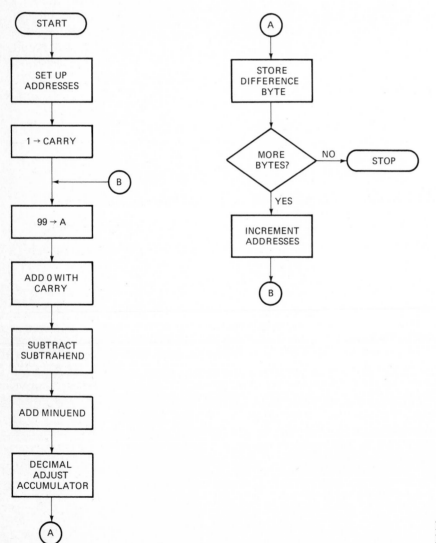

Figure 7-5. Multibyte BCD Subtraction Flowchart.

5. What error would occur if the flowchart for this routine were altered and the connector labeled "B" reentered the flow above the "1 → carry" process box?

CHAPTER REVIEW

1. Jump instructions transfer control to an instruction that is not in the normal sequence. Unconditional jumps always transfer control. Conditional jumps make the transfer only if the tested condition is true.

2. The conditional jumps can test the condition of the carry, zero, sign, or parity bits. Prior to executing the jump instruction, the status bits must be correctly set. Usually this action is the result of an arithmetic or a logical instruction.

3. Multiple-precision arithmetic is necessary to prevent overflow of large numbers. The multibyte addition algorithm relies on the add with carry instruction to produce sums of more than one byte. The algorithm permits the summing of any size numbers.

4. Multibyte subtraction is a simple modification of the addition algorithm. A subtract with bor-row operation replaces the add with carry in this process.

5. Multibyte BCD addition and subtraction are also possible in the 8080A. The decimal adjust accumulator instruction is the key to these functions. The subtraction algorithm depends on the 9's complement because the auxiliary carry status bit is not correctly set after subtraction.

6. A summary of all jump instructions is presented in Table 7-1.

Table 7-1
Jump Instruction: Summary*

Instruction	Machine Code	Number of Bytes	Execution Time, μs
JC	DA	3	5
JM	FA	3	5
JMP	C3	3	5
JNC	D2	3	5
JNZ	C2	3	5
JP	F2	3	5
JPE	EA	3	5
JPO	E2	3	5
JZ	CA	3	5
PCHL	E9	1	2.5

*Status bits not affected by jump instructions.

KEY TERMS AND CONCEPTS

Unconditional jump	Jump if minus	Multibyte addition
Conditional jump	Jump if plus	Multibyte subtraction
Jump if carry	Jump if parity even	Multibyte BCD addition
Jump if no carry	Jump if parity odd	Multibyte BCD subtraction
Jump if zero	Double-precision arithmetic	9's complement
Jump if not zero		

PROBLEMS

7-1 Draw a flowchart for the multibyte subtraction algorithm.

7-2 In the following situations, what will be the next address to be executed after the last instruction given?

a. **Address**   **Machine Code**

Address	Machine Code
1000	87
1001	32
1002	00
1003	0F
1004	FA
1005	02
1006	14

Initial values

Program counter $\boxed{1000}$

A register $\boxed{79}$

b. **Address**   **Machine Code**

Address	Machine Code
1000	47
1001	02
1002	FA
1003	00
1004	14

Initial values

Program counter $\boxed{1000}$

A register $\boxed{F0}$

7-3 Demonstrate the use of the multibyte addition algorithm, in a manner similar to Example 3, for the problem below.

$$\begin{array}{rrr} 6A & B2 & DD_{16} \\ +72 & 97 & F0_{16} \\ \hline \end{array}$$

7-4 Draw a memory map and list the final contents of the A, C, D, E, H, L registers, the program counter, and the status register after the multibyte subtraction routine has run to completion for the following problem.

$$\begin{array}{rr} 9A & 1F_{16} \\ -62 & BC_{16} \\ \hline \end{array}$$

7-5 For the BCD addition below, show the iterations of the algorithm necessary to produce the correct sum.

$$\begin{array}{r} 1\ 9\ 5\ 6 \\ +3\ 8\ 7\ 5 \\ \hline \end{array}$$

7-6 In a manner similar to Example 5, record the steps for each iteration of this BCD subtraction.

$$\begin{array}{r} 6\ 3\ 1\ 2\ 0\ 4 \\ -5\ 8\ 9\ 5\ 3\ 7 \\ \hline \end{array}$$

7-7 Write a routine which will branch to address 5600_{16} after reading a number with odd parity from memory cell 0111_{16}. (The routine must first fetch that information prior to attempting to examine it.)

7-8 Write a routine that will make a decision based on the sign of a number stored in memory:

If the number is positive, go to address 0100_{16}.
If the number is negative, go to address 0200_{16}.
If the number is 0, go to address 0300_{16}.

The quantity of interest is stored at location 0513_{16}.

7-9 Assume that you have an NEC 8080A available and choose to avoid the 9's complement. The auxiliary carry will always be correctly set or reset after subtraction in this processor, so the DAA will work properly after subtraction. Rewrite the BCD subtraction routine, taking advantage of the unique NEC 8080A features.

7-10 Using the routine of Prob. 7-9, draw a memory map and list the final contents of the A, C, D, E, H, L register, the program counter, and the status registers after the routine has run. (The NEC 8080A subtract status bit is bit 5. It is set after any addition and cleared after any subtraction. The AC bit is cleared after subtraction if a borrow from bit 4 occurred during subtraction; otherwise, it is set. The NEC 8080A does not alter the status of the carry or auxiliary carry bits when executing Boolean instructions.) Use the same variables for the minuend and subtrahend as those given in Example 5.

EXPERIMENT 7

PURPOSE: To investigate conditional jump instructions and masking.

PROCEDURE: Data is stored at address 0030_{16}. If bits 0 through 5 in that memory location are greater than or equal to 20_{16}, set address 0031_{16} to -1. Otherwise, clear address 0031_{16}.

Data Set	Address 0030_{16}
1	20
2	E0
3	1F
4	21
5	FF

STEP 1. Lay out a mask to select only bits 0 through 5 of the data word. (An AND instruction will be used to obtain the desired bits.)

STEP 2. Prepare a flowchart for your program.

STEP 3. Write the program to perform the required operation.

8

SHIFTING

The 8080A processor can function as a shift register by use of the group or shift commands. These operations, also called *rotate the accumulator* instructions, are handy for manipulating individual bits in a data word and also provide the means for multiplying or dividing numbers in the MPU. The shift instructions only modify the contents of the accumulator; no other registers or memory cells are referenced by them.

CHAPTER OBJECTIVES

Upon completion of this chapter, you should be able to:

1. Show how shift instructions can be used for scaling.
2. Explain the rotate accumulator instructions.
3. Distinguish between a normal rotation and a rotation through carry operation.
4. Write a multiplication routine based on shift instructions.
5. Describe the function of shift instructions in a division routine.

SHIFTING CONCEPTS

Shifting a register causes each bit in that register to move left or right one position. Before examining the actual 8080A shifting methods, let's consider a simplified form of shifting. Figure 8-1a shows the result of left shifting an 8-bit register. As Fig. 8-1 shows, each bit has replaced the one in the next higher order position. That is, bit 0 becomes bit 1, bit 1 becomes bit 2, and so on. The most-significant bit is discarded, and a 0 enters from the right. In a right shift (Fig. 8-1b), the bits move down one order. The least-significant bit is lost, and a 0 is entered as the most significant bit. Another effect of shifting that can be seen in Fig. 8-1 is multiplication or division by 2. By left shifting the number, we have multiplied it by 2 ($97_{16} \times 2_{16} = 12E_{16}$). Because of overflow, the most-significant digit has been lost in this example. By performing multiple left shifts, we multiply by powers of 2. After n shifts, the original number is multiplied by 2^n. Care must be exercised to prevent overflow when this technique is used. Right shifting produces the opposite effect. A right shift divides by 2 as Fig. 8-1b demonstrates: $AD_{16}/2_{16} = 56_{16}$.

Shifting to produce binary multiplications or divisions is sometimes called *scaling*. Numbers may be scaled down to avoid overflow or scaled up to obtain greater precision. Scaling is often used with double-precision arithmetic.

As an example of scaling, consider the problem of adding 1.6_{16} to 5_{16} in the 8080A. There is no way of representing a radix point directly because all numbers are treated as integers. The programmer, however, can use scaling to overcome this difficulty. The person writing the program must remember to properly treat the scaled numbers from then on. By examining the numbers, we note that the smaller number must be scaled up at least four binary places to preserve its full significance.

Four places

$$1.6_{16} = 0001. \quad 0110_2$$

Radix point   Last position of significance

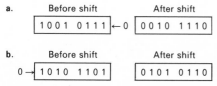

Figure 8-1. Shifting (a) Left Shift (b) Right Shift.

In scaling we must always balance preserving significance against preventing overflow. We can check for overflow by seeing how many places the larger number can be scaled without producing an overflow in the sum.

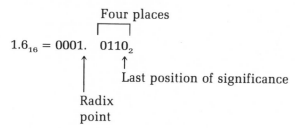

These bits can be shifted off

$$05_{16} = 0000 \quad 0101._2$$

Radix point

A zero must be kept in the sign bit position

The final scaling and sum would look like this:

$$
\begin{aligned}
1.6_{16} \text{ scaled up 4 places} &= 0001\ 0110_2 \\
5_{16} \text{ scaled up 4 places} &= +0101\ 0000_2 \\
\hline
&0110\ 0110_2
\end{aligned}
$$

We must remember the implicit radix point in the sum. It must be treated as 5.6_{16}, not as 56_{16}.

Every scaling situation requires that the magnitude of the numbers involved be examined. Many times a single-byte word length is inadequate, so double precision is needed. What would have happened in the scaling example above if we had wanted to add 1.6_{16} to 7_{16}? By using the same 4 bits of scaling, we have

$$
\begin{aligned}
1.6_{16} \text{ scaled} &= 0001\ 0110_2 \\
7_{16} \text{ scaled} &= +0111\ 0000_2 \\
\hline
&1000\ 0110_2
\end{aligned}
$$

Overflow
Sum is negative

The sum overflowed the 8-bit length. Now we may choose to either decrease the precision (to 3 bits, for instance) or to employ multibyte arithmetic.

To show that scaling need not always be in 4-bit increments, we will work this problem with 3 bits of precision. The digits will no longer be directly recognizable in hexadecimal because of the shifting, but the correct answer can be retrieved in spite of this complication (by writing the number in binary).

$$
\begin{aligned}
1.6_{16} \text{ scaled 3 bits} &= 0000\ 1011_2 \\
7_{16} \text{ scaled 3 bits} &= +0100\ 1000_2 \\
\hline
&0100\ 0011_2
\end{aligned}
$$

(The augend appears to be $0B_{16}$ and the addend 38_{16}.) The least significant bit of 1.6_{16} has been lost. The answer appears to be 43_{16}, but properly scaled, the correct sum appears

$$0100 \quad 0011_2 = 0 \quad 1000. \quad 0110_2$$

Radix point   Zero brought in

$$= 8.6_{16}$$

The trailing zero had to be reinserted in the LSB position.

CARRY BIT

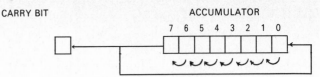

Figure 8-2. Rotate Accumulator Left.

Shifting Concepts Review

1. Explain why a left shift can be considered to be equivalent to multiplication by 2.

2. What happens to the MSB in a right shift? The LSB?

3. What two errors must you guard against when using scaling?

4. Why did the sum appear to be 43_{16} in the 3-bit scaling example? How was that problem resolved?

ROTATE ACCUMULATOR INSTRUCTIONS

These are four instructions that rotate, or shift, the accumulator in the 8080A. All the instructions use the carry status bit together with the accumulator for the rotation. The carry bit may be thought of as an independent single-bit register in conjunction with shift operation.

Rotate Accumulator Left

This instruction places the most significant bit of the accumulator in the carry bit. The accumulator is shifted left, and the previous MSB is also put in the least significant bit position of the register. Figure 8-2 shows the movement of the bits. This instruction may be thought of as a circular left shift, in that the accumulator content is circulated out the left side of the register and into the right side.

Operation code	07
Mnemonic	RLC
Addressing mode	none
Status bits affected	carry
Clock periods	4
Execution time	2 μs
Format	

bit number

7 6 5 4   3 2 1 0

Memory cell   m | 0 0 0 0   0 1 1 1 |

□ EXAMPLE

Before execution		After execution	
Program counter	0400	Program counter	0401
A register	B7	A register	6F
Status register	02	Status register	03
Memory 0400	07	Memory 0400	07

The A register is shifted left. The MSB causes the carry bit to be set. These changes may be more easily seen in a binary format.

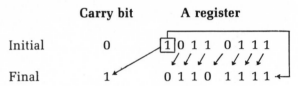

	Carry bit	A register
Initial	0	1 0 1 1 0 1 1 1
Final	1	0 1 1 0 1 1 1 1

Rotate Accumulator Right

This operation causes the LSB of the accumulator to be moved to the carry bit and the MSB of the register. The remaining bits in the register are right shifted. Figure 8-3 shows the result of executing the instruction.

Operation code	0F
Mnemonic	RRC
Addressing mode	none
Status bits affected	carry
Clock periods	4
Execution time	2 μs
Format	

bit number

7 6 5 4   3 2 1 0

Memory cell   m | 0 0 0 0   1 1 1 1 |

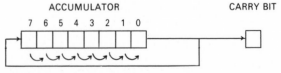

Figure 8-3. Rotate Accumulator Right.

□ EXAMPLE

	Before execution		After execution	
Program counter	0370	Program counter	0371
A register	E8	A register	74
Status register	06	Status register	06
Memory	0370	0F	Memory	0370	0F

There is no change in the status register because the LSB of the A register is 0.

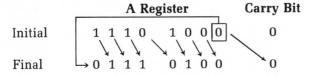

Rotate Accumulator Left Through Carry

Rotating through the carry is equivalent to a 9-bit shift. The carry bit is moved into the LSB of the accumulator, the accumulator is shifted left, and the MSB of the register goes to the carry bit. Figure 8-4 shows this operation.

Operation code	17
Mnemonic	RAL
Addressing mode	none
Status bits affected	carry
Clock periods	4
Execution time	2 μs

Format

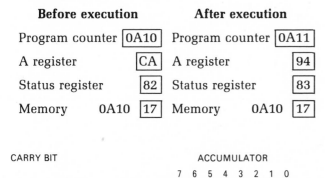

□ EXAMPLE

	Before execution		After execution	
Program counter	0A10	Program counter	0A11
A register	CA	A register	94
Status register	82	Status register	83
Memory	0A10	17	Memory	0A10	17

Figure 8-4. Rotate Accumulator Left Through Carry.

The MSB of A sets the carry condition bit.

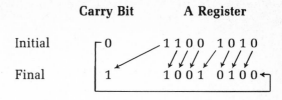

Rotate Accumulator Right Through Carry

This command right circular shifts the accumulator and the carry status as a 9-bit entity. The carry status goes to the MSB of the register, the accumulator is right shifted, and the LSB is transferred to the carry bit. Figure 8-5 illustrates the rotation.

Operation code	1F
Mnemonic	RAR
Addressing mode	none
Status bits affected	carry
Clock periods	4
Execution time	2 μs

Format

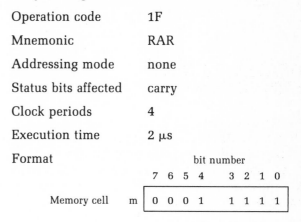

□ EXAMPLE

	Before execution		After execution	
Program counter	0880	Program counter	0881
A register	6F	A register	87
Status register	03	Status register	03
Memory	0880	1F	Memory	0880	1F

The carry status remains unchanged because the LSB of the accumulator is 1.

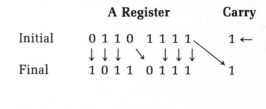

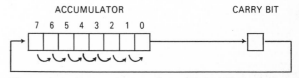

Figure 8-5. Rotate Accumulator Right Through Carry.

Rotate Accumulator Review

1. Explain why the rotate accumulator right instruction may be called a "circular shift."

2. Distinguish between the rotate accumulator left and the rotate accumulator left through carry instructions.

3. In the example for the RRC instruction, why is the carry bit 0 after execution?

4. If the instruction sequence RLC and then RAR were executed, what change, if any, would occur in the A register and the carry register contents?

SOFTWARE MULTIPLICATION

Combining rotations with other instructions will allow us to multiply numbers in the microprocessor. While relying on a program cannot duplicate the speed of high-speed multiplication circuits, software can adequately satisfy the needs for many applications. The algorithm in this section will multiply two unsigned, 8-bit quantities and produce a 16-bit product. (In general, multiplying two numbers m bits long will generate a product 2m bits in length.)

There are two approaches to solving the problem of multiplication. We could use repetitive addition, such as adding $2A_{16}$ to itself 59_{16} times to find $2A_{16} \times 59_{16}$. A faster method relies on a combination of shifting and adding. Our algorithm uses the latter procedure.

MULTIPLICATION ALGORITHM

STEP 1. Clear the product storage area.

STEP 2. If the LSB of the multiplier is 0, go to Step 3. Otherwise, add the multiplicand to the most significant byte of the product.

STEP 3. Right shift the multiplier and the 2-byte product. Have all 8 bits of the multiplier been examined? If not, go to Step 2.

An example showing all steps of the algorithm to calculate

$$\begin{array}{ll} 4F_{16} & \text{multiplicand} \\ \times\ 3D_{16} & \text{multiplier} \\ \hline 12D3_{16} & \text{product} \end{array}$$

is given in Table 8-1. You should trace the algorithm through each iteration to assure your understanding of the addition and shifting concept.

In iteration 1, the LSB of the multiplier is 1, so the multiplicand is added to the most-significant byte of the product. There is no addition of the multiplicand in iteration 2 because the multiplier

TABLE 8-1
Multiplication Algorithm Example

Iteration	Step	Multiplier		Product			
				Most Significant Byte		Least Significant Byte	
1	1	0011	1101	0000	0000	0000	0000
	2	0011	1101	0100	1111	0000	0000
	3	0001	1110	0010	0111	1000	0000
2	2	0001	1110	0010	0111	1000	0000
	3	0000	1111	0001	0011	1100	0000
3	2	0000	1111	0110	0010	1100	0000
	3	0000	0111	0011	0001	0110	0000
4	2	0000	0111	1000	0000	0110	0000
	3	0000	0011	0100	0000	0011	0000
5	2	0000	0011	1000	1111	0011	0000
	3	0000	0001	0100	0111	1001	1000
6	2	0000	0001	1001	0110	1001	1000
	3	0000	0000	0100	1011	0100	1100
7	2	0000	0000	0100	1011	0100	1100
	3	0000	0000	0010	0101	1010	0110
8	2	0000	0000	0010	0101	1010	0110
	3	0000	0000	0001	0010	1101	0011

is $1E_{16}$. Addition does take place for iterations 3 through 6. From that point on the multiplier is 0, so no more additions are needed. Each pass through the algorithm results in a right shift of the double-byte product and the multiplier.

Before examining the program for multiplication, let's discuss the technique to be used in shifting the 2-byte product. As Fig. 8-6 shows, the shifting requires two operations. In the first operation the most significant byte is right shifted through the carry. Then the least significant byte is rotated right through the carry. Because only the accumulator can be used for shifting, other registers must be used for temporary storage of the data in between shifts. The program will use the B and the C registers for that purpose.

The multiplication program below uses three registers to hold the values involved in the process. The C register must be set to the multiplier value before starting into the routine, and the D register is initially set to the multiplicand. The double-length product will be developed in the BC register pair, with the B register holding the most significant byte. By using the C register for both the multiplier and the least-significant half of the product, both quantities can be shifted by using a single instruction.

The instruction at address 1000_{16} simply clears the most significant byte of the product. Next, the index (E register) is set to stop the process after

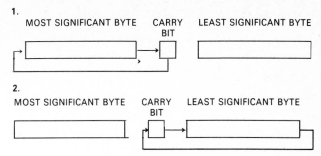

Figure 8-6. Shifting a Double Length Product.

nine iterations. Starting into the main body of the routine, the multiplier and least-significant product byte are rotated through the carry. After the counter has been decremented and nine iterations have been completed, the process examines the LSB of the multiplier (which had been moved to the carry bit by the instruction at 1005_{16}). If the bit is a 1, the multiplicand (in the D register) is added to the upper product. The routine then jumps to the next iteration. After eight times through the main program, the process is halted. Now we can understand why the index had to be set to 9, although only eight iterations were needed. A final right shift of the least-significant byte of the product was needed after the last pass through the routine.

Multiplication Routine

Label	Mnemonic	Operand	Address	Machine Code	Comment
	MVI B	0	1000	06	Zero MSH product
			1001	00	
	MVI E	9	1002	1E	Set counter for 8 iterations
			1003	09	
STEP 2	MOV	A,C	1004	79 ⎫	Rotate bit of multiplier to carry and shift
	RAR		1005	1F ⎬	
	MOV	C,A	1006	4F	Restore register
	DCR	E	1007	1D	Decrement counter
	JZ	STOP	1008	CA	Jump to stop if 8 iterations have been completed
			1009	15	
			100A	10	
	MOV	A,B	100B	78	If not, MSH product → A
	JNC	STEP 3	100C	D2	If bit of multiplier is zero skip addition
			100D	10	
			100E	10	
	ADD	D	100F	82	Add multiplicand to MSH of product
STEP 3	RAR		1010	1F	Shift MSH of product
	MOV	B,A	1011	47	Restore register
	JMP	STEP 2	1012	C3	Jump to next iteration
			1013	04	
			1014	10	
STOP	HLT		1015	76	Halt

Software Multiplication Review

1. Explain why the algorithm works only with unsigned numbers.

2. Why is an add and shift multiplication algorithm more efficient than repetitive addition?

3. In Table 8-1, why does the upper product change at step 2 of iteration 3? At step 3 of iteration 3?

4. Discuss the procedure for shifting a double-length product by means of two rotations.

5. What does the instruction at address $100B_{16}$ of the multiplication routine accomplish?

SOFTWARE DIVISION

It is also possible to divide numbers by using a program. The unsigned 16-bit divisor, an 8-bit quotient, and the 8-bit remainder are provided by the algorithm. A sequence of subtractions and shifts are used to perform the operation; the rotate left instructions are used in shifting.

DIVISION ALGORITHM

STEP 1. Obtain the next MSB of the dividend by left shifting. Subtract the divisor from the partial dividend.

STEP 2. Did a borrow from the MSB position occur? If so, add the divisor back to the result.

STEP 3. Left shift the borrow (carry) bit into the quotient.

STEP 4. Have eight iterations been completed? If not, go to Step 1.

STEP 5. Complement the value in the quotient.

A few comments should clarify the algorithm. We will use a simple binary division problem to illustrate key points.

$$11_2\,\overline{)\,110_2}\quad \begin{array}{c}010_2\end{array}$$

In Step 1 the leftmost bit of the dividend is obtained, and then the divisor is subtracted from it. In our example we obtain the first partial dividend by left shifting 110_2 1 bit.

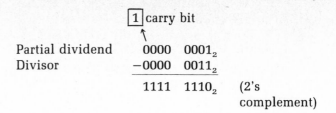

Partial dividend	0000	0001_2
Divisor	-0000	0011_2
	1111	1110_2 (2's complement)

The carry bit is set by the SUB instruction whenever a borrow occurs. (Review the instruction if your memory is hazy on this point.) The divisor "won't go into the partial dividend." The divisor must be added back to restore the original dividend value.

Next time through the algorithm we have a different situation. Left shifting 110_2 another bit gives a new partial dividend.

		⓪ carry bit
Partial dividend	0000	0011_2
Divisor	-0000	0011_2
	0000	0000_2

Now the carry bit is cleared, thus indicating the fact that the divisor can be divided into the partial dividend. After all 8 bits have been examined, the quotient that has been generated must be complemented. The reason for this step is clearly shown in the two examples above. In the first subtraction the carry (acting as a borrow bit) is set, but the quotient bit should be 0. The second subtraction cleared the carry, but the quotient should be 1. Because the carry is always the complement of the quotient, taking a 1's complement of the final value will produce the correct result.

The division routine is listed below. The most-significant part of the dividend must have been placed in the B register and the least-significant part, in the C register. The divisor is in D. After nine cycles of the routine have been completed, the quotient will be in the C register and the remainder will be in the B register.

Software Division Review

1. What does a borrow at Step 2 of the algorithm signify?

2. How does the algorithm compensate for the fact that the borrow bit is always the complement of the quotient bit?

3. Why is it sometimes necessary to add the divisor back to the partial dividend?

4. Where are the quotient and the remainder to be found after the division routine has halted?

Division Routine

Label	Mnemonic	Operand	Address	Machine Code	Comment
	MVI H	9	1000	26	Preset counter
			1001	09	
	MOV	A,B	1002	78	Initialization
STEP 3	MOV B	A	1003	47	Store partial result
	MOV	A,C	1004	79	Shift carry into LSB of quotient; MSB of
	RAL		1005	17	lower half dividend → carry
	MOV	C,A	1006	4F	Save partial lower dividend
	DCR	H	1007	25	Are all bits processed?
	JZ	STEP 5	1008	CA	Yes, go to final step
			1009	15	
			100A	10	
	MOV	A,B	100B	78	No, obtain upper half dividend
	RAL		100C	17	Shift bit from lower half to upper
	SUB	D	100D	92	Subtract divisor
	JNC	STEP 3	100E	D2	If no borrow (divisor < dividend), go to
			100F	03	Step 3
			1010	10	
	ADD	D	1011	82	Otherwise, restore original dividend
	JMP	STEP 3	1012	C3	Go to Step 3
			1013	03	
			1014	10	
STEP 5	RAL		1015	17	Final shift
	MOV	E,A	1016	5F	Temporary storage
	MVI A	FF	1017	3E	
			1018	FF	Complement the quotient
	XRA	C	1019	A9	
	MOV	C,A	101A	4F	
	MOV	A,E	101B	73	
	RAR		101C	1F	
	HLT		101D	76	Stop

CHAPTER SUMMARY

1. Shifting can move bits in a register either left or right. A single-bit left shift is equivalent to multiplication by 2; a right shift is the same as division by 2.

2. Scaling is used to maintain precision of numbers. Scaling a value too many bits can lead to overflow.

3. Instructions which rotate the accumulator left or right are also referred to as the *circular shifts*.

4. Rotating through the carry status bit effectively produces a 9-bit shift. The two rotate through carry instructions are often used for multi-byte shifting functions.

5. Two 8-bit, unsigned numbers can be multiplied by using an algorithm. The product will consist of 16 bits. A series of right shifts and additions are the basis for the algorithm.

6. A similar routine for division can be derived. In this case a series of subtractions and left shifts are used. The quotient must be complemented as a final step in the process.

7. Table 8-2 lists the rotate accumulator instructions. The only status condition possibly changed by these instructions is the carry bit.

Table 8-2
Shift Instruction Summary

Instruction			
Mnemonic	Machine Code	Number of Bytes	Execution Time, μs
RAL	17	1	2
RAR	1F	1	2
RLC	07	1	2
RRC	0F	1	2

The carry bit only is affected by each shift instruction.

Shifting	**Rotate accumulator left or right**	**Rotate through carry**
Scaling	**Circular shifts**	**Software multiply and divide**

PROBLEMS

8-1 The initial contents of the accumulator is 93_{16}, and the status register is 03_{16}. How would these values be changed after the following instructions have been executed

    a. RAL   *c.* RLC
    b. RAR   *d.* RRC

8-2 Write three instructions that perform the series of operations listed. (Overflow will not occur.)

Multiply the A register contents by 2.
Add 6 to that value.
Divide the result by 4.

8-3 Prepare a two-instruction sequence which will subtract $1.A_{16}$ from 7_{16}. (Choose the scaling that will preserve the precision of the difference but not cause overflow.)

8-4 In the addition problem below, the numbers have been scaled up 2 bits. Express the sum with the radix point in the proper position.

$$\begin{array}{r} 63_{16} \\ +\,1B_{16} \\ \hline \end{array}$$

8-5 Find the resulting values in the registers after execution of the routine listed.

Before execution		Machine Code
A register	46	78
B register	79	17
C register	B2	47
Status register	83	07
		76

8-6 Prepare a table similar to Table 8-1, showing the step-by-step changes in the multiplier and product when the multiplication algorithm is used to calculate

$$\begin{array}{r} 5E_{16} \\ \times\,47_{16} \\ \hline \end{array}$$

8-7 Write a program to shift a 16-bit quantity in the DE register pair right by 2 bits. (The D register contains the most significant byte of the number.)

8-8 Prepare a step-by-step table for the first and the second iterations of the division algorithm when the dividend is $DB04_{16}$ and the divisor is 3_{16}.

8-9 The carry bits resulting from all iterations of the division algorithm are listed below. What is the quotient?

Iteration	1	2	3	4	5	6	7	8
Carry	0	1	1	1	0	0	1	0

8-10 The division routine has been used to solve

$$\frac{19BC_{16}}{25_{16}}$$

What will the final contents of the B and the C registers be? (You do not have to use the division algorithm to solve this problem.)

EXPERIMENT 8 _____

PURPOSE: To investigate shifting instructions.

PROCEDURE: In this experiment a value is entered in the accumulator and a program executed. After execution, the A register and status register are to be examined and recorded.

STEP 1. Place the value 55_{16} in the data cell. Then write a program to load the data into the A register and rotate the accumulator left 2 bits. Explain the final values in the status register and the accumulator.

STEP 2. Using the value of AA_{16}, write a similar program to rotate A right 3 bits. What are the contents of the carry bit and the accumulator? Explain your answers.

STEP 3. Repeat Step 1 using an RAL instruction. How do the results compare to the case in the first step?

STEP 4. Repeat Step 2 using an RAR instruction. How do the accumulator and carry compare to Step 3?

9

LOOPS AND INDEXING

The processor is well suited for performance of repetitive tasks. It never gets bored or tired, so every iteration will be the same as the last. The multibyte arithmetic routines in the preceding chapters were examples of such repetitive or *looping* processes. This chapter will further our study of loops, primarily to develop a full understanding of the concept and to learn how loops may be implemented by using the 8080A instructions. Our study will not include advanced applications of loops, however, because such topics are more appropriate in a programming course.

CHAPTER OBJECTIVES

Upon completion of this chapter, you should be able to:

1. List the component functions required in every loop.
2. Calculate the initial and the final values for all counting loop configurations.
3. Explain noncounting loop constructions.
4. Use timing loops to introduce delays in a program.
5. Describe the operation of address modification loops.
6. Show how loops can be combined by nesting.

LOOP FUNCTIONS

Although loops can become quite complicated sequences, every one must have certain essential parts. The looping process, also called *recursion,* depends on the processor being able to (1) complete a sequence of instructions over and over again and (2) stop the iterations at the proper time. Consider the flowchart in Fig. 9-1a, for example. This process will add one to the contents of the variable x and place the answer back in the same variable. The loop is shown on a flowchart by a process arrow leading back to the process that is to be repeated. Unfortunately, this loop has a fatal flaw; it never stops. Once the processor begins to execute the loop, it can only be halted by the intervention of the operator.

Figure 9-1b corrects this problem. The decision operation checks the value of x each pass through the loop. Once x exceeds 10, the processor no longer takes the flow path back to the addition process. Instead, it exits the loop routine.

Even this loop has a problem. Can you spot it? We are using a register or memory cell to hold x. When the processor is first started, we have no way of telling what the value of x is. To ensure that x starts from the correct value, that variable must be initialized. What would happen if the initial value of x had been 96_{16} and we had forgotten to set it to 0? Would the test have worked correctly?

A generalized loop structure is shown in Fig. 9-1d. As you can see, every loop must contain three operations. Initialization occurs before the actual loop logic is entered to assure the proper starting point. The repeated processing is the working portion of the loop. Whether the loop is to be terminated or repeated is decided in the test portion. Analysis of any looping routine requires identification of its component parts. Look for them in the examples that follow.

Loop Functions Review

1. List the three parts of any loop.

2. What two errors were made in the loop of Fig. 9-1a?

3. Explain what would happen, in Fig. 9-1c, if the flowline from the "no" exit of the decision reentered the diagram above the "0 → x" block. Would operation be satisfactory?

COUNTING LOOPS

Loops that count the number of passes are a simple extension of the basic loop. As Fig. 9-2 shows, a counting loop adds a fourth component to modify a variable called the *index.* The index is simply a register or memory cell that holds the count of the number of times the loop has been executed. When the proper count has been reached, the "yes" branch from the test block is taken.

Let's write a counting loop, using the 8080A instructions to more clearly illustrate how a counting loop works. The flowchart is shown in Figure 9-3. This routine will multiply an unsigned 8-bit number by 3 using repeated addition. The program corre-

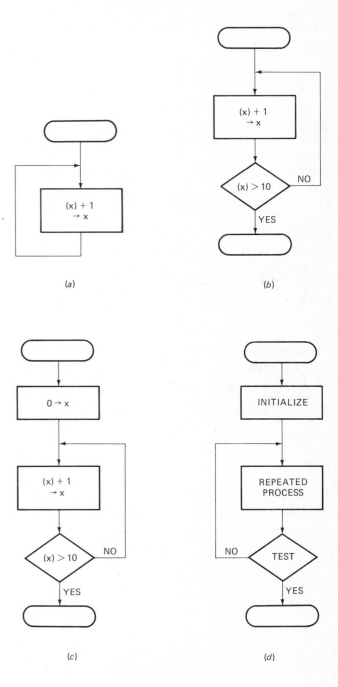

(a)

(b)

(c)

(d)

Note: (x) means the contents of the address of register x

Figure 9-1. Loop Examples.

Step	Label	Mnemonic	Operand	Address	Machine Code	Comments
1		MVI	B,1	0200	06	1 → index
				0201	01	
2		LDA	NUMBR	0202	3A	(Number) → A
				0203	00	
				0204	03	
3		MOV	C,A	0205	4F	(A) → C
4	LOOP	ADD	C	0206	81	(A) + (C) → A
5		MOV	D,A	0207	57	Temporary storage
6		INR	B	0208	04	(Index) + 1 → Index
7		MVI A	3	0209	3E	Test count → A
				020A	03	
8		CMP	B	020B	B8	Compare index with test count
9		JZ	DONE	020C	CA	Jump to DONE if index equals 3
				020D	13	
				020E	02	
10		MOV	A,D	020F	7A	Otherwise, restore A value
11		JMP	LOOP	0210	C3	Go to next iteration
				0211	06	
				0212	02	
12	DONE	HLT		0213	76	Stop

sponding to that flowchart is listed above. (The B register contains the index. The answer is stored in D.) A step-by-step analysis of the program is shown in Table 9-1. After initialization, the number is placed in both the A and the C registers to facilitate addition. After addition, the partial product is put into the answer register. Next, a comparison is made to see if the index equals 3. (Remember that the compare instruction does an internal subtraction and sets the zero status, if the two numbers are equal.) In the first iteration the count is not satisfied, so the loop is repeated. When the comparison is made again

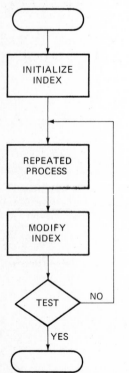

Figure 9-2. Counting Loop.

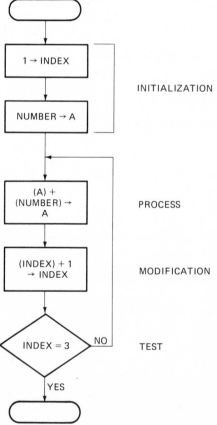

Figure 9-3. A Simple Counting Loop.

Table 9-1
Loop Analysis

| Iteration | Step | Register | | | Comments* |
		A	B	D	
Before start		?	?	?	
1	1	?	01	?	B is initialized
	2	02	01	?	A receives the number
	3	02	01	?	Number to C also
	4	04	01	?	Add
	5	04	01	04	Partial product to D
	6	04	02	04	Increment index
	7	03	02	04	Test count to A
	8	03	02	04	Compare index with count
	9	03	02	04	Comparison is not satisfied
	10	04	02	04	Restore A
	11	04	02	04	Go to next iteration
2	4	06	02	04	Add
	5	06	02	06	Store answer
	6	06	03	06	Increment index
	7	03	03	06	Test count to A
	8	03	03	06	Compare
	9	03	03	06	Comparison is satisfied, so jump
	12	03	03	06	Halt

*Memory cell 0300_{16} contains 02_{16}.

(Table 9-1, iteration 2, step 8), the values are equal, so the jump-on-zero condition does get executed and the processor halts.

Index Values

Perhaps you noticed that only two iterations were completed in Table 9-1, yet the index incremented to 3. Why did that happen? To answer this questions, we must examine the relationships between loop components and loop count. The order of modification, testing, and processing is not fixed. Figure 9-4 shows some of the possible arrangements.

In Fig. 9-4a modification and testing of the counter precede the processing. In all these examples, assume that the counter is initialized to 0. How many times

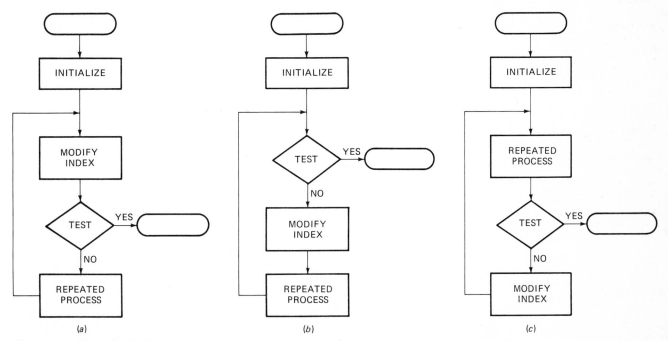

Figure 9-4. Some Loop Sequences.

is the process repeated if we test for the index being equal to 2? In Fig. 9-4*a* we see that before the first time the process is executed, the index is set to 1. On the next iteration the count is incremented prior to the test, so the process was only accomplished one time.

Moving to Fig. 9-4*b*, the first pass through, the count is 0 at the time of the test. After the first iteration the counter is 1. The second time through the counter increments to 2. Having reached the decision for the third time, the index now equals 2, and the loop stops. The process was done twice.

Finally, in Fig. 9-4*c*, the process is done the first time with an index value of 0. The process repeats for an index value of 1, and again for 2, before the test is satisfied. Therefore, the process was iterated three times. Table 9-2 summarizes the manner in which the number of repetitions depends on the arrangements and the index value. See Prob. 9-1 for other loop arrangements that affect the count.

Negative Stepping Index

The samples in the last section all used an index that incremented to some terminal value from its initial value. Frequently, a decrementing index is more useful. The choice of counting up or counting down is made on the basis of the ease of programming and the minimum memory requirements. In the 8080A, a decrementing loop is usually more efficient. As an example of the memory savings that a decrementing loop can provide, the previous multiplica-

Table 9-2
Loop Repetitions*

Order	Final Index Value	Number of Repetitions
Modify—test—process	N	N − 1
Test—modify—process	N	N
Process—test—modify	N	N + 1

*Assuming that the index is initialized to 0.

tion program will be recoded with a down-counting index.

There is a savings of four memory cells with the program rewritten in this way. There would be a further savings if the answer could be left in the accumulator rather than being moved to the D register. In the earlier case the D register was required to hold the answer while the accumulator was used in the comparison. Here no comparison is needed, so the D register storage is redundant.

The number of times a decrementing loop is repeated depends on the component arrangement in the same way as shown in Table 9-2 for incrementing loops. The only change needed to convert Table 9-2 to decrementing loops is to initialize the counter to the final value shown in that table and then count down to 0. In the present program the order is process—modify—test, corresponding to the second row in that table. By stepping through the program, we see that the addition is done two times if the starting value of the index is 2.

MULTIPLICATION BY REPETITIVE ADDITION
(Decrementing Index)

Step	Label	Mnemonic	Operand	Address	Machine Code	Comments
1		MVI B	2	0200	06	2 → index
				0201	02	
2		LDA	NUMBR	0202	3A	(Number) → A
				0203	00	
				0204	03	
3		MOV	C,A	0205	4F	(A) → C
4	LOOP	ADD	C	0206	81	(A) + (C) → A
5		MOV	D,A	0207	57	Store result
6		DCR	B	0208	05	(Index) − 1 → index
7		JZ	DONE	0209	CA	Decrementing affects status bits. Go to
				020A	0F	DONE if index is 0
				020B	02	
8		JMP	LOOP	020C	C3	Go to next iteration
				020D	06	
				020E	02	
9	DONE	HLT		020F	76	Stop

Variable Stepping Index

Often there will be a need to increment or decrement the index contents by some value other than 1. The index may be incremented or decremented by any number. When this method of indexing is used, care must be exercised in performing the test properly. Figure 9-5 illustrates the problem that can occur, if one is not properly concerned with the counting process.

The problem which the flowchart attempts to solve is to produce the sum of all even integer less than n, where n is a given input to the routine. But there is no requirement that n be even, because the sum is for all positive numbers *less* than n. If n is odd, the test will never be satisfied and the loop will not terminate. This error would be eliminated if the test were changed to checking for i greater than or equal to n. The test would terminate the loop after the highest valid integer had been added to the previous count regardless of n being even or odd. It is this type of subtle problem that accounts for many computer bugs.

The programmer is anticipating data within certain ranges, but the data does not actually have to satisfy those constraints. There was no stated requirement for n to be even, so an odd number is (or should be) a valid input. The program to properly calculate the sum is listed below. (The initial value of n is

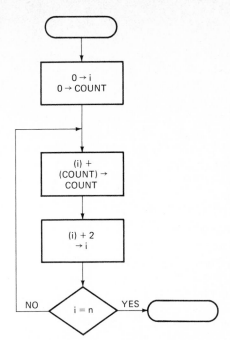

Figure 9-5. Incorrect Counting Loop.

placed in the A register, and the answer is found in the D register.)

Note that the index is decremented twice to produce a step of 2. This routine uses only single-byte arithmetic. To prevent overflow, the value of n must not exceed 63_{10}. A check for the input being within

Label	Mnemonic	Operand	Address	Machine Code	Comments
	MOV	B,A	0400	47	Store n in register B
	SUI	64	0401	D6	Subtract one greater than maximum legal value
			0402	40	
	JP	ERROR	0403	F2	If A is positive, overflow will occur, so go to error exit
			0404	16	
			0405	04	
	MVI	C,0	0406	0E	Zero index
			0407	00	
	MOV C	C	0408	79	Zero count
LOOP	ADD	C	0409	81	
	INR	C	040A	0C ⎫	Increment i by 2
	INR	C	040B	0C ⎭	
	MOV	D,A	040C	57	Temporarily store result
	MOV	A,B	040D	78	Obtain n
	SUB	C	040E	91	Subtract i
	JM	END	040F	FA	If result is negative, we are done
			0410	17	
			0411	04	
	MOV	A,D	0412	7A	Restore count
	JMP	LOOP	0413	C3	Go to next iteration
			0414	09	
			0415	04	
ERROR	CMA		0416	2F	Complement A to set it negative
END	HLT		0417	76	Stop

Notes: n is placed in the A register prior to start. The answer is in A at completion. To prevent overflow n must be 63 or less; otherwise, the A register is set to a negative value.

limits is made at the beginning of the routine, and a special output is generated if n is too large. Another error in the input which would not be detected by this test is a negative value for n. By mistake, the person using this routine could insert a negative input. A meaningless answer would be generated in that case (see Prob. 9-2).

Counting Loops Review

1. What element is added to the basic loop structure for counting?

2. List three sequences for the parts of a counting loop. How does that order and the terminating value for the index in the test affect the number of repetitions completed for each sequence?

3. What impact does use of decrementing index in a counting loop usually have on memory requirements in an 8080A-based microcomputer?

4. What error is frequently made when a variable stepping index is used? How can the mistake be avoided?

NONCOUNTING LOOPS

Every loop need not depend on an index value to stop it. Many computer processes continually repeat until a particular event is detected. For example, consider a microprocessor that is used in a communications system. The system requires that all data being received be tested for errors before any processing is started. The data are 8-bit ASCII characters which are transmitted with odd parity.

Each character will be placed in the A register by an input instruction. (Here we simply assume that the instruction causes the character to be placed in the accumulator; the input sequence is fully explained in Chap. 11.) The routine will continue

to receive characters as along as the parity is odd; if a parity error is ever detected, the processor is to halt. An input instruction does not affect the status register, so the OR operation is needed to set the status condition bits to reflect the present value in the accumulator. If the parity is odd, the jump causes the processor to repeat the input process.

Noncounting loops are frequently used in I/O processing. The chapter covering that subject provides additional examples. These loops are also used for error detection. For example, the summation program in the previous section could be rewritten to halt on the proper count or when overflow was detected. If the test for overflow were added, the initial verification of the input value would be unnecessary.

Noncounting Loops Review

1. List some conditions that could be used in the test portion of a noncounting loop.

2. Why was an OR instruction required in the parity checking routine?

3. What instruction(s) could be used to check for overflow in the summation routine, if we wanted to add that test?

TIMING LOOPS

The processor is sometimes too fast in executing its program. When some external system is being controlled, the mechanical devices cannot react as quickly as the 8080A. Such devices as valves, synchros, relays, or even the human operator must be given enough time to complete a task before the processor goes on to its next instruction.

Delays are frequently added to programs to allow

PARITY CHECKING ROUTINE

Label	Mnemonic	Operand	Address	Machine Code	Comments
LOOP	IN	0	0600	DB	Receive one character
			0601	00	
	ORI	FF	0602	F6	Cause the parity to be computed
			0603	FF	
	JPO	LOOP	0604	E2	If parity is odd, go to obtain next character
			0605	00	
			0606	06	
	HLT		0607	76	Stop

Label	Mnemonic	Operand	Address	Machine Code	Comments
	MVI B	1B	1000	06	$27_{10} \rightarrow i$
			1001	1B	
LOOP	NOP		1002	00	No operation
	DCR	B	1003	05	Decrement counter
	JNZ	LOOP	1004	C2	Repeat if count is not exhausted
			1005	02	
			1006	10	
	HLT		1007	76	Stop

for this reaction time. Assume that a teletype must be given time for printing between each character that is sent to it. We want to delay the program a minimum of 250 μs between every output. A routine that causes this delay is listed above.

By referring to the timing data on the instructions, the time elapsed in one iteration of the loop can be calculated. These values are listed in Table 9-3. The total delay each time through the loop is 9.5 μs. To calculate the number of iterations for a delay of 250 μs, we simply divide (250 μs total/9.5 μs per iteration) = 26.3 iterations. We actually use 27 iterations because we wanted a minimum of 250 μs.

Remember that the instruction execution time depends on the clock frequency. Here a standard 2-MHz clock rate is assumed. Suitable adjustments must be made for a slower clock. Furthermore, timing loops of this type are not particularly precise. Variations in the clock frequency or contention for the buses, possibly because of an input or output, will affect the accuracy of the delay. We also did not include the delay from the MVI or the HLT instructions in the routine. Generally speaking, delay loops like this one are adequate for I/O timing. If a more precise interval is needed, another method must be used. Chapter 11 discusses other timing techniques.

Timing Loops Review

1. Why are delay loops necessary?

2. If the delay from the first and last instructions of the example were included, what would be the total time interval consumed?

3. Explain why delay loops should not be used to control timing of processes that rely on precise time intervals.

ADDRESS MODIFICATION LOOPS

Computers have the powerful ability to manipulate masses of data. When large quantities of data must be processed, a well-organized data structure must be created. One type of data organization that is often used is the *table* or the *array*. Tabular data is placed in consecutive memory cells (see Fig. 9-6). Once the data has been placed in the table, updating is readily accomplished by use of an index. Let a table of 100 records be placed in memory starting at address 0650_{16}. Now we want to change the value of each record in the table. Every data word must be decreased by 1. An *address modification* loop will be used for this purpose.

ADDRESS MODIFICATION

Label	Mnemonic	Operand	Address	Machine Code	Comments
	LHLD	TBADR	0210	2A	Place the starting address of table in HL pair
			0201	0C	
			0202	02	
	MVI B	64	0203	06	Initialize index to 100_{10}
			0204	64	
LOOP	DCR	M	0205	35	Decrement one word in table
	DCX	H	0206	2B	Adjust HL to next table address
	DCR	B	0207	05	Decrement counter
	JNZ	LOOP	0208	C2	Go to next iteration
			0209	05	
			020A	02	
	HLT		020B	76	Stop
TBADR			020C	50	Table starting address
TBADR + 1			020D	06	

Table 9-3
Execution Time Delay

Instruction	Delay, μs
NOP	2.0
DCR	2.5
JNZ	5.0
Total	9.5

ADDRESS

m	RECORD 1
m + 1	RECORD 2
m + 2	RECORD 3
m + 3	RECORD 4
	⋮
m + n − 1	RECORD n

Figure 9-6. A Data Table.

This routine uses two register—one for the current table address and the other for a loop index. The HL register pair holds the address of the data word being decremented. The B register is used as the index. The index is started with a value of 100_{10} (64_{16}). When the register contains 0, all 100 words have been updated.

Address Modification Loops Review

1. Define the term "table."

2. Why was the HL register pair used in the address modification routine?

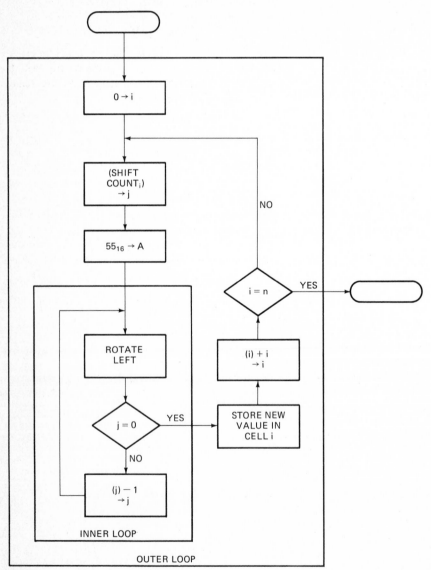

Figure 9-7. Nested Loops.

3. What is the purpose of the LHLD instruction in the routine?

4. How does the routine determine when all the records in the table have been updated?

NESTED LOOPS

When the process to be repeated is a loop itself, then *nesting* of iterative procedures is called for. Nesting of two or three loops offers an efficient programming tool. Theoretically, the concept of a loop within a loop can be continued without limit, but as the level of nesting increases, the program becomes difficult to debug and almost impossible to understand. Every level of looping requires its own index if counting loops are used.

Given the task of taking a number from a table, rotating the quantity 55_{16} left by that number of bits, and then replacing the original value by the shifted value is a good problem for nested loops. Figure 9-7 gives a flowchart for this routine. The number of left shifts will always be in the range of 1 to 8, and no verification check is required. The table is 10 words long and begins at address 1000_{16}.

In the program below, the HL register pair represents the address index i, and the B register the shift count index, j. After the HL registers have been set to the starting address of the table, they are used as an index to obtain the shift count. In the inner loop the B register decrements from that value to 0, at which time all rotations have been accomplished. Then the answer is stored and a check is made to see if all 10 (A_{16}) records have been processed. If not, the outer loop is reentered.

Nested Loops Review

1. How many indices would be needed in three nested counting loops?

2. What is the purposes of the outer loop in the example? The inner loop?

3. Which index is used for the inner loop? Which register(s) is (are) used to hold that value?

4. How is the termination value for the word count index determined?

CHAPTER SUMMARY

1. A looping or a recursive process repeats a sequence of instructions until the specified conditions have been met.

NESTED LOOP ROUTINE

Label	Mnemonic	Operand	Address	Machine Code	Comments
	LHLD	ADDR	2000	2A	Initialize word counter, i
			2001	17	
			2002	20	
AGAIN	MOV	B,M	2003	46	Set shift counter, j
	MVI A	55	2004	3E	Place shift pattern in A
			2005	55	
NEXT	RLC		2006	07	Rotate left
	DCR	B	2007	05	Decrement j
	JZ	STORE	2008	CA	If j = 0, go to store answer
			2009	0E	
			200A	20	
	JMP	NEXT	200B	C3	Go to shift again
			200C	06	
			200D	20	
STORE	MOV	M,A	200E	77	Store answer
	INX	H	200F	23	Increment i
	MVI A	0A	2010	3E	Terminating value for i is 10_{10}.
			2011	0A	
	SUB	L	2012	95	Subtract i
	JNZ	AGAIN	2013	C2	If not zero, get next value
			2014	03	
			2015	20	
	HLT		2016	76	Stop
ADDR			2017	00	Table starting address
			2018	10	

2. The variable controlling the number of iterations must be initialized prior to entering the loop.

3. Every loop consists of an initialization, a process, and a test section.

4. Counting loops use an index to control the number of cycles. A modification section is added to the basic loop structure to update the index on each pass.

5. The relationship between initial and final values of the index and the number of repetitions depends on the order of the processing, the modification, and the testing in the loop.

6. The index in a counting loop can decrement as well as increment. In the 8080A a decrementing loop will usually be more efficient in memory usage than will an incrementing loop.

7. Variable stepping indices are used when the value must be modified in units other than 1. If a variable step is used, the test must be written to properly stop the loop. The simplest way of accomplishing a proper test value is by checking for equaling or exceeding the final value.

8. Noncounting loops are terminated when a specific event occurs. The status bits are often used as flags to show that the condition was satisfied.

9. Time delays, which slow the processor to allow an external action to be completed, can be implemented by executing a series of instructions in a loop. Timing loops are easily written, but the delay is only an approximation. If precision timing is called for, another method must be used.

10. Address modification loops are well suited for indexing through tables or arrays.

11. Nested loops are used when two or more processes must be repeated. The inner loop runs to completion with each pass through the outer loop. Each nested loop must have a unique index if counting is required.

KEY TERMS AND CONCEPTS

Loops	**Index**	**Noncounting loops**
Recursive processes	**Index modification**	**Timing loops**
Loop components—initialization, processing, and testing	**Loop count determination**	**Address modification loops**
Counting loops	**Decrementing index**	**Tables and arrays**
	Variable stepping index	**Nested loops**

PROBLEMS

9-1 Complete the table (in a manner similar to that used in Table 9-2) for the loop configurations given below. The index is initialized to 0.

Order	Final Index Value	Number of Repetitions
Modify—process—test	N	
Test—process—modify	N	
Process—modify—test	N	

9-2 Write the instructions needed to detect a negative input to the summation program. Begin at address 0406_{16}. The address of the error exit, to be taken if n is less than 0, is $041A_{16}$. Do not rewrite the entire program.

9-3 What should the initial value for the index be in Figs. 9-8a and 9-8b?

9-4 What value should be used in the test portion of the flowcharts for Figs. 9-9a, 9-9b, and 9-9c?

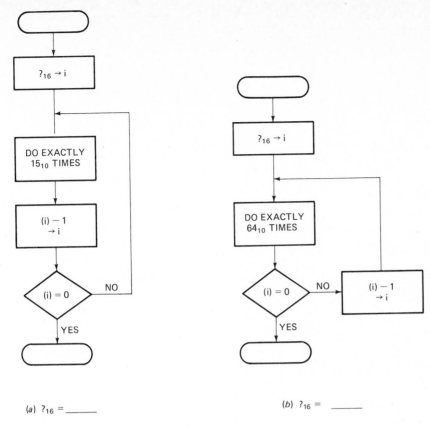

(a) $?_{16} = \underline{\hspace{1cm}}$

(b) $?_{16} = \underline{\hspace{1cm}}$

Figure 9-8. Problem 9-3.

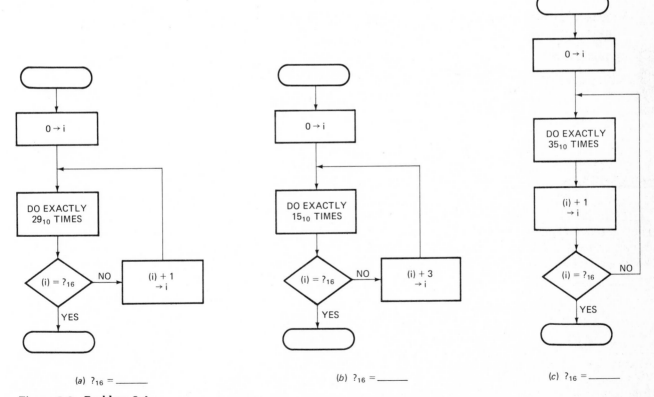

(a) $?_{16} = \underline{\hspace{1cm}}$

(b) $?_{16} = \underline{\hspace{1cm}}$

(c) $?_{16} = \underline{\hspace{1cm}}$

Figure 9-9. Problem 9-4.

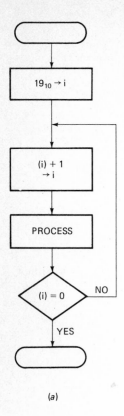

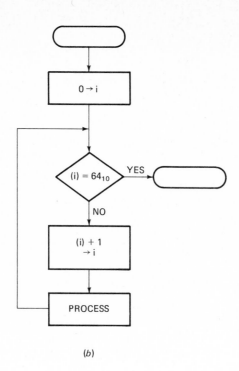

(a)

(b)

Figure 9-10. Problem 9-5.

9-5 In Figs. 9-10a and 9-10b, how many times is the process done?

9-6 A timing loop is needed to cause a delay of 2 ms. Write a routine, using the same instructions as the loop in the example in this chapter, which will create the appropriate delay. (*Hint*—consider use of the NOP instruction more than once.)

9-7 Draw a table that consists of five records. Each record is 3 bytes long. Then show two ways in which the table could be stored in memory.

9-8 The address modification problem given in this chapter is changed to require that the records only at even addresses be increased by 3. The contents of odd addresses are to remain unchanged. Rewrite the address modification routine for the new requirements.

9-9 A program is needed to do the following:

1. Take the next value from a table.
2. Rotate the quantity 06_{16} right by that number or until the sign bit is set.
3. Replace the original table value by the shifted number.

The table values range from 1 to 8, and no verification of the values is required. The table is 10_{10} words long and begins at address $05AE_{16}$. Prepare a flowchart and then code the routine.

9-10 Write a program to carry out the actions shown in Fig. 9-9c.

EXPERIMENT 9

PURPOSE: To investigate timing loops.

PROCEDURE: A long timing loop is to be written. Because the register can hold only an 8-bit value, nested loops will be required to produce as long a delay as is called for.

STEP 1. Prepare a flowchart for a timing delay loop 10 s in duration.

STEP 2. Write the program to create a timing delay of 10 s. At the completion of the delay, output FF_{16} at an I/O port.

STEP 3. Run the program and time the delay by using a watch with a second hand.

STEP 4. Increase the delay to 1 min or more. After revising your program, run it and time the delay. What can be concluded about the accuracy of this delay method?

10

SUBROUTINES

Earlier chapters covered routines for multibyte addition and subtraction, multiplication, and division. The task of rewriting those routines every time we wanted to perform the arithmetic operations would be quite cumbersome and would also waste a lot of memory space. When a group of instructions is to be used many times in a program, defining these instructions to be a subroutine eliminates the need to rewrite the same code over and over. This chapter investigates the subroutine concept.

CHAPTER OBJECTIVES

Upon completion of this chapter, you should be able to:

1. Describe subroutine construction and referencing.
2. Explain the operation of 8080A instructions used to call and return from subroutines.
3. Describe conditional subroutine calls and returns.
4. Discuss the use of the stack in initiating and terminating subroutines.
5. Show how subroutines can be nested.
6. Describe the process of parameter passing by means of registers or memory.

SUBROUTINES IN GENERAL

A subroutine is simply a group of instructions which can be executed many times in one program. The group of instructions is coded like any other set of commands, but it is assigned a unique name, thus allowing the instruction sequence to be referenced as an entity. The name of the subroutine is the label assigned to the first instruction. The label symbolically represents an address, so we reference the routine by that address in the 8080A. Figure 10-1 illustrates the subroutine idea. The main routine in a payroll program must perform a multibyte addition three times; after the instruction at addresses 0110_{16}, 0125_{16}, and $01B1_{16}$, the subroutine is referenced or *called.* At completion of the subroutine, note that the main program sequence must continue from the address immediately following the one calling that subroutine. A distinguishing feature of a subroutine is its ability to *return* to the main program in this manner.

How is this return to an arbitrary address arranged? In the 8080A the proper exiting from a subroutine relies on the stack. Although there are slight variations, the process is essentially the same for any subroutine call and return. Executing the calling instruction pushes the contents of the program counter on the stack. (Remember that the program counter is set to the address of the *next* instruction.) Then the address of the subroutine is loaded into the program counter register. This action causes the first address of the subroutine to be referenced. The remaining instructions of the subroutine are executed in a normal manner until the return instruction is reached. The return instruction causes the stack to be popped, and the data on top of the stack (the next address in the main program) is placed in the program counter. The main program then continues from the next instruction following the call. A specific example will be given following a more complete description of the unconditional call and return instructions.

Call Instruction

The call instruction is something like a jump in that the contents of the program counter are changed to transfer control to a new address. In addition, the return address is placed on the stack. The stack is located in RAM, and the stack pointer is set to the address of the item currently at the top of the stack. Pushing the new return address on the stack results in three actions:

1. The most-significant byte of the program counter value is placed on the stack at the location which is 1 less than the current stack pointer contents.

2. The least-significant byte of the program counter is placed on the stack at the location which is 2 less than the current stack pointer contents.

3. The stack pointer is decremented by 2.

Operation code	CD
Mnemonic	CALL
Addressing mode	direct
Effect on status bits	none
Clock periods	17
Execution time	8.5 μs
Format	

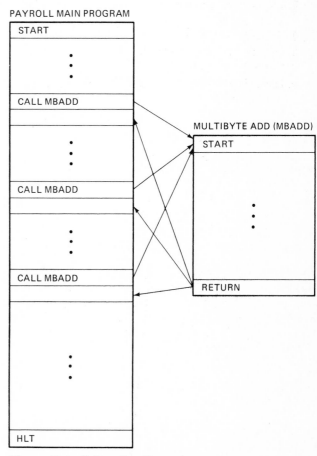

Figure 10-1. Subroutine Example.

□ EXAMPLE

Before execution		After execution	
Program counter	0400	Program counter	0200
Stack pointer	1025	Stack pointer	1023

Memory   Memory

Instruction	0400	CD	0400	CD	
	0401	00	0401	00	
	0402	02	0402	02	
Stack	1022	00	1022	00	
	1023	22	1023	03	
	1024	FC	1024	04	
	1025	EB	1025	EB	

The program counter is changed to the starting address of the subroutine (0200_{16}). The address of the next instruction in the main program is 0403_{16} (because the call instruction occupies 3 bytes). That address is pushed on the stack (high byte to location 1024_{16} and low byte to location 1023_{16}). The stack pointer is updated to indicate the new top of stack.

Return Instructions

A CALL instruction must always be paired with a return instruction for the subroutine referencing to complete properly; otherwise, a totally confused program would result. The return instruction is always the last one in a subroutine. The routine takes the address information previously pushed on the stack and updates the pointer in three steps:

1. The contents on the location equal to the current stack pointer value are placed in the least significant byte of the program counter.

2. The contents of the location equal to the current stack pointer plus 1 are placed in the most-significant byte of the program counter.

3. The stack pointer is incremented by 2.

Operation code	C9
Mnemonic	RET
Addressing mode	none
Effect on status bits	none
Clock periods	10
Execution time	5 μs
Format	

bit number

		7	6	5	4		3	2	1	0
Memory cell	m	1	1	0	0		1	0	0	1

□ EXAMPLE

Before execution		After execution	
Program counter	0240	Program counter	0403
Stack pointer	1023	Stack pointer	1025

Memory   Memory

Instruction	0240	C9	0240	C9	
Stack	1022	00	1022	00	
	1023	03	1023	03	
	1024	04	1024	04	
	1025	EB	1025	EB	

The program counter is set to proceed with execution of the instruction immediately following the last call. The stack pointer indicates the new top of stack.

Comprehensive Example

A complete subroutine example will serve to show how the call and the return instructions work together. Figure 10-2a shows the situation prior to calling the subroutine. The subroutine calling instruction is at location 2046_{16} in the main program; the subroutine starting address is 3010_{16}.

After the instruction to reference the subroutine is executed (see Fig. 10-2b), the program counter and the stack pointer have been changed, with the former to the beginning instruction in the routine and the latter to the new top of stack. The return address (2049_{16}) has been pushed on the stack.

When the subroutine completes, (see Fig. 10-2c), the return instruction causes the stack to be popped. The contents of the two top memory cells of the stack are put into the program counter for continuation of the main program. The stack pointer is decremented to reflect the change in stack length.

Subroutines in General Review

1. Which instruction is used to reference a subroutine? Which is used to exit a subroutine?

2. List the operations performed by each of these instructions.

3. How is the stack changed between Figs. 10-2a and 10-2b? Why must the stack pointer value be altered in that case?

4. Explain how the next instruction to be executed in this main program is found after a subroutine has finished its processing.

5. Why must the two instructions associated with subroutines always be used as a pair?

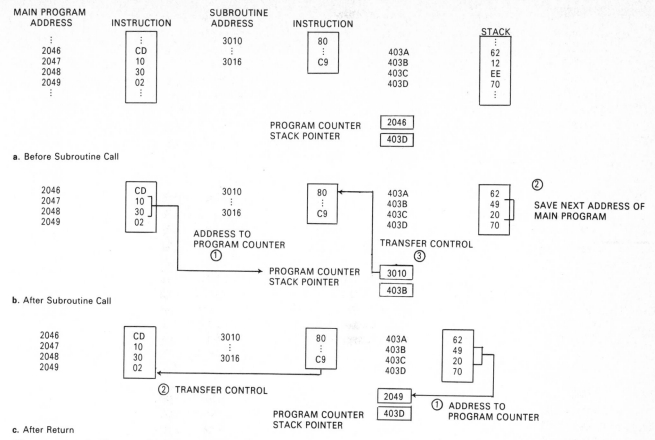

MAIN PROGRAM
ADDRESS   **INSTRUCTION**   **SUBROUTINE ADDRESS**   **INSTRUCTION**   **STACK**

⋮		3010	80		403A	62
2046	CD	⋮	⋮		403B	12
2047	10	3016	C9		403C	EE
2048	30				403D	70
2049	02					⋮

PROGRAM COUNTER   2046
STACK POINTER   403D

a. Before Subroutine Call

ADDRESS TO PROGRAM COUNTER ①

SAVE NEXT ADDRESS OF MAIN PROGRAM ②

TRANSFER CONTROL ③

PROGRAM COUNTER   3010
STACK POINTER   403B

b. After Subroutine Call

② TRANSFER CONTROL

① ADDRESS TO PROGRAM COUNTER

PROGRAM COUNTER   2049
STACK POINTER   403D

c. After Return

Figure 10-2. Register and Memory Operations.

CONDITIONAL SUBROUTINE CALLS

Just as with jump instructions, the 8080A supports conditional calling of subroutines. The status register condition is examined here to decide whether the subroutine will be called. If the condition is true, the reference is made just as in the unconditional call instruction. None of the calling instructions affects the status register, so it is the responsibility of the program to establish the condition being tested before executing a conditional subroutine instruction. Normally, an arithmetic or a logical instruction will precede the call to cause the status bits to be properly set. Notice that two execution times are given for these instructions. The instruction is completed faster if the condition being tested is false because no memory reference is needed to fetch the subroutine address. The decision requires three machine cycles, and the address fetch, if required, takes two more machine cycles (see Fig. 10-3).

Call if Carry

If the carry bit is 1, the subroutine is called. Otherwise, the following instruction in the main program is executed immediately.

Operation code	DC
Mnemonic	CC
Addressing mode	direct
Status bits affected	none
Clock periods	17 (11 if the condition is false)
Execution time	8.5 μs (5.5 μs)
Format	

bit number

		7 6 5 4	3 2 1 0
Memory cell	m	1 1 0 1	1 1 0 0
	m + 1	low address byte	
	m + 2	high address byte	

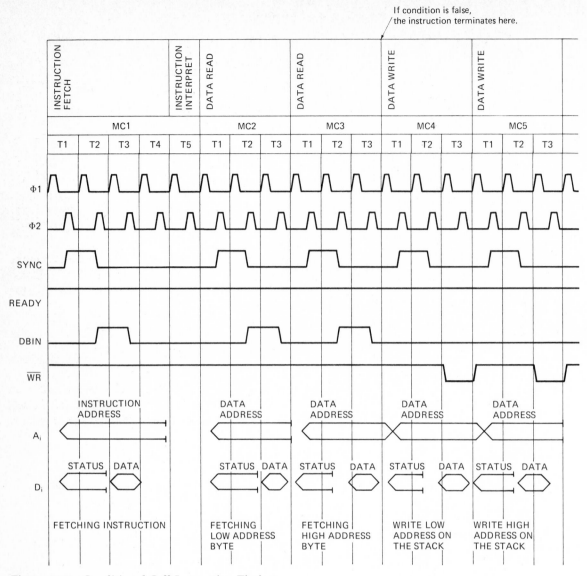

Figure 10-3. Conditional Call Instruction Timing.

□ **EXAMPLE**

Before execution		After execution	
Program counter	0B40	Program counter	0A03
Stack pointer	00F0	Stack pointer	00EE
Status register	03	Status register	03
Memory		Memory	

Stack	00EE	00		00EE	43
	00EF	00		00EF	0B
	00F0	00		00F0	00
Instruction	0B40	DC		0B40	DC
	0B41	03		0B41	03
	0B42	0A		0B42	0A

The carry bit was set, thus indicating that there was a carry out of bit 7 from the last operation. The subroutine at $0A03_{16}$ will be referenced by having that address put into the program counter. The next address in the main program ($0B43_{16}$) is stored in the top two cells of the stack and the stack pointer is updated.

Call if No Carry

This instruction makes a subroutine reference if the carry bit is cleared. The return address is pushed on the stack in the normal manner if the call is made. A carry bit that is set results in the subroutine not being referenced.

Operation code	D4
Mnemonic	CNC
Addressing mode	direct

Status bits affected	none
Clock periods	17 (11 if the condition is false)
Execution time	8.5 μs (5.5 μs)
Format	

bit number
7 6 5 4   3 2 1 0

Memory cell	m	1 1 0 1 0 1 0 0
	m + 1	low address byte
	m + 2	high address byte

□ **EXAMPLE**

Before execution		**After execution**	
Program counter	08C2	Program counter	08C5
Stack pointer	01B7	Stack pointer	01B7
Status register	87	Status register	87
Memory 08C2	D4	Memory 08C2	D4
08C3	20	08C3	20
08C4	06	08C4	06

The carry bit is set, so that subroutine will not be referenced. Instead, the instruction as $08C5_{16}$ will be executed next.

Call if Minus

If the last arithmetic or Boolean instruction produced a negative result, thus causing the sign bit to be set, the subroutine is called. No subroutine action follows if the sign bit is 0.

Operation code	FC
Mnemonic	CM
Addressing mode	direct
Status bits affected	none
Clock periods	17 (11 if the condition is false)
Execution time	8.5 μs (5.5 μs)
Format	

bit number
7 6 5 4   3 2 1 0

Memory cell	m	1 1 1 1 1 1 0 0
	m + 1	low address byte
	m + 2	high address byte

□ **EXAMPLE**

Before execution		**After execution**	
Program counter	2012	Program counter	5905
Stack pointer	0369	Stack pointer	0367
Status register	D2	Status register	D2
Memory		Memory	

Stack	0367	03	0367	15
	0368	00	0368	20
	0369	1D	0369	1D
Instruction	2012	FC	2012	FC
	2013	05	2013	05
	2014	59	2014	59

Because the sign bit is set, a subroutine sequence follows. The return address is saved on the stack, and the program counter is set to the first address in the subprogram.

Call if Plus

A subroutine will be called if the last result was positive (sign bit is 0). In case the sign bit is set, the normal program counter incrementing will occur.

Operation code	F4
Mnemonic	CP
Addressing mode	direct
Status bits affected	none
Clock periods	17 (11 if the condition is false)
Execution time	8.5 μs (5.5 μs)
Format	

bit number
7 6 5 4   3 2 1 0

Memory cell	m	1 1 1 1 0 1 0 0
	m + 1	low address byte
	m + 2	high address byte

□ **EXAMPLE**

Before execution		**After execution**	
Program counter	06A8	Program counter	06AB
Stack pointer	8801	Stack pointer	8801
Status register	82	Status register	82
Memory 06A8	F4	Memory 06A8	F4
06A9	20	06A9	20
06AA	0E	06AA	0E

The status bit for the sign is set prior to the conditional call instruction execution; thus no subroutine calling occurs. The following instruction in the main program will immediately be fetched.

Call if Zero

An earlier zero answer, which set the zero condition bit, will cause this conditional command to make a subroutine call. A nonzero value produces the equivalent to no operation.

Operation code	CC
Mnemonic	CZ
Addressing mode	direct
Status bits affected	none
Clock periods	17 (11 if the condition is false)
Execution time	8.5 μs (5.5 μs)

Format

bit number

		7 6 5 4	3 2 1 0
Memory cell	m	1 1 0 0	1 1 0 0
	m + 1	low address byte	
	m + 2	high address byte	

□ **EXAMPLE**

Before execution		After execution	
Program counter	34CD	Program counter	1140
Stack pointer	701F	Stack pointer	701D
Status register	56	Status register	56
Memory		Memory	

Instruction	34CD	CC		34CD	CC
	34CE	40		34CE	40
	34CF	11		34CF	11
Stack	701D	00		701D	D0
	701E	00		701E	34
	701F	D2		701F	D2

The call is made because the zero bit was set.

Call if Not Zero

A zero condition bit which is clear causes this instruction to make a call. On the other hand, a zero bit which is set disables the calling process.

Operation code	C4
Mnemonic	CNZ

Addressing mode	direct
Status bits affected	none
Clock periods	17 (11 if the condition is false)
Execution time	8.5 μs (5.5 μs)

Format

bit number

		7 6 5 4	3 2 1 0
Memory cell	m	1 1 0 0	0 1 0 0
	m + 1	low address byte	
	m + 2	high address byte	

□ **EXAMPLE**

Before execution		After execution	
Program counter	0147	Program counter	014A
Stack pointer	08C5	Stack pointer	08C5
Status register	46	Status register	46
Memory	0147 C4	Memory	0147 C4
	0148 EC		0148 EC
	0149 02		0149 02

No reference is made because the zero status bit is set, thus indicating that the previous result was equal to 0.

Call if Parity Even

An even parity answer to an arithmetic or a logic instruction will set the parity condition bit. A call will be made only if the parity bit is set prior to this conditional command.

Operation code	EC
Mnemonic	CPE
Addressing mode	direct
Status bits affected	none
Clock periods	17 (11 if the condition is false)
Execution time	8.5 μs (5.5 μs)

Format

bit number

		7 6 5 4	3 2 1 0
Memory cell	m	1 1 1 0	1 1 0 0
	m + 1	low address byte	
	m + 2	high address byte	

Before execution		After execution	
Program counter	0445	Program counter	0EA1
Stack pointer	1182	Stack pointer	1180
Status register	06	Status register	06
Memory		Memory	

Instruction	0445	EC	0445	EC
	0446	A1	0446	A1
	0447	0E	0447	0E
Stack	1180	20	1180	48
	1181	11	1181	04
	1182	4A	1182	4A

The three operations required to make a subroutine call have been completed as a result of the parity being set prior to executing the instruction.

Call if Parity Odd

An odd parity indication in the status register triggers this conditional operation. If the bit is set (an indication of even parity), this instruction is essentially ignored.

Operation code	E4
Mnemonic	CPO
Addressing mode	direct
Status bits affected	none
Clock periods	17 (11 if the condition is false)
Execution time	8.5 µs (5.5 µs)
Format	

bit number

		7 6 5 4	3 2 1 0
Memory cell	m	1 1 1 0	0 1 0 0
	m + 1	low address byte	
	m + 2	high address byte	

Before execution		After execution	
Program counter	09FC	Program counter	09FF
Stack pointer	1187	Stack pointer	1187
Status register	17	Status register	17
Memory	09FC	E4	Memory	09FC	E4
	09FD	0C		09F0	0C
	09FE	2D		09FE	2D

The parity was even, as shown by a condition bit of 1. No call is made.

Conditional Subroutine Call Review

1. List the conditions that can be tested to decide whether a subroutine should be referenced.

2. Explain the change in the stack and the stack pointer in the example for the CC instruction.

3. How is the value to be placed in the program counter obtained if the condition is true for a CM instruction. If the condition is false?

4. What would be the result of a CPE instruction if the preceding instruction had been ADC B? Before the add, the A register was equal to 4_{16} and the status register, to 93_{16}.

CONDITIONAL RETURN INSTRUCTIONS

The next family of instructions to be discussed provides parallel capabilities for returning from subroutines to the ones just discussed for calling the subprograms. An excellent use for a conditional return is the termination of counting loops. If the subroutine uses an iterative process, like the multiplication routine, for example, the test for final count could be made with a conditional return instruction. One instruction could both decide if the loop should complete on the current pass and also transfer control back to the main program.

If the condition is satisfied, popping the stack, incrementing the stack pointer, and loading the program counter proceed in a manner identical to the unconditional return. There is no requirement for matching conditional calls to conditional returns, of course. Any combination of conditional and unconditional calling and returning instructions is allowed. The execution time for these instructions is variable. One machine cycle is used to make the decision, and an additional two cycles are needed to fetch the address if the condition is satisfied as shown in Figure 10-4.

Return if Carry

If the carry bit is set, a return will be made to the program which called the subroutine. If the carry bit is not set, operation continues with the instruction following the return if carry command.

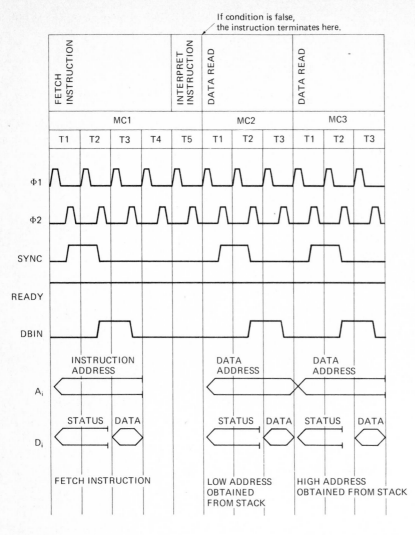

At top of figure: If condition is false, the instruction terminates here.

Column labels (vertical): FETCH INSTRUCTION | INTERPRET INSTRUCTION | DATA READ | DATA READ

Machine cycles: MC1 | MC2 | MC3
Timing states: T1 T2 T3 T4 T5 | T1 T2 T3 | T1 T2 T3

Signals: Φ1, Φ2, SYNC, READY, DBIN, A_i, D_i

A_i: INSTRUCTION ADDRESS | DATA ADDRESS | DATA ADDRESS
D_i: STATUS DATA | STATUS DATA | STATUS DATA

FETCH INSTRUCTION | LOW ADDRESS OBTAINED FROM STACK | HIGH ADDRESS OBTAINED FROM STACK

Figure 10-4. Conditional Return Instruction Timing.

Operation code	D8	
Mnemonic	RC	
Addressing mode	none	
Status bits affected	none	
Clock periods	11 (5 if the condition is false)	
Execution time	5.5 μs (2.5 μs)	

Format

bit number

7 6 5 4   3 2 1 0

Memory cell   m | 1 1 0 1 | 1 0 0 0 |

□ **EXAMPLE**

Before execution		After execution	
Program counter	01AD	Program counter	07BB
Stack pointer	2146	Stack pointer	2148
Status register	83	Status register	83
Memory		Memory	

	Instruction	01AD	D8		01AD	D8
Stack		2146	BB		2146	BB
		2147	07		2147	07
		2148	1A		2148	1A

The condition being tested is true. The contents of the cell addressed by the stack pointer go to the lower half of the program counter; the upper half of the counter is loaded from the following location in the stack. Then the stack pointer counts up by 2.

Return if No Carry

A 0 value of the condition carry bit causes a return if this instruction is used. No return occurs if that bit is set. The next instruction in the subroutine will be executed instead.

Operation code	D0
Mnemonic	RNC
Addressing mode	none
Status bits affected	none

Clock periods	11 (5 if the condition is false)
Execution time	5.5 μs (2.5 μs)

Format

bit number

		7 6 5 4	3 2 1 0
Memory cell	m	1 1 0 1	0 0 0 0

□ EXAMPLE

Before execution		After execution	
Program counter	3111	Program counter	3112
Stack pointer	0A2D	Stack pointer	0A2D
Status register	43	Status register	43
Memory 3111	D0	Memory 3111	D0

The condition is not satisfied, so the program counter merely increments to the next instruction address.

Return if Minus

A return is made if the sign bit had been set prior to this instruction. If that bit is clear, no return takes place.

Operation code	F8
Mnemonic	RM
Addressing mode	none
Status bits affected	none
Clock periods	11 (5 if the condition is false)
Execution time	5.5 μs (2.5 μs)

Format

bit number

		7 6 5 4	3 2 1 0
Memory cell	m	1 1 1 1	1 0 0 0

□ EXAMPLE

Before execution		After execution	
Program counter	2A36	Program counter	420C
Stack pointer	3014	Stack pointer	3016
Status register	92	Status register	92
Memory		Memory	
Instruction 2A36	F8	2A36	F8
Stack { 3014	0C	3014	0C
3015	42	3015	42
3016	90	3016	90

The return to the instruction at $420C_{16}$ in the main program results from the sign status bit being set.

Return if Plus

If the sign bit is 0, thus indicating a positive result, the return operation is performed.

Operation code	F0
Mnemonic	RP
Addressing mode	none
Status bits affected	none
Clock periods	11 (5 if the condition is false)
Execution time	5.5 μs (5.5 μs)

Format

bit number

		7 6 5 4	3 2 1 0
Memory cell	m	1 1 1 1	0 0 0 0

□ EXAMPLE

Before execution		After execution	
Program counter	0CA2	Program counter	0CA3
Stack pointer	118E	Stack pointer	118E
Status register	86	Status register	86
Memory 0CA2	F0	Memory 0CA2	F0

The sign bit is set, so the return operation is not done. The instruction following the conditional return will be executed next.

Return if Zero

The status register is examined, and if the zero condition bit is set, the return is accomplished. If the tested condition is not fulfilled, the next successive instruction follows.

Operation code	C8
Mnemonic	RZ
Addressing mode	none
Status bits affected	none
Clock periods	11 (5 if the condition is not satisfied)
Execution time	5.5 μs (2.5 μs)

Format

bit number

		7 6 5 4	3 2 1 0
Memory cell	m	1 1 0 0	1 0 0 0

Before execution		After execution	
Program counter	4763	Program counter	0E24
Stack pointer	6211	Stack pointer	6213
Status register	46	Status register	46
Memory		Memory	
Instruction 47C3	C8	4763	C8
⎧ 6211	24	6211	24
Stack ⎨ 6212	0E	6212	0E
⎩ 6213	78	6213	78

The previous result was zero (condition bit is set), so the return goes through. The return address from the stack is moved to the program counter and the pointer value revised.

Return if Not Zero

If the zero condition bit shows that the previous answer was other than zero, the return is effective. Otherwise there is no change from normal program counter incrementing.

Operation code	C0
Mnemonic	RNZ
Addressing mode	none
Status bits affected	none
Clock periods	11 (5 if the condition is false)
Execution time	5.5 μs (2.5 μs)
Format	

bit number

7 6 5 4   3 2 1 0

Memory cell   m | 1 1 0 0   0 0 0 0 |

EXAMPLE

Before execution		After execution	
Program counter	314B	Program counter	314C
Stack pointer	2182	Stack pointer	2182
Status register	46	Status register	46
Memory 314B	C0	Memory 314B	C0

No return is made because the zero condition bit was set.

Return if Parity Even

Even parity in the last arithmetic or logical result (condition bit set) will cause a return. No action is produced if the bit is clear.

Operation code	E8
Mnemonic	RPE
Addressing mode	none
Status bits affected	none
Clock periods	11 (5 if the condition is false)
Execution time	5.5 μs (2.5 μs)
Format	

bit number

7 6 5 4   3 2 1 0

Memory cell   m | 1 1 1 0   1 0 0 0 |

EXAMPLE

Before execution		After execution	
Program counter	1A84	Program counter	3103
Stack pointer	53D2	Stack pointer	53D4
Status register	47	Status register	47
Memory		Memory	
Instruction 1A84	E8	1A84	E8
⎧ 53D2	03	53D2	03
Stack ⎨ 53D3	31	53D3	31
⎩ 53D4	14	53D4	14

The parity was even, so the stack is popped. The address is loaded into the program counter to transfer back to the calling program.

Return if Parity Odd

An odd parity designation in the status register will allow the return to be made with this instruction.

Operation code	E0
Mnemonic	RPO
Addressing mode	none
Status bits affected	none
Clock periods	11 (5 if the condition is false)
Execution time	5.5 μs (2.5 μs)
Format	

bit number

7 6 5 4   3 2 1 0

Memory cell   m | 1 1 1 0   0 0 0 0 |

Before execution		After execution	
Program counter	4C01	Program counter	4C02
Stack pointer	0FEE	Stack pointer	0FEE
Status register	07	Status register	07
Memory 4C01	E0	Memory 4C01	E0

The parity status bit was set, thus indicating even parity. The return is not taken.

Conditional Return Review

1. How many machine cycles does the example for the RC instruction require? With a 2-MHz clock, what is the execution time?

2. Why does the return if plus example require only five clock periods to execute?

3. What is the purpose of DBIN going high during T2 of MC2 in Fig. 10-4?

4. Explain the settings of all status register bits in the RM instruction example.

5. What status register setting would have enabled the return in the $E0_{16}$ op code instruction example?

ADVANCED SUBROUTINE CONCEPTS

So far in this chapter we have considered only a main program calling a subroutine. What would we have if one subroutine called another? Can a subroutine call itself? Both situations are handled properly by the 8080A through the stack. When one subroutine calls another, we refer to the inner one as a *nested subroutine.* If a subroutine can call itself, it is a *recursive subroutine.*

Nested Subroutines

As an example of a nested subroutine, we will use the multiplication program from Chap. 8 with a slight modification. We only need to add a return instruction at the end of the program to convert it to a subroutine. Remember that the program works only with positive numbers. We will complete the multiplication capability by writing a routine that checks for a difference in the sign of the multiplier and the multiplicand. If they are different, a negative product must be produced. The sign routine will also convert negative multipliers and multiplicands to positive numbers and will then properly adjust the sign of the product. The calling sequence is shown in Fig. 10-5 and the two programs listed below. (Only the operation codes for the multiplication routine are given because this program was fully discussed in the earlier chapter.)

The sequence as shown in Fig. 10-5 begins with calling of the sign program to convert any negative inputs to positive. The sign program calls the multiplication routine, which performs the operation and returns to the sign program. After adjusting the product, the sign subroutine gives control back to the main program. The flowchart for the sign program is given in Fig. 10-6.

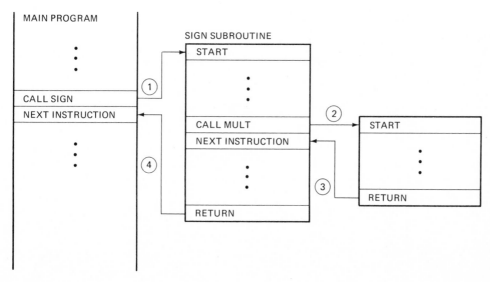

Figure 10-5. Multiplication Calling Sequence.

Label	Mnemonic	Operand	Address	Machine Code	Comments
SIGN	MOV	A,D	1460	7A	Obtain operand 1
	XRA	B	1461	A8	Exclusive OR with operand 2
	MVI A	0	1462	3E	Clear accumulator
			1463	00	
	JP	STRFLAG	1464	C3	Jump to store sign if positive
			1465	68	
			1466	14	
	CMP	A	1467	BF	Complement A
STRFLAG	STA	FLAG	1468	32	Save results of comparison
			1469	90	
			146A	14	
	CALL	MULT	146B	CD	Call subroutine
			146C	00	
			146D	10	
	LDA	FLAG	1470	3A	If product does not need to be
			1471	90	complemented, return
			1472	14	
	ADI	0	1473	C6	
			1474	00	
	RP		1475	F0	
	MVI A	0	1476	3E	Complement product
			1475	00	
	SUB	C	1476	91	
	MOV	C,A	1477	4F	
	MVI A	0	1478	3E	
			1479	00	
	SBB	B	147A	98	
	MOV	B,A	147B	47	
	RET		147C	C9	
DATA	FLAG		1490		Data storage

Label	Mnemonic	Operand	Address	Machine Code	Comments
MULT	MVI B	0	1000	06	
			1001	00	
	MVI E	9	1002	1E	
			1003	09	
MULT1	MOV	A,C	1004	79	
	RAR		1005	1F	
	MOV	C,M	1006	4E	
	DCR	E	1007	1D	
	JZ	DONE	1008	CA	
			1009	15	
			100A	10	
	MOV	A,B	100B	78	
	JNC	MULT2	100C	D2	
			100D	10	
			100E	10	
	ADD	D	100F	82	
MULT2	RAR		1010	1F	
	MOV	B,A	1011	47	
	JMP	MULT1	1012	C3	
			1013	04	
			1014	10	
DONE	RET		1015	C9	

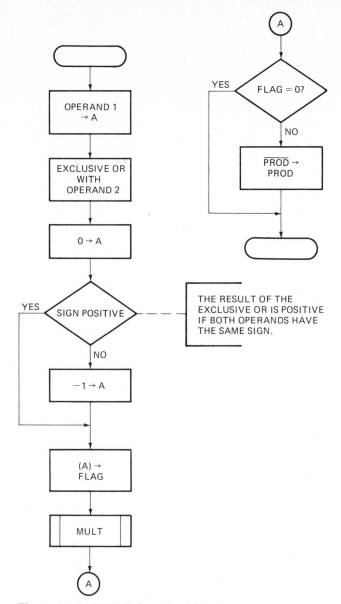

Figure 10-6. SIGN Subroutine Flowchart.

SIGN PROGRAM

The multiplier must be in the C register and the multiplicand in the D register prior to calling. The product will be in the double-length BC register pair on return. Figure 10-7 shows how the stack

changes for each call or return. We will assume that an instruction in address 4526_{16} called the sign program. (Because the call instruction occupies 3 bytes, the next instruction is located at 4529_{16}.) The stack pointer contained 5689_{16} before the process started.

The return address to the main program (4529_{16}) is pushed onto the stack (see Fig. 10-7a). When the SIGN program calls MULT, the return address 1470_{16} is also placed on the stack and the pointer increased by 2 to show the new top of stack (Fig. 10-7b).

Returning is simply a reverse process. To transfer control back to the SIGN program after MULT is through, the stack is popped to load address 1470_{16} into the program counter (see Fig. 10-7c). The final return, to the main program, is made in the same way (see Fig. 10-7d).

This process can continue until the stack is completely filled, so that the level of nested subroutines is limited only by the amount of memory available. Of course, the program, the data, and the stack must share the memory. Figure 10-8 shows an efficient way of allocating a 4K RAM to these processes which must compete for memory space. This allocation permits the maximum program and the stack size simultaneously. Memory is filled when the program and the stack overlap, because the instructions and data fill increasing memory addresses while the stack grows toward decreasing addresses.

Recursive Processes

Some problems are well suited to a repetitive use of a subroutine. In such cases the nested subroutine calls itself, thus increasing the level of nesting. A simple example of recursion is an algorithm which sums the numbers from 1 to n. We can easily calculate the sum of the jth digit to the previous ones by the formula

$$\sum_{i=1}^{j} i = j + \sum_{i=1}^{j-1} i \qquad (10\text{-}1)$$

By continuing this process until j is equal to n, we arrive at the required sum. A recursive subroutine to calculate the sum is listed below. The value for

SUM

Instruction	Address	Machine Code	Comments
ADD B	1000	80	Add next number to sum
DCR B	1001	05	Decrement n
CNZ	1002	C4	If nonzero, call again
	1003	00	
	1004	10	
RET	1005	C9	Return

STACK POINTER	STACK ADDRESS	CONTENTS
5687	5685	20
	5686	FF
	5687	29
	5688	45
	5689	A2

a. MAIN PROGRAM CALLS SIGN

STACK POINTER	STACK ADDRESS	CONTENTS
5685	5685	70
	5686	14
	5687	29
	5688	45
	5689	A2

b. SIGN CALLS MULT

STACK POINTER	STACK ADDRESS	CONTENTS
5687	5685	70] TO PROGRAM COUNTER
	5686	14
	5687	29
	5688	45
	5689	A2

c. RETURN FROM MULT

STACK POINTER	STACK ADDRESS	CONTENTS
5689	5685	70
	5686	14
	5687	29] TO PROGRAM COUNTER
	5688	45
	5689	A2

d. RETURN TO MAIN PROGRAM

Figure 10-7. Dynamic Stack Contents.

n must be placed in the B register and the accumulator set to zero prior to the call. The answer is left in the accumulator. No check for overflow is made, so if

$$\sum_{i=1}^{n} i > 7F_{16} \qquad (10\text{-}2)$$

the result will be wrong. There is another possible bug in the program if n is not selected properly (see Prob. 10-1). An example of the stack sequences for n = 3 is shown in Fig. 10-9. The pushing and the popping sequences guarantee that the instructions will be executed in the proper order, and control will eventually return to the main program. We see that the same address (1007_{16}) is placed on the stack twice (see Figs. 10-9b and 10-9c). In fact, that address would be pushed onto the stack every time the sum procedure is called by itself. After the first return (see Fig. 10-9d), the next instruction to be executed is the *same* return. This execution causes the stack to be popped again (see Fig. 10-9e), and for the second time in a row, the instruction at 1007_{16} is performed. Then the address popped from the stack is that of the return to the main program.

This example clearly shows the two characteristics of recursive programs. They are usually quite compact, requiring little memory space; however, they often consume a great deal of running time. The repeated execution of the return instruction at location 1007_{16} is a good illustration of the ineffi-

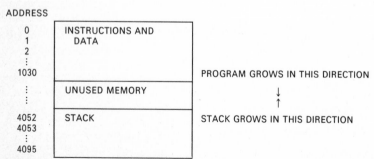

Figure 10-8. Memory Allocation.

STACK POINTER	STACK ADDRESS	CONTENTS
1027	1020	00
	1021	00
	1022	00
	1023	00
	1024	00
	1025	00
	1026	00
	1027	40
	1028	20

a. Initial call when n = 3, return address in main program is 2040_{16}

STACK POINTER	STACK ADDRESS	CONTENTS
1025	1020	00
	1021	00
	1022	00
	1023	00
	1024	00
	1025	07
	1026	10
	1027	40
	1028	20

b. Call when n = 2

STACK POINTER	STACK ADDRESS	CONTENTS
1023	1020	00
	1021	00
	1022	00
	1023	07
	1024	10
	1025	07
	1026	10
	1027	40
	1028	20

c. Call when n = 1

STACK POINTER	STACK ADDRESS	CONTENTS	
1025	1020	00	
	1021	00	
	1022	00	
	1023	07	] TO PROGRAM COUNTER
	1024	10	
	1025	07	
	1026	10	
	1027	40	
	1028	20	

d. First return

STACK POINTER	STACK ADDRESS	CONTENTS	
1027	1020	00	
	1021	00	
	1022	00	
	1023	07	
	1024	10	
	1025	07	] TO PROGRAM COUNTER
	1026	10	
	1027	40	
	1028	20	

e. Second return

STACK POINTER	STACK ADDRESS	CONTENTS	
1029	1020	00	
	1021	00	
	1022	00	
	1023	07	
	1024	10	
	1025	07	
	1026	10	
	1027	40	] TO PROGRAM COUNTER
	1028	20	

f. Third return to main program.

Figure 10-9. Recursive Stack Processes.

ciency in processor utilization. As n gets larger, even more instruction executions are required to simply pop the stack. Because computers are good at repetitive tasks, it may be a good idea to trade off longer running time for memory space. See Prob. 10-2 for another way of dealing with this issue.

Parameter Passing

The input data of all the subroutines used in this chapter was loaded into specific registers before the subroutine was called. The answer was also available in some register on return. Getting the information back and forth between the subroutine and the calling program is more formally designated *parameter passing*. The input and the output numbers are the parameters which the subroutine processes.

The number of registers is limited, so if the number of parameters to be passed exceeds the number of registers, another method must be used. A frequently used technique is a *parameter pointer*. In the 8080A the HL register pair can be put to use in that fashion.

Assume that we want to call a subroutine that will arrange 100 numbers in ascending numerical order. The numbers are located in a table that may begin at any memory location. Figure 10-10a shows how the HL registers can be used to point to the starting address. By selecting instructions which use the HL registers to address the operand (such as ADD M, MOV B,M, and SUB M), the routine can efficiently manipulate items in the table. It is obviously the responsibility of the *calling* routine to establish the proper values in the H and the L registers before the subroutine reference.

Sometimes the number of parameters to be passed is variable. Consider a communications system that receives and processes messages of any length. The messages are received in the form of ASCII characters, and every transmission ends with an end of text (EOT = 04_{16}) control code. A subroutine is to examine each character for proper parity until the EOT character is encountered. Again, the HL registers can be used to show the starting address of the table, but the end is signaled by the control character.

Exactly the same technique can be used by the subroutine to pass the output parameters. As an example of such a situation, the parity checking program above can indicate correct or incorrect parity for each character in an answer table. The answer table is the same length as the character table. The answer table corresponds item for item with the input. Correct parity is shown by a 0 value in that byte of the answer table and incorrect parity, by FF_{16} in the answer table. The HL register pair is set to the starting address of the answer table by the subroutine before the return.

Advanced Subroutine Concepts Review

1. Distinguish between nested and recursive subroutines.

2. Explain how the stack manages the four transfers of control shown in Fig. 10-5.

3. How does the SIGN program decide if the product must be complemented?

4. Why was some register, instead of the flag cell, not used to temporarily store the decision value in the SIGN subroutine?

5. Describe the most practical memory allocation scheme when a stack is being used.

6. What limits the number of times a recursive subroutine can call itself?

7. Calculate the number of times the return instruction of the SUM program would be performed if $n = 8$.

8. Discuss the tradeoff of memory space and running time of recursive routines.

9. Explain how a pointer register pair can be used to pass a fixed or a variable number of parameters to a subroutine.

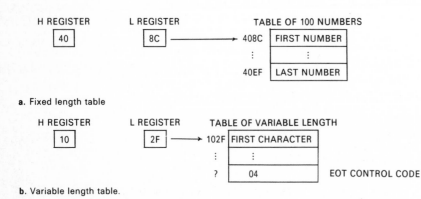

a. Fixed length table

b. Variable length table.

EOT CONTROL CODE

Figure 10-10. Parameter Passing with Pointers.

OTHER STACK INSTRUCTIONS

In addition to being useful for calling and returning from subroutines, the stack can also be used for data storage. Normally, such storage would be of a temporary nature when declaring a memory variable is unnecessary. The stack will hold the information until it is again needed in the calculations.

Push

Any register pair, or the status register and the accumulator, can be pushed onto the stack by using this instruction. (This is the only command that permits a direct examination of the status bits.) The contents of the first register are saved at the location preceding the stack pointer value and the second register, at the address 2 less than the pointer. The stack pointer is then decremented by 2. Figure 10-11 shows how this operation is performed. As Fig. 10-11 shows, the value in the B, D, H, or program status word (condition bits) is stored at the higher address in the stack. The corresponding register of the pair (C, E, L, or A) is stored in the lower address. The stack pointer is modified to the new top of stack.

Operation Code	Mnemonic
C5	PUSH B
D5	PUSH D
E5	PUSH H
F5	PUSH PSW

Addressing mode	register
Status bits affected	none
Clock periods	11
Execution time	5.5 μs
Format	

bit number

7 6 5 4   3 2 1 0

Memory cell   m   1 1 r r   0 1 0 1

STACK POINTER	STACK ADDRESS	CONTENTS
2B3D	2B3B	FF
	2B3C	FF
	2B3D	FF

a. Before execution

STACK POINTER	STACK ADDRESS	CONTENTS
2B3B	2B3B	REGISTER 2 (C, E, L, OR A)
	2B3C	REGISTER 1 (B, D, H, OR PSW)
	2B3D	FF

b. After execution

where rr = 00 for registers B and C
01 for registers D and E
10 for registers H and L
11 for PSW and A registers

□ EXAMPLE

Before execution		After execution	
Program counter	2240	Program counter	2241
Stack pointer	3565	Stack pointer	3563
A register	CD	A register	CD
Status register	97	Status register	97

	Memory				Memory	
Instruction	2240	F5			2240	F5
	3563	22			3563	CD
Stack	3564	0F			3564	97
	3565	07			3565	07

After the status register is placed in location 3564_{16} and the accumulator in 3563_{16}, the pointer is set to the address for the new top of stack (3563_{16}).

Pop

Data can be removed from the stack and placed into a register pair with this command. The byte at the address of the stack pointer is moved to one register of a pair (C, E, L, or A), and the byte from the next higher stack location is placed in the corresponding register for that same pair (B, D, H, or PSW). The stack pointer increments by 2.

Operation Code	Mnemonic
C1	POP B
D1	POP D
E1	POP H
F1	POP PSW

Figure 10-11. PUSH Instruction.

Address mode	register
Status bits affected	none (op codes C1, D1, and E1), S, Z, A$_C$, P, and C (op code F1)
Clock periods	10
Execution time	5 µs

Format

```
                           bit number
                     7 6 5 4   3 2 1 0
Memory cell   m  │ 1 1 r r   0 0 0 1 │
```

where rr = 00 for registers B and C
01 for registers D and E
10 for registers H and L
11 for PSW and A register

□ **EXAMPLE 1.** Register pair.

Before execution		After execution	
Program counter	10FC	Program counter	10FD
Stack pointer	30FE	Stack pointer	3100
B register	FF	B register	19
C register	00	C register	B0

Memory				Memory		
Instruction	10FC	C1		10FC	C1	
	30FE	B0		30FE	B0	
Stack	30FF	19		30FF	19	
	3100	27		3100	27	

□ **EXAMPLE 2.** Status register and accumulator.

Before execution		After execution	
Program counter	027B	Program counter	027C
Stack pointer	058A	Stack pointer	158C
A register	11	A register	00
Status register	02	Status register	86

Memory				Memory		
Instruction	0278	F1		027B	F1	
	058A	00		158A	00	
Stack	158B	86		158B	86	
	158C	FF		158C	FF	

There is no requirement for popping the data off the stack and into the same registers that pushed it onto the stack. In fact, a clever means of moving data from one pair of registers to another can be accomplished by using the stack:

```
PUSH   B
POP    D
```

This moves the value in the B register to the D register and the contents of the C register to the E register.

Load Stack Pointer

The stack pointer was used in all the examples in this chapter, but until now no mention has been made of how the pointer is initiated. If the stack is to be used by a program, either to call subroutines or to push and pop register pairs, the stack pointer must be set to some starting value. Otherwise, it will be equal to some unknown, random address. As Fig. 10-8 showed, this value is frequently the highest memory address, although it does not have to be. Loading the stack pointer is normally one of the first instructions performed in the main program.

One way of loading the stack pointer is with the LXI instruction discussed in Chap. 5. There is also another instruction for the 8080A which places the HL register pair data in the pointer. Of course, the registers must have been set to the proper values prior to executing this instruction. Once the stack pointer has been initiated, it should not be reloaded because its previous value will be lost.

Operation code	F9
Mnemonic	SPHL
Addressing mode	register
Status bits affected	none
Clock periods	5
Execution time	2.5 µs

Format

```
                           bit number
                     7 6 5 4   3 2 1 0
Memory cell   m  │ 1 1 1 1   1 0 0 1 │
```

□ **EXAMPLE**

Before execution		After execution	
Program counter	47F1	Program counter	47F2
Stack pointer	021D	Stack pointer	58FF
H register	58	H register	58
L register	FF	L register	FF
Memory	47F1	F9	Memory	47F1	F9

The upper byte of the pointer is set equal to the H register and the lower byte, equal to the L register.

Exchange Stack

This command causes the value in the top 2 bytes of the stack and the HL register pair to be interchanged. The L register is swapped with the contents of the location equal to that of the stack pointer and the H register, with the contents of the cell at the pointer address plus 1. The stack pointer value is unchanged.

Operation code	E3
Mnemonic	XTHL
Addressing mode	register
Status bits affected	none
Clock periods	18
Execution time	9 μs

Format

		bit number
		7 6 5 4 3 2 1 0
Memory cell	m	1 1 1 0 0 0 1 1

□ EXAMPLE

Before execution		After execution	
Program counter	18A9	Program counter	18AA
Stack pointer	2546	Stack pointer	2546
H register	11	H register	01
L register	B0	L register	FF
Memory		Memory	
Instruction 18A9	E3	18A9	E3
Stack { 2546	FF	2546	B0
2547	01	2547	11

The quantities in the stack and the register pair were switched. The stack pointer final address is equal to the initial one.

Other Stack Instructions Review

1. When the accumulator and the status register are pushed onto the stack, which register goes to the lower address?

2. All the registers and the counters in Example 1 of the POP instruction are changed. Explain the reason for their final values.

3. Name two instructions that can be used to load the stack pointer.

4. At what point in the program should the stack pointer be loaded? When should another load

stack pointer instruction be executed once the program is running?

5. How is the stack pointer affected by the exchange stack instruction? Explain why this action is logical.

CHAPTER SUMMARY

1. A subroutine is a group of instructions that is assigned a name. The instructions can be referenced to perform a certain task that is usually repeated many times in a problem.

2. A subroutine is called to reference it. After execution, the subroutine returns control to the address immediately following the call instructions.

3. The stack facilitates calling and returning from subroutines in a 8080A. The address following the call is pushed on the stack, and then the first address of the subroutine is loaded into the program counter. When the subroutine completes, the return causes the stack to be popped. The data on top of the stack, the return address, is forced into the program counter. Control is then transferred to the main program.

4. The call and the return instructions must always be used as a pair for proper operation.

5. Conditional calling and returning instructions are included in the 8080A repertoire. The subroutine operation will proceed only if the designated condition of the status register is true.

6. The timing for conditional call and return instructions depends on whether the status being tested for is true. If true, an additional two machine cycles are appended to the instruction to fetch the subroutine address from memory.

7. Subroutines may be nested to any level in the 8080A. Only the RAM space available for the stack limits the number of levels.

8. Allocation of the stack initially to the highest address provides for the maximum utilization of memory space.

9. Recursive subroutines are constructed with the ability of calling themselves. Another return address is added to the stack as a result of each call.

10. Subroutine parameter passing can be implemented by using registers or memory. When memory is used, a parameter pointer shows where the data table starts. The data table need not always have the same length.

11. Register pairs, including the program status word and the accumulator, can be pushed on the stack. The register values can be restored by popping the stack.

12. The stack pointer must be initiated whenever the program is restarted. Either of two instructions may be used to establish the pointer address.

13. Table 10-1 lists each of the subroutine and stack instructions.

Table 10-1
Subroutine and Stack Operations

Mnemonic	Machine Code	Number of Bytes	Execution Time, μs	Status Bits Affected				
				C	A_c	Z	S	P
CALL	CD	3	8.5					
CC	DC	3	5.5/8.5					
CM	FC	3	5.5/8.5					
CNC	D4	3	5.5/8.5					
CNZ	C4	3	5.5/8.5					
CP	F4	3	5.5/8.5					
CPE	EC	3	5.5/8.5					
CPO	E4	3	5.5/8.5					
CZ	CC	3	5.5/8.5					
POP B,D,H, PSW	C1,D1,E1,F1	1	5	X*	X	X	X	X
PUSH B,D,H, PSW	C5,D5,E5,F5	1	5.5					
RC	D8	1	2.5/5.5					
RET	C9	1	5†					
RM	F8	1	2.5/5.5					
RNC	D0	1	2.5/5.5					
RNZ	C0	1	2.5/5.5					
RP	F0	1	2.5/5.5					
RPE	E8	1	2.5/5.5					
RPO	E0	1	2.5/5.5					
RZ	C8	1	2.5/5.5					
SPHL	F9	1	2.5‡					
XTHL	E3	1	9§					

*F1 only.
†NEC 8080A = 5.5 μs.
‡NEC 8080A = 2 μs.
§NEC 8080A = 8.5 μs.

KEY TERMS AND CONCEPTS

Subroutine

Call

Return

Calling program

Stack usage for subroutines

Unconditional and conditional call

Unconditional and conditional return

Timing diagrams

Nested subroutines

Memory allocation for stack and program

Recursive subroutine

Parameter passing

Parameter pointer

Register pair storage on stack

Loading the stack pointer

Exchange stack and register pair

10-1 What would happen if the n input to the SUM subroutine were 0? What if $n = -120$?

10-2 Rewrite the SUM routine by using a loop instead of a recursive subroutine call. Compare the number of memory locations required for each version. Compare the execution times of the two routines for $n = 3$.

10-3 What would happen if the instruction at 1475_{16} of the SIGN routine were changed to RET (C9)? No other changes are made in the SIGN program.

10-4 The status register in the example for the CNC instruction is changed to 86_{16} before execution. Show the contents of all counters, the registers, and the stack after the instruction completes with the new initial condition.

10-5 Write a routine equivalent to the SIGN program that properly processes negative dividends and divisors for the division program in Chap. 7, calls the division routine (which has a return instruction appended to it), and corrects the sign of the quotient, if necessary.

10-6 Write an equation expressing the number of times the return instruction at location 1005_{16} of the SUM program is executed for an arbitrary value of n.

10-7 Write the instructions to prevent an error if the condition of Eq. (10-2) is true. These instructions will set the accumulator negative and return if the sum is going to be greater than $7F_{16}$.

10-8 If the n input to the SUM program is 16_{10}, how many recursive calls are made? What value is found in the A register on return?

10-9 The initial call on the SUM program is made from location 3601_{16}. (That is, the op code for the call instruction is at that address.) Show the final configuration of the stack after all calls and returns have been made if $n = 4$. The original stack pointer value is 6400_{16}.

10-10 The end of text character in Fig. 10-10*b* may be received incorrectly. That is, some bits may be erroneously set or cleared because of line noise. Devise a scheme for detecting the end of the parameter table that will be able to accommodate such errors and still find the last character of the text.

EXPERIMENT 10

PURPOSE: To investigate nested subroutines.

PROCEDURE:

STEP 1. Enter the multiplication and sign programs given earlier in this chapter.

STEP 2. Write a main program to call these routines and compute the product of these inputs:

Multiplier$_{16}$	Multiplicand$_{16}$
4	2
−4	3
FF	FF
F6	31
B4	AB
77	77

(Remember to use complement arithmetic for negative numbers.) Record the products you obtain and prove them correct by using hexadecimal arithmetic.

STEP 3. Record the stack pointer value for the last set of values. Also record the contents of 10 memory locations starting with the address on top of the stack and going toward *increasing* addresses. You can set up a table something like this:

Stack Pointer		
Cell	**Address**	**Contents**
1		
2		
3		
4		
5		
6		
7		
8		
9		
10		

Explain the reason for each value in the 10 memory cells.

11

INPUT AND OUTPUT

After all the calculations have been completed by the computer, the results must be presented in a form that a human being can read. The computer must also be able to accept new data or programs so that it can continue to process.

The input/output (I/O) sections of the computer provide facilities for these transfers under control of the software. As you will see in this chapter and in Chap. 12, moving information between the microcomputer and the external devices requires a good understanding of hardware and software interactions.

This chapter discusses the 8080A instructions used to send or receive data in parallel on the bus. Consideration is given to accumulator and memory-mapped I/O, direct memory access, and interrupts. Chapter 12 then explores typical hardware available for I/O and how the peripheral devices interface with the buses.

CHAPTER OBJECTIVES

Upon completion of this chapter, you should be able to:

1. Distinguish between accumulator and memory-mapped I/O.
2. Explain the function of the 8080A I/O instructions.
3. Discuss the use of interrupts in information exchange.
4. Explain the differences between single, multiple, and vectored interrupt architectures.
5. Define the term "direct memory access."

INPUT/OUTPUT CONCEPTS

Before starting the detailed study of specific I/O methods, let's briefly consider the various ways of exchanging data between the microcomputer and the external devices, often referred to as *peripheral equipment*. Such devices might include printers (Fig. 11-1) CRT terminals (Fig. 11-2), or floppy disk drives (Fig. 11-3).

Data can move in either direction to the computer as shown in Fig. 11-4. The direction is always relative to that computer. That is, output means that the computer is sending and input, that the computer is receiving. This convention prevents the confusion that sometimes arises when discussing the exchange from the peripheral equipment point of view. That equipment must receive output data and send input data. Notice in Figure 11-4 that every device need not handle two-way data exchange. Only device 3 has that ability. Device 1 accepts output data only, like a printer. Device 2 can only send data, such as a temperature sensor.

The 8080A microprocessor can accept or send data by using either *accumulator I/O* instructions or by *memory-mapped I/O* techniques. The input and output instructions and an I/O port are used in the former situation, while the peripheral is treated as part of memory in the latter case. An external device, suitably equipped, can notify the processor when it has input data to transmit or of any other special event by means of *interrupt* signals. The microprocessor must be able to process this signal at any time. An even more sophisticated I/O device can cause the microcomputer memory to allow that device to read or write data by mimicking the processor on the system buses. The microprocessor and the *direct memory access* (DMA) device share memory accesses in this scheme. The sections in this chapter will more fully explain these techniques.

Figure 11-1. Printer and Paper Tape Reader *(Teletype Corporation).*

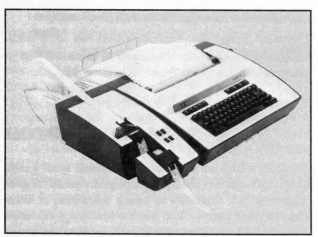

Figure 11-2. CRT Terminal *(Hewlett-Packard).*

Figure 11-3. Floppy Disk Drive *(Billings Computer Corp.).*

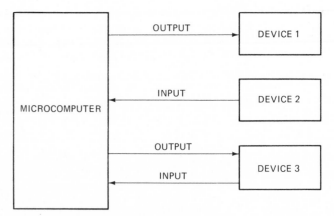

Figure 11-4. Data Transfer Directions.

ACCUMULATOR INPUT/OUTPUT

Accumulator I/O permits transfer of data between the microprocessor and the external device in either direction. Special instructions in the repertoire use the accumulator to send or receive data. Outgoing data must be in the A register before the output instruction is executed, and input data is placed in the accumulator upon input instruction completion. Accumulator I/O is most similar to the data transfer operations of minicomputers. Many microprocessors do not provide this capability, but the 8080A does support it. An *I/O port* is used with accumulator I/O.

The I/O port is a buffer which is connected to the system buses. Figure 11-5 shows a generalized I/O port. Only eight of the address bus lines need be decoded, for reasons that will become apparent when the instructions are discussed. Also, only the appropriate control bus signals need be accepted. In this situation only $\overline{I/OR}$ (input) and $\overline{I/OW}$ (output) are used by the I/O port.

The port must access the system bus at the proper time in the instruction cycle to prevent confusing other users of the buses. By proper sharing of the time available, many I/O ports can be attached to one MPU. The MPU selects the I/O port it wants to access in a manner not too different from reading or writing memory.

Input/Output Instructions

There are two instructions available for accumulator I/O, one for input and the other for output. Each instruction can select up to 256 independent devices. Therefore, we can input from a maximum of 256 devices and output to another 256. Some of the devices (e.g., device 3 in Figure 11-4) would need both input and output, while others would require only one or the other. The number associated with each input or output device is called the *device code* (DC).

The device code is an 8-bit number which uniquely addresses one peripheral device. Examples might be:

14_{16} (output)	printer device code
02_{16} (input)	temperature sensor
02_{16} (output) and $F6_{16}$ (input)	CRT terminal

Note that the input and output device codes need not be the same, as the CRT terminal assignment shows. Furthermore, the same code number may be used for input and output, as above, without any interference between the two.

INPUT. The input instruction causes the 8-bit data byte to be read from the I/O port with the device code found in the second word of the instruction. The data is placed in the accumulator. There is no need to clear the A register before this instruction because all bits are changed by reading the input data. No status bits are affected by this instruction. A timing diagram is shown in Fig. 11-6. The first machine cycle is a normal instruction fetch. During MC2 the device code is obtained from memory. This will be a hexadecimal value from 00_{16} to FF_{16}. Data transfer occurs during MC3. During the first clock period of that machine cycle the device code is set on bits A0 through A7 of the address bus. The same code is also placed on bits A8 through A15 of the address bus, so the device need only decode 8 bits. Either the upper or the lower byte may be used. The device must recognize its code and hold data stable on the data bus during the portion of T2 and T3 when DBIN is high. The processor accepts the data during this interval. By the end of T3 the external device drops the data, and the device code is removed from the address bus.

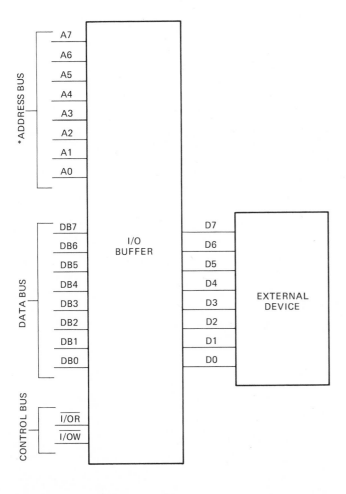

*ALTERNATIVELY A8–A15

Figure 11-5. I/O Port.

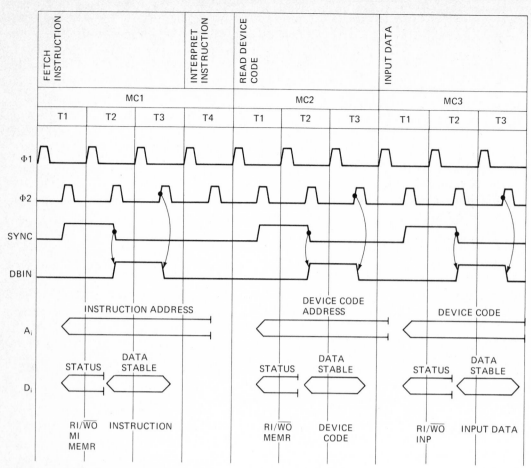

Figure 11-6. Input Instruction Timing.

Operation code	DB
Mnemonic	IN
Addressing mode	immediate
Status bits affected	none
Clock periods	10
Execution time	5 μs

Format

		bit number	
		7 6 5 4 3 2 1 0	
Memory cell	m	1 1 0 1 1 0 1 1	
	m + 1	device code	

□ **EXAMPLE**

Before execution	After execution
Program counter [1406]	Program counter [1408]
A register [03]	A register [4A]
Memory 1406 [DB]	Memory 1406 [DB]
1407 [02]	1407 [02]

The device on I/O port number 02_{16} has transmitted $4A_{16}$ to the processor, thus changing the value of the accumulator.

OUTPUT. This instruction sends the current accumulator contents to the equipment on the I/O port indicated by the device code. A timing diagram of the output sequence is shown in Fig. 11-7. The instruction is fetched during MC1 and the device code, during MC2. Just as in the input instruction, the device code is set on A0 through A7 and A8 through A15 during MC3. The device recognizes its address and samples the data bus when $\overline{WR}$ goes true (low).

Operation code	D3
Mnemonic	OUT
Addressing mode	direct
Status bits affected	none
Clock periods	10
Execution time	5 μs

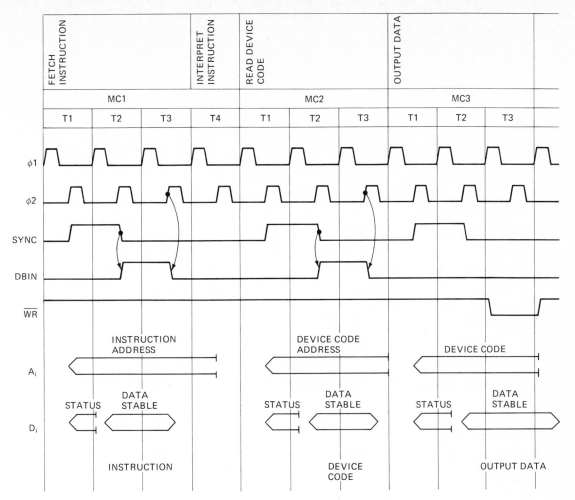

Figure 11-7. Output Instruction Timing.

Format

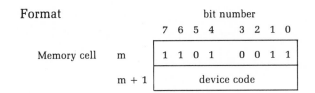

bit number

		7	6	5	4		3	2	1	0
Memory cell	m	1	1	0	1		0	0	1	1
	m + 1				device code					

☐ EXAMPLE

Before execution		After execution	
Program counter	350A	Program counter	350C
A register	22	A register	22
Memory 350A	D3	Memory 350A	D3
350B	14	350B	14

The A register value (22_{16}) is sent out I/O port number 14_{16}.

Programmed I/O Review

1. List four types of I/O used with microprocessors.

2. Which method of input/output uses an I/O port?

3. Why is it unnecessary for the device to decode more than eight address lines?

4. Where is the device code obtained?

5. What operation occurs during T2 of machine cycle 3 of the input instruction?

6. When is the data sampled by the external device during output instruction execution?

MEMORY-MAPPED I/O

Memory-mapped I/O treats external devices as memory locations in contrast to accumulator I/O, which assigns them device codes. Because the devices are considered to be memory by the MPU, any of the memory transfer instructions such as MOV, STAX, LDAX, and ADD can be used. In fact, 2 bytes

Table 11-1

Comparison of Accumulator I/O and Memory-mapped I/O

	Accumulator I/O	Memory-mapped I/O	

Instructions	OUT
	IN
		MOV B,M
		MOV C,M
		MOV D,M
		MOV E,M
		MOV H,M
		MOV L,M
		MOV A,M
			MOV M,B
			MOV M,C
			MOV M,D
			MOV M,E
			MOV M,H
			MOV M,L
			MOV M,A

		STAX B STAX D LDAX B LDAX D ADD M ADC M SUB M SBB M SHLD LHLD	ANA M XRA M ORA M CMP M INR M DCR M MVI M STA LDA
Control Signals	$\overline{I/OW}$ $\overline{I/OR}$	$\overline{MEMW}$ $\overline{MEMR}$	
Data transfer	Between accumulator and device	Between any general-purpose register (A, B, C, D, H, and L) and device	
Device decoding	Device select pulse decoded from 8-bit device code (A0–A7 or A8–A15)	From address in an instruction or a register pair	
Source of device address	From immediate data byte of I/O instruction	From address in an instruction or a register pair	

can be transferred, for example, by using SHLD. Furthermore, any of the general-purpose registers can be used as the source of destination for the data. Table 11-1 compares these two I/O techniques.

There are several advantages to memory-mapped I/O. The ability to use any of the general-purpose registers instead of just the accumulator can shorten the program. By storing the 16-bit address for the peripheral device in the HL register pair and using register addressed instructions, a memory-mapped I/O transfer can proceed faster than can accumulator I/O because the device code need not be fetched from memory. More than 256 device codes are allowed (though would probably never be required in a microcomputer). Two-byte data transfers are available, and input data can be directly used in either arithmetic or logic instructions.

Among the disadvantages of memory-mapped I/O is the need to decode a 16-bit address, even if the device code is only 8 bits long. To clarify this statement, consider how the device with address

$F3_{16}$ would distinguish between its address $01F3_{16}$, $02F3_{16}$, $03F3_{16}$, and so on, unless the upper address byte were also decoded. Some memory addresses are sacrificed for device codes also. This loss is probably not a serious problem in a processor that can address a 65K memory, like the 8080A.

Figure 11-8 shows the basic difference between the control signals used for memory-mapped and accumulator I/O. The memory and device codes available in each scheme are also indicated, assuming that addresses above $7FFF_{16}$ are reserved for devices in the memory-mapped case. One way to assign the 16-bit address space in a memory-mapped system might be as follows:

bit number

15	14 13 12 11 10 9 8 7 6 5 4 3 2 1 0

Address

0 = memory address
1 = I/O device code

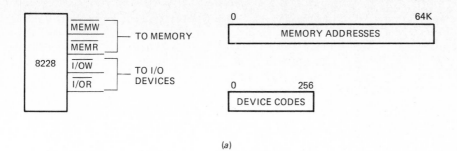

(a)

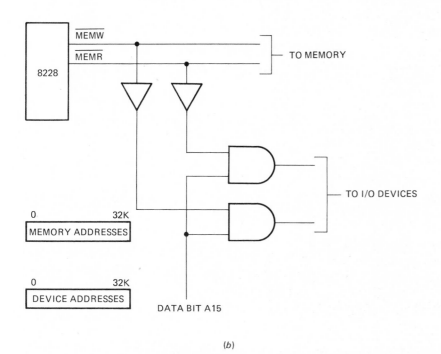

(b)

Figure 11-8. I/O Signal Comparison. (*a*) Accumulator I/O; (*b*) Memory Mapped I/O.

Memory-Mapped I/O Review

1. What is the distinguishing characteristic of memory-mapped I/O?

2. True or false? A device with address 0314_{16} must use memory-mapped I/O.

3. List the instructions that can be used with memory-mapped I/O.

4. Discuss the advantages and the disadvantages of memory-mapped I/O.

INTERRUPTS

An interrupt is a signal that arrives at any time and causes the processor to break out of its normal execution sequence and begin a special interrupt sequence instead. This section will describe the type of interrupt that a microprocessor may receive, the

instructions available to process and control interrupts, timing, and priority.

MPU Interrupt Configurations

When only one line is available to input of interrupt signals to the MPU, the configuration is called a *single* interrupt system. As Fig. 11-9a shows, many devices are ORed on one line. The processor must interrogate, or *poll*, the devices to find the particular one that has requested service.

A *multiple* interrupt structured microprocessor furnishes several independent interrupt request lines (see Fig. 11-9b). In this situation the processor does not need to poll the devices because the one requesting service is uniquely identified. By adding hardware for multiple interrupts, and thus elimination of polling, the programming burden has been reduced. The MC6800 is an example of a microproces-

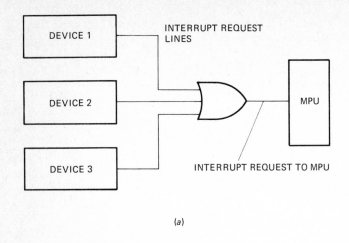

(a)

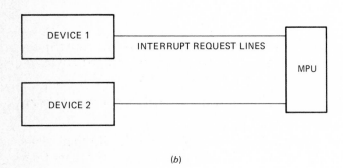

(b)

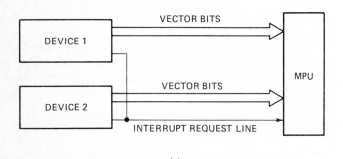

(c)

Figure 11-9. Interrupt Request Configurations. (a) Single; (b) Multiple; (c) Vectored.

Interrupt Handling Instructions

The 8080A supplies a substantial capability for accommodating vectored interrupts. When combined with supporting ICs, a powerful I/O handling capability can be constructed. There are two classes of instruction in the 8080A repertoire that relate to interrupts: control and vectoring.

CONTROL INSTRUCTIONS. The 8080A contains an interrupt enable flip-flop that dictates whether interrupt requests will be honored. If the flip-flop is set, the MPU will recognize and respond to the interrupts. When the flip-flop is reset, the processor ignores all interrupt requests. As you might expect, there is one instruction which sets the flip-flop, enabling interrupts (EI), and another that clears it, disabling interrupts (DI).

Operation code	FB	F3
Mnemonic	EI	DI
Addressing mode	none	
Status bits affected	none	
Clock periods	4	
Execution time	2 μs	

Format

			bit number								
			7	6	5	4	3	2	1	0	
Memory cell	m		1	1	1	1	1	0	1	1	
			7	6	5	4	3	2	1	0	
Memory cell	m		1	1	1	1	0	0	1	1	

Examples of the use of these instructions are presented in the following section.

sor with a multiple interrupt arrangement. It has two interrupt lines.

Most sophisticated is the *vectored* interrupt method supported by the 8080A microprocessor. In this architecture (see Fig. 11-9c) each interrupting device provides a unique address which specifies the program that services its interrupt. Once again, more complexity of hardware is traded off for simpler software in going to vectored interrupts. Not only must the processor be able to support the vectoring, but the external devices must be able to supply the vector address in this arrangement.

VECTORED INTERRUPT INSTRUCTIONS. A vectored interrupt instruction is a special-purpose subroutine call. The instruction is supplied not from computer memory, but by the interrupting device. The device provides a 3-bit number or *vector* in the instruction. When one of these instructions is received, the processor enters a special interrupt state. (In all cases we will assume that interrupts are enabled, except when explicitly disabled.) After the interrupt state has been initialized, the processor causes the program counter to be set to a vector address. The instruction format is as follows.

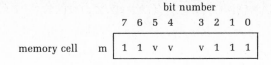

where vvv is the 3-bit vector as follows:

Vector	Address
000	0
001	1
010	2
011	3
100	4
101	5
110	6
111	7

In normal use, the vector is used with routines stored in the lower 64 bytes of memory. Each of these routines is 8 bytes long (see Fig. 11-10). Their length is dictated by the lower three bits of the vector address. These routines each service their respective interrupts. Table 11-2 lists the instructions together with their vector addresses.

COMPREHENSIVE INTERRUPT EXAMPLE.

In this section we will work a comprehensive example, showing how the interrupting device causes a particular RST instruction to be executed, in turn forcing control to be transferred to the interrupt processing routine. We will see that interrupt processing routine must execute a return (RET) instruction on exiting to give control back to the main program.

Let the interrupting device be a floppy disk which generates an RST 3 instruction. Decoding the instruction shows that the interrupt vector is 3.

$$RST\ 3 = DF_{16} = 11\ \underbrace{011}_{vvv\,=\,3}\ 111_2$$

ADDRESS$_{16}$	ROUTINE
0000	VECTOR SERVICE ROUTINE 0
0008	VECTOR SERVICE ROUTINE 1
0010	VECTOR SERVICE ROUTINE 2
0018	VECTOR SERVICE ROUTINE 3
0020	VECTOR SERVICE ROUTINE 4
0028	VECTOR SERVICE ROUTINE 5
0030	VECTOR SERVICE ROUTINE 6
0038	VECTOR SERVICE ROUTINE 7

Figure 11-10. Address of Interrupt Servicing Routines.

Table 11-2
RST Instruction

Machine Code	Instruction	Vector	Vector Address$_{16}$
C7	RST 0	0	0000
CF	RST 1	1	0008
D7	RST 2	2	0010
DF	RST 3	3	0018
E7	RST 4	4	0020
EF	RST 5	5	0028
F7	RST 6	6	0030
FF	RST 7	7	0038

Addressing mode	none
Status bits affected	none
Clock periods	11
Execution time	5.5 μs

When the processor recognizes the interrupt request (assuming that interrupts are enabled), it automatically enters the interrupt state by:

1. Waiting until the current instruction is completed.

2. Clearing the interrupt enable flip-flop. (This action will prevent any other interrupts from disturbing the process.)

3. Taking the RST 3 instruction from the data lines instead of from memory.

4. Pushing the program counter on the stack (just as a normal call instruction would do). The address of the next sequential instruction in the main program is thus saved.

5. Forcing a jump to the 0018_{16} vector address when vvv = 3.

Figure 11-11 diagrams this series of operations.

Once we are in the interrupt servicing routine, we must be very careful not to disturb the settings of registers or status bits. If we must use any register, it must first be pushed on the stack. The stack is popped just prior to returning to the main program, so the register contents before and after the interrupt remain unchanged. Before the interrupt servicing routine is exited, there are two other tasks that must be completed. First, interrupts must be reenabled if we ever want to receive another (remember that in honoring the interrupt request the processor cleared the flip-flop). Second, as mentioned above, we must execute a return instruction to cause the next address to be popped from the stack and placed in the program counter. Listed below is a typical interrupt servicing routine. Figure 11-12 is a flowchart for the routine.

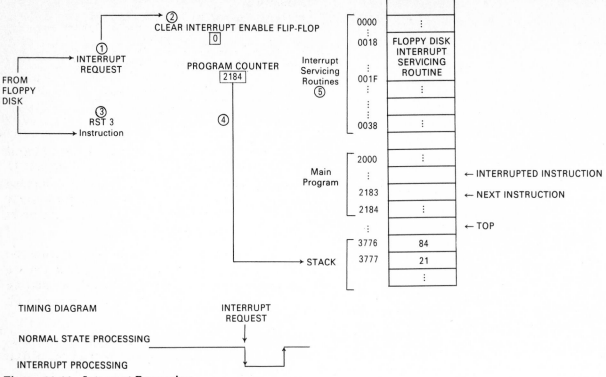

Figure 11-11. Interrupt Processing.

INTERRUPT SERVICING ROUTINE

Instruction	Address	Machine Code	Comments
PUSH A	0018	F5	Save accumulator and status bits
MVI D,3	0019	3E	Store indicator of interrupt vector in D register
	001A	03	
POP A	001B	F1	Restore accumulator and status bits
EI	001C	FB	Reenable interrupts
RET	001D	C9	Return
	001E	00	Not used.
	001F	00	Not used.

As you can see, there is not much memory space for processing. If more is needed, a jump to some other memory location can be made. Then all the memory needed becomes accessible.

Interrupt Process Timing

Having discussed the instructions available for interrupt handling and the general sequence of events, we will now look in more detail at the timing and the control signals involved. Figure 11-13 shows the relationships between the signals from the microprocessor and the external device.

As explained earlier, the interrupt is initiated by the external device setting the interrupt request signal (INT) to the processor high. The processor will acknowledge the request, unless interrupts have been disabled by either a (1) disable interrupt (DI) instruction, (2) reset condition, or (3) previous processor acknowledgment clearing the flip-flop. External devices can tell when interrupts will be accepted because the 8080A holds the interrupt enabled (INTE) line high to indicate that the flip-flop is set. The INTE signal falls on the rising edge of Φ2 in T1 when the interrupt is acknowledged, as the 8080A automatically disables other interrupts to service the current one.

The external device receives an acknowledgment on the data bus during T1 with the data bits in Table 11-3 set to indicate status. The primary interrupt status indicator is INTA, which is converted to a separate acknowledge signal if the 8228 system controller is used with the 8080A.

After acknowledging the interrupt request, the

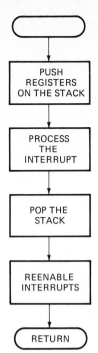

PUSH
REGISTERS
ON THE STACK

PROCESS
THE
INTERRUPT

POP THE
STACK

REENABLE
INTERRUPTS

RETURN

Figure 11-12. Interrupt Servicing Routine Flowchart.

Table 11-3
Interrupt Response Data Bit Settings

Bit	Meaning
D0	Interrupt acknowledge (INTA)
D1	Read/write control ($\overline{WO}$)
D5	Fetch cycle initiated (MI)

memory reference for instruction fetch. (Recall that memory read, MEMR, is set high on D7 in a normal instruction fetch.) This difference informs the device that the processor expects the next instruction to be supplied externally and not from memory.

3. The processor fetches an instruction from the device that causes the program counter to be pushed on the stack and gives the starting address of the servicing routine (either CALL or RST).

4. The processor references the appropriate interrupt service routine as a result of the CALL or RST.

The two instructions that can be supplied by the device require different hardware for implementation. An explanation of each approach is given below.

8080A initiates the special interrupt instruction fetch sequence:

1. The program counter is not incremented.

2. The status bits on the data lines during T1 and T2 indicate interrupt acknowledge and no

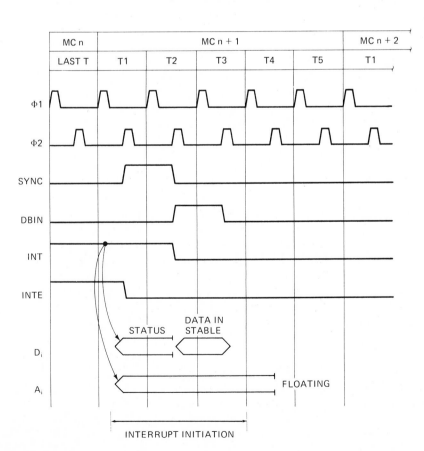

Figure 11-13. Interrupt Initiation Sequence.

USING RST. The external device senses the transition of INTA from low to high during T2. A circuit like the one shown in Fig. 11-14 then generates the RST instruction. The chip is enabled by INTA (data bus bit D0) going high during T1, when SYNC is also high. Inputs D0, D1, D2, D6, and D7 of the buffer are tied to V_{CC}. The bits selecting the vector are either grounded or tied to 5 V. For example, bits D5 and D3 would be high and D4 low for a vector value of 5.

SPECIAL 8228 FEATURE. A simplified approach to generating the RST instruction can be taken if a single interrupt configuration is suitable in the system. In this case the 8228 is used and its INTA output is tied to the 12-V power supply through a 1-kΩ resistor. Then the external device does not supply the RST instruction. Instead, the 8228 inserts the op code for RST 7 in response to the microprocessor setting INTE true. Now all interrupts must be handled by the RST 7 subroutine at address 0038_{16}.

USING CALL. There are two possible configurations to consider using when a CALL instruction is to be generated by the device. If the system does not include the 8228, fairly complex logic is needed. The external device must first send the CALL op code (CD_{16}) to the 8080A when INTA is high. It must then suppress normal memory referring during the next two machine cycles and transmit the low and high address bytes for the subroutine entrance to the MPU. The 8259 priority interrupt control unit, described in Chap. 12, can perform these functions.

If there is an 8228 in the microcomputer, the task of the external device is simplified. The 8228 generates a separate $\overline{INTA}$ signal. The external device responds to a true $\overline{INTA}$ with the op code of the CALL instruction. Then the 8228 automatically generates two more $\overline{INTA}$ low transitions during the next two machine cycles. The external logic can use these pulses to disable memory selection and respond with the address bytes.

NEC 8080A DIFFERENCE. The NEC 8080A facilitates the issuing of a CALL instruction by external logic. When the NEC 8080A receives a CALL instruction operation code in response to INTA true, it holds INTA true for the following two machine cycles as well. In effect, the 8080A signals replace those of the 8228 in this situation.

The Halt State and Interrupts

Recall that the halt instruction causes the processor to stop executing instructions. Once stopped, how is the processor restarted? The halt state can be terminated by an interrupt request (INT high). In servicing the interrupt, the processor will reference the servicing routine which will reinitiate operation.

If interrupts are inhibited when the processor is halted, the interrupt request will not be acknowledged. What does the operator do then? In such a case the only way to leave the halt state, is to turn the power off and back on again.

Interrupts Review

1. Distinguish between single, multiple, and vectored interrupt configurations. Which configuration requires polling?

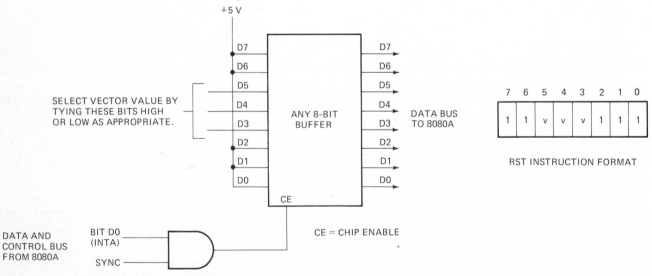

Figure 11-14. Circuit for Generating RST.

2. What instructions control the interrupt enable flip-flop in the 8080A?

3. How can you determine the entrance address for the servicing routine of an RST instruction?

4. Why must the external device issue an instruction that causes the program counter to be pushed on the stack in response to an interrupt acknowledge?

5. What instructions should be included in every interrupt servicing routine?

6. Describe the timing of interrupt signals in the 8080A.

7. What is the responsibility of an external device that generates an RST instruction after the MPU acknowledges the interrupt? What if a CALL instruction is used? How can the 8228 simplify each situation?

8. How are interrupts handled if the processor is in the halt state?

DIRECT MEMORY ACCESS

At times the data transfer to peripheral equipment may be so rapid that interrupts will not provide an adequate data exchange rate. Furthermore, a large number of interrupts will severely reduce the processing speed of the main line program. In such cases a special controller can be used to perform high-speed transfers between memory and external devices directly. Such a direct memory access controller uses the buses in a manner quite similar to that used by the processor.

In an 8080A system, the hold state is used for direct memory access. With other processors DMA may proceed after suspending the processor or by "stretching" clock pulses. Turning our interest to the 8080A, though, we will want to understand how the DMA controller emulates the MPU on the address, data, and control buses. To accomplish the emulation, each DMA channel must have a 16-bit address register and a counter for the number of bytes to transfer. A status register is usually provided as well. Because the processor and external devices cannot access memory simultaneously, one must wait for the other. This *memory cycle stealing* by the external device does slow the processor down because it cannot execute instructions without accessing memory.

A simplified DMA system is shown in Fig. 11-15. The processor and the DMA controller indicate to each other which of them is presently directing the system buses by means of the HOLD and the hold acknowledge (HLDA) signals. The devices, in turn,

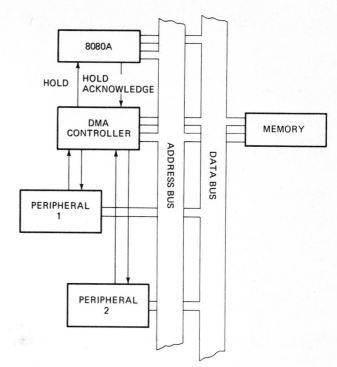

Figure 11-15. Simplified DMA Controller Block Diagram.

request use of the data bus and are granted it by the control signals between each of the peripherals and the DMA controller. Although the DMA controller is connected to the data bus, data from the external devices do not pass through the controller. Instead, once a device has been granted access to the data bus, data passes directly between the device and memory. The data bus is used by the DMA control only to accept commands from the processor or to send status information to the processor.

Direct Memory Access Review

1. When is DMA the preferred method of I/O?

2. What state in the 8080A is used during DMA data transfers?

3. True or false? Data from the peripheral device to be written into memory passes through the DMA controller on the data bus.

CHAPTER SUMMARY

1. The moving of data between the peripheral devices and the microcomputer is the responsibility of the I/O circuitry and programs. Input and output are always relative to the processor; the computer receives input data and transmits output data.

Table 11-4
Input/Output Instructions*

Instruction	Machine Code	Number of Bytes	Execution Time, µs
DI	F3	1	2
EI	FB	1	2
IN	DB	2	5
OUT	D3	2	5
RST 0	C7	1	5.5
RST 1	CF	1	5.5
RST 2	D7	1	5.5
RST 3	DF	1	5.5
RST 4	E7	1	5.5
RST 5	EF	1	5.5
RST 6	F7	1	5.5
RST 7	FF	1	5.5

*Status bits are not affected by these instructions.

2. Normally, either accumulator I/O or memory-mapped I/O instructions are used in exchanging information. Accumulator I/O instructions require an I/O port, while memory-mapped commands treat the device as a memory address.

3. Interrupt signals allow the device to request service from the MPU. Direct memory access devices can read or write memory just as the processor can.

4. An I/O port is a buffer between the system buses and the external device. The port is addressed with either the upper or the lower eight lines of the address bus. The port address is called its device code.

5. Devices are addressed as memory locations in a memory-mapped I/O architecture. Memory-transfer instructions are used to move data between the processors and the external equipment.

6. The microcomputer can use single, multiple, or vectored interrupts. The 8080A has special instructions in its repertoire to support vec-tored interrupt processing and other instructions to control interrupts. A summary of the input/output instructions is provided in Table 11-4.

7. The interrupt device supplies the starting address of the servicing routine in an RST instruction. The processor enters the interrupt state by clearing the interrupt enable flip-flop, taking the next instruction from the data lines, and pushing the program counter on the stack. The servicing routine must reenable interrupts and exit with a return instruction to pop the stack and load the program counter with the address of the instruction following the interrupted one.

8. The external device can respond to an interrupt acknowledgment from the processor by supplying either an RST or a CALL instruction.

9. The halt state can be terminated with an interrupt.

10. The peripheral can bypass the processor in accessing memory by using DMA. The 8080A hold state is employed when DMA is used.

KEY TERMS AND CONCEPTS

Input/output (I/O)	Interrupts	Single, multiple, and vectored interrupts
Peripheral equipment	Direct memory access (DMA)	
Accumulator I/O	Device code	Polling
I/O port	Handshaking	Interrupt servicing routine
Memory-mapped I/O		Halt state

11-1 A 128-byte block of data is stored in sequential addresses starting at 1200_{16}. Write a routine to transfer this data to a floppy disk on I/O port 27_{16}. (A loop will be required.)

11-2 The keyboard CRT terminal is to send ASCII (8-bit) characters to the processor. Write a routine to input 1 parallel byte from I/O port 32_{16} and store the word in cell 1010_{16}.

11-3 Write a program to input one word from a CRT terminal with accumulator I/O. The input will consist of an ASCII character packed in 8 bits. The program is to check to see if the character is the letter "L." If it is, store the character in location 1000_{16}. If not, discard the character. Repeat nine times.

11-4 Repeat Prob. 11-3 with memory-mapped I/O. Compare the efficiency of the two programs.

11-5 Write a routine to receive a 256-word record from a memory-mapped cassette recorder. The device address is 8237_{16}, and the data is to be stored beginning at address 0210_{16}.

11-6 The recorder in Prob. 11-5 sends an interrupt whenever a CRC error is detected in the data being sent to the processor. An RST 3 instruction is provided by the device. Write an interrupt handling routine which will process the interrupt by executing the program of Prob. 11-5 again. Be sure to also reenable interrupts and take care of other normal interrupt servicing tasks.

11-7 Write a memory-mapped I/O routine to output two sequential words to device 3700_{16}.

11-8 Assume that a temperature-sensing device provides values based on a reference of 30°C. That is, when the device reports 0°C, the temperature is actually 30°C; a report of 10°C corresponds to 40°C, and so on. Write a program that will add 30_{10} to every value of the input and store the results in location 5100_{16}. (You must decide whether to use a memory-mapped or an accumulator I/O to do the job most efficiently.)

11-9 A table of data is to be filled by reading an instrument connected to the 8080A. Only the lower 6 bits of the byte contain valid data. The upper 2 bits may be randomly set or cleared and are invalid. Write a program that receives the data, removes bits 6 and 7 (which are erroneous values), and stores the results in the 100_{10} word table beginning at address $17A0_{16}$. (Why would memory-mapped I/O be well suited for this transfer?)

11-10 If the interrupt that resulted in calling the servicing routine in this chapter occurred while the instruction in address $1A20_{16}$ was being executed, draw the stack configuration:

a. Prior to entering the servicing routine.
b. After the instruction in cell 0018_{16} was executed.
c. On exiting the servicing routine. Assume that register contents at the time of the interrupt were:

A	01	E	2E	SP	2000
B	16	H	B7	PC	1A22
C	A2	L	14		
D	F0				

PURPOSE: To investigate an I/O port.

PARTS LIST:

Item	Quantity
8212	1
5082–7340 hexadecimal display	2
74LS00	1

IC DIAGRAMS:

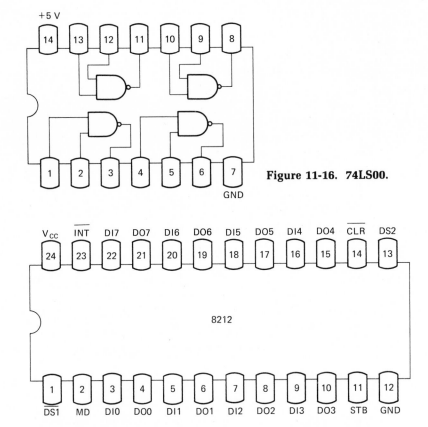

Figure 11-16. 74LS00.

Figure 11-17. 8212.

PROCEDURE: This experiment is the first of a two-part experiment. The circuit constructed and tested here is to be used in the following experiment. It should not be disassembled until experiment 12 is completed.

STEP 1. Construct the circuit shown in Fig. 11-18.

STEP 2. Connect the DI0 input to 5 V and ground DI1 through DI7. The value shown in the hexadecimal display is ____.

STEP 3. The value in the previous step should have been 01_{16}. If not, check your circuit over carefully.

STEP 4. Using this circuit, display the numbers below. Indicate the voltage on the input pins to produce the proper output.

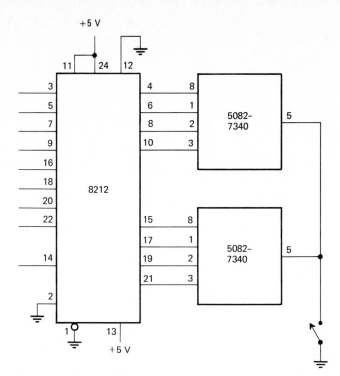

Figure 11-18. I/O Port Experiment.

| Display | Input Pins | | | | | | | |
	DI7	DI6	DI5	DI4	DI3	DI2	DI1	DI0
01								
03								
07								
70								
1F								
3F								
FF								

12

INTERFACING

The microprocessor I/O logic is only a part of the solution to the problem of sending data back and forth between the computer and the external environment. The software to control the sequences of I/O events is a second important component. Yet another is the device that properly synchronizes the movement of data on the data bus with the I/O signals on the control bus.

This chapter will continue our study of data transfer, but from a point outside the MPU. In addition to consideration of typical peripheral devices, we will analyze the programs necessary to drive the I/O.

CHAPTER OBJECTIVES

Upon completion of this chapter, you should be able to:

1. Decide whether a given family of interfacing logic is suitable for 8080A applications based on fan-out considerations.
2. Distinguish between fully decoded and linear selection address decoding of device addresses.
3. Explain the purpose of a three-state buffer on the data bus.
4. Describe the way in which an I/O port can be used for either input or output.
5. Analyze the operation of a priority interrupt control unit.
6. Show how a direct memory access controller is used in a microcomputer.

INPUT/OUTPUT DEVICES

The 8080A is supported by a family of integrated circuits which help solve the problem of interfacing the microprocessor to the I/O peripherals. General-purpose ICs can be used in this application also. When any device is connected to the 8080A buses, the output drive capability of the MPU must be considered.

The fan-out of the 8080A is such that the device can drive a maximum current of 1.9 mA. The fan-in of standard 7400 series TTL is 1.6 mA—very close to the limit. A better choice for interfacing logic is the 74LS low-power Schottky logic with a fan-in of 0.2 to 0.34 mA or the 74L series with a fan-in of 0.1 to 0.16 mA. Other alternatives are the specially designed 8080A devices such as the 8205 decoder and 8212 8-bit I/O port with a fan-in of 0.15 to 0.25 mA.

If the signals must travel more than 3 inches (7.6 cm), the outputs should be *buffered*. The 8228 system controller can be used to satisfy this requirement. When signal runs are over 12 inches (30.5 cm), special *bus drivers* and *termination networks* are necessary.

Address Selection

Interpreting every bit of a device code or an address is referred to as *fully decoded address selection*. Otherwise, only certain bits could be decoded to generate the device select pulse by using *linear selection*. For example, if only device codes 00_{16} through 07_{16} were used, then only address bits A0 through A2 need be examined. The shortcoming of this latter approach is that someday one may want to expand the system, and increasing the number of bits in the device code could require a major rebuild.

A fully decoded address selection decoder can be constructed by use of the 74LS30 8-input NAND gate shown in Fig. 12-1b. The device code used is $B6_{16}$. The pin assignment for the 74LS30 is shown in Fig. 12-1a. The output for this particular NAND may be expressed as

$$\overline{A7\ \overline{A6}\ A5\ A4\ \overline{A3}\ A2\ A1\ \overline{A0}} \qquad (11\text{-}1)$$

and only an input of $B6_{16}$ will produce a low-output $\overline{ADDR}$ signal. Assuming that we want to use the decoder with an output device, the chip select signal can be generated by ORing this output ($\overline{ADDR}$) with the processor output strobe ($\overline{I/OW}$) as shown in Fig. 12-1c. A low output from the OR gate selects the device.

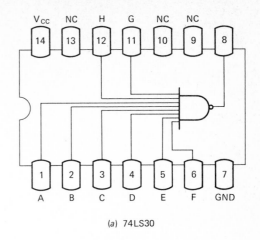

(a) 74LS30

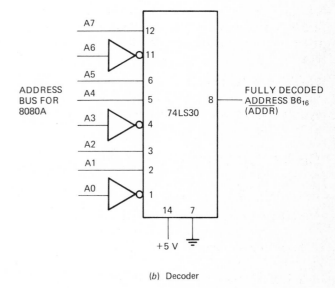

(b) Decoder

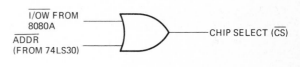

(c) Generating Chip Select Strobe

Figure 12-1. 8-Bit Fully Decoded Address Selection.

Buffering

Either input or output signals can be buffered to supply the necessary signal stability. A frequently used IC in 8080A applications is the 8095 three-state buffer. Because it is a three-state device, such buffers can be attached to the devices on the data bus, but only one can send an input to the 8080A at any time. Good design practice calls for absolutely decoding the device code.

The buffer IC is shown in Fig. 12-2a. A low input on pins 1 and 15 (DIS1 and DIS2, respectively) enables the buffer to transfer data. The chip select ($\overline{CS}$) from

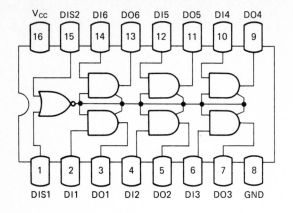

(a) 8095 Pin Assignment

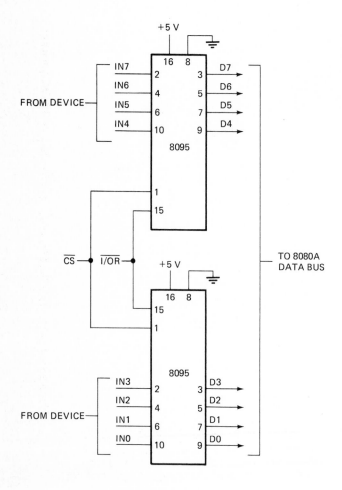

(b) 8-bit Buffered Input

Figure 12-2. Input Buffer.

a decoder similar to Fig. 12-1 and the processor input ($\overline{\text{I/OR}}$) signal are applied to these enabling inputs. When $\overline{\text{I/OR}}$ goes low and $\overline{\text{CS}}$ go low, data is sent, or *jammed*, into the MPU.

Two 8095 can be used to provide a full 8-bit data input as shown in Fig. 12-2b. The external device

first places the data on the input lines. When the $\overline{\text{CS}}$ and the $\overline{\text{I/OR}}$ signals go low, the three-state AND gates are enabled passing the signals through to the MPU.

Input/Output Ports

Input/output ports are well suited for small microprocessor systems or for the special needs of larger systems. The ports usually consist of data latches, buffers, and interrupt logic. The 8212 is an 8-bit I/O port with eight D flip-flops for the latches. The Q outputs of the flip-flops are connected to three-state, noninverting output buffers, as shown in Fig. 12-3a. A pin assignment diagram for the port is shown in Fig. 12-3b.

From Fig. 12-3 and a little Boolean algebra, we can readily determine

$$\text{ENB} = \overline{\text{DS1}} \cdot \text{DS2} + \text{MD}$$
$$\text{CK} = \underline{\text{STB} \cdot \overline{\text{MD}}} + \text{MD} \cdot \overline{\text{DS1}} \cdot \text{DS2}$$
$$\text{SET} = \overline{\text{CLR}} + (\overline{\text{DS1}} \cdot \text{DS2})$$
$$= \overline{\text{CLR}} \, (\text{DS1} + \overline{\text{DS2}}) \text{ by De Morgan's theorem}$$

A brief description of the 8212 input and output signals is listed in Table 12-1.

Next we will analyze the 8212 operation. The 8212 I/O port is selected by setting $\overline{\text{DS1}}$ low and DS2 high. Each of the flip-flops will react to the D inputs only when the clock input (CK) is high. When the clock is low, the previous Q output will be held constant.

The mode input (MD) decides whether the IC will be in the output mode or the input mode. If the mode input is high (referred to as the output mode), the output of the buffer enable or gate (gate G of Figure 12-3a) is high, thus allowing output data to pass through to the buffers. The D flip-flop input clock is also set high by the output of OR gate D (MD $\cdot$ $\overline{\text{DS1}}$ $\cdot$ DS2 is true), so the D flip-flops will react to new inputs. After the propagation delay, the new inputs will appear at the Q output terminal of each flip-flop.

When MD goes low (input mode), the three-state enable line (output of gate G) reacts to the output of gate C. Whenever the device select inputs are false (that is, $\overline{\text{DS1}}$ high or DS2 low), the output of gate G will go low, thus causing the buffer outputs to float. The clocking of the D flip-flops will then depend on the state of the strobe (STB) input. A high on STB causes clocking of the flip-flops regardless of the state of the device selection inputs. Figure 12-4 summarizes these input mode relationships in a timing diagram.

The D flip-flops can be reset at any time by making the $\overline{\text{CLR}}$ input low. For normal operation, $\overline{\text{CLR}}$ must be high. The interrupt request signal is used to inform

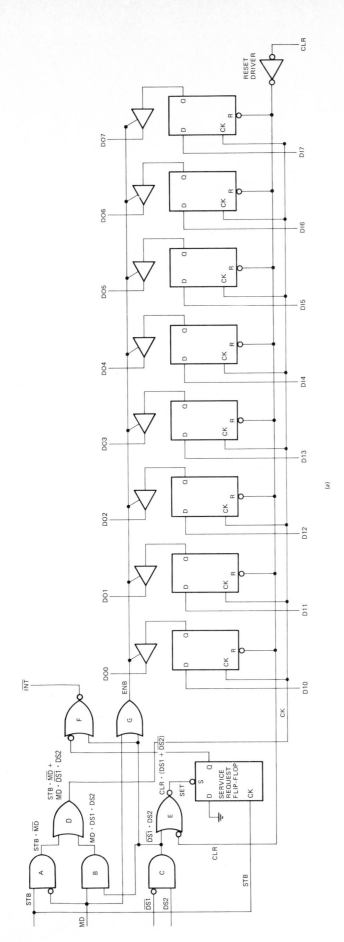

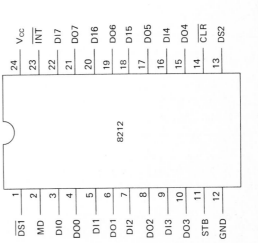

Figure 12-3. 8212 I/O Port (a) Internal Circuitry (b) Pin Numbering.

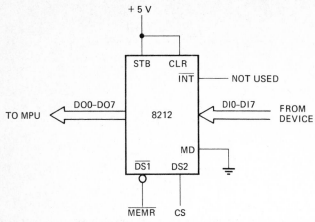

Figure 12-7. Memory-Mapped I/O Port.

MEMORY-MAPPED I/O PORTS. The same I/O devices that were used with accumulator I/O can be used with memory mapping. Essentially the changes that must be made in the circuits previously discussed are to change $\overline{I/OR}$ to $\overline{MEMR}$ and $\overline{I/OW}$ to $\overline{MEMW}$. As an illustration of how straightforward the conversion is, Fig. 12-7 shows how the 8212 input port of Fig. 12-5a converted to memory-mapped addressing. Of course, the software must be changed to use instructions which meet the requirements of the revised hardware configuration. Instead of the input (IN) instruction, MOV A,M or other memory data transfer instruction would be used.

I/O Devices Review

1. Why is the fan-out of the 8080A important?

2. List two ways of accommodating the limited drive current of the 8080A.

3. What should be done with output signal lines that are 16 inches (40.6 cm) long?

4. Define fully coded address selection.

5. How does the 8095 buffer design provide for placing only one input on the data bus at a given time?

6. Describe the operation of the 8212 in the output mode. In the input mode.

7. Why must the MD input be grounded in Fig. 12-6a?

8. What does setting the STB input high in Fig. 12-6c accomplish?

PRIORITY INTERRUPT CONTROL UNIT

The 8259 priority interrupt control unit (PICU) is a 28-pin DIP designed to work with the 8080A. All 8259 outputs are TTL-compatible. An 8228 system controller is necessary in any microcomputer that uses the 8259. The 8259 can coordinate a maximum of eight external interrupts. Alternatively, one device can serve as the master for up to eight slave 8259s providing 64 levels of interrupt priority. Such high-level inplementation would not normally be used with a microcomputer, however.

8259 Signals

The pin assignments for the 8259 are shown in Fig. 12-8, and each of the signals is briefly described in Table 12-2. The 8259 can be used in a memory-mapped I/O, or I/O port fashion. As Fig. 12-9 shows, bit A15 of the address bus is attached to the A0 input of the chip. As you will see, the 8259 is treated as a device with two addresses—a low address when the A0 input is zero and a high address when A0 is low.

A system with master-slave 8259s is shown in Fig. 12-10. An important feature to note is that the $\overline{SP}$ input is high for the master unit and grounded for the slave.

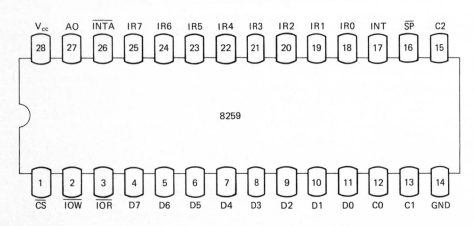

Figure 12-8. 8259 Pin Assignments.

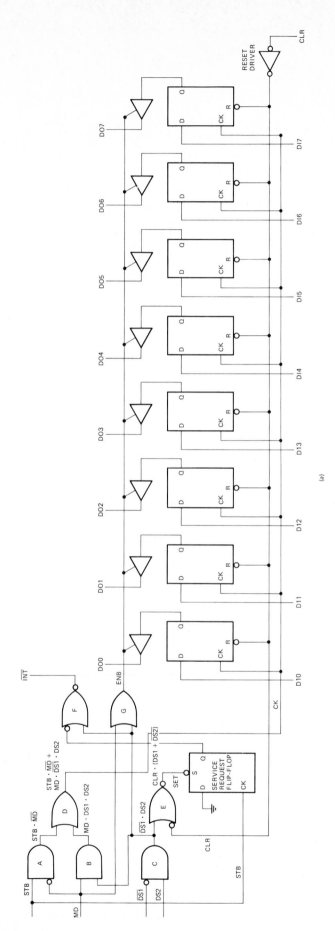

(a)

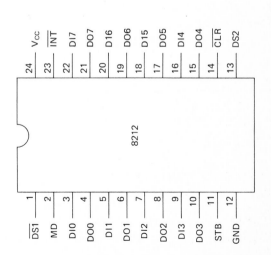

(b)

Figure 12-3. 8212 I/O Port (a) Internal Circuitry (b) Pin Numbering.

Priority Level of Device Interrupt Request Lines

	Lowest							Highest
Initially	IR7	IR6	IR5	IR4	IR3	IR2	IR1	IR0
After an IR3 interrupt is acknowledged	IR3	IR7	IR6	IR5	IR4	IR2	IR1	IR0
After an IR6 interrupt is acknowledged	IR6	IR3	IR7	IR5	IR4	IR2	IR1	IR0

ROTATING PRIORITIES, MODE B. In this mode the processor can specify the lowest priority level at any time. The priorities of the other IR lines are then assigned sequentially, but the highest level can be freely chosen. Consider the following examples. As can be seen, the highest priority IR line is always one greater than that selected to have lowest priority. Where IR2 is the lowest level, IR3 has the highest and with IR5 lowest, IR6 is highest.

polling request from the processor then goes to that slave. For example, the master unit provides a status word of

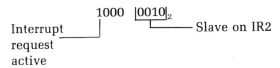

Then slave 2 is polled and responds with

Priority Level of Device Interrupt Request Lines

	Lowest							Highest
Initially	IR7	IR6	IR5	IR4	IR3	IR2	IR1	IR0
After MPU specifies IR2 lowest level priority	IR2	IR1	IR0	IR7	IR6	IR5	IR4	IR3
After MPU specifies IR5 lowest level priority	IR5	IR4	IR3	IR2	IR1	IR0	IR7	IR6

POLLED MODE. The priority arbitration can be bypassed entirely by using the polled mode. Then the 8259 is referenced by the processor to find the status of I/O devices, but no interrupts are generated. When the MPU interrogates the 8259, a status word provides an indication of the highest-level IR line that is requesting an interrupt and an indication that an interrupt request is active. The format for that word is shown below.

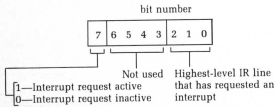

When polling is used in a master-slave configuration, the master is polled first. The slave with an active interrupt is shown in bits 0 through 2. Another

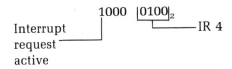

The microprocessor has found that the highest-priority interrupt request is from the device on IR 4 of slave unit 2.

SIMPLE MASK MODE. Masking permits enabling or disabling interrupts on an individual IR line level. There are two modes available in the 8259. Either mode can be superimposed on the fully nested priority or rotating priority modes A or B. In the simple mask mode, the MPU outputs an 8-bit mask—each bit represents the respective IR line. Any bit that is set disable interrupts on the corresponding IR line.

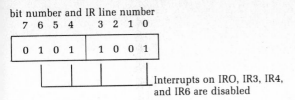

Interrupts on IRO, IR3, IR4,
and IR6 are disabled

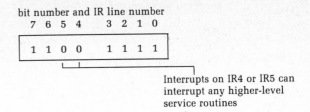

Interrupts on IR4 or IR5 can
interrupt any higher-level
service routines

PECIAL MASK MODE. This mask permits the pro-
essor to allow interrupts from a lower-priority
evice to interrupt the service routine of a higher-
riority mode. The 8-bit mask is interpreted to mean
hat 0 will allow that IR level to interrupt a service
equest for a higher level; 1s in the mask disable
his feature.

8259 Architecture

An understanding of some of the internal registers
of the 8259 is needed before we look into how to
program it. As Fig. 12-13 shows, the 8259 has eight
functional components. The data bus buffer temporarily holds data transiting between the internal bus

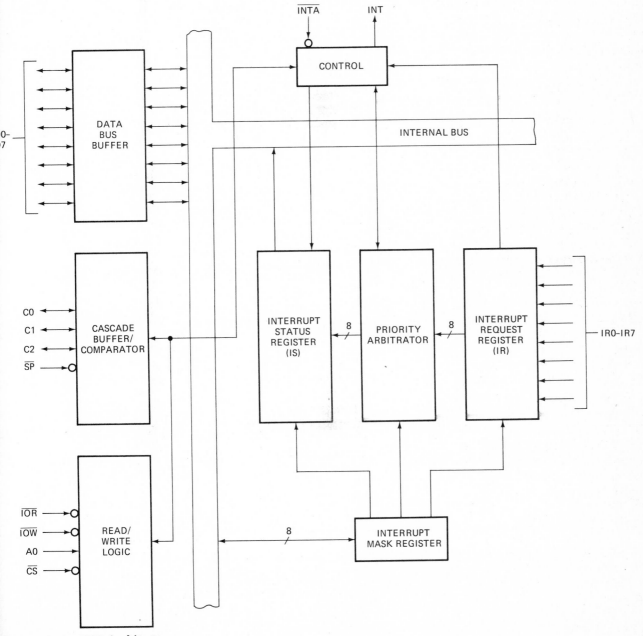

Figure 12-13. 8259 Architecture.

and the system data bus. The cascade comparator recognizes a slave unit's address. Read/write logic informs the control unit of the direction of data flow.

The interrupt request (IR) and interrupt status (IS) registers maintain the bookkeeping for the priority arbitration logic, as controlled by the processor-supplied mask (if used). The IR register latches all input from the external devices. Any device with a pending interrupt request sets the appropriate bit in the IR register to 1. Only the bit for the highest-level IR line will be set in the IS register. The IS register reflects the result of the arbitration logic. That bit remains set until the interrupt handling program in the processor clears it by issuing an "end of interrupt" command. Should a higher-level interrupt request come along while that routine is running, its bit is also set in the IS register. If the IS register contains

$$0 1 0 0 \quad 1 0 0 0_2$$
$$\uparrow \qquad \uparrow$$
$$\text{Level 6} \quad \text{Level 3}$$

we know that the interrupt handler for level 6 was interrupted by a request from IR3.

Because the interrupt request from the external device is not latched until the bit is set in the IS register, the device must hold the IR line high until acknowledged. A mask from the processor can prevent bits in the IR and the IS registers being set.

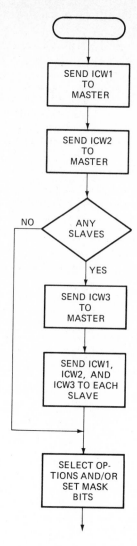

Figure 12-14. 8259 Initiation Sequence.

Programming the 8259

The 8259 is programmed by the processor sending a series of initiation and operational control words. The processor addresses the 8259 as two I/O ports or memory locations. All address bits except one are the same for the ports. The final bit is used to set or clear the A0 input.

The initiating sequence of commands that must be sent is diagrammed in Fig. 12-14. Two initialization control words (ICWs) are always used. In a master-slave system a third ICW must be sent to the master, and then sets of three words are passed to each slave. Finally, options and mask bits can be selected if desired.

Table 12-3 lists the control words for the 8259. After the initialization sequence has been sent, writing data in the high port (A0 = 1) will cause the 8259 to interpret the 8 bits as a mask, unless preceded by ICW1. The operational control words can be sent at any time after the initialization. A typical control word sequence for the configuration shown in Fig. 12-10 is given in Table 12-4.

Table 12-3
8259 Control Words

A0 Setting	Control Word	Bit Number	Meaning
0	Initialization control word 1 (ICW1)	0	Not interpreted
		1	Set, this is only a master 8259 system; clear, this is a master-slave system

ble 12-3 *(Continued)*
59 Control Words

A0 Setting	Control Word	Bit Number	Meaning
		2	Set, address vector option 1 (4 words between entrance cells); clear, address vector option 2 (8 words between entrance cells)
		3	Not interpreted
		4	Always set
		5–7	Bits 5–7 of constant portion of vector address (see Fig. 12-11); bit 5 not interpreted if option 2 was selected
1	Initialization control word 2 (ICW2)	0–7	Bits 8–15 of constant portion of vector address (see Fig. 12-11.)
1	Initialization control word 3 (ICW3)	0–7	To master unit: any bit set means that a slave is attached to that IR line
		0–2	To a slave unit: identifies slave's IR lines number at master unit
		3–7	Not interpreted
0	Operational control word 2 (OCW2)	0–2	See bits 5–7 for explanation
		3	Always 0
		4	Always 0
		5–7	Operation 0—No operation 1—End of interrupt (ignore bits 0–2) 2—No operation 3—Special end of interrupt, reset IS register bit specified in bits 0–2 4—No operation 5—End of interrupt, start rotating priority mode A (ignore bits 0–2) 6—Start rotating priority mode B (bits 0–2 specify lowest level) 7—End of interrupt, start rotating priority mode B (bits 0–2 specify lowest level)
0	Operational control word 3 (OCW3)	0–1	Set status 0—Illegal 1—Illegal 2—Select reading of IR register 3—Select reading of IS register
		2	Set, polled mode selected; clear, other mode selected
		3	Always 1
		4	Always 0
		5–6	Mask mode 0—Illegal 1—Illegal 2—Cancel special mask mode 3—Select special mask mode
		7	Not interpreted

Table 12-4
Control Word Sequence

	A0	Output	Control Word	Meaning
Initialize master in fully nested mode	0	10	ICW1	Master-slave system, 8 words between vectors
	1	10	ICW2	Base address for master vector is 1000_{16}
	1	80	ICW3	Slave on IR7
Initialize slave	0	10	ICW1	Master-slave system
	1	18	ICW2	Base address for slave vector is 1800_{16}
	1	07	ICW3	Slave is on IR7
	0	A0	OCW2	Rotate priorities mode A with end of interrupt
	0	68	OCW3	Select special mask mode
	1	02	MASK	Allow level 1 to interrupt level 0 service routine

Priority Interrupt Control Unit Review

1. What are the $\overline{I/OR}$ and $\overline{I/OW}$ inputs to the 8259 used for?

2. How is the $\overline{SP}$ input used to designate master and slave units?

3. Describe the two addressing options for the entrances to interrupt handling routines provided by the 8259.

4. How is the priority of an interrupt level established in the fully nested mode?

5. How does rotating priority mode A differ from mode B?

6. How does the processor locate pending interrupts in the polled mode?

7. How do the two types of masks influence the priority arbitration?

8. List the types of ICWs that must be issued in a master-slave system with two slave units.

THE 8257 DMA CONTROLLER

The 8257 DMA controller, used in 8080A systems, supports four DMA channels. Each channel can be assigned to a different peripheral device. All signals to or from this DIP are TTL-compatible. A diagram of pin assignments for the chip is shown in Fig. 12-15. Each of the signals is briefly explained in Table 12-5.

For the 8257 to mimic the processor, it must duplicate all signals needed to control memory reading and writing. Table 12-6 compares the 8257 signals with those of the 8080A and the 8228. Table 12-6 indicates that the 8257 multiplexes the upper 8 bits of the address of the data bus. For this reason an 8212 I/O port (or its equivalent) must be used to demultiplex the data bus output pins from the 8257. A system consisting of the 8080A with its support chips 8212 and 8257 is shown in Fig. 12-16. Only signals involved with DMA transfers are included in this figure. Memory would be connected to the address and system data buses in the normal manner.

Figure 12-16 illustrates how the low-order address bits (A0 through A7) are derived directly from the 8257, but the high-order bits (A8 through A15) are furnished by the 8212 I/O port, which obtains their values by demultiplexing the data bus from the 8257 at the proper time.

8257 Registers

Every DMA channel of the 8257 has two registers, an address register and a byte-count register. The 16-bit address registers contain the next memory location that will be written or read. The byte count and direction control registers satisfy two purposes. The lower 14 bits are the number of bytes that will be transferred, and bits 14 and 15 indicate the direction or transfer. A ninth register is used by the 8257 for commands and a tenth, for status.

To transfer any block of data by DMA, the starting address, the number of words, and the direction

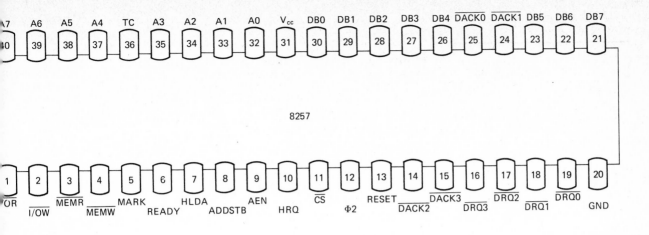

Table 12-5
8257 Signal Summary

Signal Name	Meaning	Type
DB0–DB7	Data bus	Three-state bidirectional
A0–A4	Low-order address bus	Three-state bidirectional
A5–A7	Remaining low-order address bus	Three-state, output
$\overline{I/OR}$	Processor input strobe	Three-state bidirectional
$\overline{I/OW}$	Processor output strobe	Three-state bidirectional
$\overline{MEMR}$	Memory read strobe	Three-state, output
$\overline{MEMW}$	Memory write strobe	Three-state, output
MARK	128 byte count strobe	Output
TC	Terminal count strobe	Output
READY	Memory ready-not ready	Input
HRQ	Hold request to MPU	Output
HLDA	Hold acknowledge from MPU	Input
ADDSTB	Address on data bus strobe	Output
AEN	DMA bus enable-disable	Output
$\overline{CS}$	Device select	Input
Φ2	Clock	Input
RESET	System reset	Input
DRQ0–DRQ3	Service request from external devices	Input
DACK0-DACK3	Service acknowledge to external devices	Output

Table 12-6
Comparison of MPU and DMA Signals

MPU Device	Signal	8257 Signal	Purpose
8080A	A0–A15	A0–A7, DB0–DB7	Address bus
8228	DB0–DB7	DB0–DB7	Data bus
8228	$\overline{I/OR}$ $\overline{I/OW}$	$\overline{I/OR}$ $\overline{I/OW}$	I/O read-write strobe
8228	$\overline{MEMR}$ $\overline{MEMW}$	$\overline{MEMR}$ $\overline{MEMW}$	Memory data strobes
8080A	READY	READY	Memory ready-not ready
8080A	RESET	RESET	System reset

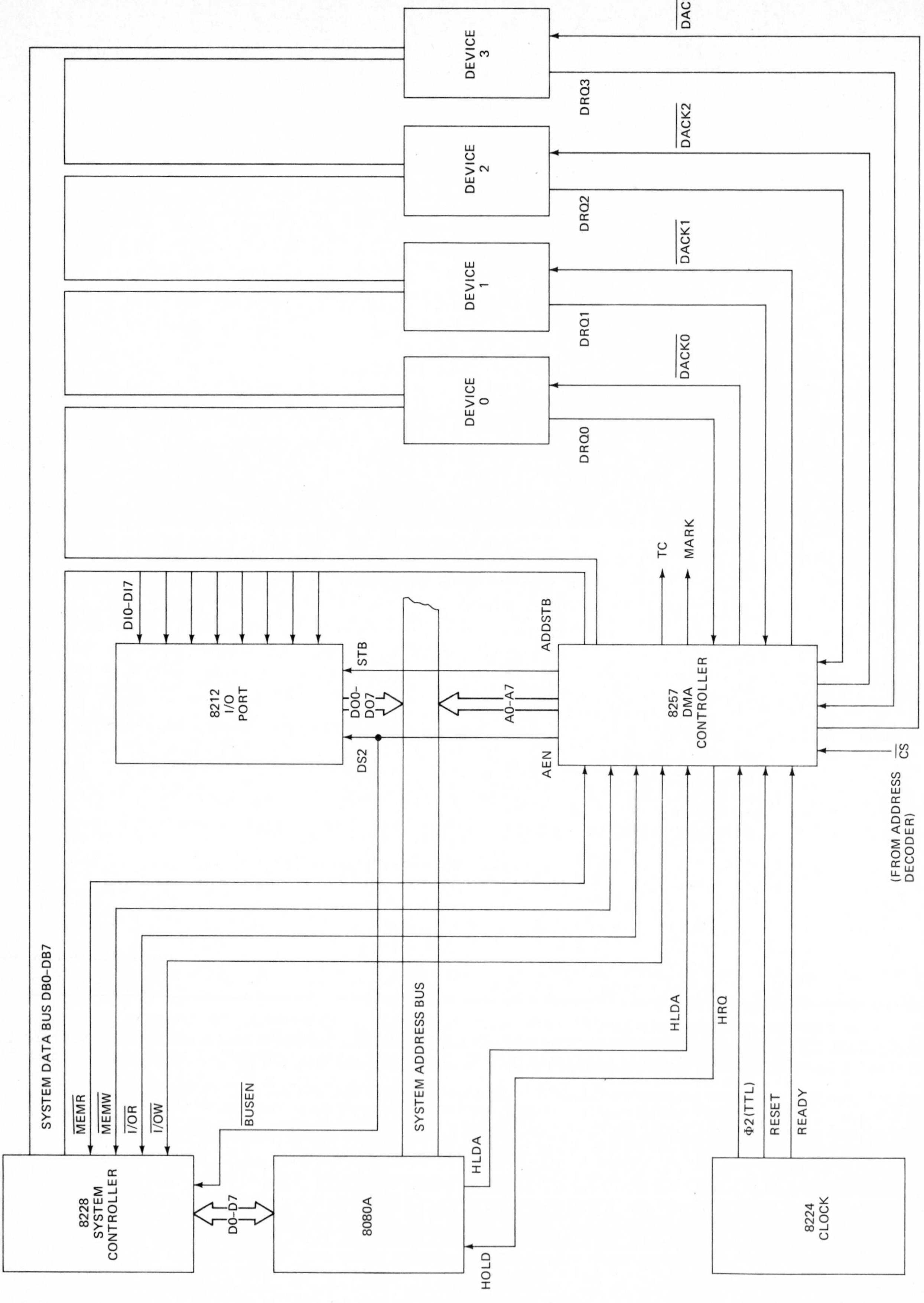

Figure 12-16. 8080A DMA System.

A3	A2	A1	A0	Destination/Source of Data
		Bits*		
0	0	0	0	Channel 0 address register
0	0	0	1	Channel 0 byte-count register
0	0	1	0	Channel 1 address register
0	0	1	1	Channel 1 byte-count register
0	1	0	0	Channel 2 address register
0	1	0	1	Channel 2 byte-count register
0	1	1	0	Channel 3 address register
0	1	1	1	Channel 3 byte-count register
1	0	0	0	Command register on output, status register on input

Addresses 1001_2–1111_2 not used.

ust be loaded into these registers by the processor. each word is transferred in the DMA operations, e register contents change as follows:

1. The address register increments to the next memory address.

2. The count register decrements, thus indicating that 1 byte has been exchanged. (Because the last byte is exchanged on a 0 count, this register should be set to $n - 1$ to transfer n words.)

To minimize pin count on the 8257 package, the ldress lines are used for a double purpose. In ldition to carrying the address information from e 8257, pins A0 through A3 also designate the gister to receive data from the processor. Table ?-7 lists the meanings of these bit values. Because e address and the byte-count registers are 16 bits ong, it takes two output operations to set the values each. The first output byte goes to the low-order bits, and the second output goes to the high-order bits of the designated register. The $\overline{CS}$ signal must e low before the MPU accesses the 8257. (To avoid roblems during DMA operations, $\overline{CS}$ must be high. his signal is automatically raised by the 8257 during ata transfer.)

Priority Arbitration

What happens if two or more devices attempt to ccess the 8257 simultaneously? A priority arbitrator, much like the one for interrupts in the previous section, decides which device gets acknowledged first. The external devices request service by setting their DRQ signal lines high. The acknowledge ($\overline{DACK}$) signal informs the device that its request is being honored.

The priority arbitration scheme to be used is selected by programming the 8257. In the *fixed priority mode* the device requests are always honored in the same order. The device on DRQ0 has highest priority and the one DRQ3, the lowest.

The *round robin mode* guarantees equal service to every device. The low-priority device cannot be locked out by higher-priority ones in this scheme. With the use of round robin, the last channel that was serviced moves to the bottom of the priority list. Table 12-8 shows the channel priorities for every situation.

DMA Options

The 8257 can transfer data in either a byte-by-byte or a burst mode. The latter method provides the highest data through-put rate. The direction of transfer is specified by the program in the processor. The DMA controller will also allow the device to specify the direction, although this is rarely done.

TRANSFER MODES. The external device can transfer its data a single byte at a time, under 8257

Channel Priority	Initialization	Last channel serviced			
		0	1	2	3
Highest	0	1	2	3	0
↑	1	2	3	0	1
	2	3	0	1	2
Lowest	3	0	1	2	3

Table 12-9
Directional Bits

Bit Numbers		8257 Acting as an I/O Port	8257 Acting as a Memory-mapped Device
15	14		
0	0	Verify cycle	Verify cycle
0	1	Write cycle	Read cycle
1	0	Read cycle	Write cycle
1	1	Not used	Not used

control. In this mode the device raises the DRQ signal prior to each transfer. When the DMA controller responds with the $\overline{DACK}$ acknowledgment, the device drops DRQ. To transfer data in a burst mode, the device holds DRQ true until the entire block has been sent or received. Only then is that signal dropped.

TRANSFER DIRECTION. The processor specifies the direction of data transfer by the settings of the upper 2 bits in the byte-count register. Table 12-9 is a tabulation of those settings. Note the reversal of meanings of two values with the use of I/O port addressing rather than memory-mapped addressing. The following section on programming the 8257 provides more background on these addressing methods.

During a *read* cycle the contents of a memory location, corresponding to the value in the 8257 address register, are transferred to the external device. The address register specifies the cell to receive data during a *write* cycle. The *verify* cycle effectively delays the data transfer, usually giving external devices that transfer data in blocks more time (possibly to compute a cyclic redundancy check calculation, for example). No data transfer occurs during the verify cycle.

DMA Timing

The timing to effect a DMA data transfer (Fig. 12-17) shows the sequence of events that occur. First, the device raises the DRQ signal to request service. After the priority arbitration logic gives that device highest

priority, or if that is the only request, the 8257 sen[ds] a true HRQ signal to the 8080A. The 8080A reco[g]nizes the signal as a hold request (HOLD) a[nd] responds with hold acknowledge (HLDA). Then t[he] 8257 can drop HRQ and set $\overline{DACK}$ true (low[)] acknowledging the request from the device a[nd] giving it access to the data bus.

Before discussing how data is strobed onto t[he] bus, a few other signals must be explained. T[he] AEN line from the 8257 goes to two other DI[P?] That signal is connected to the $\overline{BUSEN}$ input [of?] the 8228 system controller. As long as $\overline{BUSEN}$ [is] high, the 8228 performs normally, but with $\overline{BUSE}$[N] low, the 8228 will float the data bus. With the 822[8] effectively disconnected, the 8257 controller ca[n] provide bus access to the external devices. The AE[N] line also goes to the 8212 I/O port. Recall that t[he] 8212 is selected by a low input on $\overline{DS1}$ and a hig[h] on DS2. The $\overline{DS1}$ input is grounded, so it is alway[s] true. Thus at the same time that AEN disables t[he] 8228, it also enables the I/O port by making DS[2] high. The AEN signal connections are shown in Fi[g.] 12-18.

The address strobe, ADDSTB, output identifies th[e] interval when the high-order address byte is on th[e] data lines for the 8212 to demultiplex it. When th[e] address strobe is high, the high-order byte is route[d] to bits A8 through A15 of the address bus throug[h] the 8212.

The 8257 also provides two other signals whic[h] indicate the progress of the data transfer. The term[i]nal count (TC), output becomes high when a byt[e] counter reaches zero. The true TC signal means tha[t] the last byte for a given DMA channel is being sen[t.] The MARK output goes true on every 128th byt[e]

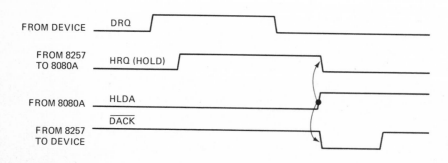

Figure 12-17. DMA Acknowledgemen[t] Timing Diagram.

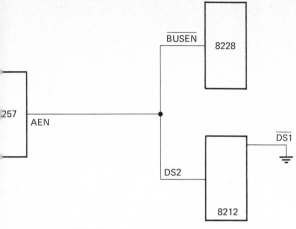

Figure 12-18. AEN Signal Connections.

changed. The signal is useful in floppy disks or ~~th~~e cassettes which block data in 128- or 256-byte ~~rec~~ords.

The remainder of the DMA transfer timing diagram ~~is~~ shown in Fig. 12-19. Prior to acknowledging the ~~de~~vice, the 8257 has set the proper address on bits ~~A0~~ through A7 of the address bus and bits DB0 ~~thr~~ough DB7 of the data bus. The 8212 latches the ~~lat~~ter onto bits A8 through A15 of the address bus. ~~Th~~at data remains latched until the next high address ~~str~~obe. The device receives the $\overline{DACK}$ signal and ~~pre~~pares to either receive or transmit. The data is ~~act~~ually transferred when the appropriate I/O or ~~me~~mory strobe signal goes low.

Programming the 8257

~~Th~~e 8257 appears as either 16 I/O ports or 16 memory ~~loc~~ations (listed in Table 12-7) to the programmer. ~~Fig~~ure 12-20a illustrates the 8257 used as an I/O ~~po~~rt. A simple interchange of wires converts the ~~DM~~A controller to a memory-mapped device as

shown in Fig. 12-20b. The programmer loads the command register with the command for the next DMA operation, after loading the address and the byte-count registers. Table 12-10 lists these commands. An example of programming the 8257 is given below in assembly language. The 8257 is used as an I/O port in this example. The addresses for the registers are:

Address register, channel 0	10_{16}
Byte-count register, channel 0	11_{16}
Command register	18_{16}

MVI	A,00	} Send low byte to address
OUT	10	} register, channel 0
MVI	A,10	} Send high byte to address
OUT	10	} register, channel 0
MVI	A,00	} Send low byte to count
OUT	11	} register, channel 0
MVI	A,41	} Send high byte to count
OUT	11	} register, channel 0
MVI	A,11	} Set control register to enable
OUT	18	} channel 0 round robin priority

The starting address for the transfer will be 1000_{16}. There will be 256_{10} words written. (The byte-count and direction register was set to 4100_{16}, which translates to 100_{16} words to transfer and a direction code for the write cycle.) Finally, the bits in the command register are set.

There are a few features in Table 12-10 that require further comment. Bit 5 allows the programmer to choose to extend write pulses. The write pulse can be advanced one clock cycle earlier than normal. This action will give a slow external device more time when sending data to memory.

Setting bit 6 in the command register disables the DMA channel involved when the TC signal goes high. Disabling the channel when the word count is exhausted ensures that the DMA operation stops

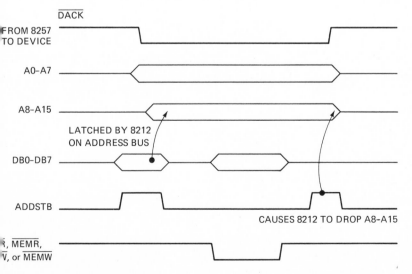

Figure 12-19. DMA Data Transfer Timing Diagram.

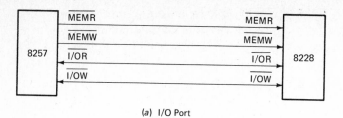

(a) I/O Port

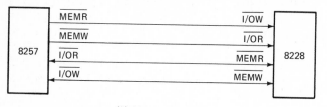

(b) Memory-Mapped

Figure 12-20. 8257 Addressing.

properly. The channel is reenabled as the processor sets its bit in the command word again. In the autoload option (see below) bit 6 does not affect channel 2.

The autoload option is selected with bit 7. The purpose of the autoload is to allow DMA to proceed without reinitiating the address and byte-count register prior to each record transfer. Autoload works only with DMA channel 2 and requires that channel 3 be reserved as a buffer. The program in the 8080A loads channel 3 with address, count, and direction for the next channel 2 transfer. When the byte count for channel 2 reaches zero, it is automatically reloaded with the values from channel 3.

Channel 3		Channel 2
Address register	$\longrightarrow$	Address register
Byte-count register	$\longrightarrow$	Byte-count register

The data exchange on channel 2 continues with the new values.

Table 12-10
Command Register* Code Words

Bit Number	Meaning
0	Set, enable; clear, disable channel 0
1	Set, enable; clear, disable channel 1
2	Set, enable; clear, disable channel 2
3	Set, enable; clear, disable channel 3
4	Clear, fixed priority; set, round robin priority
5	Clear, normal write pulse; set, extended write pulse
6	Set, for TC disable option
7	Set, autoload option

*The command register is cleared by a system reset.

If the address and byte-count registers of chan 2 (instead of channel 3) are loaded in the autolo mode, the information from the channel 2 registe is copied into channel 3. Thereafter the values the address and the byte count are refreshed channel 2 from channel 3.

The condition of the 8257 can be read by executi an input from the same address as the comma register (see Table 12-7). The status bits are list in Table 12-11. If any of bits 0 through 3 is s a true terminal count (TC) signal has been issu on that channel. Bit 4 is used with the autolo option. In autoload the value in the channel registers must not change as they are being writt into the channel 2 registers. As long as bit 4 set, the data can be written in channel 3 registe without disturbing the process. Every time the stat register is read, all the bits except bit 4 are cleare

8257 DMA Controller Review

1. How many external devices can be connecte to the 8257 in normal operations? With th autoload option selected?

2. What signals are used by devices to reque service? Which signals are used by the 825 to acknowledge the devices?

3. Why is the AEN output of the 8257 connecte to the $\overline{\text{BUSEN}}$ input of the 8228 system con troller and the DS2 input of the 8212 I/O po in Fig. 12-18?

4. List the 10 8257 registers. Describe how the are addressed.

5. Distinguish between the fixed and round robi priority arbitration schemes of the 8257.

6. How does an external device signal that it i using burst mode data transfers?

7. Describe the three transfer direction cycles use on the 8257.

8. Explain the purpose of the HRQ signal in Fi 12-17.

Table 12-11
8257 Status Registers

Bit Number	Meaning
0	TC status on channel 0
1	TC status on channel 1
2	TC status on channel 2
3	TC status on channel 3
4	Update status
5–7	Not used

9. How is an 8257 controller addressed as an I/O port different from one addressed by memory-mapped I/O?

CHAPTER SUMMARY

1. A family of support devices simplifies the task of interfacing the 8080A to external equipment. If these devices are not used, low-power Schottky TTL integrated circuits are recommended for use in the interface logic. Outputs should be buffered, and bus drivers, together with termination networks, should be used on long transmission paths.

2. Fully decoded address selection interprets every bit of the device code. Linear selection decodes only a few bits.

3. The 8095 three-state buffer is frequently used on 8080A input or output lines. The buffer is enabled by a device selection strobe from the processor.

4. The 8212 I/O port consists of eight D flip-flops used to latch data. Its output is compatible with the three-state system data bus.

5. The 8259 priority interrupt control unit can coordinate up to eight external interrupts. In a master-slave system, even more interrupts can be handled. The 8259 provides arbitration of simultaneous interrupts. The 8259 is initialized and controlled by the program in the microcomputer.

6. The 8257 DMA controller can support four channels of DMA. The 8257 modes are selected by the software in the 8080A.

KEY TERMS AND CONCEPTS

Interfacing	8095 buffer	Mask mode
Buffered signals	8212 I/O port	8257 DMA controller
Bus drivers	8259 priority interrupt control unit	Fixed priority mode
Termination networks	Interrupt priority arbitration	Round robin mode
Fully decoded address selection	Fully nested mode	Byte-by-byte transfer
Linear selection	Rotating priorities	Burst transfer
Jamming data	Polled mode	

PROBLEMS

12-1 Why is the 8257 permitted to drop the data lines representing bits A8 through A15 so early in the timing diagram of Fig. 12-19?

12-2 Why are two processor outputs necessary to load an address register of the 8257?

12-3 Explain the result of setting bit 6 in the command register of the 8257. What happens if bit 7 is set at the same time?

12-4 How many 74LS30 NAND gate input lines can be safely connected to a single 8080A output line?

12-5 If the 74LS30 NAND gate in Fig. 12-1 is to be used to fully decode the device address $D7_{16}$, which inputs require inverters?

12-6 Draw a circuit diagram similar to Fig. 12-2*b*, showing how two 8095 buffers can be used for output on the data bus.

12-7 An 8259 master-slave system consists of two slaves attached to IR6 and IR7 of the master. Devices 0 through 5 are also attached to the master, 6 through 13 to the IR6 slave, and 14 through 21 to the IR7 slave. Prepare a table similar to Table 12-4, with the proper output data to:

1. Initialize the master. Use four words between vector addresses and a base address for the master of 4300_{16}.

2. Initialize each slave. The base address for vector addresses of the slave on IR6 is 5100_{16}, and the one on IR7 has a base address of 5900_{16}.

3. Start rotating priorities mode B. End of interrupt.

4. Allow interrupts from devices 4 and 5 to interrupt any other service request.

5. Return to the fully nested mode.

6. Cancel the mask of step 4.

7. Start the polling mode.

12-8 There is a simple mask of 51_{16} active in the 8259. Rotating priority, mode B is in effect, and the current order of priority is:

Lowest							Highest
IR5	IR4	IR3	IR2	IR1	IR0	IR7	IR6

The processor issues an OCW2 of $E3_{16}$. When the devices on IR 4 and IR7 simultaneously request interupts, which will be serviced first?

12-9 The address for the 8257 channel 2 addre register is 50_{16}. Write a program to input 128_{10} wor from the floppy disk by DMA transfer. The starti address for storing the data is 0500_{16}. Fixed priori with extended write pulses and the TC disable opti are to be selected.

12-10 The CRT terminal is receiving DMA da in the burst mode controlled by channel 1 of t 8257. The floppy disk uses channel 0, also in bu mode. Round robin priority and the autoload opti have been selected. After initialization, the followi DMA transfers have occurred:

1. Terminal—read 200_{10} words.

2. Floppy disk—verify cycle.

3. Floppy disk—read 126_{10} words.

4. Terminal—read 350_{10} words.

Until this time, no conflicts have occurred, but n the terminal and disk simultaneously request a DM transfer. The disk wants to write 256_{10} words, a the terminal wants to read 100_{10} words.

a. Which one gets first access to the bus?

b. How many words are transferred?

c. Answer the same questions with fixed priori mode selected.

PURPOSE: To investigate computer output.

PARTS LIST:

Item	Quantity
8212	1
5082–7340 hexadecimal display	2
74LS00	1
74LS20	1

IC DIAGRAMS:

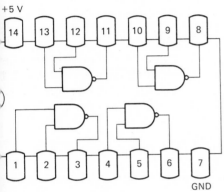

Figure 12-21. 74LS00.

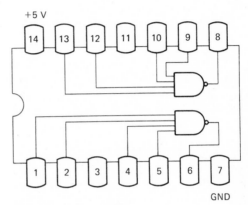

Figure 12-22. 74LS20.

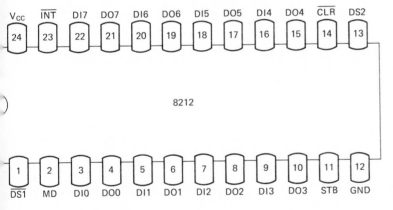

Figure 12-23. 8212.

PROCEDURE: This experiment builds on the circuit of Experiment 11. After the output port has been checked for proper operation, continue with the steps below.

STEP 1. The purpose of the 74LS20 NAND gate shown in Fig. 12-24 is to decode the device address which selects the I/O port. What device address(es) will produce a high STB signal with this type of address decoder?

STEP 2. Wire the circuit as shown in Fig. 12-24.

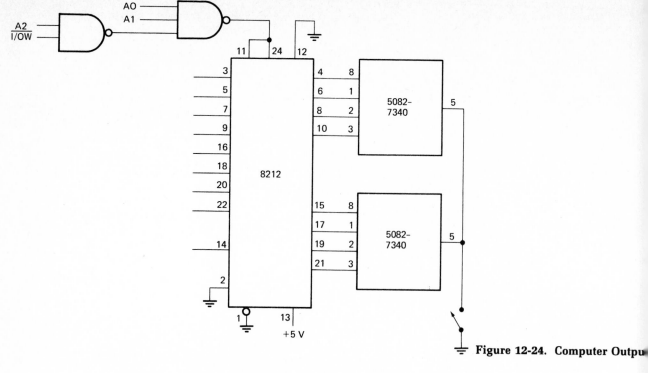

Figure 12-24. Computer Output

STEP 3. Load the program into the computer.

Instruction	Address	Machine Code
LDA DATA	0000	3A
	0001	06
	0002	*00*
OUT 7	0003	D3
	0004	07
HLT	0005	76
DATA	0006	01

STEP 4. Execute the program and record the hexadecimal display value. (The strobe switch on the display must be closed to read the value.) The output should be 01_{16}. If your results do not agree, check to assure that the program was correctly loaded. If this operation does not correct the problem, review your circuit connections.

STEP 5. Write a program to output the numbers 00_{16} through FF_{16} with a 0.01 s delay between each output. Comment on the operation of the program.

APPENDIX

While the experiments and examples given in the text are based on the 8080A microprocessor, with little or no change most apply to the 8085 or Z80 processors as well. The following sections will comment on the differences between the 8080A and the other processors to indicate how the experiments or examples might be modified for those machines.

THE 8085 MICROPROCESSOR

The architecture of the 8085 is extremely similar to that of the 8080A. For this reason, 8080A programs can be run on the 8085 without modification. Considerable savings in software costs can be realized in this manner, even though the hardware itself is upgraded if a commercial product is converted from being based on the 8080A to an 8085 system.

Many of the 8085 signal lines, however, do not correspond to those of the 8080A. As can be seen in Fig. A-1, and as listed in Table A-1, the pin arrangement differs considerably from the 8080A. Immediately obvious is the requirement for only a single 5-V power supply. This refinement makes use of the 8085 in a circuit less costly. Another modification is inclusion of clock logic on the microprocessor chip. Providing the clock on the chip eliminates the need for the 8224 clock generator. Timing signals for the 8085 consist of a more straightforward single-phase clock. The standard clock period in the 8085 is 320 ns, as compared to the slower 500 ns of the 8080A.

The lower 8 bits of the address (A0 through A7) and the data lines (D0 through D7) are multiplexed on the same bus. These dual-purpose lines are designated AD0 through AD7. The remaining address bits (A8 through A15) use dedicated lines. The memory or I/O device can distinguish data from addresses on AD0 through AD7 by the level of the ALE signal. It is high when data is on the bus and low when the bus signals represent an address.

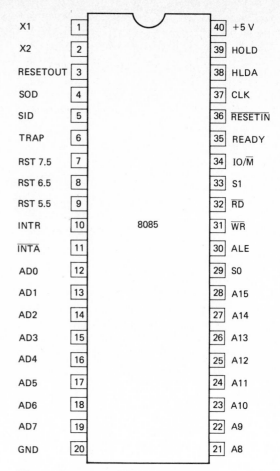

Figure A-1. 8085 Pin Arrangement.

Table A-1
8085 Signals

Signal	Description
AD0–AD7	Multiplexed three-state address and data bus
A8–A15	Three-state high-order bits of address bus
ALE	Address latch enable
$\overline{RD}$, $\overline{WR}$	Read, write strobe
IO/$\overline{M}$	I/O or memory indicator
S0, S1	Bus status indicators
READY	Wait state request
SID, SOD	Serial data I/O
HOLD, HLDA	Hold request, acknowledgment
INTR	Interrupt request
TRAP	Nonmaskable interrupt request
RST 5.5, RST 6.5, RST 7.5	Hardware vectored interrupt requests
$\overline{INTA}$	Interrupt acknowledgment
$\overline{RESETIN}$	System reset input
RESETOUT	Peripheral reset output
X1, X2	Crystal inputs
CLK	Clock signal output

…he 8085 employs new signals in reading and …ting of data. The $\overline{RD}$ signal is used to read either …mory or input data, and the $\overline{WR}$ is used for writing …mory or output data. Another signal is necessary …distinguish between the two types of reading and …ting. When memory operations are in progress, … auxiliary signal, IO/$\overline{M}$, is low. For input or …put, IO/$\overline{M}$ is high.

…he purpose of the signals currently on the data … can be interpreted by referring to the S0 and …control signals. These two signals specify whether … intent is data reading, data writing, instruction …ching, or a halt state. The meanings of these signals … listed below.

Control Signals

S1	S0	Meaning
0	0	Halt
0	1	Memory or output write
1	0	Memory or input read
1	1	Instruction fetch

…erial input and output are supported by the 8085 …well. With the SIO instruction, the program can …smit only the most-significant bit of the accu… …lator. A serial input is provided by the SID …truction. The data bit is received in the MSB … …he accumulator.

…eripherals can coordinate functions with the …trol bus signals. If a memory or I/O device needs …re time to respond to an I/O request from the …cessor, the READY signal can be used. External …ic can request control of the address bus with … HOLD signal; the processor acknowledges with …DA. The microprocessor is reset by the $\overline{RESETIN}$ …nal, which need not be synchronized with the …ck. The processor then provides a reset signal … the remainder of the system with RESETOUT.

…he interrupt structure of the 8085 is quite power… …. General-purpose interrupt requests are handled …th the INTR input. (This input corresponds to … 8080A interrupt request.) The TRAP interrupt …nnot be disabled and has the highest priority. For …s reason, the TRAP is best suited to be a power …lure interrupt. Three other interrupts are supplied … hardware vectoring. Each (as well as INTR) can … individually enabled or disabled with the SIM …truction. (All interrupts, except TRAP, can be …abled or disabled as a group with the EI and DI …structions, like on the 8080A.) The TRAP interrupt …ll respond to either edge or level triggering. The …T 5.5 and RST 6.5 interrupts are level triggered, …ile RST 7.5 is edge triggered. All interrupts are …cknowledged by the processor issuing a true $\overline{INTA}$ …nal.

THE Z80 MICROPROCESSOR

All the 8080A instructions are a subset of the Z80 repertoire. This provision means that the 8080A programs will also run on the Z80. (The Z80 instructions number 158, while the 8080A has 78.) Although the operation codes are identical, you will note that different mnemonics are used in Z80 manuals. The Z80 requires only a 5-V power supply and uses a single-phase clock. Clock logic is on the chip.

As shown in Fig. A-2 and listed in Table A-2, the Z80 does not separate read and write into memory or I/O operations. An I/O or memory selection pulse is provided to distinguish between them, as with the 8085. A nonmaskable interrupt, which is usually used to detect power failure, is supported. The Z80 also supplies a dynamic memory refresh signal, thus simplifying the interface to dynamic RAM.

This processor has more registers than the 8080A and has expanded the addressing modes. The additional registers are indicated in Fig. A-3. The alternate set of registers (indicated by prime marks, such as A′ and E′) can be used in exactly the same way as the main set, thus doubling the number of programmable registers. The alternate set is also con-

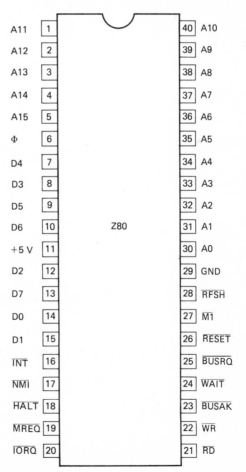

Figure A-2. Z80 Pin Arrangement.

Table A-2
Z80 Signals

Signal	Description
D0–D7	Three-state data bus
A0–A15	Three-state address bus
$\overline{RD}$, $\overline{WR}$	Read, write strobes
$\overline{M1}$	Instruction fetch cycle
$\overline{MREQ}$	Memory access indicator
$\overline{IORQ}$	I/O operation indicator
$\overline{RFSH}$	Dynamic memory refresh indicator
$\overline{HALT}$	MPU in halt state
$\overline{WAIT}$	Wait state request
$\overline{INT}$	Interrupt request
$\overline{NMI}$	Nonmaskable interrupt request
$\overline{RESET}$	Reset MPU input
$\overline{BUSRQ}$	Request for control of the data, address, and control buses
$\overline{BUSAK}$	Bus acknowledge
Φ	Clock input

venient to reserve for interrupt servicing routines. Then no registers need be saved before processing the interrupt.

The interrupt vector register extends the interrupt processing capacity of the MPU. The refresh counter indexes the address when rewriting the values into dynamic memories which is necessary to prevent data loss. Thus separate memory refresh circuitry is eliminated from the microcomputer.

The index registers allow the address of the operand to be offset by a displacement value. T programming feature is frequently applied to t or list processing and also frees the register p for other purposes. The operand address in indexed instruction is calculated as

$$address = (IX) + D \quad \text{or}$$
$$address = (IY) + D \qquad (A$$

where (IX) = contents of the X index register
(IY) = contents of the Y index register
D = displacement, a signed 8-bit valu be added to the index (the data be located within ± 128 bytes of index register contents)

The relative jump instruction also uses a displa ment. This instruction allows the programmer branch to an address equal to

$$address = (PC) + 2 + D \qquad (A$$

where (PC) = contents of the program counter
D = displacement

Individual bits can be maniplulated by a grou instructions that can set or reset any single bi a word. Block move instructions can transfer number of contiguous memory cells to anot memory area or to an output port. The block comp can scan a memory area for a specific data va The Z80 status register provides a subtraction dicator, so the DAA instruction used in B arithmetic programs is simplified.

Main Register Set

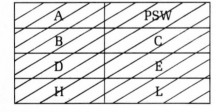

Alternate Register Set

A′	PSW′
B′	E′
D′	E′
H′	L′

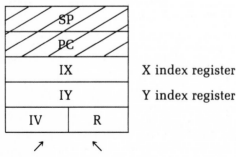

IX — X index register
IY — Y index register

Interrupt vector address — Dynamic memory refresh counter

Legend

Equivalent to the 8080A

Unique to the Z80

Figure A-3. Z80 Regis

Table A-3
Numerical Listing of 8080A Operation Codes

									Least Significant Digit							
Most Significant Digit	**0**	**1**	**2**	**3**	**4**	**5**	**6**	**7**	**8**	**9**	**A**	**B**	**C**	**D**	**E**	**F**
0	NOP	LXI B	STAX B	INX B	INR B	DCR B	MVI B	RLC	X	DAD B	LDAX B	DCX B	INR C	DCR C	MVI C	RRC
1	X	LXI D	STAX D	INX D	INR D	DCR D	MVI D	RAL	X	DAD D	LDAX D	DCX D	INR E	DCR E	MVI E	RAR
2	X	LXI H	SHLD	INX H	INR H	DCR H	MVI H	DAA	X	DAD H	LHLD	DCX H	INR L	DCR L	MVI L	CMA
3	X	LXI SP	STA	INX SP	INR M	DCR M	MVI M	STC	X	DAD SP	LDA	DCX SP	INR A	DCR A	MVI A	CMC
4	MOV B,B	MOV B,C	MOV B,D	MOV B,E	MOV B,H	MOV B,L	MOV B,M	MOV B,A	MOV C,B	MOV C,C	MOV C,D	MOV C,E	MOV C,H	MOV C,L	MOV C,M	MOV C,A
5	MOV D,B	MOV D,C	MOV D,D	MOV D,E	MOV D,H	MOV D,L	MOV D,M	MOV D,A	MOV E,B	MOV E,C	MOV E,D	MOV E,E	MOV E,H	MOV E,L	MOV E,M	MOV E,A
6	MOV H,B	MOV H,C	MOV H,D	MOV H,E	MOV H,H	MOV H,L	MOV H,M	MOV H,A	MOV L,B	MOV L,C	MOV L,D	MOV L,E	MOV L,H	MOV L,L	MOV L,M	MOV L,A
7	MOV M,B	MOV M,C	MOV M,D	MOV M,E	MOV M,H	MOV M,L	HLT	MOV M,A	MOV A,B	MOV A,C	MOV A,D	MOV A,E	MOV A,H	MOV A,L	MOV A,M	MOV A,A
8	ADD B	ADD C	ADD D	ADD E	ADD H	ADD L	ADD M	ADD A	ADC B	ADC C	ADC D	ADC E	ADC H	ADC L	ADC M	ADC A
9	SUB B	SUB C	SUB D	SUB E	SUB H	SUB L	SUB M	SUB A	SBB B	SBB C	SBB D	SBB E	SBB H	SBB L	SBB M	SBB A
A	ANA B	ANA C	ANA D	ANA E	ANA H	ANA L	ANA M	ANA A	XRA B	XRA C	XRA D	XRA E	XRA H	XRA L	XRA M	XRA A
B	ORA B	ORA C	ORA D	ORA E	ORA H	ORA L	ORA M	ORA A	CMP B	CMP C	CMP D	CMP E	CMP H	CMP L	CMP M	CMP A
C	RNZ	POP B	JNZ	JMP	CNZ	PUSH B	ADI	RST 0	RZ	RET	JZ	X	CZ	CALL	ACI	RST 1
D	RNC	POP D	JNC	OUT	CNC	PUSH D	SUI	RST 2	RC	X	JC	IN	CC	X	BI	RST 3
E	RPO	POP H	JPO	XTHL	CPO	PUSH H	ANI	RST 4	RPE	PCHL	JPE	XCHG	CPE	X	XRI	RST 5
F	RP	POP A	JP	DI	CP	PUSH A	ORI	RST 6	RM	SPHL	JM	EI	CM	X	CPI	RST 7

X = not assigned.

Mnemonic	Operation Code	Bytes	Description
ACI	CE	2	(A)+(DATA)+(CARRY) → A
ADC A	8F	1	(A)+(A)+CARRY → A
ADC B	88	1	(A)+(B)+(CARRY) → A
ADC C	89	1	(A)+(C)+(CARRY) → A
ADC D	8A	1	(A)+(D)+(CARRY) → A
ADC E	8B	1	(A)+(E)+(CARRY) → A
ADC H	8C	1	(A)+(H)+(CARRY) → A
ADC L	8D	1	(A)+(L)+CARRY → A
ADC M	8E	1	(A)+(M)+CARRY → A
ADD A	87	1	(A)+(A) → A
ADD B	80	1	(A)+(B) → A
ADD C	81	1	(A)+(C) → A
ADD D	82	1	(A)+(D) → A
ADD E	83	1	(A)+(E) → A
ADD H	84	1	(A)+(H) → A
ADD L	85	1	(A)+(L) → A
ADD M	86	1	(A)+(M) → A
ADI	C6	2	(A)+(DATA) → A
ANA A	A7	1	(A) AND (A) → A
ANA B	A0	1	(A) AND (B) → A
ANA C	A1	1	(A) AND (C) → A
ANA D	A2	1	(A) AND (D) → A
ANA E	A3	1	(A) AND (E) → A
ANA H	A4	1	(A) AND (H) → A
ANA L	A5	1	(A) AND (L) → A
ANA M	A6	1	(A) AND (M) → A
ANI	E6	2	(A) AND (DATA) → A
CALL	CD	3	(PCH) → (SP)−1, (PCL) → (SP)−2, (SP)+2 → SP, ADDR → PC
CC	DC	3	CALL if CARRY=1
CM	FC	3	CALL if SIGN=1
CMA	2F	1	$(\overline{A})$ → A (1's complement)
CMC	3F	1	$(\overline{CARRY})$ → CARRY
CMP A	BF	1	(A)−(A) set condition bits, $A_f = A_i$
CMP B	B8	1	(A)−(B) set condition bits, $A_f = A_i$
CMP C	B9	1	(A)−(C) set condition bits, $A_f = A_i$
CMP D	BA	1	(A)−(D) set condition bits, $A_f = A_i$
CMP E	BB	1	(A)−(E) set condition bits, $A_f = A_i$
CMP H	BC	1	(A)−(H) set condition bits, $A_f = A_i$
CMP L	BD	1	(A)−(L) set condition bits, $A_f = A_i$
CMP M	BE	1	(A)−(M) set condition bits, $A_f = A_i$
CNC	D4	3	CALL if CARRY=0
CNZ	C4	3	CALL if ZERO=0
CP	F4	3	CALL if SIGN=0
CPE	EC	3	CALL if PARITY=1
CPI	FE	2	(A)−(DATA) set condition bits, $A_f = A_i$
CPO	E4	3	CALL if PARITY=0
CZ	CC	3	CALL if ZERO=1
DAA	27	1	Decimal adjust A
DAD B	09	1	(HL)+(BC) → HL
DAD D	19	1	(HL)+(DE) → HL

Mnemonic	Operation Code	Bytes	Description
AD H	29	1	(HL)+(HL) → HL
AD SP	39	1	(HL)+(SP) → HL
CR A	3D	1	(A)−1 → A
CR B	05	1	(B)−1 → B
CR C	0D	1	(C)−1 → C
CR D	15	1	(D)−1 → D
CR E	1D	1	(E)−1 → E
CR H	25	1	(H)−1 → H
CR L	2D	1	(L)−1 → L
CR M	35	1	(M)−1 → M
CX B	0B	1	(BC)−1 → BC
CX D	1B	1	(DE)−1 → DE
CX H	2B	1	(HL)−1 → HL
CX SP	3B	1	(SP)−1 → SP
I	F3	1	0 → INTE
I	FB	1	1 → INTE
LT	76	1	Stop processor
N	DB	2	Input → A
NR A	3C	1	(A)+1 → A
NR B	04	1	(B)+1 → B
NR C	0C	1	(C)+1 → C
NR D	14	1	(D)+1 → D
NR E	1C	1	(E)+1 → E
NR H	24	1	(H)+1 → H
NR L	2C	1	(L)+1 → L
NR M	34	1	(M)+1 → M
NX B	03	1	(BC)+1 → BC
NX D	13	1	(DE)+1 → DE
NX H	23	1	(HL)+1 → HL
NX SP	33	1	(SP)+1 → SP
C	DA	3	Jump if CARRY=1
M	FA	3	Jump if SIGN=1
MP	C3	3	Jump
NC	D2	3	Jump if CARRY=0
NZ	C2	3	Jump if ZERO=0
P	F2	3	Jump if SIGN=0
PE	EA	3	Jump if PARITY=1
PO	E2	3	Jump if PARITY=0
Z	CA	3	Jump if ZERO=1
DA	3A	3	(ADDR) → A
DAX B	0A	1	(Address=(BC)) → A
DAX D	1A	1	(Address=(DE)) → A
HLD	2A	3	(ADDR) → L, (ADDR+1) → H
XI B	01	3	(DATA) → BC
XI D	11	3	(DATA) → DE
XI H	21	3	(DATA) → HL
XI SP	31	3	(DATA) → SP
MOV A,A	7F	1	(A) → A
MOV A,B	78	1	(B) → A
MOV A,C	79	1	(C) → A

Mnemonic	Operation Code	Bytes	Description
MOV A,D	7A	1	(D) → A
MOV A,E	7B	1	(E) → A
MOV A,H	7C	1	(H) → A
MOV A,L	7D	1	(L) → A
MOV A,M	7E	1	(M) → A
MOV B,A	47	1	(A) → B
MOV B,B	40	1	(B) → B
MOV B,C	41	1	(C) → B
MOV B,D	42	1	(D) → B
MOV B,E	43	1	(E) → B
MOV B,H	44	1	(H) → B
MOV B,L	45	1	(L) → B
MOV B,M	46	1	(M) → B
MOV C,A	4F	1	(A) → C
MOV C,B	48	1	(B) → C
MOV C,C	49	1	(C) → C
MOV C,D	4A	1	(D) → C
MOV C,E	4B	1	(E) → C
MOV C,H	4C	1	(H) → C
MOV C,L	4D	1	(L) → C
MOV C,M	4E	1	(M) → C
MOV D,A	57	1	(A) → D
MOV D,B	50	1	(B) → D
MOV D,C	51	1	(C) → D
MOV D,D	52	1	(D) → D
MOV D,E	53	1	(E) → D
MOV D,H	54	1	(H) → D
MOV D,L	55	1	(L) → D
MOV D,M	56	1	(M) → D
MOV E,A	5F	1	(A) → E
MOV E,B	58	1	(B) → E
MOV E,C	59	1	(C) → E
MOV E,D	5A	1	(D) → E
MOV E,E	5B	1	(E) → E
MOV E,H	5C	1	(H) → E
MOV E,L	5D	1	(L) → E
MOV E,M	5E	1	(M) → E
MOV H,A	67	1	(A) → H
MOV H,B	60	1	(B) → H
MOV H,C	61	1	(C) → H
MOV H,D	62	1	(D) → H
MOV H,E	63	1	(E) → H
MOV H,H	64	1	(H) → H
MOV H,L	65	1	(L) → H
MOV H,M	66	1	(M) → H
MOV L,A	6F	1	(A) → L
MOV L,B	68	1	(B) → L
MOV L,C	69	1	(C) → L
MOV L,D	6A	1	(D) → L
MOV L,E	6B	1	(E) → L

Mnemonic	Operation Code	Bytes	Description
OV L,H	6C	1	(H) → L
OV L,L	6D	1	(L) → L
OV L,M	6E	1	(M) → L
OV M,A	77	1	(A) → M
OV M,B	70	1	(B) → M
OV M,C	71	1	(C) → M
OV M,D	72	1	(D) → M
OV M,E	73	1	(E) → M
OV M,H	74	1	(H) → M
OV M,L	75	1	(L) → M
VI A	3E	2	DATA → A
VI B	06	2	DATA → B
VI C	0E	2	DATA → C
VI D	16	2	DATA → D
VI E	1E	2	DATA → E
VI H	26	2	DATA → H
VI L	2E	2	DATA → L
VI M	36	2	DATA → M
OP	00	1	No operation
RA A	B7	1	(A) OR (A) → A
RA B	B0	1	(A) OR (B) → A
RA C	B1	1	(A) OR (C) → A
RA D	B2	1	(A) OR (D) → A
RA E	B3	1	(A) OR (E) → A
RA H	B4	1	(A) OR (H) → A
RA L	B5	1	(A) OR (L) → A
RA M	B6	1	(A) OR (M) → A
RI	F6	2	(A) OR (DATA) → A
UT	D3	2	(A) → output
CHL	E9	1	(HL) → PC
OP A	F1	1	(STACK) → A-PSW
OP B	C1	1	(STACK) → BC
OP D	D1	1	(STACK) → DE
OP H	E1	1	(STACK) → HL
JSH A	F5	1	(A-PSW) → STACK
JSH B	C5	1	(BC) → STACK
JSH D	D5	1	(DE) → STACK
JSH H	E5	1	(HL) → STACK
AL	17	1	Rotate A left through CARRY, (CARRY) → A_0
AR	1F	1	Rotate A right through CARRY, (CARRY) → A_7
C	D8	1	Return if CARRY=1
ET	C9	1	Return
LC	07	1	Rotate A left, (A_7) → CARRY
M	F8	1	Return if SIGN=1
NC	D0	1	Return if CARRY=0
NZ	C0	1	Return if ZERO=0
P	F0	1	Return if SIGN=0
PE	E8	1	Return if PARITY=1

Mnemonic	Operation Code	Bytes	Description
RPO	E0	1	Return if PARITY=0
RRC	0F	1	Rotate A right, $(A_o) \rightarrow$ CARRY
RST 0	C7	1	$(PCH) \rightarrow ((SP)-1)$, $(PCL) \rightarrow ((SP)-2)$, $(SP)+2 \rightarrow SP$, $00_{16} \rightarrow PC$
RST 1	CF	1	$(PCH) \rightarrow ((SP)-1)$, $(PCL) \rightarrow ((SP)-2)$, $(SP)+2 \rightarrow SP$, $08_{16} \rightarrow PC$
RST 2	D7	1	$(PCH) \rightarrow ((SP)-1)$, $(PCL) \rightarrow ((SP)-2)$, $(SP)+2 \rightarrow SP$, $10_{16} \rightarrow PC$
RST 3	DF	1	$(PCH) \rightarrow ((SP)-1)$, $(PCL) \rightarrow ((SP)-2)$, $(SP)+2 \rightarrow SP$, $18_{16} \rightarrow PC$
RST 4	E7	1	$(PCH) \rightarrow ((SP)-1)$, $(PCL) \rightarrow ((SP)-2)$, $(SP)+2 \rightarrow SP$, $20_{16} \rightarrow PC$
RST 5	EF	1	$(PCH) \rightarrow ((SP)-1)$, $(PCL) \rightarrow ((SP)-2)$, $(SP)+2 \rightarrow SP$, $28_{16} \rightarrow PC$
RST 6	F7	1	$(PCH) \rightarrow ((SP)-1)$, $(PCL) \rightarrow ((SP)-2)$, $(SP)+2 \rightarrow SP$, $30_{16} \rightarrow PC$
RST 7	FF	1	$(PCH) \rightarrow ((SP)-1)$, $(PCL) \rightarrow ((SP)-2)$, $(SP)+2 \rightarrow SP$, $38_{16} \rightarrow PC$
RZ	C8	1	Return if ZERO=1
SBB A	9F	1	$(A)-(A)-$CARRY $\rightarrow A$
SBB B	98	1	$(A)-(B)-$CARRY $\rightarrow A$
SBB C	99	1	$(A)-(C)-$CARRY $\rightarrow A$
SBB D	9A	1	$(A)-(D)-$CARRY $\rightarrow A$
SBB E	9B	1	$(A)-(E)-$CARRY $\rightarrow A$
SBB H	9C	1	$(A)-(H)-$CARRY $\rightarrow A$
SBB L	9D	1	$(A)-(L)-$CARRY $\rightarrow A$
SBB M	9E	1	$(A)-(M)-$CARRY $\rightarrow A$
SBI	DE	2	$(A)-$DATA$-$CARRY $\rightarrow A$
SHLD	22	3	$(L) \rightarrow$ ADDR, $(H) \rightarrow$ ADDR+1
SPHL	F9	1	$(HL) \rightarrow SP$
STA	32	3	$(A) \rightarrow$ ADDR
STAX B	02	1	$(A) \rightarrow$ address=(BC)
STAX D	12	1	$(A) \rightarrow$ address=(DE)
STC	37	1	$1 \rightarrow$ CARRY
SUB A	97	1	$(A)-(A) \rightarrow A$
SUB B	90	1	$(A)-(B) \rightarrow A$
SUB C	91	1	$(A)-(C) \rightarrow A$
SUB D	92	1	$(A)-(D) \rightarrow A$
SUB E	93	1	$(A)-(E) \rightarrow A$
SUB H	94	1	$(A)-(H) \rightarrow A$
SUB L	95	1	$(A)-(L) \rightarrow A$
SUB M	96	1	$(A)-(M) \rightarrow A$
SUI	D6	2	$(A)-(DATA) \rightarrow A$
XCHG	EB	1	$(H) \leftrightarrow (D)$, $(L) \leftrightarrow (E)$
XRA A	AF	1	(A) exclusive OR $(A) \rightarrow A$
XRA B	A8	1	(A) exclusive OR $(B) \rightarrow A$
XRA C	A9	1	(A) exclusive OR $(C) \rightarrow A$
XRA D	AA	1	(A) exclusive OR $(D) \rightarrow A$
XRA E	AB	1	(A) exclusive OR $(E) \rightarrow A$
XRA H	AC	1	(A) exclusive OR $(H) \rightarrow A$

Mnemonic	Operation Code	Bytes	Description
RA L	AD	1	(A) exclusive OR (L) → A
RA M	AE	1	(A) exclusive OR (M) → A
RI	EE	2	(A) exclusive OR (DATA) → A
THL	E3	1	(L) → (SP), (H) → ((SP)+1)

end:

)	Contents of register or memory location
→	Transfer
+	Plus
−	Minus
C	Program counter
CL	Lower byte of PC
CH	Higher byte of PC
P	Stack pointer
Ā	Complement of A
A_i	Initial contents of A (before instruction execution)
A_f	Final contents of A (after instruction execution)
A_o	Least significant bit of A
A_7	Most significant bit of A
NTE	Interrupt enable flip-flop
ADDR	Memory address bytes of the instruction
DATA	Data byte of the instruction
CARRY	Carry bit
CARRY	Complement of CARRY
M	The memory address in HL register pair
IGN	Sign status bit
ZERO	Zero status bit
PARITY	Parity status bit
SW	Program status word

GGESTIONS FOR FURTHER EADING

rden, William, Jr.: *The Z-80 Microcomputer ndbook,* Howard W. Sams & Company, India-polis, 1978.

rsen, David G., Peter R. Rony, and Jonathan A. us: *The Bugbook VI,* E & L Instruments, Inc., rby, CT, 1977.

CS-85™ *User's Manual,* Intel Corporation, Santa ara, CA, 1978.

borne, Adam, Susanna Jacobson, and Jerry Kane: *Introduction to Microcomputers, Volume II Some al Support Products,* Osborne & Associates, Berke-, 1977.

sahow, Edward, J.: *Digital Integrated Circuits for ctronics Technicians,* McGraw-Hill Book Com-ny, New York, 1979.

sahow, Edward J.: *Microprocessor and Microcom-ter Interfacing for Electronics Technicians,* Mc-aw-Hill Book Company, New York, 1981.

atman, John B.: *Microcomputer-Based Design,* Graw-Hill Book Company, New York, 1977.

Z80®-CPU, Z80A®-CPU Technical Manual, Zilog, Inc., Cupertoin, CA, 1977.

Z80 Microcomputer System Micro-Reference Manual, Mostek Corporation, Carrollton, TX, 1978.

8080 Assembly Language Programming Manual, Intel Corporation, Santa Clara, CA, 1974.

SUPPLIERS OF THE 8080A

Intel Corporation
3065 Bowers Avenue, Santa Clara, CA 95051

Advanced Micro Devices
901 Thompson Place, Sunnyvale, CA 94086

National Semiconductor Corporation
2900 Semiconductor Drive, Santa Clara, CA 95050

NEC Microcomputers, Inc.
5 Militia Drive, Lexington, MA 02173

Texas Instruments, Inc.
PO Box 1444, Houston, TX 77001

SUPPLIERS OF THE Z80

Zilog, Inc.
10460 Bubb Road, Cupertino, CA 95014

Mostek, Inc.
1215 West Crosby Road, Carollton, TX 75006

SUPPLIERS OF THE 8085

Intel Corporation
3065 Bowers Avenue, Santa Clara, CA 95051

ANSWERS TO ODD-NUMBERED PROBLEMS

2-1. (a) 702 (b) 1936 (c) 3965

2-3. (a) 1442 (b) 23417 (c) 0.C (d) C4.04

2-5. (a) 111 111 010 (b) −001 001 (c) 1 010 010 111 (d) 011 011

2-7. (a) E70 (b) 25D (c) 6.2F5 (d) 363.E3

2-9. (a) 110 111 000 001 100 (b) 1111 1100 0111 0101 (c) 010 001 110.100 010 101 (d) 101 1011 0010.0110 0001 0111 0101

2-11. (a) even (b) even (c) even (d) odd

2-13. $Q(x) = x^5 − x^3$, $R(x) = 1$

2-15. An odd number of bits changed state

3-3. See Fig. A-4

3-7. See Fig. A-5

3-9. 3.033, 3, 879, 726.9, 0.03033, 3879.7269

4-1. 3, 0000_{16},$−5FFF_{16}$

4-3. Inverter on A13, none on A14 or A15

4-5. (a) 44 (b) 43

4-7. 12_{16}

4-9. 08FF = 4_{16}, AA0C = 95_{16}

5-1. A = AA_{16}, PC = 4094

5-3. D = 40, E = 95, PC = 4097, H = 02, L = A0

5-5. B = FF, 0F0B = 0F, PC = 4096

5-7. 0002 = 0B, 0003 = 0F, PC = 4096

5-9. A = 50, 0F0B = 0B, PC = 4094

6-1. ANI FF

6-3. ADD L, A = 20, L = 27

6-5. A = F9, 1412 = F9

6-7. LDA 2000, CMA

6-9. A = 68

7-3. DD4ACD

7-5. 5831

7-7. LDA 0111, ORI FF, JPO 5600

7-9. Eliminate setting the carry to 1 initia and do not set A to 99

8-1.

A	Status	A	Status
(a) 27	03	(c) 27	03
(b) 49	02	(d) 149	03

8-3. MVI A,70, SUI 1A

8-5. A = E8, B = F3, status = 83

8-7. Use the division routine by first movi DE to BC, set D to 4

8-9. 8E

9-1. N, N, N

9-3. (a) F_{16} (b) $3F_{16}$

9-5. (a) 19 (b) 64

9-7.

	A	B	C
1			
2			
3			
4			
5			

Method 1	Method 2
1A	1A
1B	2A
1C	3A
2A	4A
2B	5A
2C	1B
⋮	⋮
5A	3C
5B	4C
5C	5C

10-1. The B register would decrement from to FF to FE until zero is reached. Simi to the first case, but B would count fro 88 to 87 and so on until zero is reached

10-3. A negative product would result if the sig of the multiplier and the multiplicand w not the same.

10-7. CPI 7F, JM ERR where the label ERR begins the sequence:

ERR MVI A 0, CMA, RET

11-3.

```
            MVI    B,A
    LOOP    DCR    B
            JZ     DONE
            IN     2
            CPI    4C
            JNZ    LOOP
            STA    1000
```

11-7.

```
            LHLD   3700
            LDA    DATA
            MOV    M,A
            INX    H
            LDA    DATA+1
            MOV    M,A
```

11-9. Use MVI A,3F and ANA M

12-1. Because the data is latched by the 8212

12-3. A high TC signal disables the channel after the last byte is sent; channel 2 is not affected by TC stop if bit 7 is set.

12-5. 3 and 5

12-7.

A0	Output		
0	14	ICW1	
1	43	ICW2	1
1	C0	ICW3	
0	14	ICW1	
1	51	ICW2	2
1	06	ICW3	
0	14	ICW1	
1	59	ICW2	
1	07	ICW3	
0	E0	OCW2	3
0	68	OCW3	4
1	CF	Mask	
0	00	OCW2	5
0	68	OCW3	6
1	00	New mask	
0	0C	OCW3	7

INDEX